The LYLE

Price Guide to Collectibles and Memorabilia
#3

merry Christmas!
love,
your sister-in-law,
maryann
1994

The
LYLE

Price Guide to Collectibles and Memorabilia
#3

compiled by Anthony Curtis

A Perigee Book

Perigee Books
are published by
The Berkley Publishing Group
200 Madison Avenue
New York, NY 10016

Library of Congress Cataloging-in-Publication Data

Curtis, Tony, date.
The Lyle price guide to collectibles and memorabilia #3 / Anthony Curtis.
p.   cm.
Includes index.
ISBN 0-399-51855-X
1. Antiques—Catalogs.   I. Title.
NK1125.C8872   1994   94-8406 CIP
745.1′075—dc20

Cover design by Jack Ribik

Printed in the United States of America
1 2 3 4 5 6 7 8 9 10

This book is printed on acid-free paper.
⊗

PRICE GUIDE TO COLLECTIBLES AND MEMORABILIA

This new edition of the Lyle Price Guide to Collectibles and Memorabilia appears at a timely moment, when the market is changing, challenging, exciting as never before. A cynic might wonder what unexpected discoveries can remain to be made in this value-conscious age, when collectibles and their worth are given such prominent and sustained attention in books and the media. Yet still the surprises come out of the woodwork.

It may be because the goalposts are moving all the time, and more and more items previously regarded as, at best, peripheral, are now moving firmly into the mainstream of major collectibles. There can be very few things now that someone, somewhere, does not collect, and it is only necessary for him or her to infect a few friends with a similar enthusiasm for the creation of a market that will become increasingly valuable as more and more people take an interest.

It is the 'one-offs' in the attic, too, that can prove surprisingly valuable, those items which have been kept for purely sentimental reasons; an old concert or baseball program, for example, or the first issue of a cherished publication. (Action Comic No. 1 has now soared to new heights, fetching a record $75,000 at auction.)

Personality items continue to make big money, with film memorabilia in particular attracting interest. The old favorites Mickey Mouse and Charlie Chaplin perform consistently well, of course, a Mickey Mouse original poster for Lonesome Ghosts bringing a bid of almost $34,000 in London recently, and Chaplin's hat and cane fetching $80,850.

The most unlikely articles in this field are often snapped up, and sometimes it seems that, when it comes to film props, the more ghoulish they are, the better they sell. A recent Christie's sale included such delights as a decapitated head (simulated!) and a battery operated pumping heart from an Indiana Jones film ($710, $372), a foam rubber Batman headdress ($3,720), a polyurethane head from Alien ($1,690) and a

Walt Disney Studios. Lonesome Ghosts 1937, original painting, poster paint on paper, 39 x 36in. framed. (Christie's) $33,825

painted foam and wire triffid from the TV series The Day of the Triffids ($540). None of which, perhaps you might care to hang on your bedroom wall....

For you might do well to consider at the outset how your innocent-seeming little collecting habit is going to fit into your lifestyle, since, once it takes hold, you're often hooked for life. The real addicts can find their homes completely taken over by their collections, sometimes to the extent that it's hard to find a place to sit, or even the bed!

For all enthusiasts, however, this new edition of Collectibles and Memorabilia provides, as always, an up to the minute guide to what's making money at the moment and what could well be fetching similar sums in the near future. For there *is* still a whole lot of money to made out there, and, perhaps even more importantly, a whole lot of fun to be had making it.

Anthony Curtis

ACKNOWLEDGEMENTS

AB Stockholms Auktionsverk, Box 16256, 103 25 Stockholm, Sweden
Abbotts Auction Rooms, The Auction Rooms, Campsea Ash, Woodbridge, Suffolk
Abridge Auction Rooms, Market Place, Abridge, Essex RM4 1UA
Allen & Harris, St Johns Place, Whiteladies Road, Clifton, Bristol BS8 2ST
Jean Claude Anaf, Lyon Brotteaux, 13 bis place Jules Ferry, 69456 Lyon, France
Anderson & Garland, Marlborough House, Marlborough Crescent, Newcastle upon Tyne NE1 4EE
Antique Collectors Club & Co. Ltd, 5 Church Street, Woodbridge, Suffolk IP 12 1DS
Auction Team Köln, Postfach 50 11 68, D-5000 Köln 50 Germany
Auktionshaus Arnold, Bleichstr. 42, 6000 Frankfurt a/M, Germany
Barber's Auctions, Woking, Surrey
Bearnes, Rainbow, Avenue Road, Torquay TQ2 5TG
Biddle & Webb, Ladywood Middleway, Birmingham B16 0PP
Bigwood, The Old School, Tiddington, Stratford upon Avon
Black Horse Agencies, Locke & England, 18 Guy Street, Leamington Spa
Boardman Fine Art Auctioneers, Station Road Corner, Haverhill, Suffolk CB9 0EY
Bonhams, Montpelier Street, Knightsbridge, London SW7 1HH
Bonhams Chelsea, 65–69 Lots Road, London SW10 0RN
Bonhams West Country, Dowell Street, Honiton, Devon
British Antique Exporters, School Close, Queen Elizabeth Avenue, Burgess Hill, Sussex
William H Brown, The Warner Auction Rooms, 16–18, Halford Street, Leicester LE1 1JB
Butterfield & Butterfield, 220 San Bruno Avenue, San Francisco CA 94103, USA
Butterfield & Butterfield, 7601 Sunset Boulevard, Los Angeles CA 90046, USA
Canterbury Auction Galleries, 40 Station Road West, Canterbury CT2 8AN
Central Motor Auctions, Barfield House, Britannia Road, Morley, Leeds, LS27 0HN
H.C. Chapman & Son, The Auction Mart, North Street, Scarborough.
Christie's (International) SA, 8 place de la Taconnerie, 1204 Genève, Switzerland
Christie's Monaco, S.A.M, Park Palace 98000 Monte Carlo, Monaco
Christie's Scotland, 164–166 Bath Street Glasgow G2 4TG
Christie's South Kensington Ltd., 85 Old Brompton Road, London SW7 3LD
Christie's, 8 King Street, London SW1Y 6QT
Christie's East, 219 East 67th Street, New York, NY 10021, USA
Christie's, 502 Park Avenue, New York, NY 10022, USA
Christie's, Cornelis Schuytstraat 57, 1071 JG Amsterdam, Netherlands
Christie's SA Roma, 114 Piazza Navona, 00186 Rome, Italy
Christie's Swire, 1202 Alexandra House, 16–20 Chater Road, Hong Kong
Christie's Australia Pty Ltd., 1 Darling Street, South Yarra, Melbourne, Victoria 3141, Australia
A J Cobern, The Grosvenor Sales Rooms, 93b Eastbank Street, Southport PR8 1DG
Cooper Hirst Auctions, The Granary Saleroom, Victoria Road, Chelmsford, Essex CM2 6LH
The Crested China Co., Station House, Driffield, E. Yorks YO25 7PY
Clifford Dann, 20/21 High Street, Lewes, Sussex
Julian Dawson, Lewes Auction Rooms, 56 High Street, Lewes BN7 1XE
Dee & Atkinson, 8 Harrisen, The Exchange Saleroom, Driffield, Nth Humberside YO25 7LJ
Garth Denham & Assocs. Horsham Auction Galleries, Warnsham, Nr. Horsham, Sussex
Diamond Mills & Co., 117 Hamilton Road, Felixstowe, Suffolk
David Dockree Fine Art, 224 Moss Lane, Bramhall, Stockport SK7 1BD
Dowell Lloyd & Co. Ltd, 118 Putney Bridge Road, London SW15 2NQ
Downer Ross, Charter House, 42 Avebury Boulevard, Central Milton Keynes MK9 2HS
Hy. Duke & Son, 40 South Street, Dorchester, Dorset
Du Mouchelles Art Galleries Co., 409 E. Jefferson Avenue, Detroit, Michigan 48226, USA
Duncan Vincent, 105 London Street, Reading RG1 4LF
Sala de Artes y Subastas Durán, Serrano 12, 28001 Madrid, Spain
Eldred's, Box 796, E. Dennis, MA 02641, USA
R H Ellis & Sons, 44/46 High St., Worthing, BN11 1LL

Ewbanks, Welbeck House, High Street, Guildford, Surrey, GU1 3JF
Fellows & Son, Augusta House, 19 Augusta Street, Hockley, Birmingham
Finarte, 20121 Milano, Piazzetta Bossi 4, Italy
John D Fleming & Co., 8 Fore Street, Dulverton, Somerset
Peter Francis, 19 King Street, Carmarthen, Dyfed
G A Property Services, Canterbury Auction Galleries, Canterbury, Kent
Galerie Koller, Rämistr. 8, CH 8024 Zürich, Switzerland
Galerie Moderne, 3 rue du Parnasse, 1040 Bruxelles, Belgium
Geering & Colyer (Black Horse Agencies) Highgate, Hawkhurst, Kent
Glerum Auctioneers, Westeinde 12, 2512 HD's Gravenhage, Netherlands
The Goss and Crested China Co., 62 Murray Road, Horndean, Hants PO8 9JL
Graves Son & Pilcher, 71 Church Road, Hove, East Sussex, BN3 2GL
Greenslade Hunt, 13 Hammet Street, Taunton, Somerset, TA1 1RN
Peter Günnemann, Ehrenberg Str. 57, 2000 Hamburg 50, Germany
Halifax Property Services, 53 High Street, Tenterden, Kent
Halifax Property Services, 15 Cattle Market, Sandwich, Kent CT13 9AW
Hampton's Fine Art, 93 High Street, Godalming, Surrey
Hanseatisches Auktionshaus für Historica, Neuer Wall 57, 2000 Hamburg 36, Germany
William Hardie Ltd., 141 West Regent Street, Glasgow G2 2SG
Andrew Hartley Fine Arts, Victoria Hall, Little Lane, Ilkely
Hauswedell & Nolte, D-2000 Hamburg 13, Pöseldorfer Weg 1, Germany
Giles Haywood, The Auction House, St John's Road, Stourbridge, West Midlands, DY8 1EW
Heatheringtons Nationwide Anglia, The Amersham Auction Rooms, 125 Station Road, Amersham,
    Bucks
Muir Hewitt, Halifax Antiques Centre, Queens Road/Gibbet Street, Halifax HX1 4LR
Hobbs & Chambers, 'At the Sign of the Bell', Market Place, Cirencester, Glos
Hobbs Parker, Romney House, Ashford, Ashford, Kent
Holloways, 49 Parsons Street, Banbury OX16 8PF
Hotel de Ventes Horta, 390 Chaussée de Waterloo (Ma Campagne), 1060 Bruxelles, Belgium
Jacobs & Hunt, Lavant Street, Petersfield, Hants. GU33 3EF
James of Norwich, 33 Timberhill, Norwich NR1 3LA
P Herholdt Jensens Auktioner, Rundforbivej 188, 2850 Nerum, Denmark
Kennedy & Wolfenden, 218 Lisburn Rd, Belfast BT9 6GD
G A Key, Aylsham Saleroom, Palmers Lane, Aylsham, Norfolk, NR11 6EH
Kunsthaus am Museum, Drususgasse 1–5, 5000 Köln 1, Germany
Kunsthaus Lempertz, Neumarkt 3, 5000 Köln 1, Germany
Lambert & Foster (County Group), The Auction Sales Room, 102 High Street, Tenterden, Kent
W.H. Lane & Son, 64 Morrab Road, Penzance, Cornwall, TR18 2QT
Langlois Ltd., Westway Rooms, Don Street, St Helier, Channel Islands
Lawrence Butler Fine Art Salerooms, Marine Walk, Hythe, Kent, CT21 5AJ
Lawrence Fine Art, South Street, Crewkerne, Somerset TA18 8AB
Lawrence's Fine Art Auctioneers, Norfolk House, 80 High Street, Bletchingley, Surrey
David Lay, The Penzance Auction House, Alverton, Penzance, Cornwall TA18 4KE
Brian Loomes, Calf Haugh Farm, Pateley Bridge, North Yorks
Lots Road Chelsea Auction Galleries, 71 Lots Road, Chelsea, London SW10 0RN
R K Lucas & Son, Tithe Exchange, 9 Victoria Place, Haverfordwest, SA61 2JX
Duncan McAlpine, Stateside Comics plc, 125 East Barnet Road, London EN4 8RF
McCartneys, Portcullis Salerooms, Ludlow, Shropshire
Christopher Matthews, 23 Mount Street, Harrogate HG2 8DG
John Maxwell, 75 Hawthorn Street, Wilmslow, Cheshire
May & Son, 18 Bridge Street, Andover, Hants
Morphets, 4–6 Albert Street, Harrogate, North Yorks HG1 1JL
D M Nesbit & Co, 7 Clarendon Road, Southsea, Hants PO5 2ED
John Nicholson, 1 Crossways Court, Fernhurst, Haslemere, Surrey GU27 3EP
Onslow's, Metrostore, Townmead Road, London SW6 2RZ

Outhwaite & Litherland, Kingsley Galleries, Fontenoy Street, Liverpool, Merseyside L3 2BE
J R Parkinson Son & Hamer Auctions, The Auction Rooms, Rochdale, Bury, Lancs
Phillips Manchester, Trinity House, 114 Northenden Road, Sale, Manchester M33 3HD
Phillips Son & Neale SA, 10 rue des Chaudronniers, 1204 Genève, Switzerland
Phillips West Two, 10 Salem Road, London W2 4BL
Phillips, 11 Bayle Parade, Folkestone, Kent CT20 1SQ
Phillips, 49 London Road, Sevenoaks, Kent TN13 1UU
Phillips, 65 George Street, Edinburgh EH2 2JL
Phillips, Blenstock House, 7 Blenheim Street, New Bond Street, London W1Y 0AS
Phillips Marylebone, Hayes Place, Lisson Grove, London NW1 6UA
Phillips, New House, 150 Christleton Road, Chester CH3 5TD
Andrew Pickford, 42 St Andrew Street, Hertford SG14 1JA
Pinney's, 5627 Ferrier, Montreal, Quebec, Canada H4P 2M4
Pooley & Rogers, Regent Auction Rooms, Abbey Street, Penzance
Pretty & Ellis, Amersham Auction Rooms, Station Road, Amersham, Bucks
Peter M Raw, Thornfield, Hurdle Way, Compton Down, Winchester, Hants SC21 2AN
Harry Ray & Co, Lloyds Bank Chambers, Welshpool, Montgomery SY21 7RR
Rennie's, 1 Agincourt Street, Monmouth
Riddetts, Richmond Hill, Bournemouth
Ritchie's, 429 Richmond Street East, Toronto, Canada M5A 1R1
Derek Roberts Antiques, 24–25 Shipbourne Road, Tonbridge, Kent TN10 3DN
Rogers de Rin, 79 Royal Hospital Road, London SW3 4HN
Russell, Baldwin & Bright, The Fine Art Saleroom, Ryelands Road, Leominster HR6 8JG
Sandoes Nationwide Anglia, Tabernacle Road, Wotton under Edge, Glos GL12 7EB
Selkirk's, 4166 Olive Street, St Louis, Missouri 63108, USA
Skinner Inc., Bolton Gallery, Route 117, Bolton MA, USA
Sotheby's, 34–35 New Bond Street, London W1A 2AF
Sotheby's, 1334 York Avenue, New York NY 10021
Sotheby's, 112 George Street, Edinburgh EH2 4LH
Sotheby's, Sommers Place, Billingshurst, West Sussex RH14 9AD
Sotheby's Monaco, BP 45, 98001 Monte Carlo
Southgate Auction Rooms, 55 High St, Southgate, London N14 6LD
Henry Spencer, 40 The Square, Retford, Notts. DN22 6DJ
Spink & Son Ltd, 5-7 King St., St James's, London SW1Y 6QS
Street Jewellery, 16 Eastcliffe Avenue, Newcastle upon Tyne NE3 4SN
Stride & Son, Southdown House, St John's St., Chichester, Sussex
G E Sworder & Son, Northgate End Salerooms, 15 Northgate End, Bishop Stortford, Herts
Taviner's of Bristol, Prewett Street, Redcliffe, Bristol BS1 6PB
Tennants, 27 Market Place, Leyburn, Yorkshire
Thomson Roddick & Laurie, 24 Lowther Street, Carlisle
Thomson Roddick & Laurie, 60 Whitesands, Dumfries
Timbleby & Shorland, 31 Gt Knollys St, Reading RG1 7HU
Venator & Hanstein, Cäcilienstr. 48, 5000 Köln 1, Germany
T Vennett Smith, 11 Nottingham Road, Gotham, Nottingham NG11 0HE
Duncan Vincent, 105 London Road, Reading RG1 4LF
Wallis & Wallis, West Street Auction Galleries, West Street, Lewes, E. Sussex BN7 2NJ
Walter's, 1 Mint Lane, Lincoln LN1 1UD
Ward & Morris, Stuart House, 18 Gloucester Road, Ross on Wye HR9 5BN
Warren & Wignall Ltd, The Mill, Earnshaw Bridge, Leyland Lane, Leyland PR5 3PH
Dominique Watine-Arnault, 11 rue François 1er, 75008 Paris, France
Wells Cundall Nationwide Anglia, Staffordshire House, 27 Flowergate, Whitby YO21 3AX
Woltons, 6 Whiting Street, Bury St Edmunds, Suffolk IP33 1PB
Peter Wilson, Victoria Gallery, Market Street, Nantwich, Cheshire CW5 5DG
Woolley & Wallis, The Castle Auction Mart, Salisbury, Wilts SP1 3SU
Austin Wyatt Nationwide Anglia, Emsworth Road, Lymington, Hants SO41 9BL

CONTENTS

CONTENTS

CONTENTS

11

CONTENTS

An unusual moyegi-ito-odoshi tosei-gusoku with a fine associated kabuto comprising a sixty-two-plate russet-iron sujibachi, unsigned, probably 18th century.
(Christie's) $12,078

An etched Italian Infantry half-armor, comprising Spanish morion, gorget of two plates pivoted together at the side, cuirass with peasecod breast plate, probably Milanese, circa 1580. (Christie's S. Ken)
                    $35,000

A composite Italian armor, comprising close-helmet with one-piece skull, high roped comb, brass plume-holders, comprehensively circa 1570.
(Christie's S. Ken.) $6,500

A composite Continental armor mainly in early 17th century style, mounted on a fabric-covered wooden dummy, with realistically-carved, painted and bearded head set with glass eyes.
(Christie's) $5,750

A rare Indian full armor for a man and horse, all finely damascened in gold with scrolling foliage and flower-heads, partly 17th/18th century.
(Christie's) $16,434

A moyegi-ito-odoshi gold lacquered domaru, comprising a fine russet-iron sixty-two-plate koboshi bachi, the interior gilt, signed *Myochin Shigenobu*, second half 16th century.
(Christie's) $15,000

An English Civil War period steel hat liner 'secret' of simple skull cap form.
(Wallis & Wallis) $450

A pair of spaulders from a late 16th century German Infantry Armor. (Wallis & Wallis) $250

A good composite late 16th century Almain collar, hinged gorget with key-hole fastening stud, medial ridge to front plate. (Wallis & Wallis) $1,250

A German gorget, of exceptionally large size, comprising front and back-plates of bright steel pivoted together, bluntly pointed and struck with Nuremberg mark, early 17th century, 6^{1}/$_{2}$in. high. (Christie's) $1,500

Early 17th century pikeman's breastplate together with associated simulated five lame tassets. $1,350

An iron mempo, Edo period, 17th century, the plain iron mask set with two 'S' cheek flanges and with a separate nosepiece. (Christie's) $1,500

An etched Italian gothic pauldron for the right shoulder, of bright steel, covering the outside and back, the top-plate pierced with point holes, circa 1510. (Christie's) $2,000

A European mail shirt entirely of riveted steel rings, with elbow-length sleeves, probably 15th century, 34in. long. (Christie's) $3,000

A rare German 'Maximilian' chanfron, in two halves riveted together horizontally, shaped to the front of the horse's head and decorated with radiating flutes, circa 1520, 24in. long. (Christie's) $17,500

A scarce WWI tank driver's face mask, leather covered, chamois lined, mail chin guard. (Wallis & Wallis) **$300**

A German codpiece probably from a black and white armor, of bright steel, traces of tinning inside, mid 16th century, 6in. high. (Christie's) **$1,850**

An iron skull cap or secrete composed of numerous flattened bars riveted together complete with its original leather liner, 17th century. (Phillips) **$1,000**

A good heavy early 19th century Moro cuirass, composed of shaped brass plates linked together by thick brass mail. (Wallis & Wallis) **$675**

A rare pair of Italian vambraces, each comprising a tubular upper-cannon made in two parts linked by a recessed turning joint, early 16th century, 18¼in. long. (Christie's S. Ken.) **$9,000**

A boldly modeled russet-iron mempo with one-piece nose and fangs (onimen), with a four-lame yodorekake covered in black leather, the facepiece early 16th century, the mounting 17th century. (Christie's) **$3,250**

A rare Gothic falling bevor composed of three plates with medial ridge, the top plate with angular outward turn and released by a spring catch, late 15th century, 13½in. high. (Christie's) **$1,650**

An etched and gilt pommel plate from a saddle, the upper edges bordered by narrow flanges, probably French, circa 1570, 8in. high. (Christie's S. Ken.) **$700**

A German burgonet and almain collar from a black and white armor, the former with one-piece four-sided skull drawn up to a point with an acorn finial, circa 1560. (Christie's) **$4,200**

Arturo Toscanini, boldly signed
card, in red ink, 2nd June 1950.
(T. Vennett-Smith) $134

Charles Chaplin, signed album
page, annotated in another hand
'London Airport 29-10-52'.
(T. Vennett-Smith) $95

Leslie Howard, signed piece,
1933.
(T. Vennett-Smith) $80

King George I, small signed
piece, as King, laid down to
album page beneath
contemporary engraving.
(T. Vennett-Smith) $124

Anna Pavlova, signed piece,
overmounted beneath 5.5" x 7.5"
reproduction photo.
(T. Vennett-Smith) $86

Gary Cooper, signed cover of
Royal Performance Program ,
at the Coliseum, Charing Cross,
9th November 1938.
(T. Vennett-Smith) $76

Ernest Hemingway, signed and
inscribed edition of Look
Magazine, to inside page, 26th
January 1954 edition featuring
large article about safari in
Africa by Hemingway.
(T. Vennett-Smith) $898

Henry Longfellow, good signed
piece, 1874, laid down to
contemporary album page
beneath contemporary sepia
photograph.
(T. Vennett-Smith) $117

Josephine Baker, autograph
letter, one page, in French, to
'Cher Christian' (her first
theatrical hairdresser).
(T. Vennett-Smith) $143

Henry M. Stanley, signed piece, also signed by his wife Dorothy Stanley, small stain.
(T. Vennett-Smith) $143

William Wordsworth, small signed piece, laid down.
(T. Vennett-Smith) $118

Georges Carpentier, signed album page.
(T. Vennett-Smith) $57

Anna Magnani, signed album page, with attached photo, overmounted beneath 7.5" x 9" reproduction photo.
(T. Vennett-Smith) $134

Samuel Pepys (1633–1703; Diarist and High Naval Officer, Secretary of the Admiralty under Charles II), one page, (London), 27 May 1671, being a warrant to the Clerk of the Stores at Chatham.
(T. Vennett-Smith) $1,184

John Garfield, signed album page, with small attached photo, overmounted beneath 9.5" x 7.5" reproduction photo.
(T. Vennett-Smith) $95

Maria Callas, signed postcard, to lower white border, head and shoulders, photo by Vivienne.
(T. Vennett-Smith) $344

Leslie Howard, signed and inscribed sheet of Canadian Pacific Cruises headed notepaper, 1935, some creasing.
(T. Vennett-Smith) $86

Vivien Leigh, signed piece, overmounted beneath color postcard, 6.25" x 11.25" overall.
(T. Vennett-Smith) $115

King Edward VIII and Queen Mary, signed by both (Edward as Prince of Wales and Mary as Queen), on behalf of King George V, 10th June 1929, appointing Nevil Reid as Second Lieutenant in the Land Forces.
(T. Vennett-Smith) $315

Horatio Nelson, autograph letter, 'Nelson & Bronte', one page, 7th May 1802, to Lieutenant Bromwich, in full "I am very sorry that you do not like your situation for it cost me more interest to obtain it for you than anything I could have asked."
(T. Vennett-Smith) $1,910

Sir Winston S. Churchill, early autograph letter, one page, 16th December 1921, on Colonial Office headed notepaper, to the Irish political leader Tim Healy, "My dear Healy", "I am glad to tell you that a vacancy has occurred in the West African Custom Service"
(T. Vennett-Smith) $1,337

William Pitt, the Elder, interesting signed letter, nine pages, Whitehall, 9th March 1759, to Commodore Moore, marked 'Secret', stating that Captain Tyrrell had arrived with his despatch that had been immediately laid before the King.
(T. Vennett-Smith) $401

Queen Elizabeth II, signed Christmas card, beneath photo showing the Royal Family, accompanied by a Corgi, 1960.
(T. Vennett-Smith) $248

King Charles II, one page, February 1649, being an order of payment of six hundred livres from William Armourer Esq.
(T. Vennett-Smith) $687

AUTOGRAPHED DOCUMENTS

D. H. Lawrence's annotated copy of
Bertrand Russell's Philosophical Essays,
given to him by Lady Ottoline Morrell,
inscribed by her in pencil on the fly-leaf
DHL from OM/1915, 1910. (Phillips
London) $6,864

Prince Charles and Princess Diana, attractive
Christmas card signed by both, featuring a
color photograph of the Prince and Princess
of Wales with their two children.
(T. Vennett-Smith) $1,910

Queen Victoria, St. James's, 1st April 1892,
being a document appointing John Lowndes
Gorst a Second Secretary of Embassies or
Legations abroad, countersigned by Salisbury.
(T. Vennett-Smith) $229

Edward Jenner, autograph letter, five pages,
'Friday Septr.' (26th added in another hand),
to Dr. Worthington, the whole letter stained,
torn at folds and generally fragile.
(T. Vennett-Smith) $726

Sir Winston S. Churchill, typed letter signed,
one page, 8th May 1949, to Captain The Lord
Teynham, 'My dear Teynham', stating that "It
was a great pleasure for Mrs. Churchill and
me to be present at the Primrose League
Meeting the other day."
(T. Vennett-Smith) $936

Charles S. Parnell, typed letter signed, one
page, 31st December 1885, to a female
correspondent thanking her for her letter.
(T. Vennett-Smith) $344

The most famous 18th century maker of automata was Vaucanson, who is best remembered for what might be termed a 'digestive duck' which voided the food it had first eaten! His finest piece was perhaps a figure playing an instrument which was presented at the Academie des Sciences in 1738.

This inspired many imitations. The greatest acclaim was given to Jacquet Droz, who brought out his Lady Musician in 1773, and this became famous at all European courts.

A 19th century French musical clock diorama featuring a village scene on the banks of a river, signed Hy Marl, 37¾in. x 26¾in. $3,750

By the 19th century automata were becoming more and more complex, with acrobats and dancing dolls, monkey orchestras and shoecleaners, while in America walking dolls became popular.

They were powered in various ingenious ways, such as compressed air, water, sand, mercury or steam. It was however the coiled spring which was to prove the most popular and efficient means of power.

It was the Victorian period which saw the heyday of the sophisticated automaton. One late 19th century maker was Gustave Vichy whose work is often characterised by its height, many of his models standing over 30 inches high. His Negro figures with musical instruments have particularly fine leather faces with expressive facial movements even to the lips.

A coin-in-the-slot ship automaton featuring a three masted vessel at full sail set in a choppy sea, contained in a fret-cut mahogany glazed case, 42¾in. wide. (Bearnes) $2,250

By the end of the 19th century, toymakers, particularly in Germany had recognised the possibilities of mass-producing automatic toys, and the tinplate toy industry began to boom. The machine-produced results, were cheap and rudimentary, and thereafter mechanical toys came to be associated mainly with children.

A picture automaton, the timepiece in the church facade activates the clock-work mechanism, probably French, 35in. long. $2,600

A hand-operated musical automaton toy of a village scene, depicting a train traveling through tunnels, circa 1900 Erzegebirge, 12¼in. wide. (Christie's S. Ken) $1,000

A boxed clockwork toy, of two composition headed dolls swinging and dancing before a mirror, 11in. wide, circa 1870. (Christie's S. Ken) $1,000

Die Sud-Nord-Eisenbahn bei Erlangen, a colored lithograph sand toy, depicting a river scene with a train crossing a viaduct, 10½in. wide, Studio of Godefrey Engelmann, Alsace circa 1830. (Christie's S. Ken) $2,500

Late 19th century French musical landscape automaton with numerous moving figures and animals, on an ebonised base with bun feet, 22in. high. $2,250

A mid 19th century German portable barrel organ automaton with numerous articulated figures, contained in a carved oak case with ormolu decoration, 52cm. wide. $12,000

Unnamed and hitherto unknown musical automat, with 5 tunes, 15cm. metal cylinders with complete 57 tooth tone comb, 2 part spring winding and two mechanical dolls, in wooden case with wall attachment, circa 1890. (Auction Team Koln) $23,500

ANIMALS

A French musical manivelle of a 'Mouse Tea-Party', each animal having glass eyes and fur covered body.
(Phillips) $1,150

A clockwork fur covered rabbit automaton, emerging from a green cotton covered cabbage, 7½in. high, French, circa 1900. (Christie's) $500

'Monkey Cobbler', automaton with papier-mâché head, glass eyes, and articulated jaw, seated on a box.
(Phillips) $1,000

An Austrian rabbit-in-the-lettuce, musical automaton, the rotating white fur-covered rabbit emerging from the painted fabric lettuce, 10in. high.
(Christie's) $925

A German hand-operated musical automaton, of three wooden fur-covered cats, having a tea party, 19th century, ¼in. wide.
(Christie's) $1,100

An R.D. France drinking bear, dark brown and white rabbit fur, glass eyes, electrical 1930's, 14½in. high. $900

A coin-operated monkey pianist automaton, with the mechanism contained in the oak base, probably French, late 19th century, 16in. high. $7,500

A clockwork automaton figure of a standing bear drummer, with moving lower jaw and front paws, 27in. high, probably Decamps, 1880. (Christie's) $1,650

A Pussy Band Printed Paper automaton, circa 1910, 18in. high. $600

CONJURORS

A musical conjuror automaton, probably Decamps, French 1880, overall height 17in. $10,000

A 19th century bisque-headed Magicienne automaton. $11,250

A musical automaton doll in the form of a magician linking together a long chain of brass rings, wearing an exotic costume in the Turkish style, 15¼in. high. (Bearne's) $1,500

Automaton magician, 52½in. high, 36½in. wide. $3,000

A musical conjuror automaton by Lambert, the bisque head impressed (Depose Tete Jumeau 4), overall height 19½in. French, circa 1880. $5,000

A musical conjuror automaton standing at her magic box, French, circa 1880, 18in. high by 12in. wide. $9,000

A musical automaton of a conjuror, probably by L. Lambert, French, circa 1880, 16in. high. $3,000

Swiss automaton music box, circa 1900, of a magician, 23in. high. $6,000

A lady conjuror automaton, lavishly dressed in pink silk, mounted on square plinth, probably French, circa 1905, 26in. high. $5,250

MALE FIGURES

An advertising display automaton on oak base, circa
1930, 25in. wide. $2,250

A bisque headed clockwork
clown standing on his hands
dressed in original outfit,
16in. high. (Christie's) $500

19th century wooden
and papier-mache auto-
maton, 36in. high.
$1,500

**A very rare early 20th century
French electrically-operated life-
size black boy magician
automaton, in painted papier-
mâché, 53½ in. high excluding
associated top hat, with Cressall
speed control.
(Tennants)** $9,250

French bisque automaton,
probably Farkas, circa
1920, 12in. high.
$1,500

A composition headed auto-
maton modeled as a standing
Chinese man, 30in. high,
French 1880. $11,250

An automaton figure of a
clown with painted composition face and black and white
costume, 18in. high, with
glass dome. $3.000

**A novelty automaton electric-
driven watch maker, with
illuminated sign to the front and
lamp to his desk, 8in. high.
(Christie's S. Ken)** $1,000

A papier mache automaton
of a clown, the head inset
with fixed blue glass eyes,
18in. high. $1,500

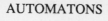

A French Manivelle automaton of a piano player and dancing couple, the pianist seated before a wooden piano, 8½in. high. (Phillips) $1,100

French musical automaton piano player, head impressed SFBJ 301 Paris, circa 1910, 13in. high. $1,250

A very fine Gustav Vichy musical automaton of a young woman playing the guitar, circa 1870. (Phillips) $10,000

A barrel organ grinder automaton, probably French, circa 1900, 17in. high. $1,250

A bisque headed clockwork musical automaton pianist, with closed smiling mouth and fixed blue eyes, by Phalibois, circa 1885, 24in. high, with label giving the airs. (Christie's S. Ken) $5,000

A black composition headed musical automaton, modeled as a smiling man seated on a stool strumming a banjo, by G. Vichy, circa 1900, 24in. high. (Christie's S. Ken.) $6,500

A painted tinplate clockwork musical Puss-in-Boots playing cello, the mechanism operating bowing right arm, probably Martin (one ear missing, spike loose), 9in. high. (Christie's S. Ken.) $1,250

A German musical automaton, 'Musical Troupe' with seven bisque dolls, circa 1880, dolls 7in. high. $4,500

A clockwork musical automaton of a papier mache headed North African girl, sitting on a stool inset with paste jewels and playing a lyre, 29in. high. (Christie's) $6,000

BAKELITE

It was in 1909 that an American research chemist, Leo Baekeland, mixed phenol with a derivative of methyl alcohol to produce an astonishing synthetic resin, which, it was found, could be molded and used for a huge variety of purposes. Not only that, it was inexpensive to produce. Bakelite, the forerunner of modern plastic, had arrived.

Its original color was amber, but later the most usual colors were cream or black. Bakelite's only real drawback was that it was brittle and could be easily cracked.

A Lalique red bakelite box and cover, of square section, the cover molded and carved, with carved signature R. Lalique, 7.5cm. x 7.5cm. (Christie's)
$1,250

Bakelite wall clock, 1930s. (Muir Hewitt) $60

Silver plated and bakelite dish, 7in. diameter, 1930s. (Muir Hewitt) $60

A German Schott bakelite hair-drier, circa 1935. (Auction Team Koeln) $20

Bakelite lemon squeezer with shaped base, circa 1930. (Muir Hewitt) $20

1930s green Bakelite thermos flask. (Muir Hewitt) $35

An Art Deco bakelite comb, brush and mirror set, by R. Amerith, France, 1920's. (Skinner Inc.) $450

A white bakelite tea box, 1940's. $10

Bradley: His Book/Christmas, 1896, published by the Wayside Press, Springfield, sheet size 42 x 29³/₈in.
(Skinner) $1,540

Decretales D. Gregorii Papae IX, Venice 1600.
(Auktionsverket) $1,276

Xenophon, Qua extant opera, Paris 1625, bears label Kimbolton Castle ex libris.
(Auktionsverket) $1,356

Hüysmans, J-K, Les soeurs Vatard, Preface L. Descaves, Paris (Librairie des Amateurs) 1909.
(Auktionsverket) $1,068

Södergran, Edith, Rosenaltaret, Hfors 1919.
(Auktionsverket) $654

An artist's album, circa 1890, wooden boards, the front decorated with a panel of cubic parquetry surrounded by a floral mosaic banding, initialed H.B., 9¹/₂in. wide.
(Sotheby's) $1,364

Leonardo da Vinci, Trattato della Pittura, with a biography of da Vinci by Rafaelle du Fresne, Paris (G. Langlois) 1651.
(Auktionsverket) $3,509

Gallus Neapolitanus J., Consilia siué iuris responsa, Naples (Octavio Beltrani) 1629.
(Auktionsverket) $1,195

Journal des Dames et des Modes I, Paris 1912–14 with 185 color plates.
(Auktionsverket) $1,770

BOOKS

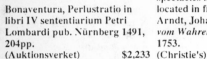

Bonaventura, Perlustratio in libri IV sententiarium Petri Lombardi pub. Nürnberg 1491, 204pp.
(Auktionsverket) $2,233

A rare pair of 'Nuremburg' grooved single wire copper nose spectacles in fitted compartment located in front cover of book, Arndt, Johann., *Sechs Bucher vom Wahren Christentum* Erfurt 1753.
(Christie's) $19,088

Fine child's exercise book, American, 18th century, reads, *The Property of Polly Runnals born April 19th 1787.*
(Eldred's) $495

Gottfried, J. L., Archontologia cosmica sive imperiorum, regnorum, principatum rerumque publicarum omnium per totum terrarum orbe, Ed. II, Frankfurt (M. Merian) 1649.
(Auktionsverket) $7,973

Melanchton, Ph-Jona. J, Heubtartikel Christlicher Lere, Wittenberg, (D. Creutzer) 1558 I-CCCLVIII.
(Auktionsverket) $1,467

Lahde, G. L., Kjøbenhavns klaedegragter eller Det dagelige liv i hovedstaden i characteristike figurer, tegnede efter naturen, Copenhagen, circa 1830.
(Auktionsverket) $1,674

Mercator, G. Atlas sive cosmographicae meditationes de fabrica mundi et fabricati figura, Amsterdam 1607.
(Auktionsverket) $17,542

Johannes Magnus, Gothorum Sveonumque Historia, Rome 1554.
(Auktionsverket) $1,547

An A. Wahnschaffe, Nürnberg softbound catalog, German, circa 1897–98, containing over two hundred and twenty five pages, illustrated throughout with wood cuts, 6 x 9in.
(Sotheby's) $1,215

Rare American Bowie knife by Alfred Hunter, circa 1845, 8¹⁵/₁₆in. clip point blade, German silver guard capped by an ornate incised carved ivory grip, bearing an escutcheon plaque, German silver mounted scabbard.
(Butterfield & Butterfield)

$6,050

Historic massive Bowie knife by Graveley & Wreaks, 16in. spear point blade, originally owned by Captain Charles Alexis Berry, sea captain and entrepreneur, born near Mt. Vernon, Virginia in 1810.
(Butterfield & Butterfield)

$27,500

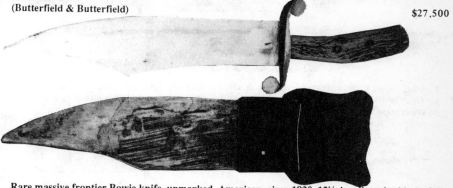

Rare massive frontier Bowie knife, unmarked, American, circa 1830, 12¹/₁₆in. clip point blade, full silver plated, silver plated crossguard and stag grip neatly incised with letter *F* on pommel, 17⁷/₁₆in. overall.
(Butterfield & Butterfield)

$28,600

Rare massive Bowie knife, unmarked, American, circa 1847, 14¹/₄in. clip point blade, the hilt composed of iron crossguard, ferrules, and incised carved ivory grip with silver pommel, inscribed on throat *J. Leach, San Antonio, 1847*, 19³/₄in. overall
(Butterfield & Butterfield)

$33,000

Bowie knife by Wolf & Clark, New York, circa 1840, 12¹/₈in. clip point blade, dark walnut grip scales, German silver hilt, studs, escutcheon plaques and turned quillons, 16³/₁₆in. overall. (Butterfield & Butterfield)　　　　$9,900

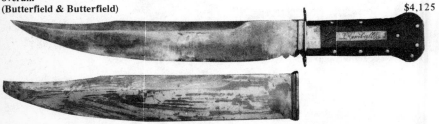

Bowie knife by English & Huber, Philadelphia, circa 1835, 9⁹/₁₆in. clip point blade, iron cross guard, German silver mounted hilt with studded ivory grip bearing two escutcheon plates, 14¹/₂in. overall.
(Butterfield & Butterfield)　　　　$4,125

Fighting Bowie knife, unmarked, American, circa 1835, 10in. clip point blade with decorative notch, coin silver mounted grip with silver studs bearing escutcheon plates marked *L. Kimball* and on the reverse *Vicksburg*, 14¹/₁₆in. overall.
(Butterfield & Butterfield)　　　　$44,000

Unmarked Bowie knife, American, circa 1845, 10⁷/₁₆in. clip point blade with sharpened false edge and decorative Spanish notch, silver mounted hilt with ivory grip bearing decorative silver studs, 14³/₈in. overall.
(Butterfield & Butterfield)　　　　$29,700

Rare American patriotic Bowie knife by Chevalier, New York, circa 1860, 8¹³/₁₆in. clip point blade stamped *Chevalier Union Knife*, on obverse *Death to Traitors*, brass mounted hilt with checkered ebony grips, 13³/₁₆in. overall.
(Butterfield & Butterfield)　　　　$5,500

AMERICAN

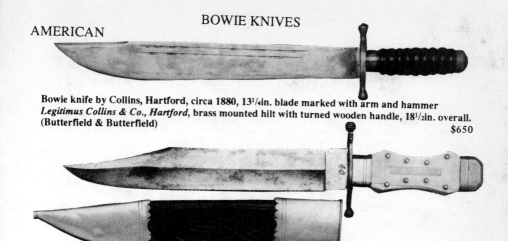

Bowie knife by Collins, Hartford, circa 1880, 13¼in. blade marked with arm and hammer *Legitimus Collins & Co., Hartford,* brass mounted hilt with turned wooden handle, 18½in. overall.
(Butterfield & Butterfield)

$650

Rare American Bowie knife, Philadelphia, circa 1835, 10⁷/₁₆in. clip point blade marked on ricasso *Sheffield Works 2,* iron crossguard, German silver and ivory hilt set with German silver studs and escutcheon plates, 15½in. overall.
(Butterfield & Butterfield)

$16,500

Rare Bowie knife by Schively, Philadelphia, circa 1835, 7¹/₁₆in. spear point blade, German silver pommel cap and guard, finely checkered horn grip, with old replacement sheath, 12¼in. overall.
(Butterfield & Butterfield)

$5,225

Rare outstanding gold mounted Bowie knife, unmarked, American, circa 1835, 10⅛in. clip point blade with decorative Spanish notch, the ivory grip surrounded by gold ricasso, crossguard, bolster, pommel cap, and set with gold studs and escutcheon plates, 14½in. overall.
(Butterfield & Butterfield)

$27,500

Rare Bowie knife by Rose, New York, circa 1830, 12⁷/₁₆in. spear point blade marked *Rose New York,* German silver mounted hilt with spiral carved grip, 17⅞in. overall.
(Butterfield & Butterfield)

$3,850

Large Bowie knife by Booth, Sheffield, circa 1850, 10³/₄in. spear point blade bearing engraved and etched panels on left side with deep serrations on the obverse and reverse, with horn and mother-of-pearl scales and two piece silver plated crossguard, 16⁷/₈in. overall.
(Butterfield & Butterfield) $6,600

Bowie knife by T. Ellin, Sheffield, circa 1845, 8¹³/₁₆in. clip point blade etched *Prarie Knife*, German silver and ivory hilt set with German silver bands, 13⁵/₈in. overall.
(Butterfield & Butterfield) $5,225

Bowie knife by Fisher, Sheffield, circa 1860, 10¹/₂in. spear point blade marked *George Fisher, Sheffield*, the ricasso stamped *S.D.*, stag handle with German silver crossguard, 15¹/₄in. overall.
(Butterfield & Butterfield) $1,100

English style Bowie knife, unmarked, circa 1880, 11¹/₂in. spear point blade, coin silver mounted hilt with celluloid grip, 17¹/₈in. overall.
(Butterfield & Butterfield) $385

Bowie knife by C. Congreve, Sheffield, circa 1835, 9¹¹/₁₆in. clip point blade with Spanish notch marked *CELEBRATED AMERICAN BOWIE KNIFE*, German silver and ivory hilt, 14¹/₄in. overall.
(Butterfield & Butterfield) $17,600

Large Bowie knife by Greaves, Sheffield, circa 1840, 11⁵/₈in. double edged spear point blade, German silver mounted hilt with ivory grip scales bearing escutcheon plates on either side, 16¹/₂in. overall.
(Butterfield & Butterfield) $8,250

WOSTENHOLM

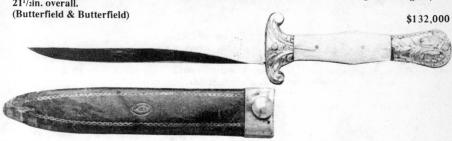

Rare outstanding exhibition Bowie knife by George Wostenholm, Sheffield, circa 1870, 13¹/₂in. clip point blade elaborately etched with panel scenes of Mt. Vernon flanked by standing Indians, mother-of-pearl grip marked *Avoir Patrie* under a raised carved profile of George Washington, 21¹/₂in. overall.
(Butterfield & Butterfield) $132,000

Small Bowie knife by Wostenholm, the 5¹/₄in. double edged spear point blade marked *I-X-L/George/Wostenholm/Celebrated/Cutlery*, hilt with ivory scales and German silver quillons and pommel.
(Butterfield & Butterfield) $520

Rare ornate Bowie knife by Wostenholm, Sheffield, circa 1850, 10¹/₄in. clip point blade, coin silver mounted hilt with full fluted ivory grips and elaborately engraved quillons in the form of dolphins, 15³/₄in. overall.
(Butterfield & Butterfield) $17,600

English IXL Bowie knife, 8in. clip point blade marked *None Are Genuine But Those/Marked IXL, G. Wostenholm & Son/Washington Works, The Real IXL Knife, The Hunters Companion*, and *IXL*, grip with tortoise shell with German silver escutcheon.
(Butterfield & Butterfield) $1,250

BREAST & BACKPLATES

A Cromwellian trooper's breast and backplate, breastplate with medial ridge, backplate struck with Commonwealth armorer's mark of helmet over "A".
(Wallis & Wallis) $1,500

An English Commonwealth period breastplate, struck with helmet over A (Commonwealth Armorer's Company mark) and maker's initials E.O.
(Wallis & Wallis) $1,100

A breastplate probably adapted in the early 19th century.
$500

A breast-plate, early 16th century, probably German, 18¹/₂in. high.
(Christie's S. Ken) $2,650

A French Carabinier trooper's breast and backplates of heavy steel overlaid in brass, dated 1832 and adapted for the 2nd Empire period with the addition of the imperial eagle.
(Phillips) $985

A breast plate for a Knight of Malta in mid 16th century style, roped neck and articulated arm cusps, vertically ribbed ensuite with two lower plates and first skirt plate. (Wallis & Wallis)
$1,250

An early 19th century officer's steel cuirass of the Household Cavalry, morocco lining and crimped blue velvet edging, leather bound borders and brass studs.
(Wallis & Wallis) $2,950

An English Cromwellian period breast and backplate, struck with Commonwealth armorer's "A", maker's initials "F.O."
(Wallis & Wallis) $900

A Victorian Household Cavalry Officer's breast and backplates, of steel with brass rivets and edging.
(Phillips) $1,350

An Innsbruck breast-plate from
an infantry armor (Harnasch),
of bright steel and rounded
form, with prominent medial ridge.
(Christie's S. Ken). $1,650

A 17th century Continental
breastplate with twin studs
for fastening and shoulder
straps. $350

A Continental articulated
breastplate, circa 1700, of
swollen form with medial
ridge. $500

A heavy German cavalry
troopers breastplate circa 1800,
musket ball proof mark,
stamped *Hartkopf*, lugs for strap
fastening.
(Wallis & Wallis) $275

A rare German gothic breastplate made in two parts
(associated) joined by a central
screw, late 15th century, 21in.
high.
(Christie's S. Ken.) $7,500

A post-1902 Household Cavalry
trooper's plated cuirass, leather
lining with blue cloth edging,
brass bound borders and studs,
leather backed brass scales with
ornamental ends.
(Wallis & Wallis) $800

An English Civil War period
breastplate, distinct medial
ridge, turned over edges, flared
narrow skirt, twin studs for
securing straps.
(Wallis & Wallis) $450

A post-1902 Household Cavalry
trooper's plated cuirass, leather
lining with blue cloth edging,
brass bound borders and studs.
(Wallis & Wallis) $825

A heavy German cavalry
trooper's breastplate circa 1800,
musket ball proof mark, lugs for
strap fastening, short raised
collar, edges pierced with holes
for lining attachment.
(Wallis & Wallis) $225

BRONZE FIGURES

France had been one of the leading countries in bronze figure production throughout the nineteenth century, and was to adopt a major role also during the Art Nouveau/ Deco periods. The medium lent itself particularly well to the flowing lines and themes of Art Nouveau, while the Art Deco period saw the increasing use of bronze in combination with ivory, or chryselephantine as it came to be known. The figures conceived in this medium have a character which is all their own.

'Valkyrie', a bronze group cast from a model by Stephan Sinding, a spear maiden astride a stallion, on the naturalistic bronze base, 56cm. high. (Christie's) $5,350

A bronze bust of an Art Nouveau maiden cast after a model by van der Straeton, circa 1900, 31cm. high. (Christie's) $650

'Anagke', (Compulsion), a bronze figure cast after a model by Gilbert Bayes, signed and dated 1918, 59cm. high. (Christie's) $16,250

Huntress, a silvered bronze figure cast from a model by G. None, Paris, 34cm. high. (Christie's) $2,000

A French bronze figure of an Aborigine maiden, cast from a model by Cordier, shown dressed only in a grass skirt decorated with shells, late 19th or 20th century, 20¼ in. high. (Christie's) $6,500

A Raoul Larche gilt-bronze figure of Loie Fuller, the veils swept up concealing two light fittings, circa 1900, 45.75cm. high.
          $22,500

Dancers, a dark and silver patinated bronze group, both dancers wearing pointed caps, elaborate bodices and panta-loons, 10in. high. (Christie's S. Ken) $1,000

'Dancer', a bronze and ivory figure by H. Fournier of a girl standing on tiptoe, holding out her skirt, 35cm. high. (Christie's) $4,000

BRONZE FIGURES

An early 20th century Italian bronze bust of a maiden in folk costume, cast from a model by E. Rubino, 44cm. high. (Christie's) $750

'Penthesilia, Queen of the Amazons', a bronze figure cast from a model by A. Bouraine, 48.2cm. long. (Christie's) $1,350

Bronze figure of a woman, signed Oscar Glandebeck, circa 1900, 12in. high. (Lots Road Chelsea Auction Galleries) $350

'Dance of the Harlequinade', a gilt bronze and ivory figure, cast and carved after a model by Th. Ullmann, 30cm. high. (Christie's) $1,500

A bronze figure of a nude dancer by Alexander Kelety, 40.2cm. high. $12,000

A bronze and ivory figure cast and carved from a model by Kovats, 39cm. high. (Christie's) $11,500

A bronze figure, 'Egyptian Priestess', 80cm. high. (Christie's) $1,350

A bronze figure of a skier in a twisting posture on a naturalistic base above a variegated marble plinth, 12½in. long. (Christie's S. Ken) $750

Bear Hug, a bronze figure cast after a model by F. Rieder, 30.8cm. high. (Christie's) $2,250

BRONZE FIGURES

An Austrian bronze of a footballer with his leg raised to kick a football, signed Fuchs, 13½in. high. (Christie's S. Ken) $750

'Thoughts', a bronze figure cast after a model by M. Giraud Riviere, circa 1930, 17.8cm. high. (Christie's) $750

A late 19th or early 20th century English bronze bust of a handsome youth, in the style of Brock, on turned red marble socle, 14.5cm. high. (Christie's) $250

A bronze figure of a naked young lady dancing, by Karl Perl, 24½in. high. (Christie's) $1,850

An early 20th century gilt bronze and ivory group of a little girl and a baby snuggled-up in an armchair signed A. Croisy, 6¾in. high. (Woolley & Wallis) $2,250

The Rejected Suitor, a gilt bronze and ivory figure, cast and carved from a model by Roland Paris, as a small bald headed man, 24.8cm. high. (Phillips London) $1,200

An Anglo-Australian early 20th century bronze figure of Diana wounded, cast from a model by Sir Bertram Mackennal, 42cm. high overall. (Christie's) $13,250

A bronze cigarette box in the form of a girl in Middle Eastern dress, 4in. high. (Capes, Dunn & Co.) $600

Sabre Dancer, a Viennese bronze figure of a scantily clad Oriental dancing girl in jeweled headdress, 55.5cm. high. (Christie's London) $7,250

BRONZE FIGURES

Dancer with Tambourine, a gilt bronze figure cast from a model by Agathon Leonard, 55.5cm. high. (Christie's) $6,000

A 20th century French bronze group of three running athletes, entitled Au But, cast from a model by Alfred Boucher, 32cm. high. (Christie's London) $2,250

A bronze and ivory figure cast and carved from a model by Marquetz and modeled as a girl with a long robe tied at the waist, 28.5cm. high. (Phillips) $600

A 20th century English green patinated bronze figure of a naked young girl, signed and dated *Pibworth, 1923,* 25in. high. (Christie's S. Ken) $750

A late 19th century Viennese bronze portrait bust of a young girl, cast from a model by Arthur Strasser, dated 1894, 42cm. high. (Christie's) $825

Eastern Dancer, a bronze and ivory figure, cast and carved from a model by G. Schmidt-Cassel, on a black marble base, 37.6cm. high. (Christie's London) $11,500

A bronze figure, cast from a model by H. Molins, as a female dancer, 58.5cm. high. (Christie's) $1,350

Morning Walk, a parcel gilt bronze and ivory group cast and carved after a model by A. Becquerel, 26.8cm. high. (Christie's) $2,000

An Art Deco bronze figure, by Fesler Felix, modeled as a naked girl with an elaborate headdress and belt, 37cm. high. (Phillips) $350

BRONZE FIGURES

An Art Deco bronze group of a male and female nude, 65cm. high. (Christie's)
$3,250

1920s bronze figurine of a lady from the demi-monde. (Muir Hewitt) $525

A gilt bronze tray cast from a model by Maurice Bouval, formed as a leaf with the figure of a nymph holding flowers, signed M. Bouval, 17.5cm. high. (Christie's) $1,100

'Bubble Dance', a bronze and ivory figure by A. Goddard, of Georgia Graves at the Folies Bergere, 1930, the female figure in short silver-patinated dress, 52.5cm. high. (Christie's)
$9,000

An Art Deco cold painted and silvered bronze figure, the young woman wearing a brief skirt, with arms outstretched, lampholders suspended from her hands, overall height 48.5cm. (Bonhams) $4,000

'Elegant', a gold patinated bronze and ivory group, cast and carved from a model by S. Bertrand, of a finely dressed woman standing with a grayhound at her side, 31.2cm. high. (Christie's) $3,350

Early 20th century bronze bust of Woman, signed Wigglesworth, stamped Gorham Co. Founders, 13¼in. high. (Skinner Inc.) $900

A green patinated bronze group cast from a model by Amy Bitter as three naked children, 'See no evil, speak no evil, hear no evil', 25cm. high. (Phillips) $3,000

A late 19th century French 'Chryselephantine' bronze and ivory figure of 'La Liseuse', base signed A. Carrier-Belleuse, 62cm. high. (Christie's) $2,650

BRONZE FIGURES

A bronze model of a fox, modeled in stylised fashion, 35cm. high, stamped on reverse Seiden-Stucker. (Phillips) $450

A bronze bust of a woman cast from a model by Dora Gordine, Paris, 1925, 36.8cm. high. (Christie's) $1,500

'Source d'Or', a bronze sculpture by Ernest Wante of a gold patinated maiden standing in a rocky enclave, 25.4cm. high. (Christie's) $1,350

Tambourine Dancer, cast from a model by D. Simon, of a nude maiden dancing with a tambourine, 44cm. high. (Christie's London)$1,000

An Art Deco bronze and ivory figurine of a young bather reclining on a large rock. (Biddle & Webb) $7,500

A stylish Art Deco bronze figure, cast from a model by Gilbert, as a naked girl with silvered body poised above a fluted bullet shaped base, 46cm. high. (Phillips London) $1,850

A bronze and alabaster figure cast and carved from a model by Lothar of a maiden tying beads in her hair, 50.5cm. high. (Christie's) $1,650

An early 20th century Belgian bronze bust of a stevedore, cast from a model by Constantin Meunier, inscribed Anvers, 58cm. high. (Christie's) $5,250

A bronze Spirit of Ecstasy showroom display, signed *Charles Sykes,* mounted on a circular marble base, 20½in. high. (Christie's London) $12,000

CHIPARUS

Of the many figurine artists who emerged during the years following the First World War one of the most important was Dimitri (Demetre is the Gallicised form) Chiparus. Chiparus was a Rumanian who came to Paris to study under A Mercié and J Boucher. He started exhibiting at the Salon des Artists Français in 1914, when he received an Honourable Mention, and continued to do so until 1928.

His figures include realistic reproductions of nudes and women in everyday clothes, as well as columbines and pierrots, and dancers, some in amazing postures and obviously influenced by the Ballets Russes.
Much of his work was executed in chryselephantine, a medium encouraged at the time by the Belgian government who were anxious to create a European market for Congolese ivory.

'Sheltering from the Rain', a bronze and ivory group cast and carved from a model by D. Chiparus, 26cm. high. (Christie's)　$2,650

'Golfer', a bronze and ivory figure, by D. H. Chiparus, of a girl swinging a golf club and wearing a green-patinated skirt, 36.8cm. high. (Christie's) $15,000

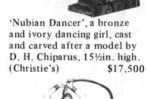

Lioness, a bronze figure cast after a model by Demetre Chiparus, 57.8cm. long. (Christie's)　$2,000

'Nubian Dancer', a bronze and ivory dancing girl, cast and carved after a model by D. H. Chiparus, 15½in. high. (Christie's)　$17,500

'Dourga', a bronze and ivory figure by D. H. Chiparus, of a girl standing on tiptoe with her arms raised above her head, 62.5cm. high. (Christie's)　$12,000

'Les Amis de Toujours', a bronze and ivory figure by Demetre Chiparus, of a standing lady, flanked by two borzois, on a rectangular amber-colored onyx base, 63cm. high. (Christie's)　$20,000

'Dancer with Ring', a bronze and ivory figure by D. H. Chiparus, of an oriental dancing girl wearing a jeweled headdress, 46.5cm. high. (Christie's) $20,000

CHIPARUS

A painted bronze and ivory
figure, 'Hush', 42cm. high,
inscribed D. H. Chiparus.
(Phillips) $4,500

'The Fan Dancer', a bronze
and ivory figure by Chiparus,
on marble and onyx base,
15in. high. (Christie's) $7,000

A painted bronze and ivory
figure, 'Oriental Dancer',
40.20cm. high, inscribed on
the marble Chiparus.
(Phillips) $7,000

A bronze and ivory figure
cast and carved after a model
by D. H. Chiparus, 16in. high.
(Christie's) $7,500

'Cleopatra', a bronze figure by
D. H. Chiparus, wearing a jeweled
headdress, bodice and wrap skirt,
48cm. wide. (Christie's) $6,000

An Art Deco period figure
in bronze and ivory of a
lady holding a muff, signed
D. H. Chiparus, 12½in. high.
(R. H. Ellis & Sons) $3,500

'Leaving the Opera', a bronze
and ivory figure by D. Chiparus
of a woman wrapped in a silver-
patinated cloak, walking down
a stepped brown onyx base,
23.4cm. high. (Christie's)
          $3,250

A gilt bronze and ivory group
of three young girls, signed
Chiparus, 6in. high. $2,750

'Fancy Dress , a cold-painted
bronze and ivory group, cast
and carved from a model by
Demetre Chiparus, as a
Pierrot wearing a green-silver
costume dancing with his
female companion, 48.5cm.
high. (Phillips) $18,000

COLINET

Claire Jeanne Roberte Colinet was born in Brussels and studied sculpture there under Jef Lambeaux. After moving to Paris she was elected a member of the Société des Artistes Français. She exhibited at their Salon from 1914, and at the Salon des Indépendants between 1937 and 1944.

It is noteworthy that Colinet was the only woman among the figurine artists who emerged in the years after the First World War. She worked in the hieratic style which was quite close to that of the artists of the 1890s, featuring mysterious dancers dressed in flowing garments of costly fabrics, laden with jewels at wrist and ankle. Colinet's best works show athletic dancers, beautifully proportioned, arranged in strange balletic poses and obviously much influenced by the Ballets Russes.

A Colinet bronze group of two dancing bacchantes, 56.5cm., 1930's. $3,750

'Snake Dancer', cast from a model by C J R Colinet of cold-painted bronze and ivory, on a marble base, 24in. high. $7,500

A Colinet bronze dancing girl in eastern costume, circa 1930, 39.5cm. high. $2,500

'Danseuse de Thebes', a bronze and ivory figure cast and carved from a model by C. J. Roberte Colinet, 25.8cm. high. (Christie's) $12,000

A bronze figure, the design attributed to C. J. R. Colinet, the female dancer dancing standing on tiptoes, 15½in. high. (Bonhams) $2,250

A bronze lamp cast and carved from a model by C. J. R. Colinet modeled as a dancing girl, her arms outstretched supporting a lamp in each hand. (Christie's) $7,000

A bronze figure by Cl. J. R. Colinet, modeled as a nude female standing on one foot, the other leg and both arms outstretched before her, supporting a ball on each, 26.7cm. high. $2,250

COLINET

Colinet cold-painted bronze and ivory figure of an 'Erotic Dancer', on an onyx base, 14in. high. $2,250

Gilt bronze and ivory figure of a girl in pantaloons, possibly by Colinet, 45cm. high. $3,000

Egyptian Dancer, a gilt bronze and ivory figure cast and carved from a model by C. J. Roberte Colinet, 42.5cm. high. (Christie's) $30,000

A cold painted bronze figure, attributed as a model by Cl. Colinet, of a naked girl with brown hair, poised above a stepped marble base, 49.5cm. high. (Phillips) $1,850

Towards the Unknown (Valkyrie), a cold painted bronze and ivory group, cast and carved from a model by Claire Jeanne Roberte Colinet, 31.5cm. high. (Phillips London) $4,000

'Oriental Dancer', a bronze figure cast from a model by C. J. Roberte Colinet, 19½in. high. (Christie's) $2,750

'Egyptian Dancer', a bronze figure, cast from a model by Cl. J.R. Colinet, of a dancing girl, with flowing skirt and Egyptian headdress, 43cm. high. (Christie's) $4,500

A gilt bronze figure of a girl, 'Modern Venus', cast from a model by C. J. R. Colinet, 47cm. high. (Phillips) $4,500

A cold-painted bronze and ivory figure of a dancing girl by Colinet on a bronze and onyx base, 18in. high overall. $6,000

FAGUAYS

Pierre le Faguays was a native of Nantes in France. A member of the Société des Artistes Français, he exhibited at their salons, where he gained an Honourable Mention in 1926. He was also a member of the La Stèle and Evolution groups, where artist craftsmen exhibited bronzes, ceramics, lamps and other decorative objects.

Le Faguays worked in the 'stylised' mode, which combined elements from many contemporary influences.

Le Faguays bronze male figure of an Olympian hero holding a palm leaf, 66cm. high, 1930's. $2,250

A bronze nude female figure of a dancer by Le Faguays, signed, 21¾in. high overall. $1,500

'Dancer with Thyrsus', a parcel gilt bronze figure cast after a model by Pierre Le Faguays, 27.6cm. high. (Christie's) $2,250

'Bacchante', a bronze green and brown patinated figure, cast from a model by Pierre Le Faguays, of a nude female kneeling on one leg, the other bent forward, 66.5cm. high. (Christie's) $10,000

A silvered bronze figure of a dancer, cast from a model by Pierre Le Faguays, the young woman wearing a pleated dress with paneled skirt, 1920s, 65cm., overall height. (Bonhams) $2,250

'Diana'. A bronze figure, cast from a model by Pierre Le Faguays, modeled as a lithe young woman wearing a short classical tunic, 66.5cm. high. (Phillips) $1,750

'Fawn and Nymph', a bronze sculpture cast from a model by Pierre Le Faguays mounted on a rectangular wooden base, 46.5cm. high.(Christie's) $10,000

'Pitcher', a bronze figure cast from a model by Pierre Le Faguays, of a young girl in a short dress, 25cm. high. $1,500

GERDAGO

Gerdago (this may or may not even be a name) is one of those producers of Art Deco bronzes about whom absolutely nothing is known. His pieces, while set firmly within the mainstream tradition of the period, i.e. having as subjects exotic dancers in wildly balletic poses, are nevertheless highly distinctive. The figures are always dressed in extravagant, angular costumes, often with tall, pointed hats, and are cold painted in the most brilliant and magnificent colors.

A bronze and ivory figure of a dancer in a floral dress by Gerdago, 12in. high. $9,000

A bronze and ivory figure of a dancer cast and carved from a model by Gerdago, 10½in. high. (Christie's) $6,000

'Dancer', a bronze and ivory figure, cast and carved from a model by Gerdago, of a female dancer poised with arms outstretched, 32.8cm. high. (Christie's) $6,000

A cold-painted bronze and ivory figure of a dancer from a model by Gerdago, on a green onyx base, 11in. high. $10,000

'Exotic Dancer', a gold-patinated bronze and ivory figure by Gerdago of a female dancer making a theatrical curtsey, 30.5cm. high. (Christie's) $20,000

GORY

'Exotic Dancer', a gilt bronze and ivory figure cast and carved from a model by A. Gory, 37.5cm. high. (Christie's) $3,500

The Cape, a gilt bronze and ivory figure cast and carved from a model by A. Gory, of a small child, 20.1cm. high. (Christie's London) $750

'Flower Seller' a gilt bronze and ivory figure cast and carved from a model by A. Gory, 38.5cm. high. (Christie's) $4,500

NAM GREB

Who is, or was, Nam Greb, the impudent sculptor of these erotic bronze figurines? You won't find the answer in any of the reference books, for the simple reason that no one by that name existed. Nam Greb is, in fact, Bergman spelt backwards!

Little enough, indeed, is known about the Franz Bergman foundry, save that it flourished in Austria during the first two decades of this century. Bergman, spelt the right way round, is known for fairly conventional cold painted bronze groups, notably of Arabs on carpets or Arabs with camels.

It is always the erotic pieces that are signed Nam Greb. These were, in fact, designed by a man called Thuss, about whom absolutely nothing more is known. It has been suggested, perhaps a little tongue in cheek, that he signed them thus because he didn't want his mother to know what he was up to!

'Sword Dancer', a large cold painted bronze figure cast from a model by Nam Greb, 21¼in. high. $2,000

A bronze rectangular casket and cover by Nam Greb, on four cockleshell feet, 4¾in. wide. $750

A cold painted bronze figure of Cleopatra cast from a model by Nam Greb, 10in. across. (Christie's) $1,250

The secret of the mummy: an encased bronze nude figure by Nam Greb, 23cm. high. $2,000

A Bergman cold painted bronze musical box, inscribed 'Nam Greb', modeled as an amorous young beau kneeling beside his willing consort, 13½in. (Lawrence Fine Arts) $3,000

A Bergman painted bronze figure, modeled as a bathing belle in one piece swimsuit and hair tied in a mobcap, 12.5cm. high. $1,250

An amusing Bergman painted bronze group, modeled as an owl, with a seal which when pressed, parts the owl's body to reveal a naked female figure, 19.5cm. high, signed *Nam Greb*. (Phillips London) $2,500

GUERANDE, JAEGER

It seems amazing today that so little should be known about so many of the sculptors whose bronzes are quite commonly sold at auction. After all, we are not talking about the dark ages, but only about sixty or seventy years back into the past. Sketchy biographical details are available on a few of the most illustrious figures, such as Chiparus and Colinet, for example, but for others, such as Guerande and Jaeger, not even as much as their dates or nationalities are freely available. Even the auction houses who regularly feature their works have little information to give.

Why should this be? One possible explanation is that many were just foundry workers, turning out pieces in a current fashion, or sometimes in imitation of more notable artists.

Also, many worked in Germany or Austria, which the Second World War would shortly leave largely in ruins, and where many records must have been destroyed. It seems a shame that the history of these bronze designers should be lost for ever, and it is certainly a subject which would amply repay some intense investigation.

KAUBA

Carl Kauba worked in Vienna in the interwar period, producing bronzes which stand a little apart from the mainstream subjects of dancers, sportsmen etc. Fairly conventional Art Nouveau type maidens do figure among his output, but he also tackled more offbeat themes such as amusing groups of children. Commonest of all, however, are his Red Indian figures, which show little Art Deco influence.

An Art Deco gilt bronze figure of a dancer kneeling with arms outstretched, signed J. D. Guerande, 21 in. high overall. $1,250

A bronze group cast from a model by Guerande of a dancing lady, 62.9 cm. high. (Christie's) $2,250

A bronze table lamp cast from a model by G. Jaeger of a naked sea nymph poised holding a conch shell to her ear, 70cm. high. (Christie's) $2,250

'The Swing', a bronze and ivory figure cast and carved from a model by Jaeger, 10½in. high. (Christie's) $2,000

A bronze group cast from a model by C. Kauba, on a variegated square marble base, signed, 14.3cm. high. (Christie's) $650

A mechanical bronze figure cast after a model by C. Kauba, on a square bronze base, circa 1920, 21cm. high. (Christie's) $1,250

LORENZL

K Lorenzl was a German Art Deco figurine modeler, who also designed ceramics for the Austrian firm of Goldscheider. He often copied well known Preiss figures, though his carving was not as skilled.

He did succeed however in capturing in bronze the 'new woman', slender and boyish, with bobbed hair, dressed either in floppy pyjamas or as an Amazon. Some of his figures are signed *K Lor* and *Ronr*.

A bronze group of a girl with a borzoi by Lorenzl. $2,750

An Art Deco bronze figure cast from a model by Lorenzl, modeled as a dancing girl, 43.9cm. high. (Phillips) $1,000

A golden-patinated bronze figure cast from a model by Lorenzl, as a dancing girl wearing a long-sleeved dress, 49cm. high. (Phillips) $1,100

'Diane', a silvered bronze group of a naked goddess flanked by two running borzois, modeled by Lorenzl, 46cm. high. $3,750

A Lorenzl silvered bronze figure, the naked maiden in dancing pose, tip-toed upon one leg, 49.5cm. high, signed. (Lawrence Fine Arts) $1,000

A Lorenzl gilt and painted bronze figure of a lady holding the hem of her skirt, on onyx base, 10in. high. (Christie's) $750

A Lorenzl gilt bronze dancing girl, poised on one leg, 15in. high. (Christie's) $1,250

A bronze figure of a nude girl, cast from a model by Lorenzl, she has bobbed hair and stands demurely with her hands clasped, 64cm. high. (Phillips) $2,750

LORENZL

A Lorenzl bronze figure of a naked dancing girl, standing on one leg, kicking the other, 28cm. high. (Phillips) $500

'Dancing Girl', a silvered bronze and ivory figure cast from a model by Lorenzl, decorated by Crejo, 22.3cm. high. (Christie's) $1,000

A bronze and ivory figure of a dancer by Lorenzl. $2,250

'Nude Girl with Shawl', a silvered bronze figure cast from a model by Lorenzl, decorated by Crejo, 37.5cm. high. $3,000

A patinated silvered bronze group of a pair of Russian dancers, cast from a model by Lorenzl, on a rectangular green onyx base, 11½in. high. $3,000

The Dancer, an enameled bronze and ivory figure, cast and carved from a model by Lorenzl, on green onyx pedestal, 27.4cm. high. (Christie's London) $2,250

A large Lorenzl silvered bronze figure of a dancing girl, 28½in. high. (Christie's) $2,750

A Lorenzl cold-painted bronze figure of a nude in dancing pose, 1930's, 23.5cm. high. $2,250

A gilt bronze and ivory figure cast and carved from a model by Lorenzl, 11in. high. (Christie's) $800

PHILIPPE

Philippe was an Austrian by birth, who created stylish models and dancers characterised by their theatrical and extravagant gestures. His treatment of the clothes is particularly striking, and often is a pure product of the new Machine Age.

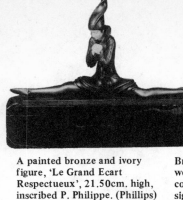

A painted bronze and ivory figure, 'Le Grand Ecart Respectueux', 21.50cm. high, inscribed P. Philippe. (Phillips) $3,450

Bronze figure of a dancing woman, P. Phillipe, 20th century, costumed figure, marble plinth, signed and titled, 15¹/₂in. high. (Skinner Inc.) $1,250

'The Swirling Dress' a cold painted bronze and ivory figure by Philippe, 40cm. high. $4,500

'Dancer', a bronze and ivory figure cast and carved from a model by P. Philippe of a girl standing on tiptoe, her hands outstretched, wearing a short flared dress and jeweled turban, 64.5cm. high. (Christie's) $13,500

'Pierrette', a cold-painted bronze and ivory figure, cast and carved from a model by P. Philippe, 37.8cm. high. (Phillips) $6,000

'Andalusian Dancer', a cold-painted bronze and ivory figure cast and carved from a model by P. Philippe, 35.3cm. high. (Phillips) $6,000

Philippe colored bronze and ivory figure of a young woman, signed, 24cm. high, 1930's. $7,500

'Rahda', a bronze and ivory figure by P. Philippe, of a dancer standing on tiptoe, arms outstretched, 43.4cm. high. (Christie's) $9,000

PROF OTTO POERZL

As with many of the sculptors of the Art Deco period, very little is known about Professor Otto Poerzl. Where did his title come from, for example? Such sketchy details as are available tell us that he was born in Scheiben, and worked out of Coburg, both in Germany. He produced figures which in many cases are so similar to those produced by Preiss that speculation has abounded that they are one and the same person. However, their respective interpretations of some examples, Bat Dancers, for instance, do show significant differences in treatment. The confusion has not been helped by the fact that both appeared to use the same foundry, and a founder's mark with the initial PK are found on both Poerzl and Preiss figures.

A Poertzel bronze and ivory group of a pierrot and partner, 1930's, 37cm. high. $11,250

'Snake Dancer', a bronze and ivory figure by Prof. O. Poertzel, on black marble base, 52cm. high. (Christie's) $13,250

Poertzel bronze and ivory group of a woman and two hounds, 49.5cm. high, 1920's. $12,000

Bronze and ivory dancer by Prof. O. Poertzel, 1930's, 32cm. high. $2,250

'Butterfly dancers', a bronze and ivory group cast and carved from a model by Prof. Otto Poertzel, of two ballerinas dancing in formation, 41.5cm. high. (Christie's) $15,000

'Page Girl' a cold-painted gilt bronze and ivory figure of a young girl by Poertzel, on a green marble base, 11½in. high. (Christie's) $2,000

'Bat Dancer' by Prof. O. Poertzel in bronze and ivory, on a marble base, 8in. high. $3,000

PREISS

Art Deco found one of its most vivid expressions in the bronze and ivory, or chryselephantine, figures of F Preiss. Virtually nothing is known about Preiss, save that he was probably born in Vienna. Even his forename is in doubt, though an Ideal Home Exhibition Catalogue of the time refers to him as Frederick, which is probably simply an anglicisation of Friedrich. His work, which appeared in the 20s and 30s, was closely copied by one Professor Otto Poerzl of Coburg, so closely in fact that there has been speculation that they may be one and the same. His figures were distributed in Britain by the Phillips and MacConnal Gallery of Arts, which published an illustrated catalog with model numbers. They chiefly featured classical and modern nudes, children, some nude and some clothed, and a few dancers. The ivory is always beautifully carved, and the subjects have sweet, pretty faces, and graceful arms and hands. The bronze is usually cold-painted in cool colors such as silver, blue and gray, and while the classical nudes can be somewhat stilted, the modern counterparts are lithe and vibrant.

Most lively of all are, however, the Olympic figures, a series including golfers, tennis players, skaters and javelin throwers. They glorify physical prowess and the body beautiful, enthusiasms which came to be hijacked by the Nazis in their preoccupation with the physical superiority of the Aryan master race. Preiss captured this so well that, rightly or wrongly, suspicion has always abounded that he was an adherent of the movement.

'Bat Dancer', a bronze and ivory figure cast and carved after a model by F. Preiss, 23.6cm. high. (Christie's) $5,500

'The Archer', a bronze and ivory figure cast and carved from a model by Ferdinand Preiss of a girl with drawn bow, in a gold-patinated tunic with train, with polychrome enameled sword and headdress, 22.3cm. high. (Christie's) $9,000

'Mandolin Player', a bronze and ivory figure by Ferdinand Preiss, the gold and silver patinated girl wearing a top-hat and loose fitting skirt, 58.4cm.high. (Christie's) $18,500

Charleston Dancer, a cold painted bronze and ivory figure, cast and carved from a model by Ferdinand Preiss, as a slender female dancer wearing silvered tights, 43.5cm. high. (Phillips London) $8,250

A painted bronze and ivory figure, 'Hoop Girl', 20.50cm. high, inscribed F. Preiss. (Phillips) $2,250

'Skater', a silver-patinated bronze and ivory figure cast by Ferdinand Preiss, of a girl skating with one leg behind her, 33.4cm. high. (Christie's) $7,000

PREISS

'Cabaret girl', a bronze and ivory figure, cast and carved from a model by Ferdinand Preiss, 38cm. high. (Christie's) $13,500

The Torch Dancer, a painted bronze and ivory figure, cast and carved from a model by Ferdinand Preiss, as a bare-breasted girl wearing floral bloomers, 39cm. high. (Phillips London) $9,000

A painted bronze and ivory figure, 'Sonny Boy', 20.50cm. high, inscribed F. Preiss. (Phillips) $2,500

'Gamin', a bronze and ivory figure by F. Preiss, of a girl dressed in a silver patinated short skirt suit, standing with her hands in her pockets, 34.3cm. high. (Christie's) $10,000

A painted bronze and ivory figure, cast and carved from a model by Ferdinand Preiss, as a female skater wearing golden, short-skirted costume 23.5cm. high. (Phillips London) $4,000

'Moth Girl', a bronze and ivory figure by Ferdinand Preiss, of a girl standing on tiptoe and examining a glass over her shoulder, 41.6cm. high. (Christie's) $7,500

Art Deco bronze and ivory figure of a young woman, after a model by Johann Philipp Ferdinand "Fritz" Preiss, circa 1930, 8³/4in. high. (Skinner Inc.) $3,500

'Con Brio', a bronze and ivory figure cast and carved from a model by F. Preiss, 29cm. high. (Christie's) $8,000

Flute Player, a bronze and ivory figure cast and carved from a model by F. Preiss, 48.5cm. high. (Christie's) $27,500

VILLANIS

No biographical details are
available for Emmanuele
Villanis. His work, however,
is set firmly in the Art
Nouveau period and also has
strong links with traditional
19th French century bronze
casting. His subject matter is
drawn very often from
Classical mythology, and
simply given an Art Nouveau
treatment. Busts, another
very traditional form, figure
largely among his output.

An early 20th century patinated
bronze figure of 'Les Nenuphars'
by Emmanuel Villanis. $3,750

Bronze bust of 'Dalila', by
E. Villanis, circa 1890, seal
of Societe des Bronzes de
Paris. $2,250

'Sapho', a cold-painted bronze
bust cast from a model by E.
Villanis, of a young maiden, her
hair tied in a bun, green and
amber patination, 58cm. high.
(Christie's) $5,000

Pair of late 19th or early 20th
century French bronze busts of
Mignon and Diana, signed on
the shoulders E. Villanis, 36.5cm.
high. $3,000

An early 20th century
French patinated bronze
bust of Omphale, cast from
a model by E. Villanis,
53cm. high. (Christie's)
                     $2,250

La Sibylie, a bronze bust
cast from a model by E.
Villanis, with Societe des
Bronzes de Paris foundry
mark, 72cm. high.
(Christie's) $3,750

An early 20th century bronze
and cold-painted figure of a
slave girl, by Emmanuele
Villanis, 16in. high. $3,000

Silvia, cast from a model by
Emmanuele Villanis, the
green patinated Art Nouveau
maiden mounted on a
pedestal, 28cm. high.
(Christie's London) $2,250

BRUNO ZACH

Bruno Zach was the post World War One artist in bronze who is generally associated with an overtly erotic style. His insolent, leather or scantily clad women, girls in slips or stockings holding a whip or naked beneath fur coats reflect the decadence of interwar Berlin with its sado-masochistic, often downright bizarre tendencies. Zach worked mostly in bronze, but he made the occasional figure in chryselephantine, and these are now particularly sought after.

A large decorative figural bronze and cameo glass table lamp, the bronze base cast from a model by Bruno Zach. (Phillips London) $2,250

'Spanish Maiden' cast from a model by Bruno Zach of a standing maiden with her hands on her hips, 30cm. high. $2,250

A bronze figure, cast from a model by Bruno Zach, 15½in. high. (Christie's) $1,500

'Dancing Satyr and Nymph' cast from a model by Bruno Zach, 36cm. high. $4,500

'Girl with a riding crop', a bronze figure cast from a model by Bruno Zach, Made in Austria, 46cm. high. (Christie's) $3,750

'The Riding Crop', an erotic bronze figure cast from a model by Bruno Zach. $3,750

'Warrior Maiden', a bronze group cast from a model by Bruno Zach of a scantily clad girl astride a galloping stallion, 45cm. high. (Christie's) $6,000

Athlete, a dark patinated bronze figure cast from a model by Bruno Zach, with impressed mark, 73.8cm. high. (Christie's London) $4,500

Books intended specially for children had appeared as early as the mid 17th century, and it quickly became clear that illustrations were of the first importance if children were to be encouraged to read with pleasure.

As the 19th century progressed, children's books became stratified into certain well-defined types, all of which, however, had the common feature of illustration. Early illustrated educational texts formed one type. Another consisted of thinly disguised moral tracts, where dreadful fates often befell the erring characters. Finally, there were books of pure entertainment, classic tales by such enduring authors as Stevenson, R M Ballantyne and Lewis Carroll. Fairy tales by the Brothers Grimm and Hans Christian Andersen trod the line between the second and third categories.

During the Victorian period, book illustrations achieved the status of an art form and three great illustrators emerged, Walter Crane, Randolph Caldecott and Kate Greenway. These three were followed by worthy successors such as Arthur Rackman, who carried the tradition forward into the 20th century.

The later 19th century also saw a wealth of ingenuity in book production, with pop-up images, sliding panels, tabs and levers all designed to amuse and appeal.

Another popular childhood book, the annual, actually predates the comics on which so many are now based, with the first, the Xmas Box, appearing in the 1820s. By the 1930s the annual was an indispensible item in many a child's Christmas stocking, and by and large their popularity has lasted to the present day.

'Little Bear And His Friends', 1st Edition, 1921. $30

'Diamond Dick', The Boys Best Weekly, 1900. $12

A Primer and Catechisme, and also the notable fayres in the Kalender set forth by the Quenes ma:iestie to be taught unto Children, T. Purfoote, assigned by W. Seres, a remarkable survival of a children's book from the late 16th century. (Lawrence) $7,500

'Walt Disney's Pinocchio', 1940. $30

'The Jolly Gnomes Annual', 1951. $25

'The Frog Prince', M. L. Attwell Illustrations, 1920's. $25

'The Little Ebony Elephant', by Fitz. $12

'The Adventures of Old Man Coyote', 1945. $8

Peter Pan and Wendy — illustrated by Mabel Lucie Attwell. $45

'The Lone Ranger Annual 1964'. $12

The Magic Doorway. $25

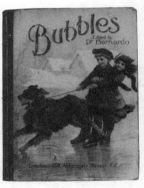

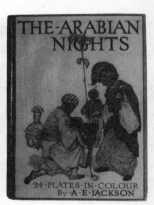

'The Companion Annual', 1924. $15

Bubbles, Volume 7. $35

Arabian Nights — illustrated by A. E. Jackson. $35

'The Ship of Adventure',
Enid Blyton, 1st Edition,
1950. $30

'Children's Outdoor-Games', by G.
B. Crozier, 1910. $20

'Alice in Wonderland',
Pears Illustrations. $12

'The Girl's Own Annual 1934'. $30

'The Wizard Book For Boys
1938'. $30

'The Brave Little Tailor',
1923. $25

'The Mickey Mouse Fire Brigade,
1936'. $60

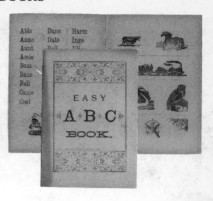

'My ABC of Nursery Rhyme Friends', Tuck, circa 1940. $20

'Easy A B C Book', circa 1850. $20

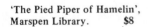

Fun and Frolic by Louis Wain and Clifton Bingham, a children's poetry book published by Nister, circa 1902. (Phillips) $250

'The Pied Piper of Hamelin', Marspen Library. $8

'See', by Dorothy Dealtry, 1950. $5

'Ameliaranne Camps Out', 1st Edition, 1939. $30

'The Book of the Teddy Bear', 1964. $25

Treasure Island 1929 —
illustrated by Rowland
Hilder. $25

'The Felix Annual', 1930's. $30

My Favourite Annual 1933.
$25

Greyfriars Holiday Annual
1921. $45

Rover Book for Boys 1940.
$25

'Blown to Bits', by R. M.
Ballantyne, 1889. $8

Chatterbox 1907. $20

Peggy and Joan — illustrated
by Honor Appleton. $20

'Nursery Fun', Dean's Picture
Book. $5

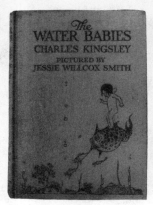

Water Babies 1938 — illustrated by Jessie Wilcox Smith.
$50

My Book of Ships 1913.
$15

Armchair Story Book 1937.
$20

'Okay Adventure Annual',
Boardman & Co. $20

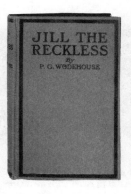

'Jill the Reckless', Eighth
Printing, 1928. $8

'The Splendid Savage', by
Conrad H. Sayce. $8

Big Book of Mother Goose,
has revolving disk of hunt
scene in cover. $30

Playbox Annual 1918.
$40

Golden Annual for Girls
1925. $20

AMPHORA

The Amphora Porzellanfabrik was established at Turn-Teplitz in Bohemia to make earthenware and porcelain. Much of their porcelain figure output was exported.

The mark consists of three stars in a burst of rays over *RSK* (for the proprietors Reissner & Kessel).

CHINA

An Amphora polychrome painted porcelain group, modeled as a young woman, being presented with a casket from a small boy, 13in. high.
(Christie's S. Ken) $250

An Amphora oviform earthenware jardinière, painted with geese walking in a wooded landscape, 8¹/₂in. high.
(Christie's S. Ken) $500

ANSBACH

Forty years after faience production began, in 1758, Johann Friedrich Kaendler, who was possibly a relative of the Meissen modeler, helped the then margrave Alexander of Brandenburg to establish a porcelain factory at Ansbach, which continued in production until 1860.

Their wares show little originality and tended to follow Meissen, Nymphenburg and particularly Berlin styles pretty slavishly. The figures in particular closely resemble those produced at Berlin, though Ansbach pieces can be distinguished by their lightweight, elongated bodies and half-closed eyes painted in red. Groups were also made based on plays written by the margrave's wife, and show lovers, hunters or allegories set against architectural arbors.

Marks, where they exist, show the shield of the Arms of Ansbach, impressed, showing a stream with three fishes. Tablewares are sometimes marked with an *A*, sometimes with a shield or the Prussian eagle.

An Amphora ceramic planter, the exterior molded and pierced in relief with mistletoe on curvilinear stems, enclosing maidens' heads, painted in green, sepia and gilt, 8¹/₄in. wide.
(Christie's) $300

An Amphora polychrome-painted pottery group modeled as a Bedouin tribesman astride a camel, 19in. high.
(Christie's S. Ken) $300

An Ansbach baluster coffee-pot and a cover, painted with two birds perched in branches flanked by scattered sprigs of puce flowers, circa 1770, 18.5cm. high overall.
(Christie's) $1,350

An Ansbach arched rectangular tea-caddy and cover painted with men fishing from a rock and in a boat before a village and distant mountains, circa 1775, 12.5cm. high.
(Christie's) $2,500

ARITA

Porcelain first appeared in Japan when the discovery of kaolin nearby in 1616 led to the establishment of a ceramic center in Saga prefecture, Hizen, which came to be known as Arita. Early Arita was painted in grayish underglaze blue and primitive red and green enamels. Enameled and blue and white wares with paneled decoration in the later Ming style were brought to the West by the Dutch from the 17th century onwards, often through the port of Imari. Kakiemon and Nabeshima wares were also made at Arita, and production continues there to the present day.

A pair of Arita blue and white candlesticks, the bell shaped lower sections decorated with buildings in a forested land-scape, late 18th/early 19th century, 25cm. high. (Christie's) $1,250

A large Arita blue and white octagonal vase decorated with karashishi prowling beneath bamboo, pine and peony with ho-o birds hovering above, late 17th century, 60cm. high. (Christie's) $6,000

A fine Arita blue and white charger, the central roundel containing a vase of cascading peony sprays on a veranda, Genroku period, 55cm. diam. (Christie's) $6,500

A Japanese Arita life-size model of an eagle, the biscuit body painted in colors, circa 1700, 59cm. high. (Christie's) $30,000

A rare Arita blue and white shallow dish, the wide everted rim with stylized lotus and scrolling foliage, late 17th century, 24.7cm. diam. (Christie's) $7,500

Late 17th century Arita blue and white ewer with loop handle, 24cm. high. (Christie's) $900

A fine pair of Arita blue and white oviform jars and covers, Genroku period, 88cm. high, wood stands. (Christie's) $10,000

A handsome Arita model of a seated dog, decorated in iron-red, brown and black enamels and gilt, its mouth agape, late 17th century, 40cm. high. (Christie's) $55,000

ASHSTEAD POTTERY

The Ashstead Pottery was established in 1923 by Sir Laurence and Lady Weaver to give employment to disabled ex-servicemen. It produced tableware, nursery novelties and figures, at first in white glazed earthenware. Painted landscape decoration and linear designs were introduced later, and the figures, usually in white glazed earthenware with touches of color, are characterised by garlands of flowers painted in bright blue, yellow, maroon, light green and yellow. The original workforce of 14 had risen to 30 by 1925, and the pottery continued in business until 1935.

The mark is usually a printed tree, with *Ashstead Potters*.

AULT POTTERY

William Ault (b. 1841) was an English potter who worked in Staffordshire before going into partnership with Henry Tooth in 1882 to open an art pottery at Church Gresley, Derbyshire. In 1887 he opened his own pottery near Burton-on-Trent, where he produced earthenware vases, pots, pedestals and grotesque jugs.

The painted decoration of flowers and butterflies was often executed by his daughter Clarissa. Between 1892-96 Christopher Dresser designed some vases for Ault, which he sometimes covered in his own aventurine glaze. Between 1923-37 the firm traded as Ault and Tunnicliffe and thereafter became Ault Potteries Ltd.

Marks include a tall fluted vase over *Ault* on a ribbon, or a monogramed *APL*.

An Ashstead lamp base, of ovoid form molded in relief on each shoulder with the head of gazelle, 11in. high.
(Christie's S. Ken) $300

An Ashtead advertising plaque, for the Ideal Home magazine, molded in relief with ballet dancer, 6in. high.
(Christie's S. Ken) $200

Three of five Art Deco Ashtead pottery wall plates. (Phillips)
          $375

'Shy', an Ashtead pottery figure modeled as young girl seated on a pedestal draped with a garland of flowers, 15¼in. high.
(Christie's S. Ken) $1,100

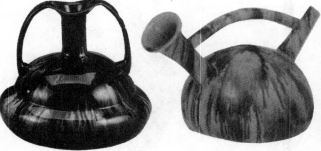

An Ault vase, designed by Dr. Christopher Dresser, with curling lip continuing to form two handles, streaked turquoise glaze over dark brown, 18cm. high. (Christie's) $1,500

An unusual Ault Pottery pouring vessel, designed by Christopher Dresser, of compressed globular shape with two pouring spouts, 28cm. wide. (Phillips) $3,350

BELLEEK

The Belleek porcelain factory was established in 1863 in Co. Fermanagh, Ireland, by David McBirney and Robert Armstrong, and continues in existence today. Its production is characterised by the use of parian covered with an iridescent glaze, and its wares consist principally of ornamental and table wares, such as centerpieces, comports, ice buckets etc. Belleek is especially noted for its frequent use of naturalistically molded shell forms, perforated decoration and woven basketwork effect.

The early impressed or printed mark from 1863–80 consisted of a crown above a harp, while later versions had a wolfhound seated alongside a harp over *Belleek*. After 1891 *Ireland* or *Co. Fermanagh* was added to comply with the McKinley Tariff Act.

A white Belleek chamber pot, the inside base with black-printed image of Gladstone, 10cm., registration mark for 1877. (Phillips) $600

A Belleek tea kettle and cover, the overhandle bound with gilt tassles and with spreading leaf molded terminals, 8¼in. across. (Christie's) $225

A fine Belleek circular basket, the looped rim applied with opalescent twig handles and sprays of lily-of-the-valley, 23.5cm. diameter. (Bearne's) $1,000

A mid 19th century Belleek porcelain honey pot and cover in the form of a beehive, 14.5cm. high. (Spencer's) $600

One of a pair of Belleek tapering jugs with fluted bodies applied in high relief with bouquets of flowers, 9in. high. (Christie's)
   Two $500

A Belleek rectangular plaque painted by Horatio H. Calder, black printed Belleek mark, First Period, 17 x 11.3cm. $3,750

A Belleek vase, modeled as three thistles supporting a larger thistle, on circular base, 22.5cm. (Lawrence Fine Arts) $300

BERLIN

Berlin ceramics date back to the late 17th century, when from 1678 faience and red earthenware was produced. In 1763 the factory came under royal patronage when Frederick the Great purchased it to become the Königliche Porzellan Manufaktur, and production turned to hard-paste porcelain. From the end of the First World War it became known as the Staatliche Porzellan Manufaktur in Berlin. Throughout its existence it has continued to produce fine table-ware with high quality painted decoration, though various designers have also pursued contemporary trends. During the late 19th century, for example, its wares were often characterised by elaborate glaze effects under oriental influence, as seen in the work of H Seeger. Notable figures were designed by Scheurich and in the early years of this century tableware was also produced to Bauhaus designs.

KPM

A Berlin blue and white cylindrical chocolate-pot and cover, circa 1775, 13cm. high. (Christie's) $600

A Berlin (Funcke Factory) blue and white faience octagonal baluster vase and cover painted with chinoiserie figures taking tea, circa 1760, 42cm. high. (Christie's) $3,000

Two Berlin faience polychrome flared octagonal vases, painted with birds perched and in flight among flowering shrubs, circa 1730, 29.5cm. high. (Christie's) $2,500

A Berlin plaque painted after Peter Paul Rubens, 39 x 31cm., KPM and scepter mark. (Phillips) $7,500

KPM Porcelain Plaque of a Young Woman, Berlin, late 19th century, hair bound at the top of her head, scepter marks, 7³/₄in. high.
(Skinner Inc) $3,000

A pair of Berlin Russian Ballet figures from models by Hubatsch, the figures in theatrical poses, each polychrome enameled and with gilt decoration, 21.5cm high. (Christie's) $1,750

A Berlin porcelain rectangular paperweight, finely painted with flowers, printed and impressed marks, 16 x 8.5cm. (Bearne's) $300

BOLOGNA

Bologna, together with Padua, is particularly associated with a rare and early type of earthenware known as sgraffito or sgraffiato. This terms refers to the technique used in their decoration. The body was of red clay covered with a white slip with the design scratched through to show the red base. The pieces were then covered with a yellow toned lead glaze and often dappled with patches of green or golden brown.

Many reproductions of the rare originals have been made by Carlo Giano Loretz of Milan. In Bologna too, in the 19th century Angelo Minghetti & Son produced fine reproductions of Renaissance maiolica.

BÖTTGER

It was J F Böttger's discovery of red stoneware and porcelain in 1708–9 which gave Augustus the Strong's Meissen factory a lead in porcelain production which it did not lose until after the Seven Years War some fifty years later. Böttger's success as an arcanist was not equalled by his success as a business man, however. He remained under Augustus's close eye almost until his death, and it was not until after that event that the factory reached the period of its true greatness and prosperity.

CHINA

A Bologna sgraffito dish, the center with a profile of a young man with curly brown hair, 16th century, 24.5cm. diam. (Christie's London) $1,500

A Bologna sgraffito trilobed jug, the bulbous body incised with scrolls of foliage, late 15th century, 20.5cm. high. (Christie's) $1,350

A Bottger red Steinzeug hexagonal tea caddy and cover molded with alternating panels of birds in trees issuing from terraces, circa 1715, 12.5cm. high. (Christie's Geneva) $42,000

A Böttger Hausmalerei saucer painted in iron-red with an equestrian figure in full dress, holding a banner, his horse dressed with plumes, circa 1720, 12.5cm. diameter. (Christie's) $1,850

A Bottger gold Chinese milk jug and later domed cover gilt in the Seuter workshop, the porcelain circa 1725, 18cm. high. (Christie's) $1,100

A rare and attractive Bottger polished stoneware tea canister, the vertical panels molded in relief and gilt with birds in flight and perched in trees, 12.5cm. (Phillips) $12,000

BOW

The Bow factory was one of the most prolific of the mid 18th century and concentrated mainly on producing 'useful' tablewares in blue and white.

Very few pieces dating from before 1750 survive, and these are mainly painted in vivid famille rose colors against a grayish paste. A selection of items were also produced unpainted but with relief decoration in imitation of Fukien blanc de Chine. The 'quail' pattern derived from Japanese Kakiemon ware is also especially characteristic of the factory as are other exotic bird patterns and botanical designs.

Blue and white production falls broadly into three periods. The first, 1749–54, saw the production of thickly potted, heavy wares painted in a vivid cobalt blue. Decoration was often in the Chinese style with a slightly blurred appearance.

During the middle, and most successful period, from 1755–63, a wide range of products were made, especially sauceboats, centerpieces, mugs, bowls etc. These were less thickly potted, often in powder blue, and favorite designs are 'Image', 'Jumping Boy', dragon, and a harbor scene, all still showing a very strong oriental influence.

From 1764 quality declined both in terms of opacity and painting. Sauceboats and plates remained a speciality, but were now much less elaborate, and after 1770 production fell considerably.

An attractive Bow polychrome cream boat, the fluted sides enameled with floral sprays detailed in black, the interior with floral and leaf sprigs, 4¹/₄in. long, circa 1765. (Tennants) $350

A most impressive Bow candlestick group modeled as a retriever chasing two grouse, standing before a colorful, flowering tree, 29cm. high. (Phillips) $3,750

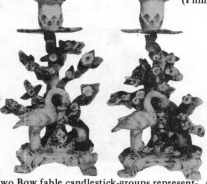

Two Bow fable candlestick-groups representing the fable of The Fox and the Stork, the stork with its beak in the neck of a bottle-shaped vase painted in a famille rose palette with a loose bouquet, the fox crouching on the other side gazing up at the bird, circa 1758, 22cm. high. (Christie's) $6,000

A Bow model of a tawny owl, its plumage in shades of yellow and brown, circa 1758, 19.5cm. high. (Christie's) $9,000

A Bow documentary cylindrical ink pot with a central circular well surrounded by five holes to the shoulder, painted by James Welsh, circa 1758, 9cm. diam. (Christie's London) $20,000

A Bow group of two dancers standing before a tree stump applied with flowers and turned towards each other with their hands raised, wearing feathered hats, circa 1765, 18cm. high. (Christie's) $4,500

A Bow porcelain figure of a nurse. (Hobbs Parker) $1,000

A Bow documentary blue and white octagonal plate, the center with the entwined monogram RC surrounded by trailing flowers, 21cm. diam. (Christie's) $3,350

A Bow figure of Pierrot with outstretched arms, wearing pale-yellow clothes edged in puce, circa 1762, 14.5cm. high. (Christie's) $1,000

A Bow figure of a seated tabby cat, a brown rat in its right paw, another disappearing into a rathole, circa 1758, 8cm. high. (Christie's) $3,000

A pair of Bow white busts of Mongolians, she with her hair plaited, he with a moustache and pointed beard, circa 1750, 27.5cm. high. (Christie's) $75,000

A rare early Bow 'Muses' figure of Hope, the lady resting one arm on a puce column, her other on an anchor, 21.5cm. high. (Phillips) $1,250

A Bow figure of a shepherd playing the bagpipes, circa 1757, 26.5cm. high. (Christie's) $1,500

A pair of Bow figures of a shepherd and a shepherdess, on circular mound bases applied with colored flowers, circa 1758, 14.5cm. high. (Christie's) $2,500

A Bow figure of Matrimony modeled as a young woman holding a turquoise square bird-cage, circa 1765, 20cm. high. (Christie's) $1,500

BRANNAM

Charles H Brannam (1855–1937) worked as a potter in Barnstaple, Devon, at first making kitchenware and ovens. From 1879 he started making art pottery, known as Barum ware, usually of brownish clay with simple designs in white slip, mostly in the form of small jugs and vases. His work is usually signed and dated.

C. H. BRANNAM
BARUM

C. H. BRANNAM LTD.

C. H. BRANNAM
BARUM DEVON

BRETBY

The Bretby pottery was founded in 1883 at Woodville, Derbyshire, by Henry Tooth and William Ault. It produced figures, jardinières, bowls, jugs, vases etc., at first in earthenware decorated with colored glazes (notably sang de boeuf), and applied with flowers, insects etc. in light colored clay. Later they also produced earthenware decorated in imitation of hammered copper, steel, and bronze with applied ceramic jewels.

William Ault struck out on his own in 1887, but Bretby continued, making 'carved bamboo' ware, and, from 1912 onwards, Clantha ware, which was decorated with geometrical designs on a matt black glaze. Art pottery was made until 1920.

From 1891 the mark was an impressed sun rising behind *Bretby*.

A large Brannam pottery oviform vase, decorated in sgraffito on one side with stylised fish swimming amid aquatic foliage, 79cm. high.
(Phillips) $600

A Charles Brannam barium blue glaze stoneware vase, incised with a mythical bird and beast below stylised foliage, dated 1881, 17in. high.
(Spencer's) $1,100

A Bretby tobacco jar and cover, inscribed 'Nicotiank', 16.5cm. high. $100

A Brannam twin-handled vase by Frederick Braddon, the handles formed as open-mouthed and scaly dragons, 23.7cm. high.
(Phillips) $200

A Brannam pottery cat, seated, his grinning face turned to one side, with the words *'Keep smiling'* modeled along the creature's tail, 24.3cm. high.
(Phillips) $300

Very fine Bretby pottery floor vase, with peasant girl figure by J. Barker, approx. 36in. high. (G. A. Key) $375

BRISTOL

Hard paste porcelain production began in Bristol in 1770, when William Cookworthy removed his factory there from Plymouth, as a place with a stronger potting tradition. Mugs, sauceboats, bowls, creamboats, coffee cups and pickle leaf dishes were among the items produced, and it is in fact often quite difficult to tell Plymouth from early polychrome Bristol.

Cookworthy and Champion's Bristol factory came to concentrate mainly on tea and coffee services, and while some decoration still shows Chinese influence, Meissen and Sèvres styles predominate. Elsewhere, sparsely decorated floral and garland patterns are common but the colors are usually sharp and clear and the gilding is superb.

There was little blue and white material produced, and creamboats, pickle leaf dishes and coffee cups are about all that will be found. The blue is very bright and the glaze relatively unflawed, and the whole approaches more nearly the Chinese original than the output of any other contemporary factory. Most Bristol blue and white ware is marked with a cross in underglaze blue.

A Bristol dessert basket of oval shape with pierced lattice sides, 1770-72, 8½in. over handles. $600

A Bristol sauceboat with foliate scroll handle, circa 1775, 7¼in. over handle. $450

A Bristol christening mug of barrel form, circa 1775, painted X in blue, 10 in gilding, 3in. high. $375

A Champion's Bristol figure of a classical female, circa 1773, 10in. high. $900

A Bristol globular teapot and cover with ear-shaped handle, Richard Champion's Factory, circa 1775, 16cm. high. $2,000

A Bristol two-handled cup and trembleuse saucer of ogee outline, marked B6 in blue enamel. $1,000

A Bristol baluster milk jug from the Smyth Service, Richard Champion's factory, circa 1776, 10.5cm. high. $800

BRITISH

The British pottery tradition before the industrial period is rooted in the medieval use of tin glazed earthenware. This was often manufactured in monasteries, such as the Cistercian pottery of the 16th century, and was the direct forerunner of the Staffordshire slipwares of the succeeding centuries, which were to form the mainstream of English potting development.

The first inspiration towards refinement came, in England as elsewhere, when the Dutch brought back the first examples of Chinese porcelain. English delft, though never in the same class as its Dutch counterpart, was made at Liverpool, Bristol and elsewhere, painted in very high temperature colors, with little overglaze enameling.

In Staffordshire, the call for a more delicate ware was answered by the development of a fine saltglazed white stoneware, and then Wedgwood's creamware, which, with its numerous imitators, soon achieved a worldwide market.

18th century English porcelain was distinguished by its variety of composition, ranging from the French style soft-paste type made at Derby, Chelsea and Longton Hall, to the soapstone pastes favored at Worcester, Caughley and Liverpool and the hard paste varieties of Plymouth and Bristol, while it was the bone ash type pioneered at Bow which was to become the standard body.

No English factory enjoyed the royal patronage which so often fostered their European counterparts, and most were short lived. Inspiration, however, did not fail, and throughout the 19th century, English potters continued to make wares ranging from simple cottage and luster ware to the fine porcelains of Worcester, Derby and Spode.

CHINA

An interesting green glazed teapot and cover, molded in relief with sprays of chrysanthemums and bell-like flowers, 14cm. (Phillips) $6,000

A ceramic chamber pot with everted rim, decorated with a design by Christopher Dresser, printed in black, brown, beige and green, 23cm. diam. (Phillips) $400

An 'Old Hall' Aesthetic movement plate, designed by Christopher Dresser, with canted corners transfer-decorated with formalised foliage, 23cm. (Phillips) $250

An English porcelain foxhead stirrup cup with gilt collar inscribed *Tallyho*, with bright eyes and pricked ears, 13cm. (Phillips) $1,250

A Fowler's phrenology head, the cranium printed with the areas of the sentiments, the base with maker's label and title, 11¾in. high. (Christie's S. Ken) $900

A Yorkshire pottery model of a horse, wearing a molded bridle, saddle cloth and surcingle, 15cm. high. (Henry Spencer) $3,000

An early 19th century English yellow ground tureen and cover, black printed with two children's scenes entitled *L'oiseau le* and *Le fit cheval*, 8in. diam. (Phillips Sevenoaks) $325

A Wiltshire inscribed and dated four-handled loving-cup, on a circular spreading foot with a lightly molded geometric pattern, 1706, 23.5cm. diameter. (Christie's) $1,250

A 19th century English drab-ware honey pot and cover in the form of a beehive, with attached dished circular stand, 9.5cm. high. (Henry Spencer) $125

'Bestiary Form', a porcelain jug form by Ruth Barrett-Danes, 28.5cm. high. (Christie's) $1,250

A pair of figures of a rifleman and an archeress, each wearing hats, blue coats, he with yellow breeches and she with a flowered dress, circa 1830, 8in. high. (Christie's S. Ken) $1,250

A pottery stick stand, formed as a bear, the naturalistically modeled beast raised upon his hind legs clutching a gnarled branch, 87cm. high. (Lawrence Fine Art) $500

A Don Pottery Orange Jumper jug, the ovoid body printed and colored with a figure of Mellish standing in profile, 18cm. (Phillips) $800

Admiral Beatty dressed in naval uniform, supporting a shell entitled *Dread-nought* between his legs, 26.5cm. high. (Phillips) $200

One of a set of twelve Elkin & Co. blue and white pottery plates, each printed with an Irish river landscape, 25.5cm., early 19th century. (Bearne's) (Twelve) $600

BURMANTOFTS

Burmantofts is the name given to products from the pottery of Wilcock and Co, which was established in 1858 in Leeds. Initially terracotta earthenware was produced, but after 1880 they also made a hard buff colored high fired earthenware with a feldspathic glaze, which became known as Burmantofts faience. This was used to make tiles and, from 1882, art pottery. Their output included vases, bowls, jardinières and figures, covered in colored glazes and showing oriental or Middle Eastern influence. Other decorations in the range included underglaze designs trailed in slip, painted or incised and copper and silver luster was also used on dark colors. From 1904 they reverted to specialising in terracotta.

Marks include the name in full or the monogram *BF*.

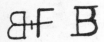

BURSLEM

Burslem was one of the major centers of the Staffordshire pottery industry in the 18th and 19th century, with scores of factories, large and small, (among the former, notably, Doulton) turning out stoneware and earthenware.

CHINA

A Burmantofts jardiniere and stand, 31in. overall, stamped marks. (Christie's) $450

A rare Burmantofts pottery plaque in shallow relief, depicting a heron in naturalistic setting, about to gorge himself on a family of frogs, 25in. approximately. (Geering & Colyer) $700

A fine Burmantofts faience charger with domed center, decorated in the Isnik manner in blue, turquoise, green and amethyst with dragons, 45.6cm. diam. (Christie's) $4,250

A Burmantofts faience vase, decorated in cobalt blue, turquoise, green and pink, on a white ground, 46.4cm. high. (Christie's London) $1,350

A Doulton, Burslem, ovoid vase, the panel painted by Fred Sutton, 17cm. high. (Phillips) $600

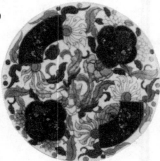

A Burslem ware ceramic wall plaque, the design attributed to Charlotte Rhead, decorated with stylised brown, and cream chrysanthemums with blue leaves and berries, 41cm. diam. (Phillips) $350

CANTON

There is a reference which suggests that earthenware cooking vessels were made in Kuangtung (Canton) as early as the T'ang dynasty (618–906). The dating of what has come to be known as Canton stoneware is, however, very difficult. It is certain they go back at least to late Ming times, and they are still made and exported in large quantities.

Canton ware is usually dark brown at the base, varying to pale yellowish gray and buff with a thick smooth glaze which is distinctive for its mottling and dappling effect. The color is often blue, flecked and streaked with gray green or white over a substratum of olive brown. Sometimes brown tints predominate, but it is the blue toned ware which is most highly prized.

Very large jars, vases etc. were made for outdoor use, sometimes with elaborate applied work, and incense burners, water pots etc. were also made in form of small animal figures.

Workshops at Canton decorated porcelain in the famille rose style for export, as well as the 'Canton enamels' painted on copper.

A Canton chamber candlestick with matching candle snuffer, each piece painted with figures. (Bearne's) $450

Canton blue and white teapot and cover, China, mid 19th century, drum shape, coastal village scene with cloud border, 5½in. high. (Skinner Inc.) $130

A pair of Canton vases, applied at the neck and shoulders with dragons and Buddhist lions, 61.8cm. high. (Bearne's) $3,750

A Canton famille rose jug and cover, the ovoid body painted with figures in a pavilion, 11¼in. high, 19th century. (Bonhams) $1,500

A Canton enamel fish tank decorated in famille rose enamels, 25.5in. $1,750

One of a pair of Canton hexagonal baluster jars and covers, 25in. high. $7,500

Late 18th century famille rose Canton enamel circular segmented supper set formed as eight fan-shaped dishes, 18in. diam. $1,000

CAPODIMONTE

The Capodimonte factory near Naples was established by King Charles III in 1742 to make soft-paste porcelain of the French type.

It was not until 1744, however, after numerous failed attempts, that Gaetano Schepers managed to produce a paste which was suitably 'white and diaphanous' and which achieved a brilliance to rival Meissen.

The most famous modeler at the Capodimonte factory was Giovanni Caselli, a former gem engraver and miniature painter. Figurines were among the earliest output of the factory, but snuff boxes, tea services and scent bottles were also made. The small objects were often mounted on gold or silver gilt, and the fine floral decoration was usually painted in finely drawn hair lines.

In 1759 Charles acceded to the throne of Spain, and the factory closed. He set up again at Buen Retiro, but the quality of products produced there is generally inferior to their Capodimonte antecedents.

A Capodimonte oviform teapot with scroll handle and spout, blue fleur-de-lys mark, circa 1750, 14.5cm. wide. $1,250

A Capodimonte baluster coffee pot and low domed cover, painted by Giuseppe della Torre, circa 1744. 26.5cm. high. $20,000

An extremely rare and finely painted Capodimonte candlestick base of triangular shape, modeled by Gaetano Fumo and Giuseppe Gricci, 18.5cm. high. (Phillips) $2,250

A Capodimonte (Carlo III) group of fisherfolk, modeled by Giuseppe Gricci, circa 1750, 17.5cm. wide. $13,000

A Capodimonte group of a youth riding a mastiff modeled by Guiseppe Gricci, the youth in peaked pale-pink cap with gilt bow, 1755–1759, 17cm. high. (Christie's) $6,000

A Capodimonte (Carlo III) shaped gold mounted snuff box, the porcelain circa 1755, 8.5cm. wide. $1,350

A Capodimonte (Carlo III) white figure of Capitano Spavento from the Commedia dell'Arte, circa 1750, 14cm. high. $6,000

MICHAEL CARDEW

Born in 1901 Michael Cardew was a pupil of Bernard Leach. His earliest products from his Winchcombe Pottery, dating from the 1920s, consist mainly of slip-decorated earthenware for domestic use, often with sgraffiato decoration. He later experimented with tin-glazed earthenware and in 1941 went out to teach at Achimota College in Ghana. Following the closure of the college in 1945 he open a pottery on the Volta river, producing stoneware often decorated with African inspired motifs. He returned to this country in 1948 and at Wenford Bridge began making light colored stoneware, often with brushed decoration, before returning to Africa to work for the Nigerian government in 1950, establishing a training center at Abuja. He died in 1983.

An oval earthenware slip decorated dish by Michael Cardew, the interior covered in a dark toffee-brown glaze with trailed mustard-yellow slip, circa 1930, 21cm. wide. (Christie's) $250

A mustard glazed stoneware two handled vase, cover and pierced liner by Michael Cardew, impressed seal mark, 11in. high. (Spencer's) $150

A small earthenware cider flagon by Michael Cardew, covered in an amber and olive green glaze over which a mustard-green, stopping short of the foot, impressed MC and Winchcombe Pottery seals, 21cm. high. (Christie's) $175

A stoneware bowl by Michael Cardew, the interior with incised decoration and blue and brown brushwork of a bird amongst grasses, MC and Wenford Bridge seals, 24.5cm. diam. (Christie's) $1,000

An earthenware coffee pot and cover by Michael Cardew, impressed MC and Winchcombe Pottery seals, circa 1933, 17cm. high. (Christie's) $425

A stoneware globular casserole by Michael Cardew with tall neck, two lug handles and a concave cover with knob finial, circa 1975, 20.7cm. high. (Christie's) $425

A small earthenware jug by Michael Cardew, impressed MC and Winchcombe Pottery seals, 12.4cm. high. (Christie's) $150

CARLTON WARE

Carlton ware was the name given to the Staffordshire earthenware produced from 1890 at the Carlton Works, Stoke on Trent, by the firm which traded until 1957 as Wiltshaw & Robinson. From January 1958 it was retitled Carlton Ware Ltd.

The factory produced ornamental ware such as vases, characterised by bright enameling and gilded floral and fanleaf decoration, black very often being used as the base color. Early products normally bear a circular printed mark with *W & R Stoke on Trent* enclosing a swallow and surmounted by a crown.

A Carlton ware ginger jar and cover, with gilt colored chinoiserie decoration depicting temples and pagodas, 31cm. high.
(Phillips) $450

A Carlton ware twin-handled boat shape bowl on splayed cylindrical column painted with an exotic bird of paradise, 23.5cm. high.
(Phillips) $275

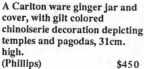

Shaped vase, 'Persian' design, marked with a gold star underneath, 280mm. high.
$600

A Carltonware service decorated in polychrome enamels, coffee pot 20.4cm. high. $1,250

Pale pink shaped vase with Art Deco design, 195mm. high. $200

'Handcraft' design vase following the Arts & Crafts movement, using a white background with blue, beige, pink and purple stenciling, 225mm. high. $300

Carlton Ware luster jug with gilt loop handle, the body painted and gilded with stylised floral and fan decoration, 5in. high. (Prudential Fine Art) $175

A leaf green Art Deco vase with large and small lustrous trees of unusual colors, black inside, 265mm. high.
$375

CARTER STABLER & ADAMS

In 1921 John and Truda Adams went into partnership with Harold Stabler and Owen Carter of Carter & Co of Poole Dorset.

Together they made hand thrown and hand decorated pottery, mostly designed either by Stabler and his wife Phoebe, or the Adams. Their shapes, mostly tableware and stoneware, were noted for their simplicity and were usually decorated in bold colors under a creamy matt glaze. Around the 1930s candlesticks were also made in the Art Deco style. The company continues today as Poole Pottery Ltd and is currently enjoying a period of great popularity, with some sales being devoted exclusively to their output.

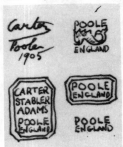

A Carter Stabler & Adams Ltd. vase, designed by James Radley Young, 25cm. high. (Lawrence Fine Arts) $300

A Carter Stabler & Adams Ltd. vase, designed by James Radley Young, with vertical panels of dots within striped borders, 15.5cm. high. (Lawrence Fine Arts) $300

A terracotta twin handled oviform vase painted by Ruth Pavely with bluebirds and foliage between contrasting borders, impressed *CSA Ltd.* mark, 6½in. high. (Christie's S. Ken) $1,000

A Carter, Stabler & Adams Ltd. biscuit fired stoneware vase, with stepped and ribbed decoration, decorated in shades of brown with geometric, linear and floral designs, 33.7cm. high. (Christie's London) $800

A terracotta plate painted by Anne Hatchard with a green spotted leaping gazelle amongst fruiting vines, impressed *CSA* mark, 12in. diam. (Christie's S. Ken) $1,250

A Carter Stabler Adams Poole pottery vase, attributed to Truda Carter, painted in blue, green, mauve, black and yellow, 22.1cm. high. (Phillips London) $175

A Carter Stabler Adams pottery dish, possibly a design by Erna Manners, painted in mauve, green and blue with stylised leaves and scrolling tendrils, 37.8cm. diam. (Phillips) $275

CASTEL DURANTE

Castel Durante, in the province of Urbino, is the birthplace of two of the outstanding figures concerned with Italian maiolica, Nicola Pellipario, the master of maiolica painting, and Cipriano Piccolpasso, who wrote the definitive work Li tre libri dell'Arte del Vasaio.

The earliest Castel Durante wares can sometimes be attributed to the painter and potter Giovanni Maria, who specialised in grotesque and trophy borders around deep-welled plates containing beautifully drawn heads of girls or youths.

Even in Pellipario's earliest works the pictorial painting style is fully developed. In 1519, he painted the d'Este service for the wife of the marquis of Mantua, where every dish and plate, in addition to heraldic arms, bears a different subject from Classical mythology, often taken from slightly earlier woodcuts.

Pellipario left Castel Durante about 1527 to join his son in Urbino.

A Castel Durante squat drug jar painted with the naked Fortune arising from the waves on the back of a dolphin, circa 1580, 23.5cm. wide.
(Christie's) $27,500

A Castel Durante tondino with a central yellow and ocher foliage mask inscribed *PACIFICAB* on a ribbon above reserved on a blue ground, circa 1525, 22cm. diameter. (Christie's) $6,000

A Castel Durante dated dish painted in green and gray about a central medallion of an Emperor to the left crowned with laurels, circa 1555, 26.5cm. diameter.
(Christie's) $3,350

A Castel Durante wet-drug jar with short yellow spout and wide strap handle, named for *S. ABSINTII* on a yellow rectangular cartouche, circa 1570, 21cm. high.
(Christie's) $4,000

A Castel Durante portrait dish boldly painted with an almost full face portrait of 'Faustina Bella', her hair coiled and braided with a white bandeau, 23cm., circa 1540.
(Phillips) $17,500

A 17th century Castel Durante baluster armorial pharmacy bottle, 22cm. high. (Christie's) $2,750

A Castel Durante Armorial saucer dish with a coat of arms above a hilly landscape, within a wide blue border, 22.5cm., circa 1570. (Phillips) $7,250

CHINA

CASTELLI

Castelli, in the kingdom of Naples, owes its fame to the maiolica made there from the late 17th century onwards, principally by the Grue and Gentili families. They produced a style which is rich in architectural detail, with borders adorned by flowers and putti, the main colors being buff, yellow and a greenish brown.

The original stylistic inspiration is generally thought to have come from Carlo Antonio Grue (d. 1723), whose four sons, Francesco Antonio, Anastasio, Aurelio and Libero continued the tradition until the death of the last in 1776.

Few factory marks were used, but the artists frequently signed their work, enabling accurate attributions to be made.

A Castelli rectangular plaque painted in the Grue workshop with the Flight into Egypt, circa 1720, 20 x 25.5cm. (Christie's) $2,250

A Castelli armorial plate painted in the Grue workshop with a traveler and companion riding a horse and a donkey, circa 1720, 24cm. diameter.
(Christie's) $3,600

A Castelli rectangular plaque painted with Abraham sacrificing a lamb, circa 1720, 27 x 20.5cm. $1,500

A Castelli rectangular plaque painted with Pan being comforted after the musical contest with Apollo seated, circa 1725, 28cm. square.
                         $1,500

Late 17th century Castelli plate painted in colors with a mounted hunting party, 23cm. diam. (Christie's)
                         $4,250

A Castelli armorial plate by Aurelio Grue, after a print from the Hunt Series by Antonio Tempesta, yellow and brown line rim, circa 1725, 29cm. diam.
(Christie's) $20,000

A Castelli scudella of circular form, painted in the Grue Workshop, with Saint Jerome holding a skull in one hand, 13.5cm.
(Phillips) $400

CAUGHLEY

Around 1772 Thomas Turner established his factory at Caughley in Shropshire. Turner had been manager at Worcester, and had trained as an engraver under Robert Hancock. He persuaded Hancock to join him in his new venture, and set out to rival the Worcester production of blue printed porcelain. He was so successful that by the 1780s Caughley was completely dominating the market, making mass produced, affordable wares in simple shapes with very elaborate decoration.

Turner then dealt his rivals a further blow by persuading their chief decorators, the Chamberlains, to set up on their own, and having done so, they gilded blue and white Caughley wares, and also made enamel pieces to order for Turner.

Turner countered elaborate Chinese patterns with transfer printing, and it is often claimed that he was the first to introduce the celebrated Willow pattern. The factory made a wide range of attractive shapes, including sauceboats, mugs, creamboats, pickle leaf dishes and bowls, as well as a number of small items, such as spoontrays, asparagus servers and egg drainers. Miniature teawares were very common and were produced in two patterns, one printed and one painted. These are very sought after today.

Both Caughley and Worcester used a number of the same transfer prints, but some are unique to Caughley, notably that commemorating the erection of the Ironbridge at Coalbrookdale in 1779.

Painted Caughley wares tend to be earlier than the more common printed pieces.

Some later printed wares were enhanced with gilding, but this tends now to detract from their value.

An important Caughley loving cup, printed in blue with a view of the Iron Bridge, 11.7cm. (Phillips) $5,000

A Caughley egg drainer, decorated in blue and white the Fisherman pattern, circa 1790, 3¹/₅in. across handle. (Woolley & Wallis) $300

A Caughley cream-jug painted with the Badge of George IV as Prince of Wales, enclosed by the crowned Royal Garter and motto within a blue dot and gilt cartouche, circa 1790, 14cm. wide. (Christie's) $1,250

A Caughley porcelain cabbage leaf molded jug, with rotund body and slant eyes to the mask spout, 22.5cm. high. (Henry Spencer) $400

A Caughley coffee pot of baluster shape, printed with 'The Fisherman' pattern, 9½in. high. (G. A. Property Services) $275

A Caughley shanked sugar bowl and cover painted with landscapes within gilt circular cartouches, circa 1792, 12cm. diam. (Christie's) $425

CHANTILLY

The Chantilly porcelain factory was founded in 1725 by Louis Henri de Bourbon, Prince du Condé, under the direction of Cicaire Cirou. The Prince was an avid collector of Arita pottery and set his factory to manufacture this type of ware. The unique feature of Chantilly is its glaze, which in contrast to the usual transparent lead glaze of soft paste porcelains was an opaque white tin glaze such as that used in the production of faience. The use of this precluded underglaze decoration, but was ideal for painting in the delicate colors of the Kakiemon style typical of Arita ware.

These Japanese designs were exquisitely painted, sometimes from the original and sometimes from Meissen copies, which they excelled both in quality of shape and decoration. After the death of the Prince in 1740 Kakiemon styles were abandoned, and a year after the death of Cirou in 1751 disaster struck the factory in the form of a Royal edict forbidding the manufacture of porcelain for a period of 12 years at any factory other than Vincennes, which was the particular pet of Louis XV and Madame de Pompadour.

While the edict was not, in fact, strictly enforced, Chantilly now abandoned the use of tin glaze in favor of a transparent lead glaze which revealed an attractive cream colored body. Over the next few years most decoration was done in camaieu (monochrome). Favorite styles were crimson cupids after Boucher and the use of a border of diapered quatrefoils in blue enamel.

Typical of the Cirou period is the red hunting horn mark, while later pieces carry a blue horn, often more crudely drawn and sometimes accompanied by *Chantilly*.

A 1870s Chantilly dish with gros bleu ground and a central gilt cartouche depicting, in puce, a chateau by a lakeside, 24cm. across.
(Phillips) $350

A Chantilly teabowl painted in Kakiemon style with a panel of flowering prunus issuing from rockwork, 4.5cm., red horn mark.
(Phillips) $750

Six Chantilly Kakiemon pistol shaped knife handles, painted with a boy (four cracked), circa 1740, mounted with contemporary silver blades, impressed swan marks, the handles 8.5cm. long.
(Christie's) $2,000

A Chantilly Kakiemon square box and cover, iron-red hunting horn mark, circa 1740, 25cm. high. $25,000

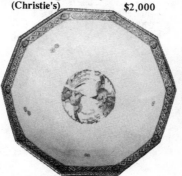

A Chantilly ten sided Kakiemon bowl, the interior with a roundel composed of two ho-ho birds, circa 1735, later French gilt metal mounts by A. Risler & Carre, Paris, 26cm. diam.
(Christie's) $2,000

A Chantilly green ground two handled pot pourri, the waisted campana body applied with swags of flowers, circa 1750, 19cm. high.
(Christie's) $8,000

CHELSEA 'GIRL IN A SWING'

The relationship between the main Chelsea factory and the Girl in a Swing factory in the mid 18th century is not clear, but it seems certain that many workmen were employed there from Chelsea, and its guiding light was probably the jeweler Charles Gouyn.

The factory was noted between 1749–54 for its scent bottles, but also produced some rare figures, modeled in a unique and dainty style, as well as some dressing table ware. Often these have been attributed to Chelsea proper, but it seems likely that the two factories were entirely separate.

A 'Girl in a Swing' cream jug with brown twig handle, circa 1750, 8cm. high. $20,000

A rare Girl-in-a-Swing scent bottle as a lady seated on a rocky mound, wearing a low cut yellow bodice, the base inscribed in red *Pour Mon Amour*, 7.5cm. (Phillips) $2,000

A 'Girl in a Swing' seal modeled as Harlequin in black mask and multi-colored checkered clothes, circa 1749-54, 3.2cm. high. (Christie's) $750

CHELSEA

The new Chelsea factory, founded in the 1740s, was largely inspired by Nicholas Sprimont, a Huguenot silversmith from Flanders, and it was probably the first of the six or so soft paste factories which sprang up in England by 1750.

Early Chelsea products were very attractive, highly translucent and based on glass ingredients. Pieces from this period often carry an incised triangle and have a strong affinity with Sprimont's silverwork, with particular emphasis on shellwork and scroll motifs. Many pieces were left in the

A 'Girl in a Swing' white Holy Family group after Raphael, the Virgin Mary wearing flowing robes seated on rockwork before a tree-stump, her left arm encircling the Infant Christ Child, circa 1750, 21cm. high. (Christie's) $51,700

A Chelsea group of two children, naked except for a pink drapery, with large fish, 24cm. high. (Lawrence Fine Art) $1,350

A 'Girl in a Swing' gold-mounted scent bottle and stopper, 1751-54, 8.5cm. high. $2,000

A Chelsea blue-ground square tapering vase, gold anchor mark, circa 1765, 32cm. high. (Christie's) $1,750

CHELSEA

white, although some were colored in Kakiemon style. Figures, often also of oriental inspiration, were made at this time and were invariably left white.

The next, or Raised Anchor Period (1749–53) saw the porcelain becoming more opaque as less lead was used. Figures are now more usually colored, this often being done in the London studio of William Duesbury. While oriental influence remained very strong, many decorations of this period are obviously of Meissen origin. Another interesting decorative development of the time was fable painting on cups, teapots etc., as was the 'Hans Sloane' plant decoration based on the drawings of Philip Miller, head gardener at Hans Sloane's botanical gardens in Chelsea. The range of shapes also widened.

By 1752 a painted Red Anchor Mark was becoming common, and this Red Anchor period, which lasted until about 1758, saw the apogee of Chelsea figure modeling. Table wares still showed oriental and Continental motifs while a new development was the manufacture of handsome vegetable and animal tureens and stands.

The final Gold Anchor period shows a departure towards the opulent and the elaborate, with colored grounds in the Meissen and Sèvres style, and figures in ornate bocages and flowery backgrounds. There was much gilding, and rich color often came to disguise inferior modeling.

By 1770 Chelsea had passed into the hands of William Duesbury of Derby, and by 1784 porcelain manufacture was concentrated there. The brilliant history of Chelsea was over.

A Chelsea fluted teabowl and saucer painted in colors with flower sprays and scattered sprigs, red anchor mark. (Phillips) $650

A Chelsea fable-decorated octagonal teapot painted in the manner of Jefferyes Hammett O'Neale with a wolf barking at a boar, circa 1752, 10cm. high. (Christie's) $4,000

A Chelsea candlestick group, with leaf molded candle nozzle and drip guard, 16.8cm. high, red anchor mark. (Phillips) $750

A fine Red Anchor period Chelsea porcelain 'Hans Sloane' plate, of shaped circular form, painted with panache in green, yellow, blue, puce, brown and burnt orange, 23.5cm. diam. (Henry Spencer) $10,000

A Chelsea octagonal dish, painted in the Kakiemon palette with pheasants, circa 1750, 20.5cm. wide. (Christie's) $1,750

A Chelsea figure of a monk seated on a stool and reading an open prayer book inscribed *Respice Finem*, 14cm. (Phillips) $1,800

CHINESE

The antiquity of Chinese ceramics and their beauty and variety down the ages make their study and collection particularly attractive, and provide scope for every taste.

The earliest unglazed earthenware jars date from as early as 2,000 BC, but it was not really until the Han Dynasty (206BC–220AD) that finer techniques, especially the art of glazing had been definitively mastered.

The next truly great period was the T'ang Dynasty (618–906AD) when the pottery was characterised by a beautiful proportion and vitality. A lead glaze was revived, which was often splashed or mottled, and many decorative themes reflect Hellenistic influence.

It was during the Sung Dynasty (960–1279AD) that the first true porcelain seems to have been made, and this period too saw the production of some of the most beautiful shapes and glazes of all time. It also saw the beginning of underglaze blue painting, which was to be perfected during the Ming period.

During the Ming Dynasty (1368–1644AD) a more or less standardised fine white porcelain body was developed which acted as a perfect vehicle for brilliant color decoration. Glazes tended to be thick or 'fat'. Colored glazes too were introduced and used either together or singly.

The K'ang Hsi period (1662–1722) marked a further flowering of the potter's art, which continued under his sons Yung Cheng and Ch'ien Lung (Qianlong). The body by now consisted of a very refined white porcelain, thinly and evenly glazed, providing the best possible base for elaborately painted decoration sometimes in the famille rose, famille verte, or famille noire palettes.

Rose Mandarin footed oval fruit platter, China, circa 1830, central panel of Mandarin figures alternating between precious antique clusters, 15½ in. wide.
(Skinner Inc.) $2,500

An ormolu mounted Chinese crackle glazed celadon vase with twin lion mask and entwined drapery handles on spreading gadrooned base, 14in. wide. (Christie's London)
                    $10,000

A magnificent Yuan blue and white jar, guan, painted around the globular body with an arching peony scroll comprising six blooms, circa 1340-50, 39cm. high. (Christie's)
                    $896,000

Rose Mandarin hot water bottle and cover, China, circa 1830, oval panels of figural courtyard scenes surrounded by floral and ornament designs, 14¾ in. high. (Skinner Inc.) $300

A large Chinese blue and white shallow dish, the center painted with deer in a landscape, the rim with a band of insects, 44cm. (Bearne's) $375

A rare Robin's egg blue Yixing wine ewer and cover, 18th century, 7¾ in. high. (Christie's)
                    $6,000

A fluted oval soup tureen and cover, enameled with bouquets and sprays of flowers, 34cm., Ch'ien Lung. (Lawrence Fine Arts) $1,000

A good heart shaped dessert dish painted in blue with the Kang Hsi Lotus pattern, circa 1770, 26cm. (Phillips London) $600

Fitzhugh blue and white salad bowl, China, early 19th century, medallion surrounded by four floral panels, 9¹/₂in. wide. (Skinner Inc.) $650

A Chinese Chien Lung bulbous shaped vase, decorated in famille verte, iron-red and other colors with mythological beast reserves, 12in. high. (Geering & Colyer) $250

A pair of Chinese blue ground flattened hexagonal vases, gilt in the London studio of Thomas Baxter, circa 1802, about 28cm. high. (Christie's London) $1,000

A blue and white baluster vase and matched cover, painted with a continuous scene of court figures, six character mark of Ch'êng-hua, K'ang-hsi, 15¹/₂in. high.(Lawrence Fine Arts) $1,000

A blue and white octagonal plate, painted in a vibrant blue with fruiting pomegranates, six character mark of Ch'êng-hua, K'ang-hsi, 10¹/₄in. diam. (Lawrence Fine Arts) $275

Important blue Fitzhugh "Pagoda" decorated footed tray, China, circa 1810, central pagoda design surrounded by four floral panels, 10in. wide. (Skinner Inc.) $1,250

A blue and white dish, the exterior with dragons chasing the flaming pearl, 7⁷/₈in., Guangxu six character mark and period. (Bonhams) $175

CHINESE EXPORTWARE

The first Chinese Exportware was produced as a result of the presence of the Jesuit fathers, who established themselves there from 1600. About fifty years later pieces of porcelain began to appear decorated with crucifixes and the letters *IHS*. Later, religious scenes were painted, mostly on plates, but sometimes even on tea sets!

Heraldic ware was the first form called for from China in great quantities in the early 18th century. Great services were manufactured with decoration often in imitation of the silver they were to replace. Punchbowls and other utilitarian pieces followed, decorated with creditable reproductions of European paintings or illustrations of events. Figures in European dress were also attempted.

The factories which produced these were grouped at Ching te Chen and they were decorated mostly at Canton. Some pieces were also made in Fukien Province, which were characterised by their creamy white appearance. These were usually decorated in Europe and were known as blanc-de-Chine.

A Chinese 18th century Export model of a pony, 26cm. wide. $13,000

A large Chinese Export punch bowl, the exterior boldly painted with the coats of arms of four Livery Companies, 40cm. diameter, Qianlong. (Bearne's) $2,000

Chinese Export "Blue Fitzhugh" platter, 19th century, 18½in. wide. (Skinner Inc.) $600

One of a pair of late 18th century Export porcelain covered urns, China, 17½in. high. $6,500

One of four late 18th century Chinese Export soup plates, 8.7/8in. diam. $2,000

An Export figure of a hound seated, Qianlong, 14.5cm. high. $2,200

A large Export armorial dish painted in shades of blue, yellow. iron-red, green and gilt, circa 1740, 17in. diam. $5,000

CLARICE CLIFF

The legendary Clarice Cliff was born in 1899 in, perhaps inevitably, Staffordshire, where she started work at 13 in one of the local potteries, painting freehand onto pottery.

Her formal training comprised a year, when she was 16, at the Burslem School of Art, and a later year at the Royal College of Art, where she studied sculpture . At 17, she had gone to work at the firm of A.J. Wilkinson, and she remained with them, and their subsidiary the Newport Pottery, for the next two decades, ending up as Art Director and marrying the boss, Colley Shorter, when she was forty.

During the 1920's she painted Tibetan ware, large jars painted with floral designs in bright colors and gold, and she also transferred on to pottery designs by such distinguished artists as Paul Nash and Laura Knight.

In 1928, however, she painted 60 dozen pieces of her own design to test the market at a trade fair. These proved so popular that by 1929 the whole factory was switched to producing her Bizarre ware.

Cliff's style is character-ised by combinations of bright colors, such as orange, blue, purple and green, or black, yellow, orange and red. Her pieces are often angular in shape and strongly Art Deco in style. Major ranges, besides Bizarre, include Crocus, Fantasque, Biarritz and Farmhouse.

At the beginning of the Second World War, the factory was commandeered by the Ministry of Supply, and Wilkinson produced only a few white pieces. After the war, the market had changed and production was not resumed.

CHINA

A 'Bizarre' grotesque mask designed by Ron Birks, covered in a dark blue Inspiration glaze, the features picked out in red. (Christie's S. Ken)　　$2,000

A Clarice Cliff 'Fantasque' ginger jar and cover decorated in the 'Melon' pattern, painted in colors, 8in. high. (Christie's S. Ken)　　$850

A pair of Clarice Cliff teddy bear book ends decorated in the 'Red Flower' pattern, painted in colors, 6in. high. (Christie's S. Ken)　　$6,000

A 'Bizarre' Yo-Yo vase decorated in the 'Orange Luxor' pattern, painted in colors, 9in. high. (Christie's S. Ken)　　$3,350

A pair of 'Bizarre' bookends, shape No. 406 decorated in the 'Honolulu' pattern, painted in colors, 6in. high. (Christie's S. Ken)　　$750

A 'Bizarre' single-handled Lotus jug decorated in the 'Blue W' pattern, painted in colors between orange borders, 11¹/₂in. high. (Christie's S. Ken)　　$3,350

CLEMENT MASSIER

Clement Massier was a French artist potter who worked around the turn of the century at Golfe-Juan in the Alpes Maritimes. He produced a luster decorated earthenware, often embellished with plant motifs.

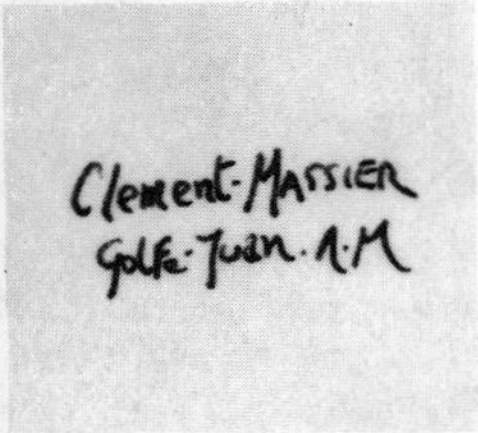

COALBROOKDALE

The Coalport or Coalbrookdale factory was established in Shropshire around 1796 by John Rose. Soft paste porcelain, sometimes in imitation of Chelsea, Swansea, or even Sèvres, continued to be made by his descendants until 1862. Around this time the factory passed into the hands of the Bruff family and in 1924 it was sold to Cauldon Potteries, moving to Staffordshire in 1926.

Pieces are often clearly marked *J Rose Coalbrookdale*, though some Chelsea pieces have an imitation blue anchor mark. Crossed tridents and *Swansea* are printed on red on imitation Swansea, and *RP* in crossed *Ls* on imitation Sèvres.

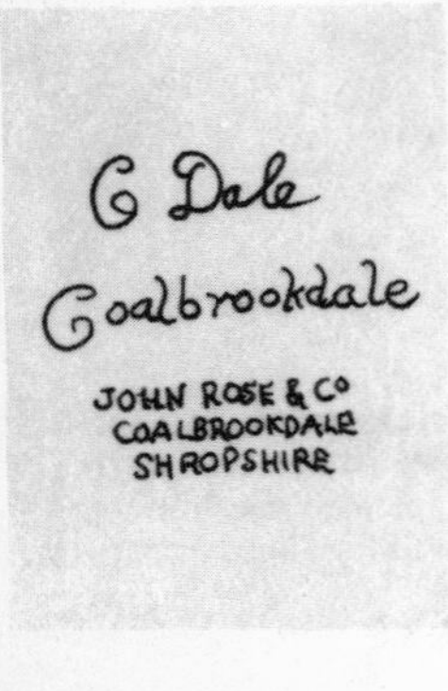

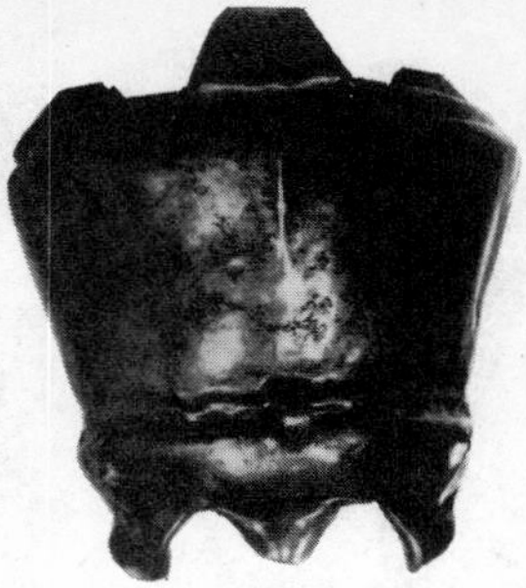

A massive Clément Massier jardinière, of irregular tapering form, decorated in an overall luster glaze of green, yellow, amethyst and amber, 56cm. high. (Christie's) $1,100

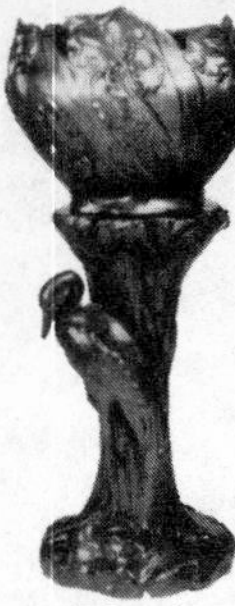

A Clément Massier earthenware jardinière with a pedestal, decorated in relief with irises, the pedestal naturalistically molded with a heron among bulrushes, 38cm. diameter of jardinière. (Christie's) $400

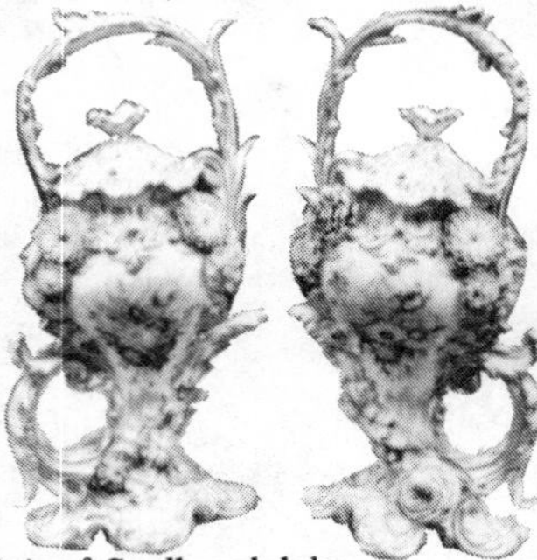

Pair of Coalbrookdale porcelain vases, mid-19th century, with handpainted floral bouquet, accented in gilt, (both handles showing breaks and repair) 15½in. high. (Skinner Inc.) $750

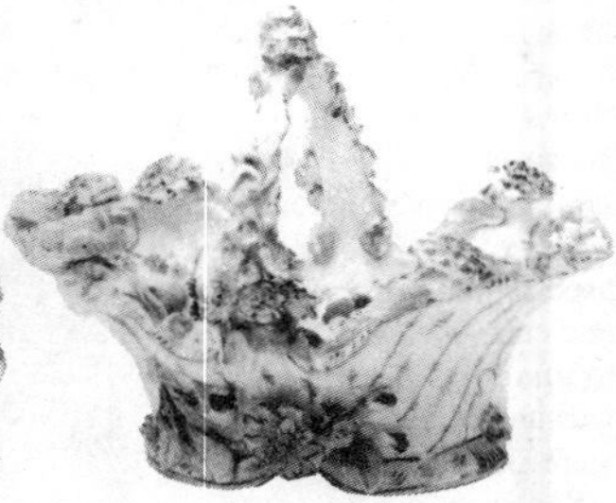

An English porcelain basket, probably Coalbrookdale, applied and painted with flowers, 27.5cm. (Bearne's) $3,000

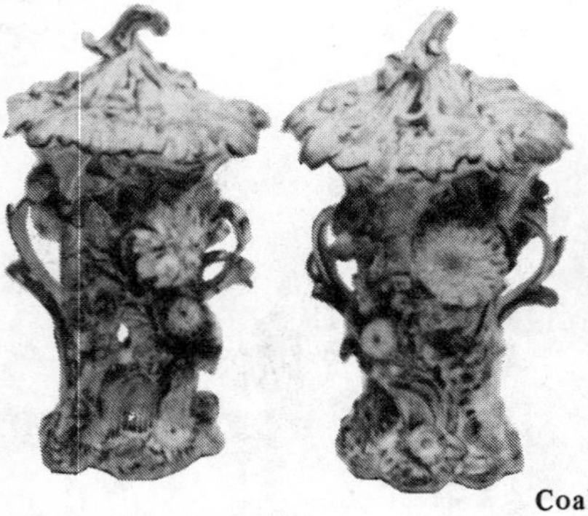

Pair of Coalbrookdale porcelain covered potpourri, mid-19th century, with scrolled leaf handles, pierced body and lid, 8in. high. (Skinner Inc.) $1,500

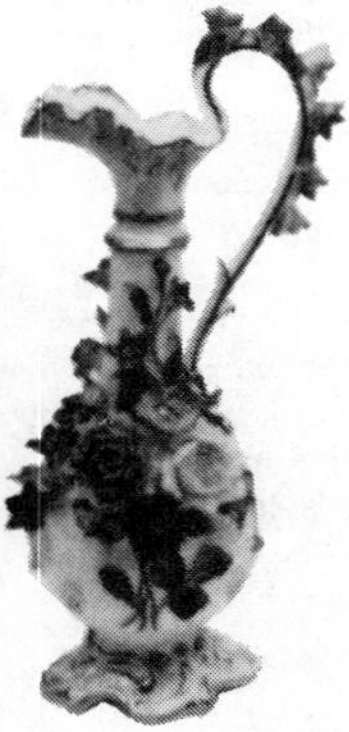

Coalbrookdale porcelain handled ewer, mid 19th century, white ground with applied flowers, leaves and vines (minor flower and petal damage), 8in. high. (Skinner Inc.) $300

COALPORT

CHINA

The Rose family established the Coalport Porcelain Works in Coalport Shropshire in 1796, and it remained in the family until the last member retired in 1862. In general, their output copied 18th century French and German porcelain, with decoration often in the Sèvres style. They employed some notable decorators, such as Jabez Ashton, who painted naturalistic flowers and fruit on large plaques, and James Rouse.

The business was declared bankrupt (1875-80) and then was acquired by Peter Bruff, who was later succeeded by his son Charles. They now turned out tableware decorated with landscapes of flower panels, or lightly decorated on pink and green grounds.

Parian and porcelain were used together for comports and centerpieces etc. and enameled jeweled decoration was used on tall vases, which were also painted with views or landscapes.

In 1924 the firm was purchased by Cauldon Potteries and in 1926 it the operation was moved to Staffordshire. It is still in existence today at Stoke on Trent.

There are numerous different marks from the various periods, usually in underglaze blue, either C, S, or N, in loops of monogram CS, or Coalport AD 1750. Later England or Made in England (from circa 1920) were added.

A rare Coalport 'D'-shaped bough pot and cover, painted with a band of geometric panels in red and black within a gold diaper frame, 20cm. (Phillips) $750

A pair of rare Coalport mantel-piece vases in neo-Classical style, painted almost certainly by Thomas Baxter, 29cm. high. (Phillips) $1,000

A pair of Coalport vases and covers in Sevres style, painted by William Cook, with ripe fruit and flowers, 37cm. (Phillips London) $1,500

A Coalport flared flower pot and stand with gilt dolphin mask handles, decorated in the London studio of Thomas Baxter, circa 1805, 16.5cm. wide. (Christie's London) $900

A Coalport pierced plate painted by Joshua Rushton, signed with a portrait of Lady Sarah Bunbury after Sir Joshua Reynolds, 23.5cm. (Phillips London) $750

An impressive pair of Coalport vases and covers, decorated with alternating panels of flowers in a vase, 40cm. (Phillips London) $2,000

93

COMMEMORATIVE

Commemorative is the word used to describe the myriad objects made and decorated to mark some person or event of special significance, coronations, jubilees, battles etc.

The first china to be made in any quantities with such intention appeared in Stuart times, and delft of the period often bears royal names and portraits.

The arrival of Queen Victoria on the throne opened the floodgates for the manufacture of commemorative china. Her predecessors as rulers were more often lampooned than venerated, but Victoria changed the popular attitude towards royalty. China commemorating events in the reigns of William and Mary, George III, George IV and William IV are rare but pieces with pictures of Victoria and Albert were made in their thousands and enjoyed pride of place on the walls and mantlepieces of rich and poor up and down the land. Plates, tobacco jars, mugs, vases, pipes, teapots, doorstops and spill jars marked every event in the royal life. The china cost little to buy and proved so popular that the range spread to include political happenings, military displays, exhibitions and even famous crimes and criminals.

Obviously age and rarity play a large part in determining the value of any piece of commemorative china, but the whole field is an attractive one. It is possible to start a collection with very little outlay, and each piece, whether modern or older, has its own intrinsic interest, which can only increase as time goes by.

CHINA

An octagonal nursery plate with embossed daisy border, printed in brown and colored with a scene entitled 'The Royal Christening', 16.5cm.
(Phillips) $45

A large brown-glazed pottery vase, gilded with a silhouette portrait of George III and inscribed in gold 'Mercy and Truth Preserve the King', 26.5cm, replacement foot.
(Phillips) $375

A Scottish molded plate, with panels of crowns and Royal emblems, the center with a profile portrait, colored and titled 'King George IIII', 21.5cm.
(Phillips) $550

A crisply molded jug of hexagonal shape, embossed with half length profile portraits of Victoria and Albert flanked by scrolling flowers, 15.5cm. (Phillips) $150

A Dillwyn & Co. pottery plate, painted in bright enamel colors, the center printed in black with the seated figure of the young Queen Victoria, 20.5cm.
(Bearne's) $450

A very rare small mug commemorating the birth of the Princess Royal, printed in black with ladies in waiting leading a horse drawn baby carriage, 6.3cm. (Phillips London) $1,350

A William Kent bust of John Wesley in clerical attire, on a mottled yellow and green base, 31cm.
(Phillips) $180

A china plate commemorating the start of the digging of the Channel Tunnel 1987/88, 27cm.
(Phillips) $60

A rare Crown Staffordshire double caricature of the Kaiser entitled 'Which'll He be', 15cm.
(Phillips) $475

A black printed jug bearing portraits of William IV and Queen Adelaide, probably commemorating the Coronation in 1830, 14cm.
(Phillips) $200

A pair of Whitman and Roth caricature figures of Gladstone and Disraeli, both standing on mottled turquoise and brown bases, 40cm.
(Phillips) $4,750

A cylindrical pottery mug printed in colors with flags and inscribed 'G.R. Peace of Europe signed at Paris May 30th, 1814', 11 cm.
(Phillips) $330

A bulbous jug with animal-headed handle, printed in puce with an unusual portrait of the young Queen Victoria, 18cm.
(Phillips) $200

A pottery jug with three medallions containing profile heads of Victoria and Albert flanking their son Albert Edward dated 1860, 26cm.
(Phillips) $225

A G.F. Bowers rope handled jug printed in colors with scenes of the Light Cavalry Charge at Balaclava, and the Sebastopol Attack, 20cm.
(Phillips) $800

COPELAND

In 1833 William Copeland bought the Staffordshire firm of Josiah Spode, and it was in 1842 that Copeland and Garrett of Stoke on Trent first produced statuary in what came to be known as Parian ware. Its success was due to the large quantity of feldspar contained in the soft paste, and a firing process which allowed an unusually large quantity of air into the kiln. The result was a porcelain notable for its lustrous transparency and delicacy of molding. A second quality parian statuary, slightly different in composition, was produced in 1850, and became known as standard parian. It lacked the silky surface of the first, but could withstand repeated firings and could be decorated in colors and gold. Copeland's were also noted for a variety of tableware produced in porcelain and earthenware and often lavishly ornamented, together with handpainted tiles.

A variety of marks were used, bearing variations of Copeland and Spode. From 1970 the firm has traded as Spode Ltd.

A pair of Copeland Crystal Palace Art Union parian ware busts, 'The Prince of Wales' and 'Princess Alexandra' by Marshall Wood and F. M. Miller. (Greenslades) $400

A fine Copeland Spode vase and pierced cover, richly decorated with a jeweled and gilded green ground, 17.5cm. (Phillips London) $600

Copeland, Parian porcelain bust 'The veiled bride', 14in. high. (Riddetts) $2,350

A rare part set of five Copeland Frog tiles, painted in shades of blue with amusing scenes of frogs variously engaged. (Phillips London) $1,000

A Copeland vase and cover, the ovoid body painted by L. Besche, signed, circa 1880, 15in. high. $2,000

A large pair of Copeland vases, each painted by C. F. Hurten, signed, circa 1870, 19¾in. high. $3,750

A Copeland bust of Juno, possibly after W Theed, in a coronet and with short ringlets, impressed mark, 20½in. high. (Christie's S. Ken) $1,500

HANS COPER

Hans Coper (1920–1981) trained as an engineer in his native Germany, but fled to England in the late '30's. During the war, he met another refugee, Lucie Rie, and went to work in her studio. They started making ceramic buttons, then graduated to domestic ware and in the evenings Coper could experiment with his own designs.

His biggest 'break' came when Basil Spence commissioned two candlesticks from him for Coventry Cathedral. His work is now established among the foremost modern pottery with prices to match.

A stoneware 'sack' form by Hans Coper, with spherical belly, the interior with cylindrical holder, the belly with incised linear decoration, the exterior covered in a buff slip, 21cm. high.
(Christie's) $6,000

An early stoneware goblet pot by Hans Coper, dark brown over a shiny 'toffee' glaze, the foot unglazed, circa 1952, 6in. high.
(Bonhams) $3,600

A stoneware 'Thistle' vase by Hans Coper, the body incised with concentric rings, the foot with incised turning, lightly burnished to reveal areas of matt manganese, 25.3cm. high.
(Christie's) $5,000

A fine stoneware 'sack' form by Hans Coper, white with bronze disk top, impressed HC seal, circa 1970, 7¹/₂in. high.
(Bonhams) $11,000

A fine black stoneware cup form by Hans Coper, made in three pieces, impressed *HC* seal, circa 1965, 6in. high.
(Bonhams) $9,000

An early stoneware cylindrical pot by Hans Coper, buff with manganese neck and rim, distinctive decoration of incised vertical lines comprised of dots, circa 1954, 8in. high.
(Bonhams) $3,000

A rare stoneware bell form pot by Hans Coper, the top third manganese merging into beige, circa 1963, 5in. high.
(Bonhams) $6,300

A stoneware 'thistle' form by Hans Coper, the disk-shaped body with flared rim, incised decoration of concentric rings, the exterior covered in a buff slip lightly burnished, 25.5cm. high.
(Christie's) $9,000

CREAMWARE

Creamware was developed by Josiah Wedgwood in response to the huge middle class demand for tableware which would be both durable and attractive. It was first introduced in 1761, at which time the glaze was not very resilient, and could be easily scratched. Nor could it withstand boiling water, which made it unsuitable for tea and coffee pots. By 1764, however, Wedgwood had solved all these problems. The final result was pleasing and modestly priced, and moreover was well suited to mechanical decoration.

It enjoyed immediate and lasting popularity. In 1765 Queen Charlotte commissioned a 60 piece tea service, which was so admired that Wedgwood was granted permission to call his new material Queensware, which name it has borne ever since. On the strength of such success, Wedgwood began using creamware for neo-Classical decorative items as well. Much creamware was sold without decoration or, in other cases, this was restricted to a simple border or pierced rims and lattice work. It was adaptable to all tastes, however, and lent itself to transfer printed scenes or painted decoration.

An attractive Derbyshire creamware teapot and cover, painted on both sides with a spray of green flowers in shell shaped panels, 11cm. (Phillips) $2,500

A Staffordshire creamware spirally molded wall-pocket of Whieldon type, circa 1760, 21cm. high. (Christie's) $750

A rare late 18th century creamware deer-head stirrup cup, decorated in brown and green streaky glazes, 12cm. long. (Henry Spencer) $1,500

A creamware baluster jug with grooved loop handle, the tortoiseshell ground applied with green swags of foliage, circa 1780, 16.5cm. high. (Christie's London) $600

A Staffordshire creamware cow-creamer milking group, of Whieldon type, spotted in brown and the milkmaid in a brown coat, circa 1765, 18cm. long. (Christie's) $1,250

A Staffordshire creamware baluster cream jug and cover of Whieldon type, applied with trailing fruiting branches, circa 1760, 12cm. high. (Christie's) $1,850

An attractive creamware tea-pot and cover, the body painted with an all over scale pattern in red and black, 14cm. probably Leeds. (Phillips London) $750

CHINA

CROWN DUCAL

Crown Ducal was a range manufactured in the 1930s by the A G Richardson factory in Staffordshire. It was decorated in the Art Deco style, notably by Charlotte Rhead who used the 'tube lining' technique. The result looks as if the decoration has been applied with an icing bag, as indeed it has!

A.G.R. & Co. Ltd.

Crown Ducal

A pair of Charlotte Rhead Crown Ducal pottery wall plaques, tubelined in brown and decorated with orange flowers and scattered blue and red flower heads, 14in. diameter. (Spencer's) $300

A Crown Ducal shaped and ribbed two handled cylindrical vase decorated with a pattern by Charlotte Rhead, printed factory mark, 5½in. high. (Christie's S. Ken) $100

DAVENPORT

Davenport's Staffordshire Pottery was established in 1773 at Longport, and produced earthenware, ironstone china, and porcelain. In the 1880s, under John Davenport, many tea services were produced, with Japanese patterns. The firm was noted for its strong and durable wares, many of which were used aboard ships of the period. Porcelain plaques, decorated both in-house and by independent artists, were also made. Marks include *Davenport* painted in blue over an anchor, or, from 1850, a crown over *Davenport* and the address. The firm finally closed in 1887.

A Davenport caneware wine cooler, molded in relief with a bust of Nelson, the reverse with naval trophies, 25.5cm., impressed mark. (Phillips) $1,000

A Davenport shaped oval two-handled foot bath, printed with the 'Mosque and Fisherman' pattern. (Christie's S. Ken) $2,500

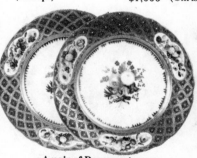

A pair of Davenport green-ground plates from the Royal Dessert Service made for William IV, the centers painted with a bouquet of rose, thistle, shamrock and leek, circa 1830, 25.5cm. diameter. (Christie's) $5,750

A Davenport stone china ice pail, liner and cover, with floral and bird decoration. $1,100

99

DE MORGAN

William Frend de Morgan (1839–1917) was an English ceramic designer, perhaps now particularly remembered for his tiles. His designs were much influenced by his friend William Morris and include, birds, fish, flowers and mythical beasts. He established his own pottery in Chelsea in 1872, producing his own tiles, and experimented with luster decoration in an attempt to reproduce the red luster of maiolica painted in Gubbio. He also designed dishes in cream earthenware decorated in red luster, and the Sunset and Moonlight suites decorated in gold, silver and copper. With Morris at Merton Abbey he continued to make tiles and dishes, and also established a factory at Fulham with Halsey Ricardo producing tiles and murals. He retired in 1905 and the factory closed in 1907

A De Morgan luster vase, decorated in ruby luster with fish swimming against pale amber waves, 15.6cm. high, 1888-97. $600

A Craven Dunhill & Co. metal mounted four tile jardiniere, each tile decorated with a design by William de Morgan, 21.2cm. high. (Christie's London) $1,000

A William De Morgan eight inch tile forming part of the Fan pattern, painted with two stylised flowers. (Phillips London) $750

A De Morgan luster vase, decorated by Fred Passenger, 1890's, 32.6cm. high. $1,350

A William de Morgan ruby luster twin-handled oviform vase, painted with scaly carp swimming in alternate directions, 37cm. high. (Phillips) $3,250

A William de Morgan circular plate, painted with a central griffin-like creature and bordered by a frieze of birds, 22cm. diam. (Phillips) $1,250

A William de Morgan 'Persian-style' vase and cover, painted with foliate fronds in turquoise, blue and pale-green against a white ground, 36cm. high. (Phillips) $7,000

DELFT

When Chinese porcelain arrived in the West, Europe was literally dazzled. Nothing of such beauty and brilliance had ever been manufactured there, and the indigenous pottery industries now had to compete with the flood of imports. Majolica had been made in small workshops throughout Holland by potters who were experienced yet open to new techniques. A result of this was delft, a decorated, tin-glazed earthenware, known elsewhere as faience. It first appeared in the early 17th century and the next 120 years were to see the steady development of both technique and quality. Majolica had been mainly multicolored, but delft was nearly all blue and white, imitating Chinese porcelain. Decoration too at first followed Chinese traditions, but later pieces saw innovative themes, such as the peacock jar, with a motif of two peacocks facing a central basket.

The finest period lasted until about 1730, when the seduction of enamel colors and the prettiness of porcelain began to sap the vitality of the medium.

CHINA

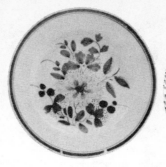

A delftware polychrome plate, painted in a bright Fazackerly palette, perhaps Delftfield factory, Glasgow, circa 1765, 23cm. diam. (Christie's) $750

A Brislington royal portrait charger with a full face, half length portrait of James II, 33.5cm. (Phillips London) $5,000

A Delft mantel garniture, comprising two covered jars and a vase, vase 13in. high. (Christie's) $250

A large mounted panel of delft tiles, the centers alternately plain or painted in polychrome with birds in branches, each 14.5cm. (Phillips London) $300

A German delft dish of silver shape, the center painted with an animal running to the left within a border of tulips, early 18th century, 13½in. diam. (Christie's S. Ken) $500

Pair of delft faience vases, painter's mark *MG*, 45cm. high. (Auktionshaus Arnold) $550

English polychrome delft bowl, early 18th century, V-outer border and scrolled inner border in blue, 9in. diameter. (Skinner Inc.) $750

A London polychrome delft Royal portrait footed dish, printed in blue and yellow with half length portraits of King William III and Queen Mary, 8¼in. diameter. circa 1690. (Bonhams) $1,850

An English delft polychrome miniature mug, painted in iron-red, blue and green with stylised shrubs and rockwork, London or Bristol, circa 1730, 5cm. high. (Christie's) $2,500

A London Royal portrait delft footed dish, printed in blue with half length portraits of King William III and Queen Mary, 8½in. diameter, circa 1690. (Bonhams) $1,100

A London delft vase painted in blue 24cm. high. (Phillips) $750

A good London delft 'Blue Dash' charger, painted with The Fall, Eve with long manganese hair handing an apple to Adam, 35cm. (Phillips) $3,500

A rare London delft white flower vase, raised on a spreading circular foot, the wavy rim encircled by three cylindrical flower nozzles, 16.5cm., mid-17th century. (Phillips London) $4,500

A very rare and interesting London delft pierced basket, attributed to Vauxhall, of circular shape supported on three bun feet, 26cm. (Phillips London) $7,000

A massive London delft dated polychrome armorial drug jar of swelling form, circa 1656, 36cm. high. $30,000

A London delft plate, painted in manganese and blue, with a half portrait of King George III, diameter 9in. (chips to rim). (Bonhams) $22,500

DELLA ROBBIA

The Della Robbia pottery was established in 1894 at Birkenhead by H. Rathbone and the sculptor, Conrad Dressler. It produced vases, bottles, jars, plates and dishes with sgraffito decoration and sometimes elaborate modeled relief with a strong Italian maiolica influence. The factory closed in 1901, but reopened and continued until 1906. Their mark consists of *Della Robbia* with a ship device and the decorator's initials.

'The Third Day of Creation', a Della Robbia tile panel after a design by Edward Burne-Jones, 55.5 x 21.5cm. (Christie's) $4,500

'Water Avens Tile', a Della Robbia tile panel designed by Conrad Dressler and decorated by E. M. Wood, 51.5 x 34.2cm. (Christie's) $900

A Della Robbia twin-handled vase, decorated by Charles Collis, with eight circular medallions, each with a sea-creature whose long tail curls round on itself, 35.8cm. high. (Christie's) $1,000

A Della Robbia bottle vase, designed by Charles Collis, with piped slip decoration of peaches and leaves covered in pink and turquoise glazes, 33.5cm. high. (Christie's) $500

A Della Robbia pottery vase by Roseville Pottery, signed with Rozane Ware seal, circa 1906, 8¼in. high. (Skinner) $900

A Della Robbia twin-handled vase decorated by Charles Collis, with a broad decorative frieze of stylised Tudor Roses, 31.6cm. high. (Christie's) $1,000

A Della Robbia wall charger, the base incised DR with a sailing ship and artist's monogram, 47.5cm. diam. (Christie's) $600

A Della Robbia pottery vase, with marks of Chas. Collis, potter and sgraffito artist and G. Russell, Paintress, circa 1903/06, 11in. high. $300

DERBY

Porcelain making in Derby commenced around the mid 18th century and has continued there ever since. During the early period, from 1750 onwards, production concentrated mainly on figures, with the result that, in contrast to most other factories of the period, comparatively few 'useful' wares were made. Emphasis from the beginning was on decoration, which was always very fine, even if some pieces of the pre–1760 period appear rather primitive and thickly potted. When more functional pieces were produced these still had decorative themes, with openwork baskets, pot pourris and frill vases featuring largely in the output. Fine tea and coffee wares were often painted with Chinese figure subjects.

William Duesbury, the London porcelain painter, became a key figure from 1756. He bought the Chelsea factory in 1770 and finally moved to Derby in 1784, where he was succeeded by his son, William II, in 1786. By the 1770s a really perfect porcelain body was being produced at Derby, and the employment of superb landscape and flower painters as decorators ensured that the finished product was of a quality second to none. In 1811 the factory was purchased by Robert Bloor, and production continued until 1848. While the quality of the body declined somewhat during this period, that of decoration remained high, and the factory continued to specialise in Imari and Japanese styles. From 1848 a new factory was opened in King Street, Derby, which continued till 1935 and specialised in copies of earlier Derby pieces. A further factory opened in 1876, called Derby

A Derby tea pot of quatrefoil outline, painted and gilt with birds and flowering plants in Chinese style, c. 1756, 17cm. high.
(Lawrence Fine Arts) $350

A Derby figure of a youth emblematic of Winter, in ermine trimmed red jacket and lemon breeches, 22.5cm.
(Phillips) $700

A pair of Derby dishes of kidney shape, painted with panels of birds in landscapes, by Richard Dodson, 25.5cm.
(Phillips) $1,250

A Derby white crayfish sauceboat modeled as a fluted shell, the handle formed as a looped coral branch resting on the back of a crayfish, Andrew Planché's period, circa 1750, 15.5cm. wide.
(Christie's) $10,000

An attractive early Derby bell-shaped mug, painted with a bouquet of colored flowers and scattered sprigs, the rim edged in brown, 11cm.
(Phillips) $1,250

A Derby trout's head stirrup-cup naturally modeled and painted in shades of green, puce and pale-pink, the rim inscribed in gilt *THE ANGLERS DELIGHT*, circa 1825, 13.5cm. high.
(Christie's) $2,000

DERBY

Crown Porcelain Co, and was continued after 1890 by the Royal Crown Derby Co, which specialised in the use of raised gold and strong ground colors.

Many early period Derby flatware pieces have 'moons' or patches in the paste which look especially bright when held up to the light. Such 'moons' can also be found on some Chelsea and Longton Hall pieces.

A Derby model of a stag at lodge in front of flower encrusted bocage, the white body dappled in brown, 17cm. (Phillips London) $1,250

A Derby vase in the form of a basket with a diaper molded globular body applied with florettes, pierced everted rim and rope handles, 13.5cm. (Phillips) $1,800

A rare Derby chocolate pot and cover, painted in a deep blue with the Walk in the Garden pattern after Worcester, 23.5cm. (Phillips London) $3,000

A pair of Derby candelabra figures of a shepherd seated playing the bagpipes, and a shepherdess playing the mandoline, 23cm. (Phillips London) $2,000

A Derby figure of a sailor's lass in yellow and claret hat, sprigged dress and black apron, 25cm. (Phillips) $900

A Derby figure group of a gallant and his companion walking with their arms entwined, he in a pink jacket, she with a lacy mob cap, 16.5cm. (Phillips) $2,000

A Derby porcelain plate, the center painted with a castle by a lake within a blue border, inscribed *View in Wales*, 23cm. (Bearne's) $300

A Derby bocage group in the form of a seated young woman with a sheaf of corn and a sickle, late 18th century, 12.5cm. high. (Bearne's) $500

DERUTA

The pottery industry in Deruta, Umbria, dates from the late 15th century. At that time wares in the usual high temperature colors were produced, together with some with metallic luster decoration. Some, too, were very distinctive in that, in order to achieve a 'near-flesh' tint, the enamel was scraped away to reveal the pinkish clay body, to which a clear lead glaze was then added.

Early 16th century Deruta luster is brassy yellow outlined in soft blue, often showing a nacreous iridescence. Later wares have a deeper tone, sometimes approaching olive green.

Large plates predominate as a form, with tin glaze on the front only and a colorless lead glaze on the underside. Some dishes and bowls with raised decoration were made using molds. Many of these feature a raised central boss, perhaps to fit the base of a matching ewer.

Reproductions of Deruta wares were made in the 19th century, notably by Ulysse Cantagalli in Florence. Most of these are marked with a blue cockerel.

A Deruta istoriato dish with Salome holding the head of John the Baptist before Herod, circa 1580, 34cm. diam. (Christie's London) $25,000

A Deruta bottle for A. Graminis painted with the figure of Santa Barbara, circa 1530, 40cm. high. (Christie's) $8,000

A Catalan colored albarello painted in the workshop of Francisco Niculoso in the Deruta style, 17th century, 31cm. high. (Christie's London) $3,350

Early 17th century Central Italian circular plaque with a raised rim dated 1606, probably Deruta, 27cm. diam. (Christie's) $850

A Deruta figural salt, the bowl supported by four three footed winged caryatids on a square pedestal with four claw feet, early 17th century, 15cm. high. (Christie's London) $3,000

A Deruta Armorial dish painted in the center with a shield with a wide band in ocher on a dark blue ground, 38cm. (Phillips) $4,500

A Deruta documentary oviform drug jar with two serpentine handles, dated 1707, 32cm. wide. (Christie's) $1,250

DOCCIA

The Doccia porcelain factory, which flourishes today, was established in 1735 by Carlo Ginori. He produced a hard gray porcelain which was at first inferior to the output from Germany factories of the time, the wares being heavily potted, with spouts in the form of snakes and high domed lids. Many pieces were painted in underglaze blue, their greyish tone suggesting that they were fired at somewhat excessive temperatures.

From 1757 to 1791 Lorenzo Ginori was running the factory and introduced many improved materials and shapes, and a fine white hard-paste product was now being manufactured. In the early 19th century, the body included kaolin, and some fine egg-shell pieces, often decorated in blue and gold chinoiserie, were produced.

As well as tablewares, plaques and vases were produced from the beginning, which were finely modeled, the vases often decorated with full relief figures overpainted in the full enamel palette with gilding.

Figures were made in a hard gray paste with an unevenly applied glaze which often shows fine cracks. Early examples were mostly based on the figures of the Commedia dell'Arte, and are usually set on a simple square base, painted to suggest marble.

After about 1780, many were left white and these are usually arranged round a tree on a hollow rock-like base. These show the true spirit of the Baroque.

The factory mark, from the late 18th century, comprised a six pointed star in red, blue or gold. It is sometimes in Star of David form, and *Ginori, Gin or GI* is often found impressed on wares dating from the mid 19th century onwards.

A Doccia slop bowl molded con basso relievo istoriato with mythological figures and monuments in landscapes (foot-rim chip repaired), circa 1770, 15cm. diam. (Christie's London) $1,500

A Doccia teacup and saucer, circa 1765. $500

A Doccia white group of the Virgin and Child, modeled after Giovanni Battista Foggini, the mother suckling her infant, last quarter of the 18th century, 42cm. high. (Christie's London) $15,000

A Doccia armorial beaker painted in colors with quartered arms on baroque mantling with rampant lion supporters, painted in the manner associated with Klinger, 1740-45, 7.5cm. high. (Christie's London) $1,250

A Doccia figure of a bearded Turk wearing a long puce and yellow striped coat over a blue and gilt flowered robe, circa 1765, 14cm. high. (Christie's London) $3,600

A Doccia baluster coffee-pot and cover painted with scattered sprays of flowers, the reeded dragon's head spout and scroll handle enriched in yellow, blue and puce, circa 1760, 20cm. high. (Christie's) $1,250

DOUCAI

Doucai, or Tou t'sai, means literally 'contrasting color' and refers to a decorative technique consisting of a pattern outlined in a thin, penciled, underglaze blue, infilled with translucent, enameled overglaze colors, principally red, yellow and green.

Examples exist from the early Ming Dynasty, and the technique seems to have been perfected in the Cheng-hua period.

Imitations and new-style wares were made under Yung Cheng and Ch'ien Lung and the 18th century saw the period of greatest output in this style.

A fine large Doucai jardiniere, Qianlong seal mark, finely painted to the side with five medallions filled with lotus flowers and feathery foliate, 13in. diameter. (Christie's) $283,870

A very fine Doucai 'dragon' saucer-dish, encircled Yongzheng six-character mark, the center of the interior enameled with a ferocious five-clawed dragon chasing a flaming pearl amidst clouds, $6^3/4$in. diameter. (Christie's) $63,870

A fine Doucai and famille rose moonflask, Qianlong seal mark, elaborately painted to each circular face with the 'three abundances', pomegranate, peach and finger citrus, $12^1/4$in. high.(Christie's) $540,000

A pair of Doucai 'Dragon' saucer-dishes, the interior with a five-clawed dragon chasing a flaming pearl amidst cloud scrolls below four stylised clouds, $5^3/4$in. diameter. (Christie's) $7,400

A Doucai Zhadou, the globular body painted with a lotus scroll, the flower-heads alternating with peaches, Qianlong seal mark, 7.9cm. diameter. (Christie's) $13,870

A Doucai bowl, finely painted to the exterior with six iron-red lotus blossoms framed within elaborate scrollwork, all between a double line below the rim, $5^3/4$in. diameter. (Christie's) $6,220

A fine Doucai dish, the interior painted with a double-centered lotus flower-head encircled by stylised ruyi-head scrolls and leaves below double blue lines, $8^1/4$in. diameter. (Christie's) $25,000

A pair of Doucai saucer-dishes, encircled Kangxi six-character marks, the central medallion painted with a crane in flight reserved on a shou character, $8^5/8$in. diameter. (Christie's) $17,750

DOULTON

The Doulton story began in 1815, when Henry's father John, known as the 'best thrower of pint pots in London' set up a pottery business in partnership with a widow called Jones and a journeyman called Watts. The Watts Doulton part of the association continued until the former's retiral in 1853, by which time the premises had moved to Lambeth High Street, where earthenware bottles, chimney pots, garden ornaments and tiles were produced.

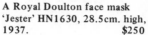

In 1835 John's second son Henry joined the company. He responded to the calls to improve urban sanitation by commencing the manufacture of sewage and water pipes, and at one time the Doulton works were producing these at the rate of 10 miles a week and exporting them all over the world.

With a solid financial base established, Henry decided he could afford to branch out and indulge some of his other interests. In the late 1850's his father had already been approached by John Sparkes, head of the newly established Lambeth School of Arts, who had requested that some of his students should try potting. It was Henry who finally responded to this request. He set up a pottery studio in a corner of the works, and it is worth noting that George Tinworth and the Barlows, Arthur, Florence and Hannah, were among the first intake.

Henry had the wisdom to show the results at the various international exhibitions which were taking place in that period,

A Royal Doulton face mask 'Jester' HN1630, 28.5cm. high, 1937. $250

Bone china teapot with raised paste gilding and exotic birds painted by J. Birbeck, 5½in. high, circa 1910. $375

A pair of Doulton Lambeth tiles painted by Margaret Armstrong, in the pre-Raphaelite style, painted in colors, each in original frame, 7 x 18½in. (Christie's S. Ken) $800

Bone china vase featuring Pan playing his pipes, in Sung glazes by Charles Noke, 7in. high, circa 1925. $1,000

A Doulton Lambeth circular pottery plaque, painted in colors with a portrait of young man in antique dress, 13½in. diameter. (Christie's S. Ken) $300

A fine Royal Doulton 'Chang' vase by Harry Nixon, Charles Noke and Fred Allen, 22.5cm., painted mark in black. (Bearne's) $3,000

109

DOULTON

and they were so enthusiastically received that by 1880 the number employed by the studio had risen to 200. Within the next twenty years it was to double again.

By this time Henry had also acquired an earthenware factory in Burslem, which he renamed Doulton and Co. Here, he began to make bone china in 1885, again creating a studio for artists and potters on the premises.

Experimentation and constant development were the keynotes for both establishments and they attracted terrific resources of talent. Charles J Noke, for example, joined the company in 1889 and finally became Artistic Director at Burslem. He experimented with Copenhagen and Sèvres type wares and in recreating oriental techniques. The results of the latter were the renowned Flambé, Sung, Chinese jade and Chang pottery. Under Noke, too, the company embarked on one of its most successful lines of all, figure models, the first of which were exhibited at Chicago in 1893.

A continuing supply of such talent ensured the survival of the Lambeth studio until 1956, while at Burslem activity continues unabated to this day.

A Royal Doulton Chang bowl by Noke, decorated with green, red, yellow, white and blue glazes on a blue ground, 7in. diameter. (Spencer's) $850

Doulton Burslem Royles Patent self pouring teapot, with pewter lid, circa 1900. $225

A large Royal Doulton Sung vase by Arthur Eaton, decorated with dragons amongst clouds, 13in. high, circa 1930. $1,250

Royal Doulton faience vase by John H. McLennan, decorated with panels representing Earth and Water, 13½in. high. $350

A Doulton cabinet plate painted by Leslie Johnson, signed, with a naked maiden seated beside a woodland pool, 22.5cm., date code for 1901. (Phillips London) $700

Doulton Burslem Morrisian Ware tobacco jar and cover decorated with a band of dancing girls, 5½in. high. $150

DOULTON CHARACTER JUGS

Charles Noke was the inspiration behind the immensely popular Doulton range of character jugs, the first of which, John Barleycorn Old Lad, was produced in the 1930s. A huge variety were made, featuring figures from folk lore and personalities past and present. Some continued in production for years. Others were quickly withdrawn, perhaps, as in the case of Churchill, because the subject didn't like them or, as in the case of Clark Gable, because it was claimed they infringed copyright. In consequence, these are now exceedingly rare, and are correspondingly valuable. Slight variations on a standard type also make an enormous difference to the value of a piece. A hatted version of Sir Francis Drake will fetch less than £100, whereas the hatless version is worth over ten times more.

'Churchill' (White), D6170, designed by C. Noke, issued 1940, withdrawn 1941. $7,500

'Mad Hatter', D6598, designed by M. Henk, issued 1965, withdrawn 1983. $75

'Gladiator', D6550, designed by M. Henk, issued 1961, withdrawn 1967. $400

'Drake' (hatless), a Royal Doulton character jug, large, D6115, designed by H. Fenton, introduced 1940, withdrawn 1941. (Louis Taylor) $2,750

Harry Fenton was one of the foremost designers of character jugs, and variations on his 'Arry and 'Arriet costermongers (when he has a blue collar and white buttons and she has a blue collar and maroon hat) will now command thousands of pounds. One useful factor for collectors is that each jug bears the back stamp of the company and is numbered according to Doulton's own system.

'Mephistopheles', D5757, designed by H. Fenton, issued 1937, withdrawn 1948. $1,350

'Clown' (Red Haired), D5610, designed by H. Fenton, issued 1937, withdrawn 1942. $2,000

Dick Whittington D6375, designed by G Blower, issued 1953, withdrawn 1960. $250

Uncle Tom Cobbleigh D6337, designed by M Henk, issued 1952, withdrawn 1960 $260

Granny (Toothless version) D5521, designed by H Fenton & M Henk, issued 1935. $675

'Ard of 'Earing D6588, designed by D Biggs, issued 1964, withdrawn 1967. $675

Mikado D6501, designed by M Henk, issued 1959, withdrawn 1969. $325

Samuel Johnson D6289, designed by H Fenton, issued 1950, withdrawn 1960. $250

Lord Nelson D6336, designed by G Blower, issued 1952, withdrawn 1969. $250

Punch and Judy Man D6590, designed by D Biggs, issued 1964, withdrawn 1969. $400

Jockey D6625, designed by D Biggs, issued 1971, withdrawn 1975. $300

DOULTON FIGURES

The first Doulton figures were made by George Tinworth, one of the original group of art potters who came to the company via the Lambeth School of Art. His output was small, however, and it was not until Charles Noke joined the firm in 1889 that figure making really became big business. Noke was inspired by the figures produced by Derby, Bow, Meissen and also, nearer home, by the Staffordshire figure making industry. Initially, the colors used tended to be rather dull, and the figures did not sell well, so their production was suspended until 1912, when a new range, including the famous 'Bedtime/Darling' by Charles Vyse, was introduced. (This was originally entitled Bedtime, but was rechristened after Queen Mary, seeing it while on a visit to the factory, exclaimed 'What a darling!')

The new figures benefited from brighter colors, and a talented team of modelers now set to work. These included Leslie Harradine, Harry Tittensor and later Peggy Harper.

More than 200 Doulton figures are still in production today, and even they can fetch surprisingly high prices.

'Lady of the Georgian Period', HN41, designed by E. W. Light, introduced 1914, withdrawn 1938, 10.25in. high. (Louis Taylor) $1,000

'The Farmer's Boy', HN2520G, 9.25in. high. (Louis Taylor) $700

A Royal Doulton porcelain figure entitled 'Carpet Vendor', H.N. 76.
(Bearne's) $1,250

A Royal Doulton group entitled 'The Perfect Pair', H.N.581, withdrawn 1938.
(Bearne's) $375

A Royal Doulton porcelain figure, entitled 'Suzette', H.N. 1696, withdrawn 1949
(Bearne's) $200

'Puppy Sitting', a Royal Doulton model of a puppy with one ear cocked, 10.4cm. high. (Phillips) $475

113

DOULTON KINGSWARE

The ware known as Kingsware was introduced at Burslem in 1899 and was used to make pottery flasks for whisky, usually in editions of 1,000, for spirit producers such as Dewars and the Hudson Bay Company. Some upmarket versions even had silver fittings. The process involved applying color slips in shades of muted greens, yellows and reddish browns to the interior of plaster molds in which a design was impressed. When another brown slip was poured in the colors blended to give a deep, soft effect to the embossed design.

The glaze was usually treacly brown in color, but another paler yellow was sometimes also used, and this much rarer effect is known as Kingsware Yellow glaze.

The principal designer of the embossed patterns was Arthur Bailey, who worked at Burslem between 1912 and 1932. They mostly consisted of drinking related motifs, and featured such popular characters as Falstaff and the Sporting Squire.

The Leather Bottle, a Royal Doulton Kingsware flask, circa 1918, 6¼in. high, 6in. long. **$450**

Micawber, a Royal Doulton Kingsware whisky flask made for Dewar's Scotch Whisky, 7in. high, issued 1909. **$200**

A Royal Doulton Kingsware jardiniere decorated with seagulls, circa 1910, 5½in. high, 9in. wide. **$210**

The Alchemist, a Royal Doulton Kingsware clock, 7½in. high, circa 1913. **$600**

Royal Doulton Kingsware single-handled jug depicting a golfer and his caddie. **$400**

Huntsman, a Royal Doulton Kingsware Toby jug, 7½in. high. **$375**

Peace flagon, a Kingsware flask with brown border, made for Dewar's, No.181, 7½in. high, circa 1919. **$375**

DOULTON SERIESWARE

It was Charles Noke who was responsible for the simple yet ingenious idea behind Seriesware. He realised that standard pottery shapes could be embellished with popular images and sold as novelty art wares to people who could not afford the artist's individual creations.

The designs were transfer printed on to pieces made of earthenware and bone china and then hand colored. The first series was called the Isthmian Games and appeared in 1889, with a new series following almost every year for the next half century. The design could be found on everything from toothbrush holders to plates, and obviously formed a rich scope for collectables.

In the 1970s Seriesware was revived, when special plates were issued for special events and anniversaries.

Oliver Twist jug designed by C.J. Noke, depicting 'Fagin and Bumble', D5617.　$100

A Royal Doulton Cecil Aldin Series ware jardiniere, the decoration from the 'Old English Scenes', 18cm. high.　$250

The Gleaners, Series ware sandwich tray.　$60

Willow Pattern Series jar and cover, 6½in. high, circa 1912.　$100

A large Royal Doulton pottery vase, decorated with an extensive fox hunting scene between bands of flowers, 57.5cm. (Bearne's)　$250

'Short Headed Salmon', a Royal Doulton rack plate, signed by J. Birbeck, 9½in. diameter, circa 1913.　$180

A Jacobean jug 'Ye Old Belle' depicting a serving wench and two cavaliers, 6½in. high. $100

DOULTON STONEWARE

Stoneware was the first material produced by John Doulton in 1815, and the company concentrated at first on mass produced items such as bottles and jugs.

When Henry Doulton joined the firm he diversified into architectural stoneware and set his protegés from the Lambeth School of Art to work. They included such famous names as the Barlows, George Tinworth and Eliza Simmance. At first their designs were fairly simple, but they subsequently embarked on pâte-sur-pâte work, whereby a raised outline was built up by delicate brush work. This led to more sophisticated designs and particularly the stylized carved foliage which presaged the Art Nouveau style.

DOULTON & SLATERS PATENT

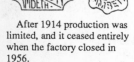

After 1914 production was limited, and it ceased entirely when the factory closed in 1956.

'Salt glazed stoneware Chine ware vase decorated by L. Mear, 9½in. high, circa 1902. $200

Doulton Lambeth stoneware jardinière, ovoid and embossed with classical profile heads and flowers within geometric borders, 8in. high.
(Hobbs & Chambers) $175

A Coronation mug commemorating the accession of Edward VII and Queen Alexandra, circa 1902, 7½in. high. $150

'Hunting', a frog and mouse group with the frogs riding mice over a water jump, circa 1884, 4½in. high. $1,500

A Doulton Lambeth stoneware jug commemorating Victoria's Diamond Jubilee, inscribed *She brought her people lasting good*, 24cm.
(Phillips) $300

'Play Goers' by George Tinworth, the group glazed pale brown with a blue and brown shaped base, 1886, 5¼in. high. $2,000

116

DRESDEN

There can be few people today who are not familiar with the term 'Dresden china', often used as a comparison when trying to convey an idea of delicacy and fragility. Try looking up 'Dresden' in any textbook, however, and it is mysteriously absent, for Dresden, in fact is simply an alternative for the more correct term of Meissen.

The misnomer dates from the 18th century itself, when 'Dresden' was enough to describe this first hard paste European factory, and when Derby was established in 1756, it became known as 'The New Dresden'.

Matters were further complicated by the fact that in the 19th century small workshops and decorators set up in the city of Dresden itself, making and decorating inferior copies of early Meissen. Often the marks were also copied.

Principal decorators in the mid-late 19th century working in Dresden were Donath, Hamann, Klemm, A Lamm and F Hirsch, all of whom decorated in the Meissen style. Many of their pieces are marked *Dresden*, with a crown or star.

A pair of Dresden salts, each shaped oval, held by a reclining male and female figure respectively, 19th century, 6½in. (Lawrence Fine Arts) $850

A Dresden group of a huntsman in 18th century costume restraining two leaping hounds, 15in. high. (Christie's S. Ken) $900

A pair of Dresden large groups of children playing round a wine press and a barrel, 30cm. and 34cm. (Lawrence Fine Arts) $7,500

Early 20th century Dresden porcelain vase and cover, white ground decorated with romantic figures and sprigs of flowers, 14in. high. (G. A. Key) $325

A massive pair of Dresden yellow ground oviform vases and covers, reserved and painted with exotic birds, blue AR marks, circa 1900, 64cm. high. (Christie's London) $5,000

A Dresden seated figure of Cupid pressing hearts in a press, on marbled circular base with gilt borders, 18.5cm. (Lawrence Fine Arts) $750

A pair of Dresden China table lamps, 19th century in the form of rose encrusted urns supported by three putti. (Lots Road Galleries) $1,100

FAENZA

It was the Italian city of Faenza, situated between Bologna and Rimini, that was to give its name to the tin glazed earthenware which came to be known as faience. From the late 14th century it had been associated with maiolica manufacture and from the mid 15th century developed a very distinctive style. Apart from the usual drug pots, fine baluster vases decorated with heraldic devices, contemporary figures or gothic foliage, were produced.

Later some large pieces in full relief were attempted. By the 16th century several Faenza painters were engaged in painting in the style now associated with Urbino, and referred to as istoriato. Far Eastern influence was also beginning to filter through and about this time a style called bianchi di Faenza, with a minimum of decoration and a white tin glaze was developed.

In 1693 Count Annibale Ferniani bought a Faenza pottery where tiles and tablewares were made, which continued almost to this day.

Full signatures of painters or potters appear only rarely on 15th century Faenza ware, but in the 16th century these become more common.

A Faenza or Tuscan vase, circa 1500-20, 32.5cm. high. (Phillips) $1,500

A Faenza crespina with fluted rim, and on a low foot, painted in the center with a standing figure of a warrior, 30cm., late 16th century.
(Phillips) $2,500

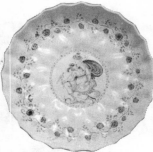

A Faenza documentary compendiaro crespina painted in the workshop of Maestro Virgiliotto Calamelli, with a falconer, circa 1565, 30cm. diam. (Christie's) $6,750

A Faenza wet drug jar of ovoid shape with an angled strap handle and straight spout, 22.5cm. high. $600

A Faenza circular tondino of Cardinal's hat form, circa 1525, 25cm. diam. $20,000

A Faenza drug vase of compressed baluster form, the contents a. api, circa 1550, 21.5cm. high. $650

A Faenza shaped dish, Cn mark to base, Ferniani's factory, circa 1770, 32cm. diam. (Christie's) $600

FAMILLE ROSE

Famille rose is a style of decoration based on Chinese porcelain painting introduced during the Yongzheng period around 1730. A deep rose pink enamel derived from gold features strongly in the palette and by mixing this with white a variety of pinks and deep rose colors were now obtainable. It was much in demand for tableware produced for the nouveau riche of the Industrial Revolution.

A pair of famille rose bowls, Qianlong seal marks and of the period, enameled on the exterior with butterflies, ripe citrus and bamboo, 4¹/₄in. diameter. (Christie's) $30,000

A famille rose yellow-ground Tibetan-style vase, iron red Jiaqing seal mark, painted to the bulbous body with stylised lotus and scrolling foliage dividing the eight Buddhist emblems, 10⁷/₈in. high. (Christie's) $15,000

A pair of famille rose flattened double-gourd vases, blue enamel Le Xian Tang Zhi hall marks, 19th century, similarly painted to both faces with the wufu (five bats), in flight amidst clouds, 7in. high. (Christie's) $5,350

A famille rose yellow-ground rose bowl, four-character Qianlong mark, painted around the exterior with four circular pink panels and ruby scrollwork each enclosing a character forming a phrase furi changming (the eternal light of Buddhism), 4¹/₂in. diameter. (Christie's) $2,650

A pair of famille rose oviform vases, Hongxian Yuzhi marks, painted in mirror image with an elegant gentleman leaning against a green bamboo fence, 11in. high. (Christie's) $4,500

A fine and rare pair of famille rose square pear-shaped vases, iron-red Qianlong seal marks, painted on the exterior in various shades of pastel enamels, 11¹/₂in. high. (Christie's) $100,000

A fine famille rose bowl, iron-red Shen de Tang Zhi mark, enameled with a continuous scene of Immortals and scholars variously engaged in dispute or relaxation, 6³/₄in. diameter. (Christie's) $15,000

A pair of 19th century famille rose candlestick figures, standing in richly decorated robes and with peacock-feather mantelet, holding a lotus-petal vase, 11¹/₂in. high. (Tennants) $4,250

FAMILLE VERTE

Famille verte is a style of
Chinese painting with
prominent use of bright green
and shades of yellow and
aubergine purple together
with line drawings in black.
It was introduced during the
Kangxi period at the end of
the 17th century.

A famille verte 'month' cup
finely painted to one side with a
flowering peach tree, inscribed
to the reverse with a couplet,
2⁵/₈in. diameter.
(Christie's) $25,000

A famille verte 'month' cup,
painted to one side with two
clumps of flowering narcissus
before rockwork and a single
long stemmed red rose,
representing the eleventh
month, 2⁵/₈in. diameter.
(Christie's) $22,500

A finely painted famille verte
rouleau vase, painted in bright
enamels with a group of
armored warriors holding
their weapons in a garden
landscape with pine trees issuing
from rockwork, 18in. high.
(Christie's) $23,500

A pair of black-ground famille
verte dishes, each painted to the
rounded exterior with a
composite floral scroll including
lotus, clematis and peony
blooms, 5⁷/₈in. diameter.
(Christie's) $20,000

A rare black-ground famille
verte baluster vase, enameled
around the body with a
composite floral scroll with
small foliate elements, all on a
dense black ground, 8in. high.
(Christie's) $20,000

A famille verte 'month' cup,
encircled Kangxi six-character
mark and of the period,
decorated to the exterior with
blossoming tree peony issuing
from a grassy patch among
pierced rockwork, 2¹/₂in.
diameter.
(Christie's) $15,000

A pair of famille verte and gilt
'duck' plates, the center of each
with a pair of swimming
mandarin ducks on a lotus pond
below another pair in flight,
8⁵/₈in. diameter.
(Christie's) $3,500

A famille verte 'month' cup,
encircled Kangxi six-character
mark and of the period, painted
to one side with two clumps of
flowering narcissus before
rockwork and a single long stem
with a red rose, 2⁵/₈in. diameter.
(Christie's) $6,500

FOLEY

The Foley pottery was established in Fenton, Staffordshire in the mid 19th century and was operated from 1903 by E Brain & Co. Its porcelain is noted for the simplicity of its design. That said, in the 1930's work was commissioned from leading contemporary artists such as Graham Sutherland and Laura Knight and is marked with the maker's name and the signature of the artist and decorator. The Foley marks include the brand name *Peacock Pottery*, with a peacock in a rectangle and Staffordshire knot.

A Foley Pastello twin handled vase of double gourd form printed and painted with rustic scene of house nestling in wooded landscape, 7in. high. (Christie's S. Ken) $700

A Foley Intarsio small oviform jardinière printed and painted in colors with a band of carp amongst waves, 4¹/₂in. high. (Christie's S. Ken) $350

A Foley Intarsio single handled jug, painted and enameled in colors with two heralds blowing trumpets, printed factory mark, 11in. high. (Christie's S. Ken) $600

A Foley Intarsio circular wall plate, designed by Frederick Rhead, the center decorated in colors with two classical maidens, 36.8cm. diam. (Phillips) $700

A Foley jardiniere and stand, each decorated in alternate green and yellow ground spiraling panels patterned with flowers and foliage, 42in. high. (Christie's) $2,500

A Foley Urbato ware vase, of globular form, decorated in white slip trailing with pink flowers and green leaves, 22.3cm. high. (Phillips) $300

A Foley Intarsio ceramic clock, painted in blue, turquoise, green, brown and yellow enamels, with Art Nouveau maidens representing day and night, 29cm. high. (Christie's) $1,250

A Foley pastello solifleur, decorated with a cottage in a landscape in shades of blue, purple and yellow, 5in. high. (Christie's S. Ken) $200

FRANKENTHAL

When Louis XV, ever jealous for his Sèvres protegé, refused Paul Hannong a licence to continue making porcelain at Strasbourg in 1755, Hannong took his know-how across the Rhine to Frankenthal, where the Elector Carl Theodor allowed him to set up in some disused barrack buildings.

Hannong quickly set to work, and within a few months was producing pieces of a standard high enough to be used as court gifts. He subsequently returned to Strasbourg, leaving his elder son, Charles-François-Paul as director at Frankenthal. Charles died in 1757, however, whereupon his younger brother Joseph Adam took over, and in 1759 bought the factory from his father. In 1762, the Elector himself bought it out, and it continued in production until 1800. On its closure, many molds went to Grünstadt, Nymphenburg and elsewhere, where they were later used to make reproductions of early Frankenthal pieces.

As they had at Strasbourg, the Hannongs made pieces which were strongly rococo in style. Their tableware owes more to Sèvres than any other German factory. Leading painters were Winterstein, who painted scenes after Teniers, Osterspey (mythology) and Magnus, who specialised in battle scenes.

Figure-making featured largely in the Frankenthal output. Early examples were designed by J W Lanz, whose subjects are characterised by their small heads and theatrical poses. J L Lück continued in a similar style, but his figures have a more robust appearance and are usually sited on extravagant scrollwork, with frequent use of arbors. The court sculptor Linck also made models for a

A Frankenthal silver shape rococo sauceboat, painted in colours with scattered sprays of roses, chrysanthemums and deutsche Blumen, incised *PH*, for Paul Hannong, circa 1755, 24.5cm. wide. (Christie's Geneva) $1,500

A Frankenthal group of four children, 23cm. wide, Carl Theodor mark in underglaze blue and dated 1783. (Phillips) $6,750

A Frankenthal group of card players modeled by J. F. Luck, crowned CT mark and letter B for Adam Bergdoll to base, circa 1765, 17cm. high. (Christie's) $8,000

A Frankenthal baluster ewer and cover probably painted by Jakob Osterspey with Bacchus and Venus reclining beside him scantily clad in brown and pink drapes, circa 1758, 23.5cm. high. (Christie's) $13,250

A Frankenthal figure of a lady emblematic of Spring modeled by J.W. Lanz, stepping forward and holding her flower-laden apron before her, circa 1760, 14cm. high. (Christie's) $1,850

A Frankenthal group of a seated young man and two young women, modeled by K. G. Luck, dating from 1778, 23cm. wide. $4,000

FRANKENTHAL

number of years on a very dramatic scale, sometimes running to entire opera scenes. Karl Lück, brother of J L, succeeded Linck as model master in 1765. He had studied under Kaendler, but his pieces, though exquisitely crafted, are notable for their fussiness and flamboyant colors.

During the later period Adam Bauer produced figures more in the neo-Classical style (though his Venuses were often rather voluptuous for a strictly Antique taste). Finally J P Melchior took over to produce groups similar to those he had been making at Höchst.

The usual mark is CT for Carl Theodor, under an Electoral crown, though PH and PHF are to be found impressed on a few early pieces. More rare is JAH with a crowned lion rampant.

A Frankenthal figure of a Chinaman modeled by K. G. Lueck, seated on a fence wearing a broad brimmed hat, date code 77, 11.5cm. high. (Christie's London) $1,100

A Frankenthal figure of Pantolone from the Commedia dell'Arte, blue lion and monogram of Joseph Adam Hannong to base, circa 1760, 11.5cm. high. (Christie's) $5,500

A pair of Frankenthal figures of Oceanus and Thetis modeled by Konrad Linck, the sea god standing extending his arm towards his companion, circa 1765, 28.5cm. and 24cm. high. (Christie's London) $93,775

A Frankenthal coffee cup and saucer, with panels painted in puce camaieu, circa 1765. $1,100

A Frankenthal group of putti emblematic of Summer modeled by J. W. Lanz, circa 1756-59, 19.5cm. high. $475

An early Frankenthal figure of Pulchinella, impressed PH3 (for Paul Hannong) on base, circa 1755, 12cm. high. (Christie's) $8,000

A Frankenthal group of a young woman embracing an elderly man, modeled by K. G. Luck, circa 1778, 15.5cm. high. $3,500

FRENCH

Early lead-glazed pottery was made in France from the 14th century onwards, The 16th century saw considerable refinements and the genre directly presages the peasant pottery made particularly in the north of France to this day.

French pottery production was always susceptible to outside influences. The 16th century maiolica production from Rouen, Nîmes, Lyons and Nevers is hard to distinguish from its Italian prototypes, although Nevers did develop a distinctive style in the 17th century with the use not only of maiolica colors but also of a deep blue polychrome.

A seminal blue-decorated faience was developed at Rouen in 1680, which influenced many other factories, such as Paris and St. Cloud, over a long period. In the 18th century Rouen again set a trend with Chinese and rococo style polychrome wares.

In the late 17th century Moustiers was influential in creating a fashion for finely painted pictorial panels, first in blue and later in yellow, green and manganese. In the mid 18th century Paul Hannong's Strasbourg factory copied the porcelain style of enamel painting for faience, and this practice was in turn copied by, among others, Niderviller, Rouen and Moustiers.

The first French porcelain was of the soft-paste type and was made at Rouen in 1673. Similar wares were subsequently produced also at Chantilly, Mennecy, St Cloud and finally Vincennes-Sèvres.

Vincennes Sèvres held the monopoly for porcelain production from about 1750-1770, after which other factories again tried to make hard-paste porcelain, and in the 19th century production became largely concentrated in the kaolin district of Limoges.

French Pottery Group of a Young Man and Woman, 19th century, both holding a molded floral decorated trunk with a hat and umbrella placed on the cover, 12¼in. wide. (Skinner Inc) $225

Late 18th/early 19th century French biscuit group emblematic of America, 29cm. high. (Christie's) $750

Two French soft-paste figures of a man playing a guitar and his companion dressed as a huntress holding a rifle, he with incised R, circa 1750, 19cm. and 20cm. high. (Christie's) $2,500

A large French ceramic jardinière and stand, the stand decorated in mottled browns and pinks flanked by bulrushes and foliage and a large naturalistic heron, total height 1.28m., signed *Jerome Massier fils, Vallauris A.M.* (Phillips) $4,000

A French oval porcelain plaque painted with a young girl wearing 18th century-style dress, late 19th century, plaque 6in. long. (Christie's S. Ken) $450

An 18th century French biscuit figure emblematic of Africa, 31.5cm. high. (Christie's) $1,000

A Le Croisic fluted dish painted with a portrait bust of a Neo Classical figure, relief epsilon mark, circa 1730, 31.5cm. diam. (Christie's London) $500

A St Clement bough pot, the bombe sides painted en camaieu with birds in landscape vignettes, circa 1785, 25.5cm. wide. (Christie's London) $1,250

A Rouen a la corne shaped, circular plate painted in high fired colors, red OD mark, circa 1750, 25cm. diam. (Christie's London) $800

A French soft paste figure allegorical of Sight, the scantily clad youth seated on a rockwork base, circa 1750, possibly Orleans or Crepy en Valois, 15cm. high. (Christie's London) $675

Two figures of jazz musicians, one with trumpet and the other with saxophone, painted in silver lustre, painted factory mark, 11½in. maximum. (Christie's S. Ken) $750

An 18th century French biscuit group emblematic of Plenty, 34cm. high. (Christie's) $750

A French 'Empire' cabinet cup decorated at the Feuillet workshop in Paris, painted with a colonnaded country house, 12cm. (Phillips) $450

A pair of French biscuit porcelain figures in the form of a man and woman, late 19th century, 42.5cm. high. (Bearne's) $500

A French faience jug of fluted helmet shape on spreading foot painted in blue, (spout riveted) 8½in. high. (Christie's S. Ken) $150

FÜRSTENBERG

For an operation which is still going strong today, the Fürstenberg porcelain factory got off to a distinctly unpromising start. In 1747, one Johann Christoph Glaser approached Duke Carl I of Bavaria, claiming to know all there was to know about making fine porcelain, and offering his services. The Duke was delighted, put a castle at Glaser's disposal, and the Duchess was so excited that she threw out all her porcelain, believing it could be ground down and formed afresh!

Glaser was a charlatan, but he managed to get a small operation going to make faience until 1753 when Johann Benckgraff was persuaded to come to Fürstenberg from Höchst. Though he brought with him the modeler Simon Feilner and the painter Johann Zeschinger, Benckgraff promptly died before he could reveal much about porcelain manufacture!

It has been claimed that the high relief and extravagant ornamentation on early Fürstenberg was used to conceal the many imperfections in the clay. However, by 1760 quality had improved sufficiently to allow the safe manufacture of simple forms which relied on enamel and gilt chinoiserie decoration, and in the 1770s some very fine figures were made by a number of modelers.

In 1795 L V Gerverot was in charge of the factory. He had worked previously at Sèvres and Wedgwood and followed neo-Classical fashions to produce black basalts and biscuit porcelain busts. In 1859 the factory was in private hands and still manufactures today.

Fürstenberg is marked with various forms of a cursive *F* in underglaze blue. Biscuit busts bear the impressed mark of a running horse.

A Furstenberg globular teapot and cover, blue script F and figure 3 to base, circa 1765, 19cm. wide. (Christie's) $3,000

A Furstenberg figure of Andromeda after a model by Desoches, seated on a rock to which she is chained by her wrist and ankle, circa 1774, 28.5cm. high. (Christie's London) $2,000

A pair of Furstenberg white portrait busts modeled by J. C. Rombrich, probably of Schrader von Schiestedt and his wife, circa 1758/9, 15cm. high. (Christie's) $9,000

A Furstenberg figure of Bagolin modeled by A. S. Laplau, circa 1775, 12cm. high. $3,500

A Furstenberg group of Perseus, modeled by Desoches, blue script F mark, circa 1780, 26.5cm. high. $600

A Furstenberg arched rectangular tea caddy, impressed no. 2, circa 1770, 10.5cm. high, silver cover. $1,100

GALLÉ

While Emile Gallé (1846–1904) is best known as an artist in glass, he also worked in other media as diverse as furniture and ceramics. He established a small workshop in 1874 at Nancy (Meurthe et Moselle) and there produced earthenware, which was first exhibited in 1890. Later, he also experimented with stoneware and porcelain.

His forms were for the most part simple, sometimes even a little clumsy, though some of his shapes were borrowed by the Rookwood pottery in the USA, who acknowledged their debt to him.

His decorative motifs included heraldic themes and scenes which were reminiscent of delft. Perhaps inevitably, too, he used standard Art Nouveau motifs such as plant designs of orchids, chrysanthemums, orchids etc, and his glazes were flowing and opaque, sometimes mingling two or more colors.

Apart from his own distinctive style, he was much influenced by Japanese styles, as reflected in some of the 'Origami' pieces he produced, the angular shapes of which presage Art Deco themes . Amongst the most charming of his pieces are his cats, which sit, regarding the onlooker with their glass eyes and an expression on their faces which is variously described as 'sweet faced' or a 'silly smile'.

All his pieces were marked, either with the impressed initials *EG, Em Galle Faiencerie de Nancy*, or with various versions of his signature.

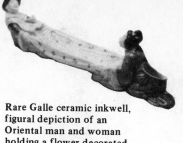

Rare Galle ceramic inkwell, figural depiction of an Oriental man and woman holding a flower decorated fabric between them, 17½in. long. (Skinner Inc.) $1,850

A Galle style pottery cat, seated with free-standing forelegs, wearing a pale blue coat scattered with gilt flowers, 34.5cm. high. (Henry Spencer) $750

A pair of Gallé faience 'Origami' models each as an abstract folded creature painted with yellow and blue bands, 8cm. high. (Phillips) $500

A Galle faience bowl of squat dimpled bulbous shape, 1890's, 14cm. $200

A Gallé faience model of a cat, the creature sitting back on its haunches and gazing with glass eyes and whiskered grin, 34cm. high. (Phillips) $1,350

A Galle faience Origami model as an abstract folded creature painted with stylised corn-flower sprays, 8cm. high. (Phillips London) $150

GARDNER

The success of the Imperial Porcelain factory in the mid 18th century and the demand for its products led private individuals to set up their own porcelain making enterprises in Russia. Among them was Francis Yakovlevich Gardner, an Aberdonian by birth, who arrived in Russia in 1746 and made his fortune in a Moscow banking office. He received an Imperial permit in 1766 and started work the following year. While early Gardner pieces cannot rival the porcelain of Meissen, he was successful in making products of a lovely off-white hue, which soon attracted royal patronage. Many commissions followed for grand services for use on ceremonial occasions in the Winter Palace, adorned with badges and ribbons of chivalric orders. Gardner also turned out a series of delightful little biscuit 'dolls', producing 800 of these in 1770 alone.

While Gardner's products showed some neo-classical influence as the century wore on, they remained resolutely Russian in spirit. The factory was made a company in 1857, and was taken over by the firm of Kuznetsov in 1892.

The marks include a *G*, either in Cyrillic or Roman, while crossed swords or a star are found towards the end of the 18th century. After the early 19th century *Gardner* appears in Cyrillic with the Arms of Moscow. From 1855–1881 the Russian two headed eagle appears above the arms encircled with a band on which is inscribed *Fabrik Gardner v Moskve*.

A porcelain figure of a naked young woman by Gardner, Moscow, circa 1840, 7½in. high. $650

A pair of Gardner figures representing a peasant couple, Moscow, circa 1850, 14.5cm. high. $400

A biscuit group of three tipsy men standing on an oval base, by Gardner, printed and impressed marks, 23.5cm. high. $1,000

A Gardener figure of a Finn in traditional costume, standing before a tree stump, in brown hat, gray jacket and breeches, 26cm., red printed mark. (Phillips) $500

A porcelain figure of a street vendor, with Gardner factory mark, Moscow, circa 1850, 15.3cm. high. $650

A biscuit group of two bearded men, by Gardner, printed and impressed marks, 22cm. high. $700

128

GERMAN

Medieval German pottery consists mainly of jugs and cups, most of which are undecorated. Cologne and the Rhineland were particularly prominent pottery areas at this time.

From the 16th century very fine salt glazed stoneware was made in the four centers of Cologne, Siegburg, Raeren and Westerwald, the last with incised decoration, while in the 15-17th centuries the Hafner, or local stove makers, were responsible for the production of earthenware with fine green and colored glazes.

The German faience industry dates from the 17th century and aimed mainly at reproducing Chinese style blue and white. It centered round Hanau and Frankfurt, and Hanau is also notable for having pioneered the work of the Hausmaler, or outside decorators, whose work was to have such importance both for faience and later for porcelain. Faience was also produced at Nuremberg (where most of the Hausmaler worked) and Bayreuth; this was notably baroque in style and used high temperature colors. A clutch of factories in Thuringia also made blue and white and high temperature polychrome faience.

Germany took the lead in true porcelain manufacture, when Böttger discovered its secret for Augustus the Strong in 1708-9. No other German factory succeeded in copying it for almost fifty years, but from the middle of the century numerous other princes endeavoured to set up their own manufactories. Interest was at its height between 1750-75, and this was when much of the finest work was done.

A Florsheim faience inkstand, modeled as a chest of three serpentine-fronted drawers, 15cm. high. (Phillips) $2,000

Late 17th century Habaner Ware inscribed and dated beer jug, 30cm. high. (Christie's) $5,750

A pair of German porcelain figures of Cupid-like figures, each with a bow and quiver, standing on a foliate base, 37.5cm. (Bearne's) $400

A Brunswick faience figure of a standing bagpiper, circa 1730, 18cm. high. (Christie's) $7,500

A German porcelain small rectangular plaque painted in colors with a mermaid and a youth seated on rocks, circa 1880, 2¾ x 2¼in. (Christie's S. Ken) $300

A German porcelain pierced tazza, with a military equestrian figure attended by a Moor, impressed numeral, 16¼in. high. (Christie's S. Ken) $575

GERMAN

CHINA

A Wallendorf figure of a fruit vendor in a black hat, gray jacket, iron-red patterned waistcoat, puce breeches and black shoes, circa 1770, 13cm. high. (Christie's) $1,250

One of a pair of German heart shaped vases on domed circular bases chased with scrolls and rocaille decoration, 6¾in. (Christie's S. Ken)
Two $500

A colored Wurzberg figure of a putto, after the Nymphenburg models by Bustelli, standing and leaning against a yellow lyre, 10cm. (Phillips) $800

A Crailsheim faience tankard (Walzenkrug) painted in colors with an exotic bird and pine trees, mid 18th century, 28.5cm. high. (Christie's) $1,350

A pair of German seated pug dogs, with blue ribbon-tied collars hung with yellow bells, possibly Braunschweig, circa 1750, 14.5cm. and 15.5cm. high. (Christie's) $5,000

A Hannoversch-Munden reticulated baluster vase and pierced cover with rosehead finial and applied leaves painted in green and manganese, three crescents mark over painter's mark K in the manganese, circa 1770, 37cm. high. (Christie's) $5,000

A Stralsund baluster vase with reticulated sides, circa 1770, 36.5cm. high. $1,350

A German porcelain rectangular plaque painted with a three-quarter length portrait of a young girl, 7½in. high. (Christie's) $750

A German shaped circular trompe l'oeil plate molded with leaves and applied with wild strawberries naturalistically colored. circa 1765, 23cm. diam. (Christie's London) $3,000

GOLDSCHEIDER

It was in 1886 that Friedrich Goldscheider founded his factory in Vienna. After his death in 1897, production continued there under the direction of his widow and brother Alois, until, in 1920, the business was taken over by his two sons Marcel and Walter. In 1927, however, Marcel broke away to form the Vereinigte Ateliers für Kunst und Keramik.

While such things as vases were produced, the factory is best known for the figures and wall masks which epitomised the Art Nouveau and perhaps even more, the Art Deco styles.

A Goldscheider figure of a woman with one hand on her hip, one on her hat, with artist's monogram, 33.5cm.high. (Christie's) $1,300

A Goldscheider terracotta wall mask modeled as the head of young girl holding a fan across her neck, 11in. high. (Christie's) $450

A Goldscheider earthenware wall mask, 1920's, 17cm. high. $375

A Goldscheider pottery figure of a dancer, in a floral lilac dress with bonnet, 12in. high, circa 1930. (Morphets) $450

Goldscheider pottery mask of an Art Deco lady, approx. 12in. (G. A. Key) $500

A Goldscheider pottery figure of a young black boy, wearing a shabby brown jacket, grayish-brown trousers and a red and white striped shirt, 56cm. high, impressed maker's mark. (Phillips) $1,650

Parisienne, a Goldscheider polychrome ceramic figure modeled by H. Liedhoff, printed factory marks, 13¾in. high. (Christie's S. Ken) $600

'Suzanne', a Goldscheider figure, the design by J. Lorenzl, the nude figure loosely draped with a patterned gray enameled robe, 33.6cm. high. (Christie's) $800

GOLDSCHEIDER

A Goldscheider pottery figure, modeled as a sailor holding a girl, 30cm. high. $500

A small Goldscheider terracotta wall mask of the head, neck and hand of a young girl, 8in. high. (Christie's) $300

A Goldscheider pottery group after a model by Lorenzl, of a flamenco dancer and a guitar player, 17in. high. $900

A Goldscheider pottery figure of a dancing girl, designed by Lorenzl, 16in. high. $1,000

A Goldscheider pottery double face wall plaque, the two females in profile, 12in. high. $600

A large Goldscheider 'Butterfly Girl', after a model by Lorenzl, circa 1930, 48.5cm. high. $2,400

A Goldscheider pottery mask of a girl looking down, Made in Austria, circa 1925, 23cm. high. $500

A Goldscheider pottery figure of a woman wearing a beaded costume, on a black oval base, 18in. high. $2,500

A Goldscheider pottery 'Negro' wall mask, 26.5cm. high. $275

GOSS

The Goss factory was established in 1858 by William Henry Goss, who had learned his trade at the Copeland Works, where he rose to become chief artist and designer. When he set up on his own, he continued to produce the parian busts and figures which he had worked on at Copelands, and also brought out a small amount of terracotta ware. Another early line was jeweled scent bottles and vases, made from pierced and fretted parian and inset with cut glass jewels. No more of these were made after 1885.

The advent of his son Adolphus into the company revolutionised production. Adolphus realised that a huge market existed among the new Victorian day-trippers for souvenirs of the places they had visited, and he hit on the idea of producing small china ornaments bearing the towns' coats of arms. William Henry did not appreciate this inspiration at first, but his son finally persuaded him and soon the factory's bust and figure output had been completely replaced by the new heraldic ware.

It was Adolphus too who arranged the marketing and distribution of his idea, and he became the firm's principal salesman. One agent per town was appointed as sole distributor, and they could only sell pieces bearing their own town's coat of arms, though after 1883 they were allowed to select from a wider range of shapes. Despite Adolphus' success, relations with his father were very strained, and when William Henry died in 1906 he was excluded from a share in the business. It fell finally to a fourth son, Huntley, in 1913, who was no business man. He tried to survive and capitalise on the Great War by introducing a range of

Preserve jar and lid with grapefruit decoration, 110mm. (Goss & Crested China Ltd.) $100

Nut Tray with South Africa 1900 commemorative decoration, 145mm. diam. (Goss & Crested China Ltd.) $100

A very rare W. H. Goss porcelain figure of the Trusty Servant, decorated in bright enamels, 20cm. high. (Henry Spencer) $2,000

Little girl Goss doll with real hair, porcelain arms, head and legs. $600

A Goss parian bust of Queen Victoria, for Mortlock's of Oxford Street, 236mm. high. (Phillips) $325

Shakespeare leaning on a lectern, parian, 175mm. high. (Goss & Crested China Ltd.) $400

GOSS

battleship and military designs, but eventually failed and sold the firm in 1929. The new owners continued to make heraldic ware for four more years, during which time all pieces were marked *Goss, Goss England* or *Made in England*. Harold Taylor Robinson tried to revive the company in 1931 as W H Goss Ltd, but failed and went bankrupt in 1932.

After this, throughout the 30s a colorful range to match the Art Deco mood of the times was produced. Cottage ware was a particularly successful line, and commemorative mugs and beakers were produced for coronations and jubilees. Production ended in 1940 and the Goss site is now owned by Portmeirion Potteries.

A number of marks were used during the production period, some of which have already been mentioned. A Goshawk with outstretched wings was in continuous use from 1862, and indeed, the factory was known locally as the Falcon Works.

Goss Oven, printed mark and legend.
(Christie's S. Ken) $400

Goss commemorative vase for the death of Edward VII *Edward the Peacemaker*, **1910.**
(The Crested China Co.) $125

Gretna Green, The Old Toll Bar, printed mark and legend.
(Christie's S. Ken) $2,000

Goss cruet set and stand.
(The Crested China Co.) $100

'Boulogne sedan chair', 70mm long.
(Goss & Crested China Ltd) $60

'London Stone', 110mm. high.
(Goss & Crested China Ltd) $200

Goss Bettwys y Coed kettle with arms of Dunkerque.
(The Crested China Co.) $30

'First and last house in England', small, 65mm. long.
(Goss & Crested China Ltd) $180

Large three handled loving cup, 120mm. high.
(Goss & Crested China Ltd) $100

GRAYS POTTERY

The firm of A E Gray & Co
was a Staffordshire pottery
operating at Hanley between
1912–33 and then at Stoke
between 1934–61. Susie
Cooper designed for them
between 1925–32. In the
1960s they amalgamated with
the firm of W Kirkham and
from then on traded as
Portmeirion Potteries.

Their marks, which are
usually printed incorporate
versions of a galleon and
Grays Pottery England.

A Gray's Pottery Art Deco
spherical lampbase, painted in
colors with a stylised scene
of golfers, 6in. high. (Christie's
S. Ken) $1,250

**A Gray's pottery tea for two,
painted with floral sprays in
blue, green, yellow and orange
on a black ground, height of
teapot 4^1/$_2$in.
(Christie's S. Ken) $600**

GRIMWADE

Grimwade Bros produced
earthenware between 1886–
1900 at Hanley, Staffs, From
1900 they became Grimwade
Ltd. Their marks include *G
Bros* on a star within a circle
until c. 1900, when it
changed to a crown and *Stoke
Pottery*. Thereafter many
fully named marks were
used, including *Winton*
(1906) *Vitro Hotel Ware* (c.
1930) *Royal Winton Ivory* (c.
1930) and *Atlas* (c. 1934–9).

Grimwade pottery plate 'Well
if you know of a better 'ole
go to it'. $60

Grimwade mug 'Well if
you know of a better
'ole go to it'. $60

Grimwade vase depicting
'Old Bill', 'At present we
are staying at a farm'. $75

Grimwade shaving mug with
transfers of 'Old Bill' and
Arms of Margate. $60

A Grimwades Cube luster teapot, printed and painted with
fairies, cobwebs and toadstools,
printed factory mark, 4in. high.
(Christie's S. Ken) $175

HADLEY, JAMES

James Hadley (1837–1903) was an English ceramic modeller who worked at the Worcester factory between 1870–5. He took his inspiration from the Japanese style, producing pieces with reticulated decoration and others in the Shibayama style.

From 1875 he worked independently, supplying models to the Royal Worcester factory until 1896. He also made a series of table figures after Kate Greenaway, carrying baskets and enriched with gilding. His own porcelain, mainly in the form of vases with molded relief decoration in tinted clay, was marketed as Hadley ware. He was succeeded by his sons, until the firm was sold to the Worcester factory in 1905. His marks include the printed or impressed monogram *JH & S* or *Hadley's Worcester*, later also with a ribbon label.

James Hadley, a majolica ware model of an elephant carrying a howdah on its back, 22cm. (Phillips London) $650

Hadley's porcelain vase and lid with cone finial, 4in. high. (G. A. Key) $275

A pair of shell sweetmeat dishes, attributed to James Hadley, 22cm. wide, impressed and printed marks for 1882. (Phillips) $900

James Hadley: a very large Cricklight figure of a Grecian water carrier holding an amphora, 79.5cm., date code for 1897. (Phillips London) $2,250

A figure of a gentleman of George III's reign wearing a top hat and tails, by James Hadley, 20.5cm. (Phillips London) $500

James Hadley, set of five figures of the Down and Out Menu Men, fully colored, and standing on gray brick bases, approx. 15cm. (Phillips) $1,800

A candle extinguisher in the form of a young lady's head, by James Hadley, 9cm. high, date code for 1892. (Phillips) $600

HAMADA

Shoji Hamada (circa 1894–1978) was a Japanese potter whose early work was influenced by the Korean ceramics of the Yi dynasty. He worked mainly in stoneware, producing vases, bowls etc. in simple sturdy shapes colored usually in brown, olive, gray and black. In 1920 he came to England with Bernard Leach, and worked with him at St Ives for the next three years. Here, he became fascinated with English medieval pottery and also participated in experiments with lead-glazed slipware. On his return to Japan, he took many ideas with him, and helped found the Japanese Craft Movement in 1929. He became a strong influence in modern Japanese ceramics, and his later pieces, made during the 50s and 60s are characterised by their use of slablike, angular forms.

A stoneware saltglazed deep bowl with flared rim by Shoji Hamada, 28.2cm. diam. (Christie's) $2,000

A stoneware bowl by Shoji Hamada, beige with olive brown vertical stripes and dark brown foliate decoration, 8in. diam. (Bonhams) $2,750

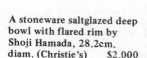

A fine slab bottle by Shoji Hamada, tenmoku glaze with abstract design, circa 1960, 8in. high.
(Bonhams) $4,500

A rare hexagonal vase by Shoji Hamada, tenmoku glaze with three floral motifs, circa 1958, 8in. high. (Bonhams) $4,500

A stoneware cut-sided bottle vase by Shoji Hamada, with short neck and shallow foot, circa 1960, 29.1cm. high. (Christie's) $2,400

A stoneware saltglazed press-molded jar by Shoji Hamada, with paper label inscribed 56, 22cm. high. (Christie's) $2,500

A stoneware elongated ovi-form vase by Shoji Hamada, 27.9cm. high. (Christie's) $1,750

137

HAN

The pottery of the Han period (206BC–220AD) is the earliest really attractive Chinese ware, for it was about this time that the ornamental qualities of the medium were realised. Also, at this time there was a certain amount of contact with the near East and even the West, which led to the general introduction of glazes, which had been in use in Egypt from ancient times.

Han pottery is usually either red or slaty gray, depending on the provenance of the clay, and varies in texture from soft earthenware to something approaching stoneware. The bulk of it is glazed, the typical glaze being a translucent greenish yellow, though this is subject to many variations. One of the characteristic features of pottery of this period is the frequent appearance of 'spur marks', usually three in number, around the mouth or base of a piece, which were made by the supports used when the ware was placed in the kiln.

Han pottery is decorated in various ways: either by pressing in molds with incuse designs, giving a low relief effect, or by the use of stamps or dies, or by applied strips of ornament, all of which would be covered by the glaze.

It was the fortunate custom to bury the dead together with many of the objects which surrounded them in life, and it is to tomb excavations that we owe most of the Han pottery in existence today.

Chinese painted pottery ding, Western Han Dynasty, with swirling red and white design, 6¹/₂ in. high.
(Skinner Inc) $900

A painted gray pottery figure of a court lady with attenuated silhouette, (firing fissure, minor chips) Han Dynasty, 44cm. high.
(Christie's) $17,500

Two gray pottery rectangular tomb bricks, one impressed to the center with five parallel rows of lozenge-shaped panels, Han Dynasty, 92cm. x 38.5cm.
(Christie's London) $6,000

A green-glazed red-pottery granary jar on three short bear feet, with ribbed mushroom-cap shoulder and short cylindrical neck, Han Dynasty, 25.5cm. high.
(Christie's London) $1,350

A gray pottery model of a mythical beast standing four-square, the thick tail curling upwards, Han Dynasty, 31cm. long.
(Christie's) $4,000

Chinese glazed pottery hill jar, Han style, conical cover with peaked terrain above cylindrical sides, 8¹/₂ in. high.
(Skinner Inc) $1,500

HIRADO

The Hirado kilns are thought to have been started in the late 16th century by Koreans brought to Japan by the daimyo Hideyoshi. Their early wares were mostly blue and white, and failed to achieve any great recognition until the late 18th and early l9th centuries. They are made of the finest white porcelain and painted in a soft cobalt blue with miniaturist landscapes. In the main they consist of faceted bottles, or narrow necked flasks, while some other vases and utensils have animals or insects molded on to their sides.

While these were very fine, in the l9th century Hirado wares developed a truly amazing delicacy and perfection.

Mid 19th century white glazed Hirado model of a stylised tiger, 20cm. long. $750

Late 18th century bowl and cover modeled as a seashell with smaller shells, probably Hirado, 14.4cm. wide. $750

A 19th century Hirado circular deep dish, 15.5cm. diameter. $675

Late 19th century well-modeled Hirado blue and white group of five playful karashishi, 18.8cm. high. (Christie's) $775

A 19th century Hirado cylindrical brush pot, 14.3cm. diam. $900

Late 19th century Hirado blue and white oviform vase, 26.2cm. high. (Christie's) $1,100

A 19th century Hirado ware netsuke of Gama Sennin, impressed signature Masakazu, 8.1cm. high. (Christie's) $900

One of a pair of late 19th century Hirado saucer-shaped dishes, each decorated in Kutani style, 61.2cm. diam. (Christie's) $5,750

139

HISPANO MORESQUE

In 711 the Moorish armies of the Caliph of Damascus invaded Spain, where they were to remain until their final expulsion by Ferdinand and Isabella in 1492. Thus for almost 800 years Spain formed the point of convergence of Eastern and Western civilizations, and nowhere is this dual influence seen more clearly than in its pottery.

Islamic potters had learned the art of tin-glazing with the addition of copper and silver oxides from their Mesopotamian counterparts. They brought this knowledge with them, and there are reports of a thriving export trade of lusterware from the Malaga region of Spain dating from as early as the mid 12th century.

Some of the forms of the early wares would be difficult to reproduce even today.

In the 14th century many Muslim potters from Malaga and Murcia moved to the Valencia area, and Manises became the renowned center of 'golden' pottery. Here it became subject to gothic influence, and the representation of a wide range of birds and animals became popular.

Towards the end of the 15th century came a demand for lighter tablewares, resulting in the introduction of a new range of shapes and more precise techniques similar to those used by Staffordshire potters, such as, for example, the greater use of molds.

In the early 17th century animal forms take on more stylized forms, and the fine draughtsmanship of earlier pieces is lacking. From the 19th century many reproductions were made. It is worth remembering that no regular marks ever appear on genuine Hispano Moresque ware.

An Hispano-Moresque tapering waisted albarello decorated in blue and copper-luster with two bands of stylised bunches of grapes, late 15th century, 18cm. high. (Christie's) $4,000

An Hispano-Moresque gold-luster armorial dish, the raised central boss with the Arms of a rampant lion within a spirally gadrooned surround, late 15th century, 48cm. diameter. (Christie's) $12,500

An Hispano-Moresque copper-luster large dish of pale colour and large size, the raised central boss with a swan surrounded by a band of stylised script, 16th century, 41cm. diameter. (Christie's) $3,350

An Hispano-Moresque blue and copper-luster large dish with a raised central boss with a quartrefoil surrounded by a band of radiating fronds, 16th century, 41cm. diameter. (Christie's) $3,750

Hispano-Moresque charger decorated in luster with plant motifs, Valencian, md 16th century. (Christie's Rome) $2,250

An Hispano-Moresque copper-luster oviform jar, the short cylindrical neck with four grooved loop handles divided by waisted panels of flowers and loop-pattern, 17th century, 22cm. high. (Christie's) $5,750

HÖCHST

Hard paste porcelain was first produced at Höchst-am-Mein in 1750 by Johann Benckgraff and Josef Jakob Ringler, who had both come from Vienna. The operation was never on a sound financial or administrative footing and the Elector had to make several reorganisations before his successor took over completely in 1778. The factory closed in 1796.

Early wares were characterised by a rather coarse body and a milky glaze, but quality soon improved and there was a large output of figures as well as of tableware. Especially important are the figures from the Commedia dell' Arte, set on high square pedestals. These are similar to those subsequently produced at Fürstenberg (the modeler Feilner may have been responsible for both) but the Höchst models are livelier and less fussy.

Höchst was among the earliest factories to make pastoral groups and arbor scenes. These were mainly by J F Lück. Laurentiis Russinger made rather larger groups in the manner of Boucher. He was succeeded in 1767 by Johann Peter Melchior, whose delightful groups of children gave way in the early 1770s to groups of classical sentimentality.

When the factory closed the molds passed on to works in Damm and Bonn, both of which made falsely marked reproductions. In the early years of this century further fakes were made at Passau.

From 1750–60 the mark is usually that of a wheel with between four and eleven spokes. Six is the most common, and eight often denotes a fake. These were either incised or impressed. A similar mark in underglaze blue was used between 1760–96; and an Electoral Hat 1760–64.

One of a pair of Höchst teacups and saucers, painted with a girl with an apron full of fish and her companion holding a net, three figures carrying packages through a marsh from a boat, circa 1765.
(Christie's)   (Two) $5,000

One of a pair of Höchst teacups and saucers painted with pastoral scenes after engravings by J.E. Nilson, circa 1765.
(Christie's)   (Two) $5,000

A pair of Hochst pot-pourri vases painted in the manner of Andreas Phillipp Oettner, circa 1765, 25 cm. high.
(Christie's) $20,000

A Höchst copper-gilt mounted oval snuff-box painted with scenes of lovers in landscape vignettes beside sheep and a masked figure, circa 1775, 9.5cm. wide.
(Christie's) $7,500

One of a pair of Höchst teacups and saucers, painted with a huntsman and hounds beside a pond, an old woman and a young boy, a gardener planting a tree helped by a girl with a rake and a gallant and companion, circa 1765.
(Christie's)   (Two) $2,750

IMARI

The name Imari derives from the port through which the porcelain of 17th century feudal Japan was exported. It has been adopted to describe the palette of underglaze blue and overglaze iron red and gilt of the Arita export wares. Most 17th century Japanese porcelain was blue and white and, due to fluxing of the cobalt with the glaze, the blue decoration characteristically bleeds into the surrounding area. It was to overcome this fault that early workmen painted iron red and gold onto the glaze to conceal the blurred edges.

An Imari molded teapot, the chrysanthemum-shaped body with chrysanthemum flowerheads and foliage in relief, circa 1700, 13.8cm. high. (Christie's) $2,250

An Imari barber's bowl decorated in iron-red enamel and gilt on underglaze blue with a vase containing flowers and foliage, Genroku period, 27cm. diam. (Christie's) $600

An Imari jar and cover decorated in iron-red and black enamels and gilt on underglaze blue, Genroku period, 63cm. high. (Christie's) $2,750

A pair of rare and unusual Imari bijin, the partially clad figures decorated in iron-red, green, aubergine and black enamels and gilt, Genroku period, 31.5cm. high. (Christie's) $20,000

A fine Imari tankard decorated in iron-red enamel and gilt on underglaze blue, the ovoid body with three shaped panels, the loop handle pierced for a mount, Genroku period, 22.5cm. high. (Christie's) $6,000

An Imari polychrome bottle vase, painted with peonies and chrysanthemums amongst scrolling foliage with birds flying above, 30.5cm., late 17th century. (Bearne's) $2,250

A pair of Imari jars of square section, each facet painted with a jardinière of chrysanthemums, 24.5cm. (Bearne's) $1,500

A Chinese Imari tankard of cylindrical form, painted in underglaze blue, iron-red and gilding, 5¼in. high, Kangxi. (Bonhams) $300

ITALIAN

CHINA

The word maiolica came into use about the middle of the 15th century to describe firstly lustered Spanish pottery and then all kinds of tin glazed earthenware. The principal centers for the production of the latter were Orvieto, Tuscany and Faenza. Deruta joined them not long afterwards and featured, from 1501, a golden and a ruby luster.

Decorative styles and themes were to some extent common, which can make identification difficult, though some characteristic features, such as the blue stained enamel of Faenza and the gray and blue of Castel Durante, did emerge. The istoriato pictorial style was perfected by Pellipario, first at Castel Durante and later at Urbino. Urbino was also the source of a new style of grotesque decoration after Raphael from the mid 16th century.

The 17th and 18th centuries saw imitations of Dutch delft emerging from Savona and elsewhere, while Florence has the distinction of producing the only porcellanous ceramic material to be made in Renaissance Europe. This 'Medici' porcelain is of an artificial soft-paste type.

As far as true porcelain is concerned, the Vezzi factory at Venice was started in 1719 with the help of a Meissen renegade, while Doccia, from 1737, drew its styles from Vienna. French-style soft-paste porcelain was made at Capodimonte from 1742, and production was resumed in Naples in 1770.

Italian porcelain is characterised by its gray color, and this is common to) the products of Nove, Treviso, Doccia and Venice.

An Italian majolica salt modeled as a figure of a woman standing at a table, 18th century, 8in. high. (Christie's S. Ken) $750

A large blue and white Italian dish painted with David, crowned and playing a harp, mid 18th century, 49cm. diam. (Christie's) $1,250

A North Italian cruet painted with birds perched among scrolling red and yellow flowers with blue berries beneath blue scroll borders, probably Turin, circa 1750. (Christie's) $1,850

A Caltagirone albarello of waisted cylindrical form, painted in ocher and pale green with scrolling foliage on a pale blue ground, 23cm. (Phillips) $600

An early 18th century Siena circular dish painted with two women with children, 31.5cm. diam. (Christie's) $1,700

A Ligurian wet drug jar of globular form with short spout and strap handle, inscribed in manganese with *Syr*Rosar Firr*, 20cm. (Phillips) $1,000

NOVE.

143

GEORGE JONES

George Jones (d. 1893) was a Staffordshire potter working at the Minton factory. In 1863 he established the Trent pottery, where he manufactured white and transfer printed earthenware for the domestic market as well as majolica. From 1872, by which time he was trading as George Jones & Sons, he was producing ornamental wares with pâte-sur-pâte decoration, such as wall pockets and vases. Porcelain was introduced in 1876 in the form of basket shaped flower holders etc and around 1880 vases with colored earthenware body and painted decoration were also being made. The factory was renamed Crescent Pottery in 1907.

A rare George Jones majolica posy holder modeled as a green crested crane with long yellow beak, seated on a blue yellow-lined base, 14cm.
(Phillips) $650

A George Jones punch bowl with Mr. Punch lying on his back supporting the holly-decorated bowl in his arms, circa 1875, 36cm. diam. $4,500

Pair of George Jones majolica garden seats of cylindrical form, circa 1874, 18.1/8in. high. $9,000

A George Jones majolica cheese dome and stand. $500

A George Jones majolica jug molded in relief with panels of a pointer and its prey reversed with a fox hunting a rabbit, 1872, 10in. high.
(Christie's S. Ken) $800

A George Jones figure of a camel, impressed with monogram GJ and Kumassie, 23.2cm. high. $1,500

A George Jones vase, the handles formed as be-ribboned rams' heads, molded maker's monogram GJ and Stoke-on-Trent, 34cm. high. $1,600

144

KAKIEMON

There is a charming tradition that Sakaida Kizai-emon, an Arita potter, made an ornament in the form of twin persimmons (kaki) for his feudal overlord, who was so pleased with it that he conferred on him the honorary name of Kaki-emon. Sakaida adopted this as his family name and it was thus that the porcelain got its name. Sakaida worked for a merchant named Toshima Tokuyemon, who had learned the secret of enameling in colors, and together they mastered the art to commence one of the most important ceramic productions.

At first, white glazed pieces were brought to the Kakiemon workshops for coloring, though they later acquired their own kiln. Their vibrant designs and colors made such an impact on the European market that within a few years every European factory was trying to produce direct imitations. Early pieces, dating from 1640–70, use thick bright turquoise and iron red in imitation of the orange–red of ripe persimmons. Additional colors are azure blue, soft orange, primrose yellow, lavender blue and grass green.

Early pieces were for the use of the patron, and were strictly in the Japanese taste. However, in time decoration became more refined, and instead of covering large areas of the piece, became sparser, showing the water-color quality of the enameling. Marks rarely appear before the 18th century, and the most common are the *fuku* (happiness) and *kin* (gold) marks. Pieces were made in a wide variety of shapes, from baluster jars to human and animal figures. From the 18th century many designs show a strong European influence.

A Kakiemon bowl, decorated in iron-red, blue, green, yellow and black enamels and gilt, the interior with two birds amongst pine, prunus and bamboo, late 17th/early 18th century, 35.9cm. diameter.
(Christie's) $75,000

A Meissen kakiemon circular two-handled tureen and cover painted with 'The Three Friends', blue crossed swords mark and *Pressnummer* 21, circa 1740, 32cm. wide.
(Christie's) $13,250

A Kakiemon ewer, the body with two panels depicting figures with fans and parasols in a garden where a bough of cherry blossom issues from rockwork, late 17th century, 20.5cm. high.
(Christie's) $11,500

A Kakiemon hexagonal teapot and cover decorated in iron-red, blue, green and black enamels, the pinched sides with panels of mixed flowers and foliage, late 17th century, 15.2cm. long.
(Christie's) $3,350

A Kakiemon octagonal tapering beaker decorated in iron-red, green, blue and black enamels, the exterior with a sarigue leaping amongst brushwood fences and floral sprays, late 17th/early 18th century, 11.1cm. x 7.5cm. (Christie's) $10,000

An early enameled kraak style dish, decorated in the Kakiemon style in iron-red, blue, green, yellow and black enamels, the center with a profusely filled flowerpot on a verandah, late 17th century, 31.7cm. diameter.
(Christie's) $10,000

KANGXI

The Kangxi period in Chinese porcelain follows directly on the so-called Transitional period (1620–82) when there was great unrest and the Dutch, forbidden to continue their activities, turned their attention to Japan.

In 1682, however, the emperor Kangxi appointed Ts'ang Ting-hsuan as director of the Imperial factory, and following this appointment Chinese porcelain was to reach an unprecedented perfection of quality. During Kangxi's reign (1662–1722) porcelain decorated in underglaze blue was produced in ever increasing quantities for the European market. These are usually far superior to late Ming export material.

During the reign of Kangxi many wares for the home market were produced with monochrome glazes including a lustrous mirror black and fine translucent greens and yellows. It was probably during the later years of the reign, too, that the rose crimson enamel derived from gold was first introduced from Europe, and it was this that was to form the basis of the famille rose palette. Wares produced during Kangxi's reign rarely bear his reign mark, which makes dating difficult.

A peachbloom-glazed beehive waterpot, taibo zun, Kangxi six-character mark, the well-potted domed sides rising to a narrow waisted neck, 5in. diameter.
(Christie's) $30,000

A blue and red square brushpot, Kangxi six-character mark, painted in underglaze-blue and copper-red on the waisted body, 6¹/₂in. square.
(Christie's) $3,000

An aubergine and green yellow-ground incised 'dragon' dish, encircled Kangxi six-character mark, the center of the interior with an aubergine and a green incised five-clawed dragon, 5¹/₂in. diameter.
(Christie's) $1,500

A famille verte 'magpie and prunus' rouleau vase, Kangxi, decorated to the cylindrical body with two magpies perched on a blossoming prunus tree amongst bamboo, 17³/₄in. high.
(Christie's) $9,000

A blue and white jardinière, Kangxi, painted to the exterior with The Three Friends, pine, prunus and bamboo below a band of key pattern, 17in. diameter.
(Christie's) $1,000

A famille verte pear-shaped vase, Kangxi, brightly enameled in iron-red, green, turquoise, aubergine and gilt, 9in. high.
(Christie's) $3,750

A fine 'green dragon' dish, Kangxi six-character mark, painted to the center of the interior with a circular panel of a scaly dragon reaching for a flaming pearl, 7³/₄in. diameter.
(Christie's) $1,100

KLOSTER VEILSDORF

Of all the many small factories which flourished in the Thuringian forests in the 18th century, the best known is probably that of Kloster Veilsdorf.

It was established in 1760 by Prince Friedrich Wilhelm von Hildburghausen and employed many specialists from other factories, such as Abraham Ripp, a kiln worker, Nikolaus Paul, the arcanist, Caspar Schumann, a painter, and most famous of all, Wenzel Neu, the modeler. With such a collection of talent, it was not surprising that they produced practical wares of excellent quality, skilfully decorated by such painters as Schumann and Döll.

Wenzel Neu is probably responsible for most of the figure output between 1760–65. The quality is not particularly high, but the style is very typical of Thuringian ware in general. Many groups were made using the same models in various guises. In about 1780 allegorical figures of the four Continents were produced, which was a completely new departure. These were probably modeled by Franz Kotta, who subsequently worked at the Volkstedt factory. He also produced a fine bust of Prince Friedrich, the factory's founder.

The factory was purchased in 1797 by the sons of Gotthelf Greiner, who then used the clover leaf mark from their Limbach factory. The earlier mark consists of *CV*, sometimes in monogram, sometimes with a shield of arms between the two letters, and sometimes drawn to look like Meissen crossed swords.

A Kloster Veilsdorf figure of Capitano Spavento modeled by Wenzel Neu, 1764-65, 16cm. high. $1,500

A Kloster Veilsdorf figure of Pierrot modeled by Wenzel Neu, 1764-65, 15.5cm. high. $8,000

A Kloster Veilsdorf figure of a crouching leopard, probably modeled by Pfranger snr., circa 1775, 12cm. long. $675

A Kloster Veilsdorf cane handle, formed as a bearded old man, circa 1770, 7.5cm. high. $800

A Kloster Veilsdorf figure of Cadi-Leskier, modeled by Pfranger, circa 1770, 14cm. high. $5,000

A Kloster Veilsdorf figure of Pantalone modeled by Wenzel Neu, 1764-65, 14.5cm. high. $3,000

KUTANI

Kutani wares, in contrast to Kakiemon, were directly derived from late Ming colored pieces. They are the most highly prized of all Japanese porcelains and are very difficult to date, as no records of the old factories survive. Broadly speaking, the early pieces are referred to as Ko- (old) kutani, as opposed to the Ao- (new) Kutani revivalist stonewares of the 19th century.

Ko-kutani pieces usually have a whitish gray body with a milky white glaze. The colors are rich and harmonious and include vivid green, egg yellow, aubergine, Prussian blue and iron red. Decoration is mainly representative of birds and insects among flowering trees and shrubs, and rarely features animals, while figures are Chinese in conception. They were probably made during the latter part of the 17th century for the use of the overlord and his court.

As the 18th century wore on the power of the Shogunate, the main patrons of such kilns, began to wane, and the Kutani kiln, which had been under the protection of the daimyo Maeda, collapsed in the last years of the century, following his fall from favor. In 1816 Yoshidaya Denyemon revived the kiln, and production continued until the 1860s. These Ao-kutani pieces lack the vitality and originality of the earlier products. They are often heavily enameled, with green or yellow grounds, and the decoration is outlined in black. They also bear a small two character mark which was lacking on the earlier pieces.

The Arita kilns, which fared much better during the early 19th century, continued to produce pieces in the Ko-kutani style.

A Kutani koro amusingly modeled in the form of a Shishi, the rounded body raised on four legs, the tail forming the handle, Meiji period, 7³/₄ in. high. (Bonhams) $300

A Kutani koro and cover of typical form, painted all over in iron-red and gilt with Shishi and cash symbols, 11³/₄ in., Meiji period. (Bonhams) $750

A garniture of three Kutani vases, the central covered jar with Buddist lion knop, each painted on one side with a woman and children in a garden, 30cm. (Bearne's) $1,000

One of a pair of Kutani vases, painted in iron-red and gilt with cockerels amongst peony between ho-o, 14in. high, Meiji period. (Bonhams) $900

A late Kutani (Kaga ware) box and cover formed as a chest attended by three karako, signed *Takayama ga,* late 19th century, 25cm. high. (Christie's London) $4,500

An important Ko-Kutani dish decorated with chrysanthemum flowerheads and foliage scattered among stylised waves, late 17th century, 21cm. diam. (Christie's) $50,000

KYOTO

Kyoto was both the seat of the Japanese Imperial court and an important area of ceramic production in the Edo period (1615–1868). In the 17th century, the potter Ninsei had developed an enameled and gilt pottery, which continued to be manufactured in the 18th century onwards, principally by Kenzan and his successors. Individual potters thrived all over the city, making not only faience, but porcelain in blue-and-white, kinrande and three-color Ming styles. Notable among them were Y Seifu in the Meiji period and later K Kawai and M Ishiguro.

A Kyoto type circular bowl with foliate rim, signed, Meiji period, 24.2cm. diam. $2,000

A Kyoto tapering rectangular vase painted with panels of a daimyo and his retainers, signed Nihon Yozan, Meiji period, 12.7cm. high. $1,000

A Kyoto compressed globular koro, signed Kinzan, Meiji period, 8.2cm. diam. $1,250

Pair of late 19th century almost life-sized stoneware models of a courtier and a courtesan, probably Kyoto ware, 149cm. high. $11,000

Late 19th century Kyoto chrysanthemum-shaped deep bowl decorated in colors and gilt, signed Kizan kore o tsukuru, 29.8cm. diam. $1,350

Late 19th century Kyoto hexagonal vase decorated in colors and gilt on a royal blue ground, signed Kinkozan zo, 43.6cm. high. (Christie's) $3,000

Late 19th century Kyoto square dish with canted corners, 15.7cm. sq. $1,000

A Kyoto trumpet-shaped beaker vase decorated in colored enamels and gilt, signed Kinkozan, Meiji period, 17.8cm. high. $1,500

BERNARD LEACH

Born in 1887, Bernard Leach was brought up in Japan, and Japanese influence predominates in his work. After studying under Frank Brangwyn in the UK, he returned to Japan in 1909 and began to develop influences which led to the Japanese folk art movement. In 1920 he settled in St Ives in Cornwall where, initially with the help of Shoji Hamada, he made stoneware and raku, using local materials. Throughout his life he returned frequently to the East, and he is noted not only for his own output but also as a teacher and a writer. His pottery is remarkable for the carefully planned relationship of body and glaze and by the variety of decorating techniques which he employed. He died in 1979.

A large stonewar jar by Bernard Leach, with lobed sides, circa 1965, 19.3cm. high. (Christie's) $1,250

A Bernard Leach stoneware jar and cover, circa 1943, 28cm. high. $1,850

A Bernard Leach stoneware St Ives four inch tile painted with a weeping willow tree, 10.2cm. square. (Phillips London) $400

A tall stoneware jug by Bernard Leach, with incised strap handle, circa 1970, 27cm. high. (Christie's) $800

A tall stoneware jug by Bernard Leach, covered in green running glaze, the body decorated with a series of indented studs, impressed BL and St. Ives seals, circa 1961, 12$^{1}/_{4}$in. high. (Bonhams) $1,750

A rare stoneware plate by Bernard Leach, decorated with a painted mountain goat, impressed BL and St. Ives seals, circa 1955, 9$^{3}/_{4}$in. diameter. (Bonhams) $2,250

A stoneware vase by Bernard Leach, decorated with brush strokes and spots, in brown and blue, impressed St. Ives, circa 1938, 4$^{3}/_{4}$in. high. (Bonhams) $600

LEEDS CREAMWARE

Very fine Leeds creamware was made under the proprietorship of Hartley Green & Co between 1780–1800. A perforated ware was typical of the output, each opening being made with a separate punch, and not, as was later the case at Wedgwoods, by a multiple tool.

Marks are *Hartley Green & Co* and *Leeds Pottery*, either alone or repeated in a cross. The old molds were reused at Slee's pottery in Leeds from 1888 and were marked like the originals.

A Leeds creamware cylindrical teapot and cover, with floral terminals and spiral molded spout, 12cm. (Phillips London) $2,500

A Leeds creamware plate, the center painted with the portraits of the Prince and Princess of the Prince and Princess William V of Orange, 24.7cm. (Bearne's) $275

A Leeds creamware tea canister of octagonal shape, 12.5cm. high, incised no. 25. (Phillips) $1,850

A Leeds creamware baluster coffee-pot and domed cover, the green striped body with entwined strap handle, circa 1775, 22.5cm. high. (Christie's) $4,500

A Leeds creamware teapot and cover with 'beaded' edges, brightly painted with Chinese figures in a garden, 17cm., late 18th century. (Bearne's) $350

A Leeds creamware baluster jug, boldly painted below the spout with a portrait of the Princess of Orange, 14cm., late 18th century. (Bearne's) $175

A creamware punch-kettle and cover, painted in a famille rose palette with Orientals among furniture, vases and shrubs, probably Leeds, circa 1775, 21cm. high. (Christie's) $1,000

A Leeds creamware figure of a bird, with green splashes to its neck, tail and breast, standing astride a slender quatrefoil base, circa 1780, 21cm. high. (Christie's) $3,500

LENCI

The Lenci pottery was active in Turin during the 1930's, and produced three distinctive types of wares. The first, consisting of wall plaques in the form of female heads in scarves, as if going to Mass and figures of the Madonna and Child, were aimed at the domestic market. In stark contrast was the second group, made up of female figures, either nude or clad in contemporary costumes.

The third, and less well-known type, consists of vases and dishes decorated with Cubist-style painted scenes.

A Lenci earthenware box and cover, cover modeled with a dozing elf, dated 4.2.32, 21cm. $500

A Lenci centerpiece modeled as a young naked girl, 46cm. high. (Christie's) $1,350

A Lenci ceramic figure, of a nude girl wearing a checkered cap kneeling on the top of a globe, with a book in one hand and a dog by her side, with painted signature *Lenci, Made in Italy, Torino*, 48cm. high. (Christie's) $6,000

A Lenci bust of a father and baby, the sleekly groomed, dark-haired man clasping and kissing a rosy-cheeked, fair-haired and somewhat reluctant baby, 18cm. high. (Phillips) $1,100

A Lenci figure group, of a bare-breasted native woman wearing an abstract patterned wrap-around skirt in yellow, green and black, 44cm. high. (Phillips) $1,350

A large figure of a native girl, marked 'Lenci Torino Made in Italy', 1930's, 55.5cm. high. $675

A Lenci figure of a rooster, painted marks Lenci 1936 S.P., 29cm. high.(Christie's) $1,500

A Lenci pottery wall mask modeled as a young girl wearing a head scarf, 11½in. wide. $300

LIBERTY

Arthur Lazenby Liberty was the archetypical Victorian entrepreneur. Starting life as an assistant in a London emporium, he rose to be the manager of a firm called Farmer and Rogers which sold Oriental imports to the rapidly increasing clientele of customers in search of beautiful things for their homes. Recognising the magnitude of the new market, Liberty took a chance and opened his own shop in Regent Street in 1875. Within five years it had proved to be a huge success and it is still thriving on its original site. His success was due to the fact that he had a discriminating taste and knew exactly what his customers wanted to buy.

With regard to pottery, Liberty sold art pottery made by Charles Brannam of Barnstaple (Barum ware) and also the Aller Vale Pottery of Newton Abbot. Liberty was, in addition, a close friend of William Moorcroft, and sold his work with the printed mark *Made for Liberty & Co.*

LIMBACH

The Limbach factory was established in the mid 18th century by Gotthelf Greiner, who had previously been a glass maker. It turned out simple, cheap tablewares, which had the unique distinction of being almost over marked, some bearing the marks of the painter, workshop, factory, and date! Figures were also made in the style of Meissen and though the quality is inferior, they do have a pleasing simplicity. Again, as if to underline their relation to that factory, they often bear the marks of crossed hayforks! Limbach marks were applied in iron red or purple The factory is in existence to this day.

CHINA

A pair of Liberty jardinières on pedestals, each with shallow hemispherical bowl decorated with entrelac border in relief. 80cm. high. (Christie's) $3,000

A Moorcroft pottery oviform vase made for Liberty & Co., in the Toadstool pattern, 10in. high, signed in green. (Christie's) $1,000

A Limbach figure of a girl emblematic of Summer in a yellow hat, orange bodice and puce skirt under a yellow-flowered apron filled with a sheaf of corn, circa 1770, 13cm. high. (Christie's) $500

A Limbach group emblematic of Winter, he wearing a puce and blue hat, she with a puce and black hat, circa 1780, 16cm. high. (Christie's London) $1,000

A Limbach bird nesting group, modeled as a boy climbing a tree and handing birds from a nest to his companion below, circa 1780, 20cm. high. (Christie's London) $2,000

A Limbach figure of a fisherman leaning against a tree-stump, one bare foot raised, holding a large fish in his arms, circa 1770, 14cm. high. (Christie's) $1,000

LINTHORPE

The Linthorpe Pottery was established in 1879, near Middlesborough, with Henry Tooth as manager, and, until 1882, Christopher Dresser as art director and designer. Their early wares were designed on simple, flowing lines with equally flowing glazes in two or more rich colors, while later sgraffito or pâte-sur-pâte decoration was introduced. It ceased production in 1890. Pieces are marked with *Linthorpe*, sometimes over the outline of a squat vase. Some are signed by Dresser, and or initialed with Tooth's monogram.

A Linthorpe vase, designed by Dr. Christopher Dresser, formed as a cluster of five pointed gourd shapes encircling a central funnel-shaped neck, 11cm. high. (Christie's) $2,250

A Linthorpe earthenware jug, shouldered tapering form with flared neck, with facsimile signature *Chr. Dresser* 19.5cm. high. (Christie's London) $300

A Linthorpe pottery jug, designed by Dr. Christopher Dresser, with everted rim continuing to form an angled handle, terminating in a rippled design, covered in a streaky caramel, green and crimson glaze, 21cm. high. (Christie's) $3,000

A Linthorpe twin-handled pottery vase designed by Christopher Dresser, the vessel of flattened oviform with bulbous neck, 20.8cm. high. (Phillips) $200

A Linthorpe vase, designed by Dr. Christopher Dresser, the gourd-shaped body with double angular spout and curved carrying-bar, streaked glaze of green and brown. (Christie's) $1,750

A Linthorpe earthenware jug designed by Dr Christopher Dresser, covered in a thick predominantly green and brown glaze, (slight restoration to lip rim) 16.7cm. high. (Christie's) $300

A Linthorpe vase, designed by Dr Christopher Dresser, decorated with four grotesque heads, each forming a handle, covered in a streaky green glaze, 22.5cm. high. (Christie's) $1,500

A Linthorpe vase, designed by Dr. Christopher Dresser, the streaky glaze in tones of green and brown, with incised decoration of a single fern encircling the gourd, 19cm. high. (Christie's) $1,500

154

LIVERPOOL

There were seven porcelain factories in Liverpool in the 18th century, of which three, Chaffers, Christians and Penningtons are generally regarded as forming the mainstream tradition from 1754–99.

The Chaffers' factory (1754–65) made a bone ash and a soapstone porcelain which are often difficult to tell apart as most of the standard shapes were identically produced in both.

Blue and white made up the bulk of production and showed a strong Worcester influence in terms of both shape and decoration, being painted in a free and pleasant style. Distinctive characteristics are the upturned lips of jugs and the fact that cream and sauceboats are often molded.

The decoration of the polychrome pieces was also of a high quality, often featuring Chinese figure and floral subjects.

The Christian factory (1765–76) produced examples which were well potted but on which the decoration was competent rather than outstanding. Blue and white teawares are very common but flatware is rare, while the polychrome output was again decorated with floral or Chinese mandarin subjects. Christian's specialised in garniture sets of vases, decorated with floral reserves on a gros bleu ground.

The output of the Pennington factory (1769–99) consisted largely of imitations of Christian's wares but was generally of inferior quality as regards both potting and painting. Again, blue and white predominates, and among the finest examples are ship's bowls, which were sometimes named and dated.

A Liverpool blue and white molded oval sauceboat, attributed to Wm. Ball's factory, circa 1758, 14.5cm. wide. (Christie's) $3,500

A Liverpool tin-glazed stoneware small cylindrical mug, circa 1760, 6.5cm. high. (Christie's) $3,000

A Pennington Liverpool ship bowl painted in blue with a ship in full sail, inscribed *Success to the Perseus, Capt. Gibson, 1790,* 25cm. (Phillips London) $5,000

A Liverpool creamware oviform jug printed in black with figures on a quayside, 10½in. high, circa 1797. (Christie's) $1,000

Liverpool creamware pitcher, England, circa 1800, black transfer printed three-masted ship flying the American flag, 10in. high. (Skinner Inc.) $1,500

A Liverpool delft transfer-printed tile by John Sadler, circa 1760, 13cm. square. (Christie's) $500

LONGTON HALL

Longton Hall was one of the first porcelain factories in the entire United Kingdom, and production commenced around 1750. Unsurprisingly, in these circumstances, initial output was somewhat primitive in quality, but the standard of both potting and decoration rapidly improved. Early pieces consisted mainly of the so-called 'Snowman' figures and mugs, plates, dishes etc. decorated in 'Littler's' blue. The underglaze was often runny and uneven, but has a brightness which was no doubt in imitation of Vincennes. The reserves were often left unfilled, giving the pieces a somewhat unfinished appearance.

William Littler had joined the venture in 1751 and by 1753–4 there was an improvement in the standard of potting, though decoration was still quite primitive. At this time the scarce Longton Hall powder blue vases, teapots and bottles were made. Between 1754–7 some really beautiful pieces were produced, including a range of leaf-molded wares in the Meissen style. A large proportion of the output of that time was in fact molded in remarkable shapes with leaf, fruit and vegetable motifs.

Decoration was carried out by, among others, the 'Castle' painter who specialised in European scenes, and the 'Trembly rose' painter whose floral motifs bear a resemblance to Red Anchor Chelsea. Bird painting was often really superb.

The polychrome wares produced between 1758–60 are also finely decorated, and the products transfer printed in black by Sadler were made at this time.

From 1754 blue and white was also made, but examples of this are now fairly rare.

A Longton Hall leaf dish, painted in the manner of the Trembley Rose painter, circa 1755, 22.5cm. wide. (Christie's) **$600**

Rare Longton Hall tureen and cover of lobed circular shape, circa 1755, 12in. wide. **$4,750**

A Longton Hall mug of cylindrical shape with a spurred handle, painted in blue with an Oriental style landscape, 6.5cm. (Phillips) **$1,000**

A rare Longton Hall pierced leaf basket of deep circular shape, the overlapping leaves with light puce ribs, 25.5cm. wide. (Phillips) **$5,000**

A Longton Hall vase of inverted baluster form with spreading neck and fluted base, the body painted in colors, 4¾in. high. (Christie's S. Ken) **$350**

A Longton Hall figure of a milkman with two pails, one on his head the other by his side, circa 1755, 27cm. high. (Christie's London) **$4,000**

LOWESTOFT

Lowestoft did not really set out to become a top-class manufacturer of porcelain, and the proprietors' diffident approach can be seen in their original description of themselves as 'China Manufacturers and Herring Curers'! The factory was established by four partners in 1757, with the humble purpose of producing useful wares for the local inhabitants, and it leapt to spurious fame when some 19th century ceramic writers wrongly ascribed to it a hard paste Chinese porcelain being made expressly for the European and American market.

The earliest Lowestoft pieces were decorated only in a soft underglaze blue in the style of Nanking and no colored enamels were introduced before 1770. The blue and white ware was often relief molded and often, too, associated with the modeler James Hughes.

The 1770s saw the introduction of enameled pieces in Imari type designs, but as the porcelain remains of the soft-paste European variety they are quite distinctive. It is mostly tea wares which received this sort of treatment. There followed a more sophisticated type of decoration in the European style, with bold flowers and no distracting borders, and some Chinese type designs were also adopted.

From about 1790 a sparse and simple sprig motif became popular, often in enamel colors but sometimes only in gold. The factory at this time also made some of the earliest seaside souvenir porcelain in the form of mugs and inkwells bearing inscriptions such as *A Trifle from Lowestoft*, for by now the town was a fashionable watering place.

An 18th century Lowestoft porcelain miniature sparrow-beak jug, 3½in. high. (Hy Duke & Son) $100

A Lowestoft miniature teapot and cover of globular shape, printed in blue with a version of the 'Three Flowers' pattern, 8.5cm. (Phillips) $700

A rare Lowestoft custard cup painted in colors with a 'Redgrave' pattern beneath an egg and flower border, 6cm. (Phillips) $500

A late 18th century Lowestoft porcelain sparrow beak jug of baluster form, painted with Long Elizas, 9cm. high. (Spencer's) $550

A Lowestoft blue and white bell shaped tankard painted with Oriental buildings among trees, circa 1764, 4¾in. high. (Christie's) $1,000

A rare Lowestoft model of a pug dog with a green collar and a brown coat, seated on a green rectangular base, 9cm. (Phillips) $2,250

LUDWIGSBURG

In 1758 Johann Jakob Ringler established a porcelain factory for Duke Carl Eugen of Württemberg. Ringler had arrived there via Vienna, Höchst and various other centers, but it was at Ludwigsburg that he remained until his death in 1802.

The factory produced a distinctive smoky brown body, which, if the exquisite detail on some of the figures is anything to go by, was nevertheless excellent for modeling. Tablewares and vases really show little originality, but some fine modelers were employed on figure production. Among the earliest were groups of dancers, reflecting the Duke's interest in ballet, probably by Jean Louis, who also is credited with having designed the tiny Venetian Fairs series. Both of these were subsequently the subjects of many inferior reproductions. Other modelers include J C W Beyer, who composed 'lean and hungry' figures, and Johann Göz.

The Duke was generous with money for the factory, but after his death in 1793 it rapidly declined, and closed in 1824.

The most common mark is two interlaced back to back Cs below a ducal crown. After the accession of Duke Ludwig in 1793 the Cs were replaced by an L and from 1796–1816 and FR monogram for King Frederick. In 1816 Frederick was succeeded by William, and the mark became WR. Three stag's horns in a shield were sometimes used around 1800.

A Ludwigsburg teabowl and saucer, painted with birds on branches, circà 1760. (Christie's) **$750**

A Ludwigsburg rococo oval two-handled tureen and cover, blue crowned interlaced C mark and impressed IP, circa 1765, 32cm. wide. **$4,000**

Four Ludwigsburg putti emblematic of the Senses, after models by Johann Heinrich Schmid, Taste eating fruit, Smell with a basket of flowers, Hearing listening to a watch and Touch holding fruit, circa 1780, 24cm. high overall. (Christie's) **$3,000**

A Ludwigsburg group of Bacchus and a Bacchante modeled by Johann Christian Wilhelm Beyer, the naked figures embracing and she squeezing a bunch of grapes into his bowl, circa 1765, 24cm. high. (Christie's) **$4,000**

A Ludwigsburg figure of a Tyrolean boy playing a pipe, standing on a shaped rectangular base (stick missing, damage to extremities), circa 1770, 10.5cm. high. (Christie's London) **$450**

A Ludwigsburg group of dancers modeled by Franz Anton Bustelli, blue crowned crossed-C mark and incised UM 3 to base, circa 1760, 16cm. high. (Christie's) **$17,500**

MAJOLICA

Majolica is a glazed or enameled earthenware often decorated in relief, and it was 16th century Italian mastery of this medium which provided the inspiration for its revival some three centuries later. In this country, Minton in particular made a wide range of objects in majolica, from garden ornaments to small figures, from 1850 onwards, under the guidance of Leon Arnoux. Some of his work was shown at the Great Exhibition in 1851. Wedgwood too revived its own 18th century green glazed ware with decoration of relief-molded leaves, using a white earthenware body. Elsewhere, in Italy production centered mainly round the Cantagalli workshop in Florence and the Ginori family in Doccia, while Scandinavian and American factories also jumped on this popular bandwagon.

An English majolica tobacco-jar and cover in the form of a pug dog, glazed in shades of brown and with a pink interior, circa 1860's, 8in. high.
(Christie's S. Ken) $450

A majolica spill-vase group of a squirrel seated on its haunches nibbling a nut beside a hollow tree-trunk, circa 1870. 4¹/₄in. high.   (Christie's S. Ken) $150

A pair of Majolica blackamoor figures of a man and woman, each standing by a tree stump, damaged, 70cm. high.
(Bearne's) $1,200

A Spanish maiolica dish painted in blue, yellow and ocher with a portrait of the Virgin in profile to the left within two bands of flowerheads, 18th century, 30.5cm. diameter.
(Christie's) $1,500

A pair of Siena maiolica vases by Bartholomeo Terchi, one vase signed Bar: Terc(h)i: Romano: 1726, 56cm. high overall. (Phillips) $3,600

A Brown, Westhead, Moore & Co. majolica group of two kittens, one climbing up the front of a lady's boot, the other chasing a ball of wool, circa 1880's, 6¹/₄in. high.
(Christie's S. Ken) $700

Early 17th century Netherlands majolica syrup jar, painted in blue with scrolling foliage and plant pods, 23.5cm. high. (Phillips) $750

MARSEILLES

Marseilles faience was made by a number of factories in the 18th century, but the name most often associated with it is that of Pierrette Caudelot, la Veuve Perrin.

After the death of her husband in 1748, she ran the factory until her own death in 1793. Until 1764, when he set up his own concern, she was in partnership with Honoré Savy who claimed to have invented the style of decoration where a translucent green enamel is applied over black painting. Other popular forms of decoration include chinoiserie scenes in the style of Pillement and scenes after the artist Teniers, while Mediterranean fish were often used to decorate large soup tureens.

Another of her former employees who set up on his own was Joseph Robert. He was responsible in no small degree for the high quality of the decoration at the Perrin factory and he set up his own factory in 1766 to produce porcelain. His products have a highly distinctive style, and the decoration is quite different from the mainstream of French production of the time. It often features individual flower painting and landscape scenes strongly reminiscent of the Meissen style of the late 1730s. The factory did not survive the Revolution and closed in 1793. While Perrin and Savy may also have manufactured porcelain, no confident ascriptions of their pieces can be made.

CHINA

One of a pair of Marseilles (Veuve Perrin) shaped circular plates painted en camaieu vert with bouquets of flowers, circa 1765, 25cm. diam. (Christie's) $700

A French faience holy water stoup, painted in colors with St Louis kneeling before an altar in a landscape vignette, third quarter of the 18th century, probably Marseilles 44cm. high. (Christie's London) $1,250

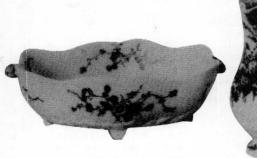

A Marseilles faience pear-shaped ewer and two-handled oval basin, 14¾in. wide, circa 1765. $450

A Marseilles faience casket in the form of an armoire, late 18th century, 14½in. high. $1,000

One of a pair of Marseilles circular dishes painted en camaieu verte, Savy's factory, circa 1770, 28.5cm. diam. $2,400

MARTINWARE

The Martin Brothers cooperative, which set up in 1873, consisted of Robert Wallace Martin, who had worked for the Fulham pottery, and his brothers Walter and Edwin, who had previously been employed by Doulton. Walter was thrower, and Edwin decorator, while a further brother, Charles, became the business manager and ran a shop in Brownlow Street, London.

Martinware comes in a wide variety of shapes. The decoration is mainly incised, with the colors reminiscent of Doulton stoneware. The most common motifs are plants, birds, animals and grotesques, of which perhaps the most notable are R W Martins 'wally birds'. These are often found as tobacco jars, with the heads forming the lids, and generally have a somewhat menacing air. Some of the later production tended more towards the abstract, relating it to later studio pottery. The works closed in 1914.

A Martin Bros. stoneware two-handled spirit flask, 9½in. high, London and Southall, 1901. $1,000

An early Martin Brothers vase, incised with birds and leafy branches in green, blue and brown, 23.3cm. high. (Phillips) $150

A stoneware Martin Bros. grotesque double-face jug, dated 1903, 19cm. high. $1,800

A Martin Brothers stoneware vase, incised with a pattern of wild roses in a cream glaze with briers and leaves in green on an oatmeal ground, 25.50cm. high. (Phillips) $950

A Martin Bros. stoneware jug, molded and painted with a 'knobbled' design in blue and brown enamels, 23.3cm., inscribed _Martin Bros, London & Southall, 10–1895._ (Bearne's) $650

An unusual ceramic and pewter inkwell, cast in the style of a Martin Brothers bird with the head forming the hinged cover, 4¼in. high. (Christie's S. Ken) $350

A Martin Brothers grotesque bird, the head incised _Martin Bros., 3–1902, London & Southall,_ mounted on circular ebonised wooden base, 25cm. high. (Christie's) $5,000

MASON

Miles Mason was a dealer in Chinese porcelain who in around 1800 set up his own manufactory at Lane Delph, to replace stock which he could no longer obtain from the East. There, he produced both bone china and 'hybrid' hard paste porcelain, mostly decorated with underglaze blue printing in simple Chinese patterns. Their teaware and dessert ware shapes were mostly unique of their type and so are readily recognisable. Later, however, the factory moved on to produce ironstone pottery, with such success that Mason's Ironstone is a leading name to this day.

Mid 19th century Mason's ironstone toilet set. (British Antique Exporters) $300

One of a pair of Mason's ironstone soup tureens, covers and stands, circa 1825, 13in. $1,000

A Masons Ironstone foot bath and jug, printed in colors in Chinese style with vases and bowls of flowers among branches. (Lawrence Fine Arts) $2,500

Part of a mid 19th century Mason's ironstone dessert service of nine pieces, plate 9in. diam. $800

A Miles Mason sugar bowl and cover painted with 'The Dragon in Compartments' pattern, 16cm. wide, with two others, 15cm. and 19cm. wide, 1810-15. (Christie's) $650

Mason's style jug and foot-bath. $1,250

Mason's ironstone jug decorated with Imari pattern, 8in. high. (G. A. Key) $120

MEISSEN

At the beginning of the 18th century the race was on in Europe to find the secret of the manufacture of Chinese-type porcelain. The winner was Augustus the Strong, Elector of Saxony, thanks to his sequestration of a young alchemist, J F Böttger, whom he originally employed to turn base metal to gold. When Böttger failed at this, Frederick set him the alternative task of porcelain manufacture under the eye of Ehrenfried Walther von Tschirnhaus, a Saxon physicist who was also fascinated by this challenge. Success finally came in 1710, and a new red and white porcelain manufactory was set up in the Albrechtsburg at Meissen.

Production problems persisted, however, and it was not until 1713 that the first pieces were offered for sale, the decoration of which was largely influenced by the court silversmith Johann Irminger, and featured molded and applied vine leaf and foliage reliefs and modeled and applied rose sprays.

The king wanted color, but Böttger was never really successful in finding enamels which would withstand the firing temperatures required to fuse them into the glaze, and much of his output remained white.

Poor Böttger never enjoyed his triumph. He was still under guard until 1714, and at the mercy of a capricious ruler who refused to entertain his plans for improved kilns etc. In 1719 the factory's arcanist, Stölzel, smuggled its secrets out to Vienna enabling a rival establishment to be set up there, and when Böttger died in March of that year, at the early age of 37, the factory was in disarray.

Immediately however a turn-round occurred. The king made instant management reforms.

A Meissen KPM baluster teapot and domed cover, painted by P. E. Schindler, circa 1724, 15cm. wide. (Christie's) $11,500

A Meissen group of two vintagers on a rocky outcrop, a young woman by their side filling a bottle from a barrel, 21 cm. (Bearne's) $1,100

A Meissen figure of the Courtesan from the Cries of London series, modelled by J. J. Kandler and P. J. Reinicke, circa 1754, 14cm. high. (Christie's) $2,500

One of a pair of Meissen circular dishes, blue crossed swords marks, Pressnummern 20 and 21, circa 1745, 30.5cm. diam. (Christie's) $3,600

A Meissen powder purple ground milk jug and cover with bud finial painted in colors with Watteau figures, crossed swords mark, circa 1745, 14cm. high. (Christie's London) $1,850

A Meissen group of a Mother and Children modeled by J. J. Kandler and P. Reinicke, circa 1740, 23.5cm. high. (Christie's) $2,500

MEISSEN

installed the new kilns he had denied Böttger, and underglaze blue was achieved. From Vienna too came the repentant Stölzel, bringing with him the enamel painter Gregorius Höroldt, who quickly perfected a superb range of overglaze enamels and used them to create fine copies of oriental wares as well as his own chinoiserie inventions. Through Höroldt, Meissen finally came to fame and fortune, and the first marks were introduced. For 15 years painted decoration remained paramount, and was only superseded by J J Kaendler's relief molding and figurines in the late 1730s.

From 1740 Kaendler's output was phenomenal. In addition to a constant supply of naturalistic figures, he designed new relief patterns for tablewares, and it is to him more than anyone that Meissen owes its long triumph, which started to wane only after the peace of 1763, when the victorious Frederick the Great of Prussia was successful in luring several fine modelers (though not Kaendler) to his new factory in Berlin.

The rococo Meissen style came to look increasingly out of date in the new Neo Classical age. Throughout the late 18th and early 19th century the factory struggled for survival in the face of disappearing markets (as imports were forbidden by several countries to protect their domestic products), and the new dominance of English creamware. Though the Napoleonic Wars temporarily cut off the supply of English goods, other German potters had learned to imitate Wedgwood cream and Jasperware, and finally Meissen too came to manufacture imitations, both of this, and their own earlier pieces.

A Meissen figure of a thrush, modeled by J. J. Kandler, circa 1745, 18cm. high. (Christie's) $4,500

A Meissen two-handled silver-shaped jardiniere, the fluted body painted with sprays of Manierblumen, circa 1755, 17cm. wide. (Christie's) $1,300

A Meissen Deckelpokal, blue crossed swords mark to the base, and gilder's mark c to both pieces, circa 1725, 18cm. high. (Christie's) $12,500

A pair of late Meissen figures of a gallant and a lady, each standing on a shaped grassy base molded with gilt scrolls, 10½in. high. (Christie's) $2,500

A Meissen figure of a recumbent pug dog on a baroque stool, modeled by J. J. Kandler, 11cm. high. (Christie's) $10,000

A Meissen hexagonal baluster teacaddy painted in the manner of P. E. Schindler with Orientals taking tea, circa 1725, 9cm. high. (Christie's) $3,000

MENNECY

The Mennecy factory was set up in 1734 in Paris by Louis François de Neufville, Duc de Villeroy under the directorship of François Barbin. For the first year it produced faience, but then turned to porcelain and in 1748 moved to Mennecy.

For its early products it drew heavily on the shapes manufactured at Rouen, and on St Cloud (blue lambrequins) and Chantilly (Kakiemon) for its decorations. Mennecy soon developed its own style however. Its paste was characterised by its lovely dark ivory color and its glaze by its wet-looking brilliance. The factory did not have a wide range of shapes, but those it did produce were admirably simple in form, tall, globular teapots with gently curving spouts, and cups and saucers which were either straight sided, tapering down or pear shaped. Among its most characteristic pieces were spirally fluted custard cups and sugar bowls with lids surmounted by a rosebud.

Painted decoration was very beautiful, dominated by cool blues and pinks and often depicting naturalistic flower or bird designs and delicate polychrome landscapes where brown and green predominate. Mennecy also excelled at figure modeling, especially under the sculptor Gouron, who came to the factory in 1753.

Mennecy continued producing rococo style, mainly useful wares into the 1770s, after which quality declined. It continued in production until 1800, by which time porcelain had been abandoned in favor of faience and cream colored earthenware. Mennecy porcelain is marked *DV* for the Duc de Villeroy. After the factory moved to Bourg la Reine in 1773 the mark *BR*, often incised, was used.

A Mennecy teapot and cover of globular shape with double ogee handle and flower finial, 9.5cm. high, incised DV mark. **$1,000**

A Mennecy hen snuff box with silver gilt mount, mark of Eloy Brichard, Paris, 1756-62, 5cm. wide. **$1,750**

A pair of Mennecy figures of pug dogs, circa 1750, 14cm. long. **$7,500**

A pair of Mennecy figures of a young man and woman, circa 1740, 17.5cm. high. **$3,000**

A French white soft paste model of an elephant, free-standing with long tusks and a curling trunk (one ear chipped, firing cracks to underside), circa 1750, probably Mennecy, 20cm. long. (Christie's London) **$9,000**

A small white Mennecy baluster jug and cover with hinged silver mount, circa 1740, 11.5cm. high. **$2,250**

METTLACH

The original Mettlach factory was established in 1809 at the Abbey of Mettlach in the Rhineland. In 1836 it merged with the factories of Villeroy and J F Boch and together this group produced earthenwares. Stoneware was also made from 1842 onwards, with a high proportion of the output being exported to America.

Art Pottery, decorated with inlaid clays in contrasting colors (Mettlach ware) was also introduced, and among the top artists working there was J Scharvogel. In the later part of the 19th century terracotta and mosaic tiles were added to the range. Marks include Mettlach castle with the monogram of *VB*, and a circular mark with Mercury looking over *Villeroy & Boch* and *Mettlach.*

A Mettlach pewter mounted 'Castle' stein, impressed marks and numbers, date code for 1898, 40cm. high. $1,650

A Mettlach plaque of a spring landscape, signed H. Cradl?, stamped Villeroy & Boch, 17½in. diam., Germany, 1910. $1,000

Late 19th century Mettlach plaque, signed C. Warth, 16¾in. high. $250

A Mettlach salt glazed stoneware jardiniere, the continuous central band incised and decorated in colors with gnomes cavorting amongst blossoming branches, 23cm. diam. (Spencer's) $600

Large Mettlach Stein, circa 1898, etched decoration depicting lovers, signed *Warth,* pewter lid, 14½in. high. (Skinner Inc.) $700

A Mettlach tankard of tapered cylindrical form with pewter cover, Germany, 1898, 7in. high. $400

A Mettlach stoneware vase, the ovoid body decorated with an encircling pattern of stylized flowers, 41.7cm. high. (Bearne's) $225

166

MING

When Chu Yuang Chang founded the Ming dynasty at Nanking in 1368, the art of producing high fired porcelain had already been mastered and was being used to make not only small pieces but also huge storage jars. The glaze on these is often cracked, so that it is possible to see clearly how the base, lower body, shoulders and neck were made separately and then stuck together with a watered down porcelain clay before drying and decorating.

Underglaze painting too had already been discovered during the previous Yuan period, and Ming decorators exploited the possibilities of both iron red, and the favored Burmese cobalt blue to the full.

Ming pieces can often be dated by appearance. Fourteenth century pieces, often painted with brilliant precision in loosely composed designs, were made from a finely mixed white clay with a thin grayish glaze, whereas on those dating from the 15th century, the glaze is often thick and clear and has allowed the blue to bleed into it during the firing, giving an effect of enhanced depth and richness.

Celadons had been produced during Sung times, and their use was continued during the Ming period, but they were used for heavily potted wares, storage jars, lanterns etc which were carved or applied with a premolded design and covered with a thick celadon glaze. These proved extremely popular in the near East, Burma and India, perhaps because it was believed that poison would boil if it touched a celadon surface!

The enamel painting of porcelain was first successfully introduced at the end of the fifteenth century.

A rare late Ming Wucai brushrest, Wanli six-character mark, molded and reticulated with an ascending yellow dragon at the center flanked by four smaller dragons in brown, red, blue and green, 6¹/₂in. wide. (Christie's) $94,000

An early Ming blue and white dish, Yongle, painted to the center of the interior with a lotus arabesque comprising a central flower-head surrounded by five smaller flower-heads, the well with a continuous foliate lotus scroll below a band of classic scroll at the rim, 11in. diameter. (Christie's) $20,000

A Ming blue and white baluster vase, 15th century, painted around the body in inky-blue tones with a foliate lotus-scroll between double lines, 5in. high, box. (Christie's) $3,700

A Ming blue and white pear-shaped vase for the Islamic market, Zhengde, the globular body painted with six roundels containing Islamic script divided by vertical flanges and amidst clouds and a flaming pearl, 10in. high. (Christie's) $16,250

A large Ming blue and white 'Hundred boys' jar, painted to the exterior with a continuous scene of boys at play, with a group acting out the scene of a high official flanked by advisers in audience and a kneeling subject, 15³/₄in. diameter. (Christie's) $53,000

A rare early Ming blue and white baluster vase and cover, guan, painted around the body in inky tones with 'heaping and piling' to depict a continuous lotus meander, Yongle, 27cm. wide. (Christie's) $96,000

MING

This was done by applying the colors to clear glazed pieces and then refiring them in a low temperature 'muffle kiln'.

The late Ming period saw the opening up of an export trade extending far beyond the traditional markets of the near East and Southeast Asia. In 1595 the Dutch established a trading post at Canton, and it was the Dutch East India Company who first brought back the Kraak porselyns which were to provide the inspiration for European porcelain manufacture.

It is worth remembering that the marks on Ming pieces should not be taken as gospel. If a potter were successful in reproducing an earlier style to the same standard as the original, he would apply the mark of the emperor of the period of the original. This was done for honorific reasons, and not, then at least, from any desire to deceive.

A Ming blue and white bowl, the deep rounded sides flaring at the rim, the exterior painted in bright blue tones with Buddhistic lions, the interior with a flaming ruyi motif centering a cash symbol, Jiajing six-character mark, 15cm. diameter.
(Christie's) $4,000

A Ming 'green and yellow' dish, Jiajing six-character mark, the interior with five ruyi connected by a leafy vine, all in olive-green enamel reserved on an ocher-yellow ground, 6³/₄in. diameter.
(Christie's) $3,750

A rare pair of celadon-glazed candlesticks, early Ming Dynasty, formed probably in three parts with small petal-molded sconces, 9¹/₄in. high.
(Christie's) $12,500

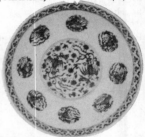

A late Ming blue and white 'phoenix' bowl, the center of the interior painted in bright blue tones with an ascending and a descending phoenix, Wanli six-character mark and of the period, 20cm. diameter.
(Christie's) $5,000

A Ming blue and white zhadou, zhengde four-character mark and of the period, the lower bulbous body, interior and exterior of the flaring neck similarly painted with two scaly five-clawed dragons striding amid dense leafy vines, 6in. diameter.
(Christie's) $50,000

A late Ming blue and white baluster jar, encircled Wanli six-character mark and of the period, painted around the broad body with large, looping leafy meanders of peony, each flower-head beneath a Daoist emblem, 5in. high.
(Christie's) $2,000

A fine and rare Ming yellow and red-glazed jar, painted in reserve on a pale mustard-yellow ground with two five-clawed scaly dragons emitting fire scrolls in a lively motion amongst cloud scrolls, 5⁷/₁₆in. high.
(Christie's) $130,000

MINTON

Thomas Minton was born in 1765 and apprenticed at the Caughley Works where he was trained in the art of engraving copper plates for underglaze-blue painted designs. In 1793 he established his own works at Stoke on Trent, where it traded as Minton & Co from 1845 and Mintons Ltd from 1873. It was noted from the first for the high quality and diversity of its output, which at first consisted mainly of blue printed earthenware, though porcelain was added to the range in 1797, The original pattern book of that period survives today.

From 1847 large quantities of parian ware were produced, and figures were made by a number of eminent modelers. Various partners took responsibility for various branches of the firm, and by 1868 these separated. Minton, Collins & Co specialised in tile manufacturing, while C H Campbell became responsible for earthenware.

Minton had a strong presence at the Great Exhibition of 1851 where they displayed Sèvres style porcelain vases, terracotta and majolica garden ornaments, parian figures and tiles, all of which attracted much favorable comment. Pâte-sur-pâte decoration was introduced by the Sèvres-trained decorator and modeler Marc Louis or Miles Solon, who worked for Minton between 1870 and 1904. Dinner services were commonly painted or printed in the Japanese taste with flowers, chickens or butterflies.

Art Nouveau vases, again decorated by Solon, were popular around the turn of the century, and were usually decorated with colored glazes contained by raised lines of trailed slip.

A Minton majolica oval jardinière, the two handles modeled as a scantily clad cherub kneeling on a scroll, 1868, 18in. wide.
(Christie's S. Ken) $1,500

A Mintons blue-ground vase and cover in the Art Nouveau style, the body and stem painted with swags of pink roses, date code for 1919, 10½in. high.
(Christie's S. Ken) $600

A pair of Minton majolica cornucopia vases, circa 1872, modeled as putti astride cornucopiae issuing from dolphins, 27in. high.
(Christie's East) $4,000

A Mintons majolica jardinière, the blue ground molded in relief with vertical flat ribs, terminating in paw feet, circa 1870's, 10¾in. high.
(Christie's S. Ken) $500

A Minton majolica garden-seat in the form of a seated monkey eating fruit and wearing a lugubrious expression, date code for 1867, 19½in. high.
(Christie's S. Ken) $1,350

A pair of Minton candleholders modeled as a youth and companion wearing broad-brimmed hats and striped and flowered dress, circa 1835–36, 9in. high.
(Christie's S. Ken) $1,350

MOCHAWARE

Mochaware was produced from about 1780 until 1914 and was named from mocha quartz. It is characterised by its decoration , by which tree, moss and fernlike effects were introduced by means of a diffusing medium, which was described as 'a saturated infusion of tobacco in stale urine and turpentine'! It was inexpensive to make, and was first made of creamware and subsequently of pearlware and cane ware. It was designed mainly for domestic use, for public house serving jugs and mugs for measures used to serve shrimps, nuts etc.

MONTELUPO

In the 17th and 18th centuries a coarse, heavy earthenware was produced at Montelupo, near Florence. It was characterised by the somewhat rough and ready painting of caricature figures of soldiers and men dressed in curious contemporary Italian costumes and bristling with weapons, striding across the plates.

In the mid 17th century, marks are found referring to Rafaello Girolamo and Jacinto or Diacinto Monti of Montelupo. Helpfully, the date also appears on these.

Mochaware pitcher, England, early 19th century, with four large brown, rust and white tobacco leaves, 9½in. high. (Skinner Inc.) $5,500

Mochaware pitcher, England, 19th century, decorated with bands of "worming" on ecru and siena grounds, 8in. high. (Skinner Inc.) $1,250

A Montelupo wet drug jar, the flat handle and the spout painted green, the pharmacy sign of a crescent beneath the terminal of the handle, circa 1560, 25cm. high. (Christie's London) $2,250

A Montelupo crespina boldly painted in ocher, yellow, blue and green with a central circular medallion of a fox surrounded by radiating panels of stylised foliage, mid-17th century, 25cm. diameter. (Christie's) $1,850

A Montelupo crespina, the center with the bust portrait of a girl draped in a green shawl and inscribed *VESTRO* within a border of radiating panels, early 17th century, 23.5cm. diameter. (Christie's) $2,750

A Montelupo wet-drug jar, with strap handle painted a foglie in blue, ocher and yellow, third quarter of the 16th century, 24.5cm.high. (Christie's) $1,350

A Montelupo à Quatieri crespina painted in blue, ocher, yellow and green with a putto in a landscape, 27cm. (Phillips) $1,800

MOORCROFT

When Macintyre's art pottery department closed in 1913, Moorcroft established his own pottery at Cobridge, employing his old colleagues. There, they made a wide range of items from pen trays to toastracks, from vases to brooches.

His flambé glazes were developed in the 1920s, and by the 1930s his range of motifs included fruit, birds, fish and boats. Matt glazes were introduced and his designs became increasingly simple. Moorcroft's signature always appears on his products, often painted in green until the 1920s and thereafter mainly in blue.

An octagonal bowl with everted rim, the interior decorated with alternate panels of peacock feathers and tulips, 10in. wide. (Christie's) $450

An ovoid vase with everted rim decorated with a band of frilled orchids, in pastel tones on a cream ground, 8½in. high. (Christie's) $400

A twin-handled square biscuit barrel and cover decorated in the 'Hazledene' pattern, in shades of green and blue, 6½in. high. (Christie's) $750

A pair of cylindrical candlesticks decorated in the 'Pomegranate' pattern, in shades of pink, ocher and green on a mottled green and blue ground, 8in. high. (Christie's) $1,500

A spherical vase decorated with stylised fish among waterweeds, in shades of red and ocher on a speckled salmon pink ground, the interior blue, 6in. high. (Christie's) $1,800

A baluster vase decorated in the 'Eventide' pattern, in shades of ocher, pink, green and blue, 13in. high. (Christie's) $1,000

A twin-handled tapering cylindrical jardiniere, made for Liberty, decorated in the 'Hazledene' pattern, in shades of blue and green, 8¼in. high. (Christie's) $800

A tapering cylindrical vase decorated with a bland of orchids, in shades of yellow, pink and purple on a graduated blue ground, 5in. high. (Christie's) $400

MOORCROFT MACINTYRE

William Moorcroft (1872–1945) was a Staffordshire potter who trained as an art teacher, but became designer for Jas. Macintyre & Co at Burslem. He designed vases, bowls etc. decorated with plant forms and scale patterned borders and panels mainly in blue, red and gold (Aurelian ware). His Florian ware (1898–1904) was decorated with violets, poppies and cornflowers in underglaze colors. His flowers were often stylized and depicted in darker shades of the base color. Landscape patterns, toadstool and pomegranate motifs were introduced later and Flammarion ware was produced from around 1905 with luster glazes, often red or green and again slip decorated with plant forms.

A Macintyre cup and saucer, decorated in the 'Eighteenth Century' pattern of floral swags and ribbons, in shades of blue, green, pink and gilt.
(Christie's) $500

A Macintyre Gesso Faience biscuit barrel with electroplate mount and cover, incised with alternate spirals of flowers and foliage, 6½in. high.
(Christie's) $700

A pair of Macintyre Green and Gold Florian Ware vases, decorated in shades of green and gilt with cartouches of poppies and curvilinear foliage, 10¼in. high.
(Christie's) $900

A Macintyre oviform pot decorated with yellow poppies and cartouches of forget-me-nots, in shades of yellow, green and blue, 3in. high.
(Christie's) $400

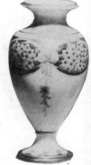

A Macintyre Green and Gold Florian Ware twin-handled coupe, with cartouches of curvilinear poppies and tulips, in shades of blue, green and gilt, 7½in. high.
(Christie's) $775

A Macintyre plate decorated with three swirling sprays of irises, in shades of green and blue, 8in. diameter.
(Christie's) $1,000

A Macintyre vase, decorated in shades of yellow, blue and gilt with oval cartouches and pendant trials of flowers and foliage, 9¼in. high.
(Christie's) $1,250

MOORE

Bernard Moore (1853–1935) was a Staffordshire artist potter who, with his brother Samuel, succeeded to his father's porcelain factory at St Mary's Works, Longton in 1870. Trading as Moore Bros. they made high quality tableware, which was sometimes highly ornamental, together with lamps, baskets etc. They used a clear turquoise glaze and metallic colors and favored decorative motifs were modeled cupids, animals, especially dogs, and plant forms. Chinese cloisonné imitations were also produced and pilgrim bottles with pale pâte-sur-pâte decoration and gilding.

The Moore Bros. factory was sold in 1905. Thereafter, at Wolfe St, Stoke, in conjunction with C Bailey of Doulton, Moore tried out flambé glazes. The pieces he produced here tended to be based on simpler earthenware forms and were sometimes decorated by leading contemporary pottery artists such as Beardmore and Billington.

Marks include *Moore*, and from 1880 *Moore Bros* impressed or incised. The name painted with a printed globe mark also occurs after 1880.

A Bernard Moore red flambe jardiniere of flared cylindrical form, 29cm. high.　$700

A flambe pottery bowl, by Bernard Moore, 8¼in. diam., and a Chinese carved wood stand.　$350

A Bernard Moore flambe baluster vase, decorated in gilt with a Japanese lady sitting at a table, 18cm. high. (Phillips)　$300

A large Bernard Moore luster pottery jardiniere, 11½in. high.　$1,100

A Morrisware pottery vase, decorated with peonies in mauve, crimson and olive-green against a sea-green ground, 16.5cm. high. (Phillips)　$425

A large S. Hancock & Sons Morrisware baluster vase, decorated with mauve and inky blue thistles on a greeny yellow ground, 32.9cm. high. (Christie's London)　$1,500

MORRIS WARE

Morris ware was produced from the 1890s into the early 20th century by the firm of S Hancock and Sons, an earthenware company in Stoke on Trent. The pieces were decorated by George Cartlidge (b. 1868) in plant forms outlined in trailed slip in the style of William Moorcroft, and usually also signed by him.

MOUSTIERS

The Moustiers factory was established in around 1670 in a remarkably remote corner of France, about 60 miles north east of Marseilles. Early wares were in the blue and white made popular by Rouen, and many fine dishes with pictorial scenes were made. Pierre Clerissy took over in 1679 and started a business that under his grandson Pierre II, was to flourish until 1757.

In about 1710 designs were adopted based on the engravings of Jean Berain, who as designer to the King in the Department of Occasional Expenses had been responsible for the backgrounds for court galas and entertainments at Versailles.

Polychrome wares were also designed at Moustiers by Jean-Baptiste Laugier and Joseph Olerys, which often depicted mythological or biblical scenes surrounded by elaborate festoon borders. They also designed some with fantastic human and animal figures, sometimes indulging in less than decorous pursuits. Their monogram *LO* is common and often faked. Genuine Moustiers is very light, finely potted and has a smooth, milky white glaze.

A Moustiers shaped oval dish painted in shades of manganese with Berainesque dwarfs, birds and a fox, circa 1740, 33cm. diam.
$2,000

A French faience oval basket and cover, Moustiers, circa 1740, 8½in. wide.
$900

A Moustiers shaped circular plate, manganese GOL and cross mark of Olerys and Laugier, circa 1740, 25cm. diam. $1,250

One of a pair of Moustiers (Ferrat) shaped circular plates painted with pairs of parrots, circa 1770, 25cm. diam. (Christie's)
$600

A Moustiers (Olerys and Laugier) shaped dish painted with garlands and the armorial device of three boots with the motto 'Forward'.
$500

A Moustiers faience 'Seau a Rafraichir' with double plumed mask handles, attributed to Olerys and Laugier, circa 1740, 21cm. diam.
$1,300

A Moustiers faience tazza with lobed rim, painted with the fable of the 'Fox and Goose', 30cm. wide. $900

NANKIN

'Nankin' is the name given to blue and white porcelain of the late eighteenth and nineteenth centuries, which was shipped through the port of Nanking.

'Nankin yellow', on the other hand is used to describe a lustrous, pale golden brown glaze used together with Kangxi underglaze blue decoration. It was used particularly for export wares to the near East.

A blue and white oval tureen, cover and stand, heavily encrusted, circa 1750, the stand 41cm. wide. $4,500

One of two blue and white spittoons, the interior with a border of trellis pattern, circa 1750, 12.6cm. diam. $3,000

One of two blue and white dishes, the borders each with three clusters of flowering branches, circa 1750, 42cm. diam. $15,000

A copper red and celadon glazed figure of a standing dignitary, circa 1750, 18.3cm. high. $30,000

A large blue and white deep dish painted with four fan-tailed fish, circa 1750, 45cm. diam. $10,000

Large mid 19th century Chinese Nanking ashet, 16½in. wide. (Peter Wilson) $600

A blue and white 'piggy-back' group formed as a standing lady and a small boy, circa 1750, 19.8cm. high. $13,500

Early 19th century Chinese Nankin porcelain decoration with Shi Shi dog and punt in a lake setting center, 17 x 13in. (G. A. Key) $325

NANTGARW

The history of the Nantgarw pottery began in 1814 when William Billingsley and his son-in-law Samuel Walker arrived there. Billingsley had been a painter at Derby and had also experimented with porcelain bodies in the hope of modifying the Derby paste to resemble that of Sèvres.

At Nantgarw, a useful site both for the proximity of coal supplies and a link with the Bristol Channel in the form of the newly opened Glamorgan canal, they succeeded in making a soft paste porcelain which was of amazing quality and translucence. To do so however had cost them all their capital, and they were lent further funds by a local surveyor, W W Young. Also, the President of the Royal Society sent the proprietor of the Swansea works, L W Dillwyn, to have a look. Dillwyn was greatly excited by what he saw at Nantgarw and arranged for Billingsley and Walker to move to Swansea. There, Billingsley oversaw the painting, while Walker experimented with a more reliable body than that which had been produced at Nantgarw.

In 1819, both returned there and the second Nantgarw period began.

Due to financial problems, Billingsley and Walker left Nantgarw again in 1820, and Young was left with the pottery. He employed Thomas Pardoe, a Derby-trained potter who had worked at Swansea, to decorate the remaining stock. Pardoe's free, slightly naive style was in stark contrast to London decorated Nantgarw. He painted birds, landscapes and figure subjects, using often broader strokes and heavier color than other painters. The pieces were sold at two auctions in 1821 and 22.

A Nantgarw coffee cup and saucer with pierced heart-shaped handle, painted by Thomas Pardoe, circa 1820. (Christie's) $500

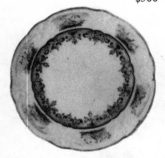

A Nantgarw plate painted by Thomas Pardoe, the border with exotic birds perched on trees in landscape vignettes within molded foliage-scroll cartouches, circa 1820, 21.5cm. diameter. (Christie's) $750

A Nantgarw armorial cabinet-cup and saucer, the central arms within a garter with the motto *Deus et Patria*, circa 1820. (Christie's) $3,000

A Nantgarw (London-decorated) ornithological soup-plate, the center painted with Black Grouse, named on the reverse, circa 1820, 24cm. diameter. (Christie's) $3,000

A Nantgarw London-decorated gold-ground circular two-handled sauce tureen and stand, the body and stand painted with garden flowers on a gilt band, circa 1820, the stand 18.5cm. diam. (Christie's) $4,250

A Nantgarw plate painted by Thomas Pardoe, the center with two pheasants perched on a tree in a landscape vignette, circa 1820, 22cm. diameter. (Christie's) $2,250

NAPLES

The Royal Factory of Naples was established in 1771 by Ferdinand IV, son of Charles III, and employed many of the ex-workers of the latter's Capodimonte factory.

Domenico Venuti was made Director in 1779. He engaged skilled modelers etc from other factories and the first really successful pieces produced at Naples were huge services, used as Royal gifts, and often featuring a biscuit figure centerpiece.

The decoration often drew heavily on themes from the new discoveries at Herculaneum and Naples and books were published explaining the various classical allusions. Commoner today are tablewares decorated with a central medallion showing peasants in traditional garb, with borders of wreaths or Pompeian fret.

With regard to body, early pieces tend to be rather yellow, but a fine white or creamy body was developed during the 1780s. Early painting shows a marked resemblance to Capodimonte of the later rococo period.

Some figures were produced, usually off white, either glazed or in biscuit. Some, of individuals strolling along alone or in pairs, are interesting for having no base, but are balanced on their own feet.

Naples, of course, first employed the much copied crowned *N* mark. Unless the piece is soft paste porcelain however the mark is fraudulent. *FRF* is also used in blue black or red enamel, under a crown.

CHINA

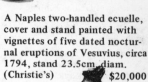

A Naples figure of a lady dressed as an Oriental wearing a plumed hat, yellow shawl and pink coat over a long dress with blue spots, circa 1790, 16cm. high. (Christie's London) $12,000

A Naples two-handled ecuelle, cover and stand painted with vignettes of five dated nocturnal eruptions of Vesuvius, circa 1794, stand 23.5cm. diam. (Christie's) $20,000

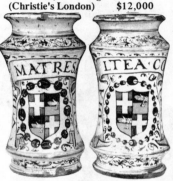

A pair of Naples armorial waisted albarelli, the central quartered Arms in ocher, yellow and blue within a beaded cartouche, mid-16th century, 23cm. high. (Christie's) $12,000

A Naples (Real Fabbrica Ferdinandea) group of a gallant and companion, he in a black top hat, she in a black shawl over a purple patterned skirt and yellow shoes, circa 1790, 18.5cm. high.   (Christie's) $13,500

A Naples creamware white group of the Madonna with the Infant Christ and St. John, inscribed Laudato Fecit 1794, 35cm. high. (Christie's) $7,000

A Naples (Real Fabbrica Ferdinandea) Royal portrait medallion with the heads of King Ferdinando IV and Queen Maria Caroline, circa 1790, 6.5cm. diameter. (Christie's) $2,500

NEVERS

When the Duke Luigi Gonzaga of Mantua became Duke of Nevers in 1565, he brought with him from Italy some leading faïenciers, notably Domenico Conrado and his brothers from the Savona area. The Conrados prospered and were to hold a virtual monopoly of faience manufacture in Nevers until around 1630. Through the influence of Guilio Gambini, an Italian potter from Lyon, who was in partnership for some time with Augustino Conrado, much early production was in the late Urbino pictorial style, with designs of biblical and mythological scenes. Some large figures were also made at Nevers and were probably made by Daniel Lefebvre, who worked there between 1629-49.

Given the brothers' origin it is unsurprising that much Nevers faience was decorated in the Savona style though both the clay and glaze were harder than those used there. Because the firing was done at unusually high temperatures, the colors sometimes have a faded look, and the final protective covering of a glassy lead glaze normally found on Italian maiolica was also omitted.

The Conrados also introduced a new painting technique, whereby cobalt was added to the basic tin glaze to make blue, and designs were painted on this base in a thick white enamel paste. It is called the 'Persian' style, but probably owes more to Limoges enamels. Pseudo oriental designs in time superseded those of Italian inspiration as the potters copied Chinese inspired Dutch faience.

Early marks often include the decorator's name with *A Nevers* or *DF* and a date incised for Lefebvre's work.

A French faience figure of an Oriental lady standing in a classical pose, her long plaited hair tied by a blue top knot, circa 1730, possibly Nevers, 37cm. high. (Christie's London) $6,250

A French istoriato tazza painted with Diana and Acteon, the alarmed Diana and her attendants covering her with drapes, probably Nevers, last quarter of the 16th century, 28cm. diam. (Christie's London) $2,250

Late 17th century garniture of three Nevers bleu persan vases, 37cm. and 59cm. high. $7,500

A pair of faience bucket-shaped jardinières, the sides painted in yellow, green, iron-red and underglaze blue with an Oriental by shrubs in a garden, probably Nevers, circa 1680, 13.5cm. high. (Christie's) $5,000

A Nevers (Conrade) armorial blue and white tondino, the center painted with a huntsman blowing a horn accompanied by his hound, circa 1680, 30cm. diam. (Christie's London) $1,500

A massive Nevers bleu persan bucket-shaped jardinière, the strapwork and foliage handles with bearded mask terminals, circa 1680, 47cm. high. (Christie's) $3,300

178

NEWPORT POTTERY

The Newport pottery was a subsidiary of A J Wilkinson Ltd operating in the 1930s, and is distinguished by having among its designers the legendary Clarice Cliff.

A large Newport pottery Bizarre wall mask, 1930's, 37cm. high. $500

A Newport pottery 'Archaic' Bizarre vase, 1930's, impressed number 373, 17.75cm. high. $1,000

A Newport pottery Bizarre vase, deep inky blue at base, printed marks, 1930's, 36cm. high. $1,300

An amusing Newport pottery model of an owl wearing a suit, signed *M. Epworth*, 18.5cm. (Bearne's) $175

A large Newport pottery Bizarre vase, 1930's, 36.75cm. high. $4,000

A Newport pottery Bizarre 'Delicia' jar and cover, 1930's, 21cm. high. $650

A Newport pottery Bizarre charger, 1930's, stylised foliate design in blue, orange and green with blue border, 33.5cm. diam. $300

A Bizarre single-handled 'lotus' vase, 29.3cm. high. Newport, late 1930's.
                    $500

NIDERVILLER

The manufacture of hard paste porcelain began at Niderviller in 1765 and continues today. The factory was originally opened in 1754 by Baron Jean Louis de Bayerlé to make faience. In 1770 it was purchased by the Comte de Custine and passed on his death to Claude Francois Lanfrey.

For its styles, it drew heavily on the wares of Strasbourg, turning out vases, clocks and large tablewares in the high rococo taste, Forms and decoration were almost identical for both its faience and porcelain output, the latter comprising mainly oriental or European flowers, sprigs or landscapes.

Figures were produced, the majority being left unglazed. Many were modeled by Charles Sauvage, known as Lemire. When Paul Louis Cyfflé's Lunéville factory was sold in 1780 many of his molds also passed to Niderviller.

Marks are *BN* in monogram, *CN* in monogram, two interlaced *C*s or *N Nider* or *Niderviller*.

NOVE

In 1728 Giovanni Batista Antonibon established an earthenware and hard paste porcelain factory at Nove near Bassano. He was succeeded there by his son and grandson, and it continued in the family until the late nineteenth century.

It is noted for its tureens in the form of fish, and for practical rococo tablewares painted in high temperature colors. The mark of a star with a tail is common on 19th century pieces.

Good quality cream colored earthenware was also made at Nove from about 1780 by Giovanni Maria Baccin and others such as Baroni, Bernardi, Viero and Cacchetto. Most of these are clearly marked.

A Niderviller faience shaped hexafoil dish, circa 1775, 25cm. diam. $8,500

One of a pair of Niderviller covered vases and covers, 15¼in. high, circa 1780. $2,250

A Niderviller miniature group of Venus scantily clad in a puce cloth leaning against billowing cloud scrolls, circa 1780, 8.5cm. high. (Christie's Geneva) $450

A Niderviller figure of 'La Jardiniere', on a circular base, 20.5cm. high. (Phillips) $360

Two Nove pistol-shaped handles painted with fruit and flowers, fitted with a steel four-pronged fork and a blade, 19th century, 7.5cm. and 8cm. long. (Christie's) $275

A Le Nove two handled ecuelle cover and stand, painted in colors with scattered sprays of flowers, iron red star marks, circa 1770, the stand 22cm. diam. (Christie's London) $2,500

NYMPHENBURG

Following the establishment of the porcelain factory at Meissen, the rulers of the other German states were anxious to set up their own ventures. One of the most successful was at Nymphenburg in Bavaria, where production began in 1753 and continues to the present.

The original factory was situated at Neudeck, under the patronage of the Bavarian Elector, who had married a granddaughter of Augustus the Strong, and it was transferred to Nymphenburg itself in 1761.

Throughout its early history a galaxy of talent was employed there, but financially things ran far from smoothly and a succession of managers were engaged to try to make it profitable. The fame of the Nymphenburg factory, however, rests essentially on the work of one man, the modeler Franz Anton Bustelli, who is to rococo what Kaendler was to baroque.

Nymphenburg porcelain is of the true hard paste variety, fairly white in color and covered with a fine and brilliant glaze. Early pieces were delicately colored and many left in the white. Flat washes of red-blue, black, pink and gold were used for coloring dresses. Small pieces, such as snuff boxes, and tablewares were also produced in profusion during this period.

Early Neudeck-Nymphenburg pieces often bear the diamond paned shield from the arms of Bavaria, and from 1765 a hexagram mark was additionally used. A lively 'seconds' market existed from the beginning, and defective pieces were sold in the white with the factory mark canceled by an engraved stroke.

A Nymphenburg oil and vinegar stand with two bottles and hinged covers, circa 1765, the bottles 18cm. high. $13,000

A well-painted Nymphenburg topographical cup, and a saucer, the cup with a view of Marsbach. (Phillips) $650

A pair of Nymphenburg figures designed by Prof. J. Wackerle of stylised 18th century fops. $3,500

A Nymphenburg baluster coffee pot and domed cover painted in colors to both sides with birds roosting in trees and perching on terraces, indistinct incised mark, circa 1760, 23cm. high. (Christie's London) $3,400

A Nymphenburg shaped circular dish from the Hof service painted with a large spray of roses, chrysanthemum and tulips, further flowers and a butterfly, circa 1762, 23.5cm. diameter.
(Christie's) $4,000

A Nymphenburg figure of a parrot modeled by Dominicus Auliczek, its plumage painted naturalistically in green, yellow, iron-red and blue, circa 1765, 15.5cm. high.
(Christie's) $6,000

181

PARIAN

In the early 19th century, Staffordshire potters were experimenting with formulae for unglazed white porcelain which could be modeled into statuary in imitation of the finest Greek marble sculptures found on the island of Paros. The firms of Copeland and Garrett and Minton were front-runners in the race, and it was Copeland who in 1842 released the first piece of 'parian' statuary, entitled Apollo as the Shepherd Boy of Admetus. Their success was due to the high quantity of feldspar in the formula and a firing process which permitted a large amount of air in the kiln. The result was a lustrous transparency and delicacy of molding.

Minton, who were the first to use the name Parian, contested Copeland's claim of a 'first', and the jury at the Great Exhibition produced a soothing statement which declared in effect a draw.

Copeland commissioned figures from many of the finest sculptors of the day, while Minton's principal modelers were John Bell and Albert Carrier Belleuse.

Wedgwood, Worcester and Coalport all produced parian ware, including some impressive tableware, where glazed and decorated bone china was successfully combined with lightly gilt statuary.

Standard parian was found to be excellent for relief molded fancy ware, with smear glazing. Colored backgrounds were achieved by tinted slip brush-applied to the appropriate parts of the mold, and the main colors were blue, sage and brown. Standard parian was criticised because the fine granular surface was easily soiled, though this was to some degree overcome from 1860 by the use of a thin coating of lead glaze.

CHINA

A Bennington Parian teapot with domed cover, squirrel finial, 5in. high. $450

A Copeland Parian bust of a young woman with flowing hair, 23in. high. $750

A Parian figural group of sleeping children 'Le Nid', circa 1875, signed 'Croisy', 15in. high.
(Skinner Inc.) $600

A Copeland Parian group of 'The Sleep of Sorrow and the Dream of Joy', after the original sculpture by Rafaelle Monti, circa 1875, 18½in. high. $750

A Bates, Brown-Westhead and Moore parian bust of Apollo after a model by Delpech, Art Union stamp and dated 1861, 14in. high. (Christie's S. Ken) $500

A Minton Parian group of Ariadne and the Panther on rectangular base, year cypher for 1867, 13.7in. high. $450

PARIS

CHINA

During the Neo-Classical period many small porcelain factories were scattered in and around Paris, most of which were under some form of noble patronage. Mainly they produced tableware and there was very little figure production.

Despite their numbers however, the porcelain they produced was surprisingly uniform in both shape and decoration, and it is often very difficult to tell the output of one from another unless they are marked. The severer neo-Classical style did not, of course, lend itself to the wilder flights of imagination in the same way as did Baroque and Rococo. Plates were usually plain and unmolded, coffee and teapots cylindrical or vase shaped, cups cylindrical and bowls often raised on feet.

One new form which did emerge at this time however was the semicircular bulb or flower pot, the fronts of which were divided into three panels with pilasters, and decorated with neo-Classical motifs.

Decoration of the period was not generally elaborate in content, consisting mainly of formal motifs, but its technical brilliance was truly amazing. There was much use of gilding and chased decoration which, together with colored grounds and borders, often matt, gave a remarkably rich effect.

Napoleon's expedition to Egypt and his elevation to Emperor saw the beginning of the Empire period, during which the Paris factories continued to thrive. In many aspects the Empire style is merely an extension of neo-Classicism, but wares now began to show a greater variety of form, with greater use of modeling for the handles and spouts of teapots etc. Vases, too, while retaining their basic shape,

Paris Porcelain Figural Desk Set, France, late 19th century, the cover modeled as three young girls, the oval base with mounted inkwell and sander, 8in. high. (Skinner Inc)　　　$500

Paris porcelain American historical pitcher, France, circa 1862, enamel decorated portraits of Grant and Farragut in military dress, 8³/₈in. high. (Skinner Inc.)　　$17,000

A pair of ormolu-mounted Paris pale blue-ground campana-shaped vases, one painted with a stag-hunt, the other with a boar-hunt, circa 1810–20, 38in. high. (Christie's)　　$7,500

A Paris (Stone, Coquerel et le Gros) plate transfer-printed in sepia with a view of Chateau de Houghton, Comté de Norfolk, circa 1820, 23.5cm. diameter. (Christie's)　　$750

A Paris tea kettle, cover and stand, iron-red monogram mark of Louis-Stanislas Xavier, circa 1780, 30cm. wide.　　$2,400

A Paris porcelain veilleuse, the globular teapot and cylindrical holder painted with peasant lovers in landscape vignettes, circa 1830, 24cm. high over-all. (Christie's)　　$425

PARIS

had more interesting handles, which were often of biscuit, or gilt unglazed porcelain. Their matt surface contrasted with the highly polished gilding on the bodies. Egyptian motifs were understandably common.

Another new form of the time was the cabinet cup, not part of a service but as an entity in itself. The saucers for these tended to be fairly plain and decorated only with gilding and they acted as a foil for the highly elaborate cups. These were often flared in shape with ornate modeled handles, richly decorated with fine enamel painting of topographical scenes, portraits etc. in panels. They were often so lavish and extravagant that it seems unlikely they were ever designed for any practical use.

Theodore Deck (1823–91) was a French artist potter from Alsace who from 1856 onwards was making ornamental earthenware in Paris. His early work was often decorated with scenes commissioned from artists, and he was greatly influenced by middle Eastern, notably Iznik styles.

A Dagoty Paris ewer and basin, the ewer with matt blue ground, decorated in white relief with acanthus leaf borders and swan neck griffins, 31cm. high. (Phillips London) $4,500

A Paris pink-ground barrel-shaped coffee-cup and saucer painted with a chinoiserie figure smoking a pipe, fabulous trees and plants, circa 1810. (Christie's) $500

A Paris gold-ground baluster coffee-pot and cover painted at Naples each side with figures watching a puppet-show and spaghetti vendors, circa 1800, 18.5cm. high. (Christie's) $3,000

A Paris biscuit roundel of Napoleon, the head of the Emperor molded with a laurel wreath, pierced for hanging, circa 1810, 15.5cm. diameter. (Christie's) $600

A Paris porcelain cabinet cup and saucer painted with geometric panels of stylised flowers and foliage, circa 1820, 2³/₄in. high. (Christie's) $296

A pair of unusual French flambé porcelain vases, Paris, circa 1880, in 18th century manner, 68.5cm. high. (Sotheby's) $27,984

A Paris porcelain vase of baluster form, painted with a bouquet of garden flowers and grapes, early 20th century, 15¹/₂in. high. (Christie's) $1,281

PEARLWARE

Pearlware was the name given in 1780 by Josiah Wedgwood to a whitened version of his celebrated creamware which he had just developed successfully.

This was made by adding a touch of blue coloring to the body. It could be just as thin as porcelain, and formed an excellent background for blue printing, enabling it to compete favorably with Chinese wares. It was quickly adopted by many other potteries, and became extremely popular in the late 18th/19th centuries.

A pearlware oval plaque molded in high relief and colored with two recumbent lions, circa 1790, 28.5cm. wide. (Christie's) $1,000

A Yorkshire pearlware model of a show horse, with an ocher and green saddle-cloth tied with a blue girth, circa 1800, 14.5cm. high. (Bearne's) $1,850

A pearlware globular teapot and cover, printed with two circular panels of female archers, circa 1800, 7½in. wide. (Christie's S. Ken) $300

An unusual Victorian bargeman's pearlware smoking companion, the tobacco jar with an antique slavery portrait and a biblical reference, 38cm. high overall. (Henry Spencer) $340

A pearlware shallow bowl on a small foot, the interior printed in blue with a double portrait busts of George III and Charlotte inscribed 'A King Rever'd, A Queen Belovd, Long May They Live', 19cm. (Phillips) $600

A dated Staffordshire pearlware globular jug, inscribed 'Samuell Piggott 1799' and flanked by the farmer's arms, 7¼in. high. (Christie's S. Ken) $160

A pearlware group depicting the marriage of John Macdonald, he and his companion flanking an anvil with a priest attending, circa 1810, 8½in. high. (Christie's S. Ken) $800

A pearlware figure of a hound seated erect with a dead bird at its feet, on a shaped base, Staffordshire or Yorkshire, circa 1785, 10.5cm. wide. (Christie's) $750

PESARO

Pesaro was another of the towns in the Duchy of Urbino with a strong potting tradition, and maiolica was made there during the late 15th and 16th centuries.

In 1462 mention was made of a loan of a large sum of money for the enlargement of a manufactory of vessels, and it is to this date that the commencement of maiolica manufacture is generally ascribed.

In 1546, Jean Sforza passed an edict in favor of Pesaro, forbidding the introduction from other factories of any but common vessels for oil and water and a similar edict was passed in 1552, naming the potters Bernardino Gagliardino, Girolamo Lanfranchi and Mo. Rinaldo as engaging to supply the town and country with vases and pieces painted with historical subjects. Girolamo Lanfranchi was succeeded by his son Giacomo, who in 1562 invented the application of gold to maiolica, fixed by fire.

A notable patron of the pottery was Guido Ubaldo II, who became Duke of Urbino in 1538, but on his death in 1572 the pottery began to decline and by 1718 there was only one potter still there who made ordinary vessels.

The manufacture of pottery was revived in the middle of the century, when Antonio Casali and Filippo Caligari from Lodi set up again to make practical wares such as drug jars, lamps and cups. These were decorated in the later French, imitation Sèvres style, with low fired enamel colors, probably by Pietro Lei, who came to the factory from Sassuolo in 1763. Favorite motifs were gold arabesques, medallions of flowers, and landscapes.

Imitation Urbino ware was made by Magrini & Co of Pesaro from 1870.

CHINA

A documentary Pesaro trilobed jug, inscribed in Greek, circa 1790, 22cm. high. (Christie's) $3,300

A Pesaro istoriato tondo painted in colors after Sforza Marcantonio with the legend of Perseus and Andromeda, circa 1570, 25.5cm. diam. (Christie's London) $35,000

A Pesaro fluted crespina painted with the Sacrifice of Isaac, circa 1570, 24.5cm. diam. (Christie's) $8,000

A Pesaro fluted crespina painted with Christ on the road to Calvary, circa 1570, 23.5cm. diam. (Christie's) $5,000

A Pesaro istoriato tazza painted in colors by Sforza di Marcantonio with Anchises and Aeneas arriving at Pallanteum, circa 1550, 27cm. diam. (Christie's) $4,500

A Pesaro cylindrical albarello boldly painted with manganese, blue and orange flowers, oranges and scrolling foliage between blue concentric bands, circa 1780, 22cm. high. (Christie's) $1,500

186

PETIT

Jacob and Mardochée Petit purchased their factory at Fontainebleu in 1830 and it remained in the family until well into the second half of the century. It was Petit perhaps more than any other who recaptured the spirit of the true rococo during its 19th century revival, and the clocks, lavish inkstands, vases and tea warmers which he modeled in the form of personages or figures are among the most popular of his works.

Many French factories of the time made products in styles attributed to Petit but those bearing the underglaze blue mark *JP* are obviously better quality and command a premium.

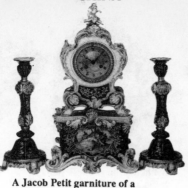

A Jacob Petit garniture of a clock and a pair of candlesticks all molded with rococo scrolls, shells and leaf motifs, 39.5cm. (Phillips)　　　$1,350

A pair of early 19th century Jacob Petit baluster vases on square bases with gilt mask handles, 71cm. high. (Wellington Salerooms)　$6,000

A Jacob Petit pot-pourri in the form of a fish, painted in iron-red and apricot and gilt scales, 19th century, 7¹/₂in. long. (Christie's S. Ken.)　　$300

An attractive pair of early 19th century Jacob Petit porcelain taper holders, modeled as a Turkish sultan and his sultana, 16.5cm. high. (Henry Spencer)　　$2,250

A Jacob Petit tapering oviform vase and domed cover with two blue rope-twist handles, blue JP monogram, mid 19th century, 20in. high. (Christie's S. Ken.)　　$800

A pair of Jacob Petit vases of ogee shape with flared rims, painted in colors with bouquets on both sides, 18cm. (Phillips)　　$600

A Paris (Jacob Petit) clock-case and stand of scroll outline, blue JP marks, circa 1835, 37cm. high overall. (Christie's)　　$1,250

A Jacob Petit porcelain figural vase, as a lady seated on a rocky mound encrusted with flowers, 27.5cm. high. (Henry Spencer)　　$450

PILKINGTON

Pilkington's Tile and Pottery Co. was set up in 1892 at Clifton Junction Lancashire, to manufacture tiles, but from 1897 the production range was extended to include buttons, vases etc. Shortly afterwards the decoration of bought-in biscuit vases also began.

Opalescent glaze effects were discovered in 1903 and from then on the production of glazed earthenware known as Lancastrian pottery began. These wares, which consisted of vases, bowls, trays etc. were usually simple in shape, but decorated in a wide palette of colors often with a crystalline or opalescent effect.

The company was run by two brothers, William and Joseph Burton, who were both ceramic chemists and who were instrumental in developing the luster decorated pottery which formed the bulk of the factory's 20th century production. Modeled, molded or incised decoration appears on these pieces, while the decorator R Joyce modeled animals and birds. Lapis ware was introduced in 1928, and tile production continued throughout.

The factory ceased production in 1937, midway between the deaths of the two brothers, though it started up again in a limited way ten years later, when potters were encouraged to produce individual pieces which were then decorated and signed with the artist's monogram.

Until 1904 the mark *P* was sometimes used, followed until 1913 by *P* and *L* and two bees. The Tudor rose was a later mark, and *Royal Lancastrian* is another variation.

A Pilkington Lancastrian luster vase and cover decorated by Richard Joyce with a frieze of antelopes and stylised trees, 15.5cm. high. (Christie's) $800

A Pilkington Lancastrian deep bowl designed by Walter Crane and decorated by Wm. S. Mycock, date code for 1913, 21.6cm. high. $1,350

A Pilkington's Royal Lancastrian luster vase decorated by Gordon Forsyth, painted in red and gold luster with bands of tudor roses, 1915, 8¹/₂ in. high. (Christie's S. Ken) $500

A Pilkington's Royal Lancastrian twin-handled vase decorated by Gordon Forsyth, 1908, 30.2cm. high. $300

A Pilkington 'Royal Lancastrian' luster vase by Richard Joyce, painted in golden luster with two mounted knights in armor 26.5cm. high. (Phillips) $1,500

A Pilkington's Lancastrian molded ovoid luster vase decorated by Richard Joyce, the body embossed with wild animals amongst grassland, 1915. (Christie's S. Ken) $1,200

PLYMOUTH

The first pottery in England to make hard paste porcelain was William Cookworthy's factory at Plymouth, where production started in 1768. There were enormous technical difficulties to overcome, with a huge amount of kiln wastage, and this made it difficult to turn the project into a commercial success.

The Plymouth paste was very hard and white, and the glaze tended to be heavily smoked. Spiral wreathing, a pattern of fine grooves which appeared on the surface of the vessels as they twisted in the kiln, is also common. However, some quite elaborate shapes were achieved, such as large vases and intricate shell salts. More common are the useful tablewares, with pickle leaf dishes, for example, often painted in underglaze blue and overglaze iron red. The decoration was often in the Chinese Mandarin or famille verte style. Most successful of all were the bird decorated mugs by the French painter Mons Saqui.

Most of the polychrome production was unmarked, and is often difficult to distinguish from early Bristol. With the blue and white output, however, this is easier, as Plymouth produced a very blackish underglaze blue, due to the high temperature at which it was fired. It is rarer than the polychrome, but a greater proportion is marked.

Marks usually comprised the chemical sign for tin with a combined 2 and 4 in underglaze blue, and naturally add greatly to the value of a piece.

After less than three years, Cookworthy transferred the whole operation to Bristol in 1770.

A Plymouth cream jug, painted in underglaze faded sepia or blue with flowers, trees and rocks, 9cm. (Lawrence Fine Arts) $600

Two Plymouth white figures of pheasants, Wm. Cookworthy's factory, circa 1768, 20cm. high. $2,000

A pair of Plymouth figures of musicians wearing pale clothes, he playing the recorder and his companion the mandolin, Wm. Cookworthy's factory, circa 1770, 14.5cm. high. (Christie's) $1,000

Rare Plymouth figure of a lady on scroll molded base, 6in. high. $1,200

A rare Plymouth figure of 'Winter' in the form of a naked boy with a robe, in mint condition. $1,200

A Plymouth group of two putti emblematic of Spring, 14.5cm. high, impressed letters S & D (flower festoon R). (Phillips) $500

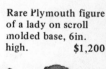

2

POOLE POTTERY

The firm of Carter & Co was established in Poole, Dorset in 1873 to manufacture earthenware and tiles. The latter it often supplied for subsequent decoration, by, among others, William De Morgan. In 1895 they took over the nearby Architectural Tile Co.

Their range of earthenware, notably ornamental pottery, was developed principally by Owen Carter, the son of the proprietor. His experiments with glazes led to the creation of the matt, cream glaze which came to be associated with Carter Stabler and Adams. This amalgamation took place in 1921, when Owen Carter went into partnership with Harold Stabler and John and Truda Adams.

It was out of this partnership that the Poole Pottery, as it was renamed in 1963, grew. Poole Pottery products from all periods are much in vogue as collectables today.

A pottery oviform jug, shape no. 304, painted by Marjorie Batt with bluebirds and foliage in typical colors, impressed *CSA Ltd* mark, 5in. high. (Christie's S. Ken) **$330**

A pottery biscuit barrel and cover with wicker handle painted by Sylvia Penney, with stylised flowers and foliage, impressed *Poole,* 5½in. high. (Christie's S. Ken) **$200**

A pair of Pheobe Stabler earthenware figures modeled as a boy and girl, each draped with a garland of flowers, impressed *Hammersmith Bridge* mark, 7in. high. (Christie's S. Ken) **$850**

The Bull, a pottery group designed by Phoebe and Harold Stabler, modeled as two infants astride a bull in ceremonial trappings of swags and garlands, impressed *CSA* mark, 13in. high. (Christie's S. Ken) **$3,500**

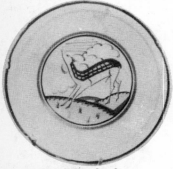

A terracotta shallow bowl, decorated by Anne Hatchard painted with a deer in an open landscape, impressed *CSA* mark, painted insignia and *RG,* 9½in. diameter. (Christie's S. Ken) **$375**

A Phoebe Stabler plaster bust of a young girl with pigtails, painted yellow, inscribed *Phoebe Stabler 1911,* 15in. high. (Christie's S. Ken) **$375**

A pottery charger painted by Nellie Blackmore with a view of the ship the Harry Paye, by Arthur Bradbury, 15in. diam. (Christie's S. Ken) **$900**

POTSCHAPPEL

The porcelain made at Meissen must surely be one of the most forged and copied artefacts of all time. One of the host of factories which sprang up in the 19th century precisely to do this, was situated at Potschappel near Dresden, the major center for Meissen copies.

The Potschappel factory was established in 1875 and traded as the Sächsische Porzellanfabrik Carl Thieme. It produced exclusively Meissen type pieces, such as the crinoline groups which had been made from the mid 18th century. Carl Thieme, the founder, was also the chief designer.

Various marks were used. Some pieces were clearly marked *Dresden* or *Potschappel*, while others have simply a cross and a *T*. Crossed *Ls* with a coronet and a flower with leaves or a bee on a hive are further variations.

19th century porcelain comport by Potschappel, circa 1872, with a rococo stem supported by two young Cupids, approx. 18in. (G. A. Key)
$450

Potschappel porcelain cabinet cup and saucer by Carl Thieme, with a pink ground with a landscape decoration. (G. A. Key)
$150

A pair of Potschappel pierced two-handled vases, painted in colors with Classical figures in landscape within borders, 22½in. high. (Christie's S. Ken) $2,000

A Carl Thieme Potschappel pierced centerpiece applied with flowers, the base with four figures, 12½in. high. (Christie's S. Ken) $575

A Carl Thieme Potschappel porcelain table centerpiece, the shaped base with an 18th century lady with two suitors, 55cm. high. (Henry Spencer)
$1,300

A Potschappel two-handled vase and an armorial cover, the vase with crossed T mark, the stand with blue beehive mark, circa 1900, 84cm. high.
$1,350

PRATTWARE

Blue printed ware proved enormously popular in the early 19th century, with just about every English pottery turning out vast quantities of the stuff.

In the 1840s however the firm of F & R Pratt of Fenton achieved a breakthrough when they introduced multi-color printing. This they did by engraving each color, using a palette of red, blue, yellow, black or brown, on a separate copper plate. When carefully arranged and engraved in stipple, the result was a full range of colors, which decoration was sometimes further enhanced with gilding.

Initially this was used mainly for decorating potlids, where even great paintings by famous artists were sometimes reproduced. Soon everyone was imitating Prattware, and the range of wares so decorated extended to include tea and dessert services, vases, ceramic picture frames and bread plates.

Pratt was blessed with a highly skilled engraver, Jesse Austin, who sometimes signed or initialed his work. His mark adds great cachet to a piece.

Pratt's pieces usually carry the mark *F & R Pratt Fenton* impressed, or more rarely, a crown with *Manufacturers to HRH Prince Albert/F & R Pratt.*

A Pratt pottery sauce boat molded in the form of a dolphin, painted in green, brown and ocher enamels, 15.5cm. long. (Bearne's) $450

A Prattware group of Saint George slaying a dragon, flanked by two female figures in ocher dress, 25cm. (Phillips) $875

A Prattware watch holder of a longcase clock decorated in Pratt colors and molded in relief with various Classical figures, 27cm. (Phillips) $1,100

A Prattware relief-molded jug decorated in colors, depicting Admiral Duncan in profile flanked by two ships, 17cm. (Phillips) $475

18th century Pratt figure of a cat with blue, green and ocher splashed decoration, 3in. high. (Prudential) $400

A Prattware George IV commemorative plate with a profile head of the King wearing a laurel wreath and naval uniform, 22cm. (Phillips) $575

QIANLONG

The Emperor Ch'ien Lung held sway for 60 years between 1736–95 and his peaceful reign marked a high point in the history of Chinese ceramics. T'ang Ying had supreme control of the Imperial Porcelain Manufactory from 1743 and he brought the Imperial wares to a peak of perfection, introducing to them many new 'foreign' colors, and the use of double glazes.

Blue and white was still made; the vases were often of archaic bronze forms decorated with bronze patterns or a pattern of floral scrolls. The blue, however, was usually a dullish indigo in tone, and the character of Kangxi ware is lacking.

On-glaze painting in famille rose enamels was widely extended in the Qianlong period, and tints were now mixed to produce the European effect of shading. Designs were taken from nature or copied from the antique, featuring brocade designs etc.

Much Qianlong ware was exported, notably 'Mandarin' wares, ewers, punch bowls and vases painted with panels of figure subjects with the surrounding space filled with composite designs of blue and white with passages of pink scale diaper or scrolls broken by small vignettes. Table ware often has elaborately molded and pierced ornament in famille rose colors. Gilding, too, was freely employed.

In Ch'ien Lung's time the art of porcelain reaches a technical apogee, but later in the period it is already beginning to lose freshness and spontaneity. The pieces are marvellous examples of neatness and finish, but there is a cold sophistication about them, and they lack the fire and vigor which characterised the Ming and Kangxi periods.

A Chinese famille rose tobacco leaf, shaped oval dish, 18¼in. wide, Qianlong. $6,000

A Woucai bowl, the exterior painted with dragons in green enamel and iron-red below a border of flowers and Buddhist symbols, 13cm., Qianlong mark. (Bearne's) $450

A pair of large Mandarin palette vases, each painted with panels of officials and ladies on terraces, 18⅞in. high, Qianlong. (Bonhams) $3,600

A fine underglaze-blue and copper-red garlic-head vase, Qianlong seal mark, the compressed globular sides vividly painted with three Buddhistic lion cubs pawing and playing with ribboned brocade balls, 10½in. high. (Christie's) $48,000

A blue and white stemcup, Qianlong seal mark, the flaring sides of the cup painted to the exterior with lanca characters divided by arches formed by lotus sprays, 3¼in. high. (Christie's) $4,500

A Qianlong export mug, of cylindrical form, with entwined strap handle, decorated with scattered sprays of flowers, 14cm. high. (Henry Spencer) $400

LUCIE RIE

Lucie Rie (b.1902) is an Austrian artist potter who trained under Powolny in Vienna. In 1938 she came to the UK as a refugee from Nazism and opened a button factory in a London mews, where she was joined by fellow refugee Hans Coper.

Her early pre-war work had consisted of simple, thinly potted stoneware, sometimes polished or covered with rough textured glazes, her style influenced both by functionalist ideals and by Roman pottery. Her mark at this time was a painted *LRG* over *Wien*.

After the war she made porcelain decorated with unglazed bands of cross-hatched decoration colored with manganese oxide, and stoneware in elegant simple shapes.

She used color sparingly, and developed a number of glazes, notably a yellow one containing uranium. Others were characterised by their rough uneven texture.

The significance of her work was recognised when she was made a Dame of the British Empire and she still flourishes today. Her mark now is an impressed monogram *LR* within a rectangle.

A stoneware baluster vase by Lucie Rie, covered in a shiny deep-blue glaze with run matt-manganese rim, circa 1955, 31.7cm. high. (Christie's) $2,500

A stoneware bottle vase by Lucie Rie, with flared waves rim, flattened cylindrical neck, circa 1975, 27.2cm. high. (Christie's) $2,000

A stoneware bowl by Lucie Rie with compressed flared sides, the exterior carved with fluted decoration, impressed LR seal 14cm. high. (Christie's) $3,000

A stoneware salad bowl with pulled lip by Lucie Rie, covered in a finely pitted bluish-white glaze with iron-brown flecks, circa 1954, 14.3cm. high. (Christie's) $1,350

A porcelain bottle vase by Lucie Rie, covered in an off-white glaze, with gray veining and a mottled pinkish-green spiral, circa 1965, 27.5cm. high. (Christie's) $4,000

A small stoneware bowl by Lucie Rie, covered in a mirror-black manganese glaze with white rim, circa 1953, 10cm. diam. (Christie's) $750

A stoneware vase by Lucie Rie, covered in a gray-lavender pitted glaze with iron-brown flecks, circa 1970, 17cm. high. (Christie's) $900

ROBJ

Robj was a French dealer who in the 1920s and early 30s commissioned small decorative porcelain items, such as inkwells, ashtrays, preserve pots etc, for sale in his Paris showroom. Lamps, bottles and incense burners often in the form of the human figure were popular as were Cubist inspired statuettes in cream colored porcelain with a crackle glaze. Robj sponsored annual competitions until 1931, and winning designs were sometimes produced in limited editions at the Sevres factory.

ROCKINGHAM

Pottery manufacture began at the Rockingham factory near Swinton in Yorkshire in the mid 18th century. During the early 19th century high quality pottery was produced mainly for export to Russia. From 1826-42, however, when the factory was run by the brothers Thomas, George and John Brameld, its porcelain became highly acclaimed at home. In quality, Rockingham's output was second only to Nantgarw, while its superior strength meant that it could be used for an astonishing diversity of forms.

It is perhaps most famous for its brown glazed ware. This glaze was applied very thickly, the object being dipped three times, to give a streaked chocolate coloration. It was used for such objects as toby jugs, tea and coffee pots, as well as the famous Cadogan pots. These were teapots shaped as a peach with foliage and fruit decoration. They were lidless, the liquid being poured in through a hole at the bottom to which was attached a tapering, slightly spiraled tube which finished just short of the top. They were thus unspillable.

CHINA

A Robj earthenware bowl and cover, formed as a Red Indian's head, with dark red glazed feather headdress, 20cm. high. (Christie's) $675

A Robj porcelain jug, modeled as a rotund lady wearing a plum colored dress, the spout modeled as an apron, 19.5cm. high. (Phillips London) $375

Pair of Rockingham figures of a young boy and a girl, inscribed no. 36, 4¾in. high. $600

One of a pair of early Rockingham primrose leaf molded plates, painted with flowers in vases on marble tables, probably by Edwin Steele, 24.5cm. (Phillips) $1,500

A Rockingham cabinet cup and stand with two gilt scroll handles, circa 1835, the stand 11.5cm. diam., the cup 10cm. high. (Christie's) $775

Rockingham-type brown glazed figure of a lion, England, mid 19th century, (chips under base rim), 11in. wide. (Skinner Inc) $275

ROCKINGHAM

Blue and white ware was also produced in the common Willow pattern and some designs peculiar to Rockingham. Rarer are green glazed and cane colored wares, the latter often decorated with raised classical or floral ornament in blue, white, chocolate or green.

Rockingham also produced a staggering diversity of ornamental ware, from baskets and scent bottles and toys down to bedknobs and door handles – the list is virtually endless, and some outstanding artists were engaged to decorate these.

Their useful ware comprised dinner and dessert services, which fall into two basic designs, one featuring coronet knobs and scrolled handles and the other rustic handles and twig finials. Several famous services were made for the nobility and royalty – William IV paid £5,000 for a Rockingham dinner service. The company, however, lost money on virtually all of these commissions, and with their huge diversity of output the factory was never really on a sound financial footing. The Bramelds relied heavily on their patron Earl Fitzwilliam, whose successor in 1841, in justifiable exasperation, refused to plow any more money into the enterprise. By the next year the factory had closed.

There is a diversity too of Rockingham marks. On pottery *Brameld* is generally found together with a + and a numeral. On cane ware this is usually in an oval plaquette. After 1826 *Rockingham* becomes more common, most often found on brown ware, and until 1830 the Earl Fitzwilliam griffin arms are found with *Rockingham Works Brameld*. After 1830 the color of the mark changes to puce.

A fine and impressive Rockingham porcelain basket, of shaped rectangular form with double entwined twig handle, griffin mark, 30cm. long. (Spencer's) $1,350

A Rockingham cylindrical patch box and screw-on cover painted in the manner of Edwin Steele, 1826-30, 10cm. diam. (Christie's) $1,250

A Rockingham porcelain neo rococo style teapot and sucrier and covers, painted in colors probably by John Randall with exotic birds. (Spencer's) $1,300

A Rockingham spill vase painted with a church in a mountainous wooded river landscape, C8 in gold and puce griffin mark, circa 1835, 11.5cm. high. (Christie's) $700

A Rockingham flower encrusted circular basket with overhead handle, the exterior applied with flower heads, circa 1830, 11.2cm. (Bearne's) $700

A Rockingham porcelain octagonal plate, decorated in famille verte enamels, 35cm. diam. (H. Spencer & Sons) $375

ROSENTHAL

Philip Rosenthal opened his porcelain factory in 1879 in Selb, Bavaria. It was noted from the first for the high quality of its products. He designed three major services, Darmstadt (1905), Donatello (1907) and Isolde (1910) which at first were left undecorated, but later painted under the glaze in various styles.

From the 1920s figures in Art Deco style were also produced, including theatrical characters and subjects in modern dress, many of which were signed by the artist. Philip Rosenthal died in 1937 and was succeeded by his son, also Philip, who appointed independent artists to work in studios in Selb on pieces which were sold in the Rosenthal studio houses. The firm continues in business today.

Marks include a crown over crossed lines and *Rosenthal*, or over crossed roses.

A Rosenthal guitar playing pierrot with poodle, seated on a mound, by Rudolf Marcuse, 1913, 33cm. high. (Kunsthaus am Museum) $800

A Rosenthal porcelain figure, 'Korean Dancer', designed by C. Holzer-Defanti, 40cm. high, printed factory marks for 1929. $850

A Rosenthal porcelain figure of Autumn, modeled by Gerhard Schliepstein, design as a kneeling, attenuated barely clad maiden holding a basket of fruit, 18cm. high. (Phillips) $825

'Fright'. A Rosenthal porcelain bust of a faun by Ferdinand Liebermann, modeled as a young bare-chested faun holding a set of pan pipes, 39.4cm. high. (Phillips) $1,600

A Rosenthal figure of a female tennis player, striding out on an oval base, by Fritz Klimsch, 1936, 51cm. high. (Kunsthaus am Museum) $750

A Rosenthal ceramic sculpture by Gerhard Schliepstein, circa 1930, 50.8cm. high. $2,100

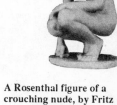

A Rosenthal figure of a crouching nude, by Fritz Kilmsch (1870–1960), matt, 1936, 36cm. high. (Kunsthaus am Museum) $435

ROYAL COPENHAGEN

As its name suggests, the Royal Copenhagen Porcelain Factory was established under the auspices of the Danish Royal family in 1775, and continued under their patronage until it was bought by Aluminia in 1867. In 1884 it was moved to the Aluminia works in the city, under the direction of Philip Schou.

A number of notable artists worked for the company, including G Rode and C F Liisburg, who painted in colored porcelain slip from the 1880s. The factory was notable for its smooth shaped figures decorated in pale colors under a smooth glaze. In the 1890s some abstract elements emerged, but naturalism reasserted itself again later in the work of G Henning and A Malinowski.

There was some experimentation with glazes, with sang-de-boeuf and crystalline glazes being introduced in the 1880s.

From the 1930s figures were almost exclusively of stoneware and relief decorated stoneware vases were also produced. Some styles and decorations also show a strong Chinese influence.

Marks are generally a crown and motif over three waves, sometimes in conjunction with *Denmark*, *Danmark* or *Royal Copenhagen*.

A Royal Copenhagen porcelain vase of compressed shape, decorated with a slightly abstract frieze of lilies and foliage, 11.5cm. diam. (Phillips) $250

A Royal Copenhagen group by Gerhard Henning, depicting an 18th century courting couple, 24cm. high. (Christie's) $1,000

A fine Copenhagen botanical campana vase brilliantly painted with a broad register of specimen flowers, roses, dahlias, asters and lilies, blue wave mark, circa 1810, 43.5cm. high. (Christie's Geneva) $42,000

A Copenhagen pale pink ground two handled oviform vase, painted with a view of a Royal residence, blue waved line mark, late 19th century, 26.5cm. high. (Christie's London) $775

A Copenhagen snuff box and cover modeled as a pug's head, circa 1780, contemporary silver reeded mount, marked for Hamburg, 6cm. wide. (Christie's Geneva) $4,500

A Royal Copenhagen porcelain figure of the Gronland girl, dressed in national costume, holding two bunches of flowers, 6in. high. (Spencer's) $500

ROYAL DUX

Royal Dux is the tradename of the Duxer Prozellanmanufaktur, which was established in 1860 in Dux, Bohemia, now Duchov, Czechoslovakia. It was noted at first for its portrait busts and extravagantly decorated vases, many of which were destined for the American market. From the 1920s onwards it produced Art Deco style figure, of single ladies, dancing couples etc. Marks include an *E* (for the proprietor Eichler) in an oval surrounded by Royal Dux Bohemia set on an embossed pink triangle.

A fine Royal Dux group of a classical Grecian horseman with his charges, 43cm. high, circa 1900. $750

A Royal Dux porcelain bottle vase with applied rustic handle, 44.5cm. high. $300

A Royal Dux porcelain group of a dancing couple in blue glazed and gilt Eastern costume, 12¼in. high. (Christie's S. Ken) $500

A pair of Royal Dux book ends in the form of clowns, cream, green and brown designs with gilt work. (G. A. Key) $450

A Royal Dux Art Deco porcelain figure, modeled as a girl with red hair, naked except for a blue cap tied with a ribbon at the side, 27.25cm. high. (Phillips) $375

A Royal Dux center piece, the trefoil base with column modeled as three bare breasted girls kneeling and supporting lily-form bowl, 6½in. high. (Christie's S. Ken) $350

A Royal Dux bust, the young Art Nouveau maiden gazing to the left, raised pink triangle mark, 20in. high. $1,000

A Royal Dux porcelain figure group of a Roman charioteer, the chariot drawn by two rearing horses, 46cm. overall. (Henry Spencer) $1,250

ROYAL DUX

A Royal Dux group in the form of Pierrot kissing the hand of a young woman wearing a flowing ball gown, after a design by Schaff, 28.5cm.
(Bearne's) $875

A pair of Royal Dux bisque porcelain figures of a rustic boy and girl, the young boy wearing a green hat, the girl wearing a décolleté pink blouse, 17in. high.
(Spencer's) $750

A Royal Dux porcelain figural posy holder, in the form of a young girl in Kate Greenaway type dress, 25cm. high.
(Spencer's) $500

A Royal Dux bisque porcelain figure group of a traveler on a camel, the traveler wearing flowing robes, an attendant at the camel's feet, 17in. high.
(Spencer's) $900

A Royal Dux bisque porcelain figure of a bathing belle, seated wearing a green head scarf, and brown bathing costume, 16in. high.
(Spencer's) $1,100

A Royal Dux bisque porcelain Art Nouveau style flower holder, as a maiden draped in a brown robe seated upon a rocky outcrop, 27cm. high.
(Spencer's) $675

A pair of Royal Dux figures, one of a goat-herd wearing a bear skin over his tunic, his companion feeding a lamb from flowers, 52cm.
(Bearne's) $1,350

Royal Dux figure of Harlequin and female companion, on oval base, 19in. high. (Phillips Manchester) $375

A pair of Royal Dux bisque porcelain figures of harvesters after F. Otto, the young boy wearing a sou'wester, the young girl wearing a white blouse and purple bodice, 21in. high.
(Spencer's) $900

RUSKIN

The Ruskin Pottery was founded at West Smethwick, Birmingham, in 1898 by William Howson Taylor (1876–1935) who had trained at the Birmingham School of Art. Throughout his career he was constantly experimenting with glazes and it is these which give his work its principal interest.

Initially, he made 'Soufflé' ware, where the predominant colors were blues, greens, purples, grays and celadons with a glaze in a single color or mottled, clouded or shaded with a harmonising tone.

Luster wares were also made in a wide range of colors and shades, and a pearl luster was introduced, sometimes with a blistered texture and often with a kingfisher blue glaze. Flambé glazes with scattered viridian spots derived from the use of copper salts were produced, and after 1929 matt and crystalline glazes were added to the range. Taylor's High Fired wares featured dramatic color contrasts, for example purple and black streaking on sea green, or black and green on cream.

With regard to the wares produced, many vases were made, some of which could be heavily potted and covered with blue, green, orange or crystalline blue with a frosted effect. The shapes were often based on Chinese styles. Other products included useful tableware, buttons, hatpins and cufflinks, some silver mounted.

Unfortunately Taylor took the secrets of his glazes with him to his grave, determined that his work should not be imitated. Production stopped at the factory in 1933.

Marks include Taylor's name up to 1903, after which *Ruskin* becomes usual, and the pieces are often dated.

A Ruskin high-fired stoneware vase, the oatmeal ground clouded with green and speckled with irregular areas of purple and blue, 1915, 21.cm. high. (Christie's) $1,750

A Ruskin high-fired stoneware bowl, the exterior glazed in deep red clouding over gray the interior red speckled with purple and green, 1933, 24.5cm. diameter. (Christie's) $1,400

A Ruskin high-fired stoneware bowl, the oatmeal ground mottled overall in dove-gray overlaid with red and purple clouding, with green speckling, 31cm. diameter. (Christie's) $3,000

A Ruskin high-fired stoneware vase, pale ground mottled overall in purples and greens fragmented with random 'snake-skin' patterning, 1914, 32.3cm. high. (Christie's) $2,500

A Ruskin high-fired egg-shell stoneware bowl, with dark mottled red glaze clouding to green and purple towards the foot, 21cm. diameter. (Christie's) $1,850

A Ruskin high-fired stoneware vase, the mottled gray ground overlaid with a cloudy red, purple and gray breaking into gray speckling, 1926, 31.5cm. high. Christie's) $2,000

ST CLOUD

Although porcelain seems to have been made at Saint Cloud as early as 1667, it was the faience factory of Pierre Chicaneau which first turned out Chinese-style soft-paste porcelain. When Chicaneau died, his widow remarried one Henri-Charles Trou in 1679, but kept the secret of soft-paste manufacture from her new family until her death, when a renewed patent in 1722 mentions the names of Henri and Gabriel Trou. It was this Henri Trou, her stepson, who eventually took over the Paris factory in the rue de la Ville l'Eveque which had been established in 1722 by the widow of Pierre Chicaneau's son!

The factory greatly benefited from the patronage of the Duc d'Orleans (Monsieur) brother of the king, and had as its mark a fleur de lys or a sun face, which latter is much more common. The body of St Cloud porcelain tends to be heavily potted, suggesting it was difficult to work with, and the paste varies in color from blue-white to ivory. Decoration was usually in the style popularised by Rouen faience with lambrequins much in evidence, from designs inspired by contemporary silver. Meissen influence was also strong, particularly in the latter period of the factory's production, though St Cloud designers were not devoid of their own ideas, and it is probable that the first trembleuse saucer came from there.

Most enamel painting was in imitation of Japanese Arita porcelain decorated in the Kakiemon style. The factory closed in 1766.

CHINA

A St. Cloud white teapot and cover with flower finial, circa 1720, 16.5cm. high.
$325

A St Cloud snuff box and cover modeled in the shape of a crouching cat, silver mounts with a decharge mark, circa 1735, 5.5cm. long.
(Christie's London) $1,500

Twelve Saint Cloud blue and white knife handles, painted with bands of lambrequin and scrolls, circa 1715, the handles 8cm. long.
(Christie's) $1,100

A St Cloud white seau a demi-bouteille with mask handles, circa 1730, 11cm. high.
(Christie's) $2,000

One of a pair of St. Cloud blue and white spice-boxes and covers, each with four compartments and standing on three paw feet, circa 1710, 14cm. wide.
(Christie's)   (Two) $2,600

A St. Cloud snuff box and cover modeled as a Chinese man, circa 1740, 5.5cm. high.
$1,500

202

SALTGLAZE WARE

A saltglaze effect is achieved by glazing during the firing with salt thrown into the kiln at a temperature above 2,000°F, where it combines chemically with the silicate in the clays to form a durable sodium silicate glaze which has the orange-peel appearance associated with Chinese porcelain.

Most early saltglaze ware is coarse and brown, but after the 1740s, when Staffordshire potters had achieved a light white stoneware body comparable in delicacy and durability with Chinese porcelain, the process was also used very successfully with this.

Later it was also colored with enamels.

A Staffordshire saltglaze small leaf dish with green stalk handle, circa 1755, 15cm. wide. (Christie's) $450

A Staffordshire saltglaze sugar sifter, molded in relief with ozier and diaper panels, 14cm. (Phillips London) $1,300

A Staffordshire saltglaze polychrome oval sauceboat, the exterior crisply molded and painted in natural colors with trailing vine, circa 1755, 18cm. long. (Christie's) $5,000

A Staffordshire saltglaze polychrome baluster jug, painted with a figure and buildings in a landscape vignette within a lobed puce feuilles-de-choux and foliate cartouche below, circa 1760, 22cm. high. (Christie's) $10,000

A Staffordshire saltglaze white teapot and cover in the form of a camel, with molded bird's head and foliage spout, circa 1755, 15cm. high. (Christie's) $12,000

A Staffordshire saltglaze white figure of Chung-li Ch'uan, the bearded Immortal, holding a fan and a peach, circa 1750, 18.5cm. high. (Christie's) $10,000

A Staffordshire saltglaze bear-jug and cover of conventional type, covered in chippings and clasping a dog, circa 1750, 26.5cm. high. (Christie's) $6,000

A Staffordshire saltglaze white snuffer figure, modeled as a lady wearing a peaked bonnet, (two cracks to skirt) circa 1745, 9.5cm. high. (Christie's) $3,000

SAMSON

Edmé Samson set up his porcelain factory in Paris in 1845 with the intention of making reproductions of the most popular pieces produced by other makers in both China and Europe.

Samson's pieces were made mainly from a grayish-hued hard paste porcelain, even where the originals had been in soft paste, and a bluish tinged glaze is found particularly on Chinese inspired examples. In fact, it can be very difficult to tell these Chinese reproductions from the originals. The body used is very similar, though Samson's wares have a smooth finish as opposed to the 'orange-peel' texture of Chinese porcelain. In the main, the Chinese wares which were imitated were 'Export' pieces decorated in the European style in famille rose and famille verte palettes, and they often featured armorial decoration. English production was not so popular on the Continent at the time. Bow, Chelsea and Derby figures were, however, produced in considerable numbers.

Reproductions of St Cloud and Chantilly pieces were very popular however, in particular their celebrated cachepots, the originals of which were already beyond most purses. Meissen was another favorite source on inspiration, and here again it is sometimes difficult to tell the original from the copy, although the Samson pieces tend to have a light speckling on the body and a blackening of the base. Their appearance overall is somewhat glassier, and the colors harsher. Strangely, Italian porcelain escaped Samson's attentions almost entirely, though many copies of tin-glazed earthenwares such as Deruta and Gubbio were made. Iznik pottery was another prime target.

An ormolu-mounted Samson porcelain vase, decorated overall with foliage, flowers and birds, late 19th century, 17¹/₂ in. high. (Christie's) $1,250

A pair of Samson figures of Autumn and Winter, on rococo bases highlighted in gilt, 14in. high. (Christie's S. Ken) $500

A pair of Samson white figures of Saints Andrew and John, the former standing before his cross, the latter holding the Book of Revelation, circa 1880, 15¹/₂ in. high.
(Christie's) $2,000

A Samson gilt metal mounted pot pourri vase and cover, painted with peasant figures in rural landscape vignettes, on a shaped square gilt metal base, late 19th century, 58cm. high. (Christie's London) $3,600

A Samson porcelain and ormolu-mounted two-handled potpourri vase and cover, with high ormolu pineapple and foliage finial, blue cross mark, circa 1880, 53cm. high. (Christie's) $4,000

Pair of Samson porcelain figure ornaments, 'Presentation of Ribbons' and 'The Hairdresser', 7in. high. (G. A. Key) $600

SATSUMA

From the 16th century pottery was made at Kagoshima (formerly Satsuma) prefecture in Japan. Korean potters provided the early inspiration - the main kilns at Naeshirogawa and Ryumonji were developed under them, and early pieces are notably Korean or Chinese in style.

From the 18th century however, Satsuma ware is essentially a hard, gray-white or vellum colored earthenware with a crackle glaze, which is embellished with extravagant gilding and enameling. It was introduced to the West at the Universal Exhibition in Paris in 1867.

CHINA

A pair of Satsuma baluster vases boldly decorated with two panels of courtiers and attendants beside a veranda and samurai beneath blossoming trees, late 19th century, 62.5cm. high. (Christie's London) $10,000

A Satsuma oviform vase decorated with a continuous pattern of sages and divines amongst rocky pools, late 19th century, 23cm. high. (Christie's London) $2,500

A Satsuma koro and cover of quatrefoil shape decorated with four rectangular panels depicting warriors, ladies and pastoral scenes, signed *Hoen Seizo*, late 19th century, 8.5cm high. (Christie's London) $1,500

A Satsuma deep bowl decorated with a bamboo grove, the stalks issuing from a central mass of peony, chrysanthemum and other flowers, late 19th century, 14cm. diam. (Christie's London) $6,750

A Satsuma koro and cover decorated with a continuous pattern of two sprays of flowers and grasses, signed *Shozan*, late 19th century, 14cm. high. (Christie's London) $4,500

Satsuma pottery floor vase, late 19th century, one side decorated with samurai, the other with birds and an overall gilt moriage enamel ground, 59in. high. (Skinner Inc.) $7,500

A pair of tapering rectangular Satsuma vases decorated with four shaped panels surrounded by flowers and foliage, signed *Ryokuzan*, late 19th century, 24.5cm. high. (Christie's London) $6,000

A Satsuma molded baluster vase decorated with various sages and scholars, oni and beasts under the boughs of a pine tree, signed *Satsuma yaki Tomonobu*, late 19th century, 45cm. high. (Christie's London) $5,600

SAVONA

The Ligurian coast thrived as a pottery center from the sixteenth century. Most commonly found today, however, are the wares marked with the arms of Savona or a crudely drawn lighthouse, dating from the seventeenth and eighteenth centuries. These tend to be heavily potted in a baroque style which imitates contemporary silver forms. The decoration is usually in blue, and in Ming style. Sometimes rather crudely painted polychrome pieces also appear.

One of the major workshops was that of Sebastian Falco, whose pieces bear a falcon mark. He specialised in a speckled manganese ground with tiny scenes in reserved panels.

The Borelli family too were making tin-glazed earthenware as early as 1735, in the Castelli style, and the family tradition was maintained into the early nineteenth century. They produced some figures, some painted and some in the biscuit state, and a pleasant butter-colored creamware.

A rare armorial wine pail, probably Savona, painted with a frieze of stylised birds, buildings and plants, 19cm. high. (Phillips London) $2,040

A Savona blue and white armorial ewer of waisted baluster form, the loop handle with mask terminal, the body with the quartered Arms flanked by foliage, circa 1740, 28.5cm. high. (Christie's) $4,200

A pair of Savona faience figures of a gardener leaning on a watering can, his companion with a hurdy-gurdy, circa 1760, 20cm. high. (Christie's London) $3,600

A Savona dated figure of Winter modeled as a bearded man clasping a fur-lined yellow cloak about his shoulders, incised with the date 1779, 33.5cm. high. (Christie's) $3,000

A Savona blue and white oviform wet-drug jar, titled in manganese *S. de Pharfara* between bands of foliage, circa 1720, 7³/₄in. high. (Christie's) $548

A Savona blue and white fountain with loop-over handle, circa 1700, 59cm. high. (Christie's) $6,000

A large Savona charger painted in blue with a figure of Neptune in a shell-shaped chariot, 46cm., shield mark. (Phillips) $2,500

SCRATCH BLUE

The term scratch blue is used to refer to a white salt glazed stoneware which is decorated with incised inscriptions in the form of stylized flowers, birds or rouletted patterns. These were filled in with a substance called zaffer before firing.

Zaffer, or sometimes zaffre, is a word of Arabic origin referring to an impure cobalt oxide which was obtained by fusing the mineral ore with sand. (Zaffer was also used, together with potassium carbonate and silica in the manufacture of smalt. This was a blue pigment which was imported into England from Saxony until native deposits of cobalt oxide were found. It was used as an enamel, as an underglaze color for underglaze grounds and for tinting certain bodies.)

With zaffer a dark, impure blue was formed.

Scratch blue wares were made between 1724 and 1776 in Staffordshire and possibly too at Liverpool and elsewhere in England.

Doulton revived the technique in the 1870s, using black and brown pigments instead of blue. This was known as scratch brown ware.

A 'Scratch Blue' saltglaze sauceboat of silver shape, incised and colored in blue with a simple flower spray on both sides, 15.5cm., circa 1750–60. (Phillips) $675

A 'scratch blue' saltglaze puzzle jug, the rim with three pinecone molded spouts (two missing), 21.5cm. high. (Phillips) $4,250

A jug with incised scrolling brown foliage and applied white bead work, c.m., 1876, 6¾in. high. $200

A mid 18th century white saltglazed stoneware scratch blue short pedestal loving cup, all-over incised with flower heads and leaves, 19.5cm. high. (Spencer's) $800

A documentary Bovey Tracey saltglaze scratch-blue inscribed and dated rectangular tea-caddy, 1768, 11.5cm. high. (Christie's) $2,750

A Staffordshire saltglaze scratch-blue dated two-handled cup, each side incised with trailing flowering branches and with the initials *H:W.* above the date 1756, 30.5cm. wide. (Christie's) $18,000

An early jug, incised in a white ground with herons standing in water, o.m., 1874, 7½in. high. $325

207

SÈVRES

Porcelain production began at Sèvres in 1756 when the Vincennes factory was moved there, and the first 14 years of its output are considered by many to be unsurpassed.

At first, a soft paste porcelain was made, with silky glazes and richly ornate decoration. It was hugely expensive to make, however, and had the further disadvantage that it could not be molded into complex shapes, which tended to fracture in the kiln. Nevertheless, it was dear to the heart of Louis XV, who was wholly responsible for funding the operation, and his mistress Mme de Pompadour. He assisted it further by issuing several decrees granting virtual monopolies in favor of Sèvres, and even acted as salesman in chief, holding annual exhibitions at Versailles and selling off the pieces to his court.

Sèvres products are remarkable for their brilliant ground colors and chemists were constantly at work developing new tones. Honey gilding, then a virtually new technique, was also widely used, while a host of flower and figure painters (Louis engaged fan painters for this) added their designs. With regard to form, tableware shapes largely followed those of the delicate lines of contemporary silver. Sèvres was also famous for its soft-paste biscuit models, notably in the period 1757-66, when Etienne Maurice Falconet was chief modeler.

By 1769, Sèvres was moving over to hard paste manufacture, and this period coincided with a change to more severe, neo-Classical forms, while decoration too became very much simpler. On many pieces, indeed, this was reduced to a simple ground color with gilding.

A Sèvres saucer painted by Falot and gilded by Prevost, the center painted with doves, date mark for 1781.
(Bearne's) $330

A Sèvres white porcelain group of Diana the huntress and two other figures on a rocky outcrop, 33cm. total height.
(Bearne's) $900

A pair of Sèvres style turquoise ground vases with pointed oviform bodies painted with figures of a lady and gentleman in 18th century costume, 29.5cm.
(Phillips) $935

A 19th century French giltwood occasional table set with a 'Sèvres' porcelain dish, the central oval panel painted with two lovers and a goat resting in a landscape signed Boucher, 1ft. 5in. wide.
(Spencer's) $625

A Sèvres Empire cabinet-cup and saucer painted with a portrait medallion of Darnalt on a silver ground with foliage swags, circa 1820.
(Christie's). $1,750

Sèvres porcelain covered urn, late 19th century, retailed by Bailey, Banks and Biddle, signed "G. Poiterin", 22in. high.
(Skinner Inc.) $1,600

SÈVRES

Ground colors changed too, not always for the better. Nor did biscuit figures adapt very well, having a grayer cast in hard paste and becoming more classical in form. After the departure of Falconet for the Russian court, various sculptors were employed to produce reduced size copies of their own works, and they sought to reproduce in the new medium, the appearance of marble, but without surface glaze or shine.

On the abolition of the monarchy Sèvres was taken over by the State in 1793. Under Napoleon's appointee Brogniart, soft paste was finally abandoned (it was revived again in the late 1840s) in favor of a new hard paste formula which was particularly suitable for tableware.

Soft paste wares are clearly marked in blue enamel with the usual crossed *Ls* motif and a date letter (doubled after 1777). In hard paste, a crown is placed above the blue mark from 1769-79. After 1793 a date appears instead of the letter.

Fake Sèvres pieces abound, and it is important to be able to distinguish between hard and soft paste wares. This can be done by viewing obliquely so that the light penetrates both the ground color and the painting. If it is soft paste, the transparency will be seen to be consistent throughout. On hard paste the painting will form a slight shadow against the close texture of the paste over which both glaze and color form a thin coating.

Genuine Sèvres soft paste porcelain has a virtually clear glaze, not uneven as found in forgeries. On more recent forgeries too the colors are not blended with the glaze as was the case with the originals.

A Sevres bleu de roi ground tasse litron and saucer, reserved with garlands of pink roses, 1766. (Christie's Geneva) $1,300

A Sevres plate, painted with fishermen in two panels, with two others of fish and shellfish, 26.5cm. (Lawrence Fine Arts) $850

A Sevres vase hollandois and pierced stand painted en camaieu bleu with cottages and figures in rural landscapes, painter's mark script N to both pieces, 1757, 20cm. wide. (Christie's London) $9,000

Pair of Sevres ormolu mounted vases, 19th century, decorated with continuous landscape containing a maiden and putto, signed *Labarre*, 28½in. high. (Skinner Inc) $2,000

A Sevres caisse a fleurs, the sides painted in colors with sprays of wild flowers within camieu bleu rose and trellis borders, date letter G for 1759, 17.5cm. (Christie's London) $5,750

A Sevres two handled seau a bouteille, painted in colors with large sprays of garden flowers, date letter H for 1760, painter's mark for Rosset, 19.5cm. high. (Christie's London) $5,500

SEVRES

SHELLEY

The Shelley Pottery grew out of the Foley factory in the 1920s. They produced very fine teawares in a strong Art Deco style, the cups sometimes in inverted conical shapes with triangular handles, or curved octagonal shapes. These were decorated with bold colored motifs, such as geometric patterns, sunbursts or peacock tails. They also produced novelty pieces such as Humpty Dumpty teapots.

They later became Royal Albert and form part of the Doulton group.

A Shelley Intarsio teapot in the form of a caricature of Austin Chamberlain. (William H. Brown) **$500**

A Shelley bone china figure, designed by Mabel Lucie Attwell, of a pixie in green costume jumping over a log, 3in. high. (Christie's) **$275**

A Shelley Regent part coffee set printed and painted with sprays of primroses. (Christie's) **$375**

A Shelley 'Pixie' part tea set designed by Mabel Lucie Attwell, comprising pixie house teapot and cover, two toadstool sugar bowls and pixie mug, 5½in. high. (Christie's) **$360**

A Shelley Vogue bone china part coffee set printed and painted with overlapping rectangles in orange and black. (Christie's) **$450**

A Shelley 'Animal' teaset designed by Mabel Lucie Attwell modeled as duck, rabbit and chick in sailor costumes. (Christie's) **$1,100**

A Shelley nursery teapot by Hilda Cowham, modeled as a marquee and printed with two seated children reading, 5in. high. (Christie's S. Ken) **$500**

Part of a forty-piece Shelley white porcelain teaset in gray, black and yellow. **$1,000**

SICILIAN

Maiolica was produced in Sicily basically in imitation of the style of the North Italian centers such as Faenze, Venice and Tuscany, though the results tend to be cruder and more rustic than their prototypes. The areas of Caltagirone and Trapani were two major potting centers on the island.

As is often the case with a devolved art, Sicily went on producing this type of maiolica long after the vogue had passed in the north, and most examples date from the 17th century.

Marks are very rare: *SPQP* is occasionally found, indicating Palerman origin.

One of three 17th century Sicilian waisted albarelli, approx. 24cm. high. (Christie's) $800

One of two 17th century Sicilian drug jars with narrow necks, 23cm. high. (Christie's) $1,250

One of a pair of 17th century Sicilian wet-drug jars with scroll handles, 25cm. high. (Christie's) $2,000

A Sicilian (Trapani) waisted armorial albarello painted in yellow, green and blue with an armorial device, circa 1620, 20.5cm. high. (Christie's) $1,350

A Sicilian oviform vase painted with a portrait of a helmeted soldier, dated 1662, 37cm. high. (Christie's) $900

One of three 17th century Sicilian waisted albarelli painted in yellow, green and blue, approx. 23cm. high. (Christie's) $1,300

A Sicilian Caltagirone albarello painted in colors with two portrait heads on yellow grounds, mid 17th century, 31.5cm. high. (Christie's London) $2,250

A Sicilian (Trapani) blue and white waisted albarello painted with stylised flowers, late 16th century, 21cm. high. (Christie's) $675

SIENA

The Tuscan town of Siena had a flourishing maiolica industry from the 13th century onwards, but reached its heyday from around the early 16th century, when apothecary pots, dishes depicting Biblical characters and tiles, many for the Petrucci palace, were produced in considerable numbers. These show a marked preference for an opaque dark orange tone.

In the 18th century dishes and panels were produced by Ferdinando Maria Campani and Bartolomeo Terchi, which lean towards Castelli in style. They feature principally buffs and light blues, and Terchi also makes use of a very dark brown.

CHINA

A pair of Siena wall-plaques, painted with an elephant and a porcupine in rocky wooded landscapes, Bartolomeo Terchi's factory, circa 1740, 28cm. high. (Christie's) $2,600

A Siena wall-plaque painted in blue with buildings in a rocky wooded landscape, within an ocher and brown marbled pierced frame molded with putti, circa 1740, 46.5cm. high. (Christie's) $3,000

A pair of Siena massive campana-shaped ewers with molded gilt-winged caryatid handles and an applied gilt foliate mask beneath the lip, the bodies painted with Bacchic fauns, circa 1730, 63cm. high. (Christie's) $32,000

A pair of Siena wall-plaques, the centers painted with a snail and a turkey in rocky wooded landscapes with a town in the distance, Bartolomeo Terchi's factory, circa 1740, 28.5cm. high. (Christie's) $5,000

SLIPWARE

Slipware is the earliest characteristically English earthenware, which gets its name from the creamy mixture of clay and water, known as slip, which was used for its decoration. Slip could either be painted on over large areas, trailed in lines or dots from a quill spouted pot, or combed into the surface of a piece. Many artists also used it to impart color interest to a piece.

A slipware dish decorated with a black-coated hussar riding a cream-slip horse with brown spots, upper Austria, circa 1790, 31cm. diameter. (Christie's) $2,000

A slipware dated dish decorated with a sgraffiato merhorse flanked by the initials *G.S.T.* and *M.S.T.*, probably upper Austria, 1790, 28.5cm. diameter. (Christie's) $1,850

SONG

It was during the Song or Sung period, from 960–1279 AD, that potters became established as respected craftsmen on a par with the bronze worker and the jade carver, and the pieces they produced were strongly impressionistic and naturalistic in style.

Their wares were made in the simplest ways with little painting or embellishment. Most were wholly undecorated or enhanced by molding, stamping, the application of clay reliefs or etching. All these processes were carried out while the clay was still unfired. The glaze was added and the whole was then subjected to a single firing.

Song glazes tend to be thick and hard, and any crackle is positive and well-defined. They consisted basically of two types, a thick, opalescent glaze of pale lavender or turquoise, and a smooth, translucent celadon glaze with a predominantly green tint. Varying color effects were achieved by the use of different oxides, doubtless at first by accident, but they were soon obviously being achieved systematically.

A Cizhou painted pillow molded from two parts as a lady recumbent, Song Dynasty, 33cm. wide. $15,000

A Ding type stem bowl, ivory white glaze, Northern Song Dynasty, 8.9cm. diam. $1,100

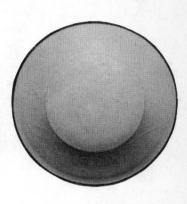

A Dingyao bottle potted in the form of a contemporary metal prototype, N. Song Dynasty, 25cm. high, fitted box. $100,000

A Dingyao dish carved with a feathery lotus spray and scrolling leaves, N. Song Dynasty, 20.7cm. diam., fitted box. $25,000

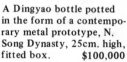

A Yingqing fluted baluster vase with S-scroll handles on the flaring neck, Song Dynasty, 17.2cm. high. $700

A Jun Yao bowl, the sides under a lightly-crackled lavender glaze, S. Song Dynasty, 11.3cm. diam. $4,000

A Henan black-glazed baluster vase, meiping, freely painted, Song Dynasty, 22cm. high. (Christie's) $4,500

SPODE

As early as 1762 Josiah Spode started developing his Staffordshire pottery, which, under his descendants, became the first in England to introduce bone china bodies at the end of the 18th century. Spode's shapes were mostly plain, with correspondingly simple but elegant decoration, or alternatively elaborate Japanese patterns. The bulk of the factory's production consisted of printed pottery and the porcelain was really only a sideline.

The company was bought in 1833 by Thomas Copeland (q.v.). From 1970, however, it has again traded as Spode Ltd.

Most pieces were marked *Spode*, with a pattern number in red. The earliest sometimes have impressed marks.

A Spode 'Beaded-Hoop' decorated with pattern no. 1106, circa 1810-20. 3½in. diam. $800

An attractive pair of Spode candle extinguishers on a small rectangular tray with loop handle, 12.5cm., impressed workman's mark. (Phillips) $750

A pair of Spode gold-ground flared cylindrical vases painted with groups of luxuriant fruit and flowers on the rich gold ground, between white beaded rims, one vase with red mark and pattern no. 711, circa 1815, 16.5cm. high. (Christie's London) $3,300

A Spode porcelain 'Beaded New Shape' jar and cover with gilt ball finial and loop handles, pattern No. 1166, 10½in. high. (Dacre, Son & Hartley) $6,000

A Spode two handled vase, painted in Imari palette with panels of flowers on a blue and gilded ground, 16cm. (Phillips London) $750

A Spode porcelain pastille burner in the form of a large house with two windows in the gable end. (Bearne's) $1,900

An early 19th century ironstone baluster jar and cover, possibly Spode, 46cm. high. $650

STAFFORDSHIRE

Devotees of Arnold Bennett's novels about the Five Towns will be aware of the names Fenton, Longton, Hanley, Burslem, Tunstall and Burmantofts – Bennett left one out – which were the center of the great pottery industry of the 19th century. It was there that Staffordshire figures were produced in their thousands and bought with eagerness to adorn chest tops and mantlepieces in homes all over the country. At one time there were over 400 factories going full blast in the area around Stoke on Trent to satisfy the demand.

Staffordshire figures were unsophisticated in their modeling and cast in the shape of popular heroes or characters from stories, plays and poetry. There was an especially popular line in politicians and heroes like Wellington and Nelson. They were press molded and decorated in underglaze blue and black with touches of color in overglaze enamel and gilding. Early examples have closed bases or a small hole in the base while 20th century pieces are usually slip cast in Plaster of Paris molds and are open ended.

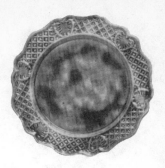

A Staffordshire small green-glazed plate, with molded dia-per-pattern border, circa 1770, 19.5cm. diam. (Christie's) **$600**

A Staffordshire spill-vase modeled as a ram, circa 1845, 4½in. high. (Christie's) **$150**

A Staffordshire jug, decorated with a band of silver luster with a pattern of scrolling flower branches, 12cm. (Lawrence Fine Arts) **$225**

A Staffordshire solid-agate tapering hexagonal choco-late-pot and domed cover, (cover restored) circa 1750, 22.5cm. high. (Christie's) **$9,000**

A Staffordshire toby jug in the form of a man seated hol-ding a jug of foaming ale, the base marked Walton, 10¼in. (Lawrence Fine Arts) **$600**

A pair of colorful Staffordshire pottery zebra vases, each animal with head held high, 27.5cm. high. (Bearne's) **$750**

A Staffordshire pottery figure of Andromache in a cream robe, leaning on an urn, circa 1790, 22.5cm. (Osmond Tricks) **$130**

STONEWARE

Salt glazed stoneware is a very old method of making pottery and there had been workshops producing this sort of ware at Lambeth in South London for many centuries when John Doulton started to work there in 1815. He made salt glazed domestic jars, bottles and barrels in brown with a slip glaze using the same methods as potters had used since the Middle Ages. John's son Henry realised the potential of stoneware when he followed his father into the business. He expanded the firm's operations into architectural stoneware and then the decorative stoneware which was to make the family fortune. In 1866 he encouraged students from the nearby Lambeth School of Art to come to work in a studio he attached to his pottery and allowed them complete licence to experiment and make everything they wanted. He was fortunate in having as protegés gifted people like the famous Barlow family, Frank Butler, George Tinworth and Eliza Simmance. Their work was shown abroad, particularly at Paris in the 1867 Exhibition, where it created a sensation that put Doulton's name on the international art map.

A stoneware jug by Thomas Samuel Haile, with strap handle, 19.9cm. high. (Christie's)　　$500

A buff stoneware 'Gothic Windows' jug, possibly Charles Meigh, 9¹/₂in. high. (Christie's S. Ken)　　$200

An Annaberg stoneware baluster jug molded and colored with a crowned king on horseback and holding his orb, with a coat-of-arms and the date 1689, 25.5cm. high. (Christie's)　　$1,300

A Pierre Fondu stoneware amphora vase, covered in an olive-brown and blue crystalline glaze, 57.9cm. high. (Christie's)　　$1,000

A Brameld light buff stoneware jug, decorated with a stag at bay and equestrian figures, having an entwined serpent handle, 7in. high. (Woolley & Wallis)　　$250

Important and unique stoneware crock with cobalt decoration of two deer flanking an eight-inch diameter pocket watch, 13in. high. (Eldred's)　　$35,000

A massive Kreussen armorial stoneware marriage Krug, molded all over and painted in enamels, possibly 17th century, with pewter mount, 49cm. high. (Christie's)　　$1,500

STRASBOURG

The Rococo style is seen at its best in the faience of Strasbourg, which was intended mostly for the German market.

The factory there was established in 1721 by Charles-François Hannong and its wares initially followed the Rouen style. In 1739 however Paul-Antoine Hannong became artistic director and he started making full use of the 'grand feu' colors, as well as gilding.

The arrival of several leading German painters in Strasbourg enabled Hannong by 1750 to become the first faience producer to decorate his wares in the full palette of enamel colors as used on porcelain. Perhaps the most striking of these was a rich crimson.

The monogram initials of Paul Hannong *(PH)* and Joseph Hannong *(JH)* are frequently seen on 19th century reproductions.

Mid 18th century Strasbourg figure of a wild boar.
$10,500

A Strasbourg oval dish with pierced border, blue H/860 mark, circa 1770, 30cm. wide. (Christie's) $325

A large Strasbourg surtout-de-table, circa 1750, 52cm. high, the plateau 64cm. wide.
$6,500

Strasbourg shaped circular dish painted with flowers, circa 1750, 47cm. diameter. $2,250

A Strasbourg blue and white octagonal dish, circa 1730, 11½in. wide.
$1,750

Mid 18th century Strasbourg figure of a dog. $7,500

One of a pair of mid 18th century Strasbourg hexafoil plates, 24cm. diam. (Christie's) $750

SUNDERLAND

In the 19th century Sunderland became a popular pottery center, where many factories specialised in producing commemorative wares and gifts for sailors. These consisted mainly of jugs, wall plaques and mugs, bearing some painted scene, a motto or doggerel, usually in a pink luster frame, which was 'splashed' to give a blotched appearance.

The pictures which appeared on these are fairly limited in range, common themes being the Wearmouth Bridge, a balloon ascent and the 'Sailor's Return' or 'The Sailor's Farewell', or simply sailing ships.

Many other factories, from nearby Newcastle to far away Swansea, copied Sunderland luster ware, and as most pieces are unmarked, it is often difficult to make a confident attribution, though many genuine Sunderland wares were made as presentation pieces, and the name and date on these can be very useful.

Genuine Sunderland commands a premium among luster wares, and another criterion is the rarity of the scene or verse which appears on a piece. Some were used again and again, while others have survived on only a few pieces.

A rare Sunderland Reform mug, printed in black with green and pink luster washes, with half length portrait of 'William the IV', 12cm. (Phillips) $600

Sunderland luster pottery chamber pot with an applied frog and cartoon face in the interior. $500

Sunderland luster jug, inscribed 'Francis & Betsy Taylor', circa 1845, 9¼in. high. $600

Early 19th century Sunderland luster pottery jug, 4¾in. high. $275

A Sunderland luster oviform jug, 9½in. high, circa 1830. (Christie's) $475

A Sunderland luster jug decorated in colours with scenes and insignia relating to the Alliance of England and France, 17cm. (Phillips) $500

A Sunderland pink luster jug printed in black with a portrait bust of Earl Grey and inscribed 'The Choice of the People and England's Glory', 19cm. (Phillips) $800

SWANSEA

The history of the Swansea pottery is closely bound up with that of Nantgarw, after the proprietor of the Cambrian pottery in Swansea, L W Dillwyn, brought William Billingsley and Samuel Walker from there in 1814.

Dillwyn, however, wanted a more reliable porcelain body than had been made at Nantgarw, and in response Walker was to produce three bodies for him. The first was a fine and light porcelain using bone ash, which had a duck-egg blue translucence. Whilst expensive to make, it found great favor in London. The second was a glassy looking porcelain using soaprock, and the third a lightly pitted glaze with a brown translucence. This was marked with a trident and is now known by that name, but it was not popular.

Like Nantgarw, Swansea styles show a strong French influence, but it is that of the Empire rather than Sèvres. There is less scroll and ribbon molding and painting is often sparing, with plates often quite plain in shape.

The Swansea body was much stronger than that of Nantgarw, and thus many more upright shapes were produced. Swansea is in fact notable for its wide range of shapes. A few biscuit figures of sheep were even produced in 1817, together with biscuit plaques with applied flowers.

Like Nantgarw, distribution in 1816–7 was mainly through Mortlock in London, but a smaller proportion of pieces was put out for decoration. It was Billingsley who supervised in-house painting at Swansea, with a predilection for flowers and landscapes in very delicate colors. Other flower painters who worked with him there were David Evans, William Pollard and Henry Morris.

A Swansea London-decorated flared cylindrical cabinet cup, painted with a continuous band of garden flowers, circa 1815, 9cm. high. (Christie's)　$750

A Swansea oviform vase, painted with a wooded landscape vignette and a lakeland scene, circa 1815, 26cm. high. (Christie's)　$6,000

A Swansea pot-pourri vase and pierced cover of campana shape, painted by David Evans, with a frieze of garden flowers, circa 1820, 13.5cm. high. (Christie's)　$3,000

A Swansea porcelain plate from the Lysaght service, painted by Henry Morris, 24.3cm., early 19th century. (Bearne's)　$600

A Swansea miniature cabinet cup and saucer painted by William Pollard with bands of wild flowers, circa 1815. (Christie's)　$1,000

A Swansea oviform vase with flared neck and gilt eagle handles, painted by David Evans, red stencil mark, circa 1815, 15cm. high. (Christie's)　$2,500

TANG

The ancient custom of
burying the dead alongside
many of the items which
surrounded them in life has
contributed greatly to our
understanding of earlier
times, and most of the pottery
which survives from the
Tang period (618–906 AD)
does in fact come from such
burial sites.

These show that Tang
potters were able to carve
figures with skill and
refinement from bodies
ranging from soft
earthenware to a hard
porcelain-like stoneware,
which varies in color from
light gray and rosy buff to
white.

They are usually covered
with a thin, finely crackled
glaze, either pale yellow or
green in color, though some
are more richly coated with
amber brown or leaf green
glazes. Splashing, streaking
and mottling are all
characteristics of Tang
pieces, which presage the
Staffordshire Whieldon and
agate ware of 1000 years
later. Marbling of the ware
by blending light and dark
clays in the body was also
achieved, and again this was
to be reproduced much later
in the 'solid agate' ware of
Staffordshire.

Of all the figures found in
Tang pottery, the horse is
conspicuous both for its
frequency and for the spirit
and character with which it is
portrayed.

Some Western influences
can be seen in Tang pottery,
and certainly there were
many contacts with the near
East at the time. Typical
examples are the egg-and-
tongue and honeysuckle
patterns to be found in border
designs, which show clear
Graeco-Roman influence.

A fine blue glazed footed bowl,
with thinly potted rounded sides,
Tang Dynasty, 11cm. diam.
(Christie's) $4,000

A red pottery figure of a
mounted attendant, Tang
Dynasty, 31.5cm. high.
                         $1,750

A Sancai pottery figure of a
horse, standing foresquare on a
rectangular base, well modeled
with strongly contoured flanks
and facial features, Tang
Dynasty, 50.5cm. high.
(Christie's) $16,500

A Sancai buff pottery
globular jar, Tang Dynasty,
16.8cm. high. $4,500

A rare blue-splashed Sancai
tripod censer, Tang Dynasty, the
body covered with blue, green,
orchid and white splashes
streaking toward the base,
7¹/₂ in. diameter.
(Christie's) $15,600

An unglazed buff pottery
figure of a seated lady
musician, Tang Dynasty,
19.5cm. high. $2,000

TOURNAI

CHINA

The Tournai porcelain factory opened in 1751 when Joseph Peterinck was granted a patent by the Empress Maria Theresa. A soft paste porcelain was manufactured, at first with a slightly grayish hue, but after 1765 it became much creamier.

The decoration owed much to Meissen styles, and commonly depicted flowers, landscapes, castle scenes etc. Much of the finest bird and flower painting is attributed to Henri-Joseph Duvivier, who was chief painter at Tournai between 1763–71.

A blue enamel ground is common on Tournai pieces and later bird painting from Buffon's *Histoire Naturelle des Oiseaux* was done by Jean-Ghislain-Joseph Mayer, who became head painter in 1774.

Many English potters and painters were employed at Tournai during the early period and much of their output bears a strong resemblance to Derby, Worcester and Chelsea pieces of the period. Groups and figures were produced by Nicholas-Joseph Gavron and by Joseph Willems, a sculptor from the Chelsea factory, and, after his death in 1766, by Antoine Gillis and Nicholas Lecreux. Groups were often left white, but sometimes painted in strong enamels.

When Peterinck died his son took over for a short time, before leaving to establish his own factory in the town in 1800. The original factory was bought by the de Bettignies family who kept it until it was taken over by the Boch brothers in 1850. It was during the de Bettignies period that many flagrant forgeries of Sèvres, Chelsea and Worcester pieces were produced.

Early marks include a tower either in enamels or gold.

A porcelain snuff box mounted in England en cage in gold, possibly Tournai, circa 1765, 7.5cm. wide. $9,000

One of a pair of mid 18th century Tournai faience pug dogs, after the original Meissen models by J. J. Kaendler, 15.5cm. high. $11,000

A Tournai ornithological oviform jar and cover from the Duc d'Orleans service, circa 1787, 18.5cm. high. $1,500

A Tournai spirally-molded plate painted by Henri Joseph Duvivier in puce camaieu with a coastal scene, a man on horseback urging his cattle towards a boat, circa 1765, 23cm. diameter. (Christie's) $2,500

A Tournai fable teacup and saucer painted in the manner of Duvivier with 'The Fox and The Crane', gilt castle marks, circa 1765.
(Christie's) $1,650

One of a pair of Tournai two-handled seaux a glace covers and liners with molded Ozier borders, circa 1770, 25cm. wide. $400

URBINO

Urbino, the capital of the Duchy of the same name, became a maiolica center only in 1520, when "Guido da Castello Durante" established a workshop there. Guido was the son of Nicola Pellipario, who had worked at Castel Durante, and his father joined him at Urbino in 1527. It was Nicola Pellipario who popularised the istoriato style, with which Urbino came to be especially associated.

Their Fontana workshop produced many pieces, including large wine coolers, salvers, pilgrim bottles and stands, with a characteristic decoration of arabesques and grotesques painted in color on a white ground edged in yellow and picked out in orange. Guido's son Orazio Fontana, started up his own workshop next door in 1565, and where pieces are unsigned, it is difficult to tell whose workmanship they are.

The work of the painter Francesco Xanto Avelli is fairly easy to distinguish, however, for he specialised in crowded scenes, almost like stage settings, featuring characters with very rounded limbs and his favorite tones were bright yellows and orange.

There are many recent imitations of the Urbino grotesque-arabesque style, but these can usually be distinguished by the pen-like draughtsmanship of the painting, which indicates that the white tin-glaze ground had been fired first to make painting easier. Beware too a pinkish purple tone which the 16th century artist did not possess.

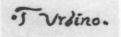

An Urbino Istoriato dish painted in the Fontana workshop with Proserpine and her companions, circa 1570, 27.5cm. diam. (Christie's)　$25,000

An Urbino istoriato plate painted with the Temptation of Adam, circa 1560, 23cm. diam. (Christie's)　$5,000

An Urbino istoriato tazza painted with Marcus Curtius leaping into the abyss on a white stallion surrounded by soldiers before a tree, circa 1545, 25.5cm. diameter. (Christie's)　$10,000

An Urbino maiolica accouchement bowl painted inside the deep bowl with an expectant mother and child, 15.5cm. diameter, Patanazzi workshop, last quarter 16th century. (Phillips)　$2,250

An Urbino Istoriato dish painted with a figure of a bearded man, possibly intended for Hercules, 26cm. (Phillips)　$2,500

A very spirited Urbino Istoriato plate painted by Francesco Durantino, showing the victorious Scipio, 29cm. (Phillips)　$18,750

VENICE

Though some pieces of Venetian faience can be dated back to 1520, production did not begin in any quantity until the middle of the century. As a major trading port, Venice was obviously open to Middle and Far Eastern influences and this is reflected in the pottery which was produced there.

Ground colors are often stained to a lavender blue, with the decoration painted in strong cobalt, relieved only occasionally with a little opaque white or yellow.

A Venice plate painted in colors with the Children of Venus, 23.5cm. diam. (Christie's) $2,500

One of a pair of mid 16th century Venetian vasi a palli, 33cm. high. (Christie's) $20,000

A Venice istoriato dish of shallow cardinal's hat form, painted with the story of Jacob and the Angel, workshop of Domenico da Venezia, circa 1560, 30cm. diameter. (Christie's) $8,000

A large Venetian Berretino albarello, painted with an elaborate scroll inscribed with the name of the contents *Mo Franda F,* 17th century, 34cm. high. (Christie's London) $4,250

A Venice vaso a palla with the portrait heads of two saints in cartouches, circa 1550, 28cm. high. (Christie's) $8,000

A Venetian drug bottle painted with portraits of a Turk and a soldier, second half of 16th century, 23cm. high. (Christie's) $4,000

A Venice Istoriato saucer dish painted with Apollo slaying the children of Niobe, circa 1560, 29.5cm. diam. (Christie's) $26,000

An attractive Venice albarello of cylindrical form, painted in colors with bands of convolvulus on a scrolling blue ground, 14.5cm. (Phillips) $1,750

VIENNA

The porcelain factory of Claude Innocent Du Paquier was established in Vienna during the early years of the 18th century. Though it received no state patronage, the Emperor granted it many privileges and it became the second factory in Europe to commence hard paste porcelain manufacture, following the defection of the Meissen arcanist Stölzel in 1719 and Böttger's half-brother, Tiemann who brought the kiln designs from that factory.

Early Vienna porcelain can be distinguished from Meissen by the flatness of the glaze, which becomes greenish when thickly applied, and footrims tend to be rough and unglazed. Like Meissen, the early designs owe much to silver shapes.

Apart from adopting architectural features in their forms, such as gadrooning and fluting, Viennese designers also borrowed shapes from Dutch delftware. Three features which became highly characteristic of Viennese decoration were plastic decoration, baroque scrollwork and Japanese 'sprigs'.

There was some copying of figures from Meissen originals, and many fine pieces were made as gifts for the Russian court. By 1725 iron red, green, purple, pink, yellow and blue enamels were being used, and these were softer in tone than the brilliance of their Meissen counterparts. Schwarzlot, black enamel painting with a brush or point, was much in evidence to depict putti, animals, mythological or hunting scenes. Tableware bearing this last decoration are known as Jagd services.

The factory's output was set firmly in the Baroque tradition, as reflected in the Laub and Bandelwerk (scroll and foliage) and naturalistic

A Vienna (Dupaquier) rect-angular casket and liner, circa 1728, in a contemporary fitted leather box, 16.5 x 12cm. (Christie's) $32,500

A Vienna (Dupaquier) two-handled, double-lipped baroque molded sauceboat painted in the Imari style, circa 1740, 24.5cm. wide. (Christie's) $7,500

One of a set of six 'Vienna' porcelain plates, signed Wagner, 9½in. diam. (Capes Dunn) $2,500

A Vienna porcelain snuff box, the interior of the lid finely painted with two gentlemen seated out-of-doors at a table, drinking wine, 9cm. (Phillips London) $1,250

A Vienna Commedia dell'Arte group of Scaramouche and Pulchinella, circa 1750, 14.5cm. high. (Christie's) $12,500

A Vienna (Dupaquier) cream-pot and cover painted by Johann P. Dannhoffer, circa 1725. (Christie's) $5,000

VIENNA

deutsche Blumen decorations which are much used. The period ends with Du Paquier offering the factory to the archduchess Maria Theresa, who bought it in 1744. Du Paquier continued as director, but retired the same year and died in 1751.

During the state-owned period from 1744 there was a noticeable improvement in the quality of the color of the clay, which became whiter. Pieces were decorated now rather in Rococo style and many decorators were persuaded to come from Meissen, among them the flower painters Johann Klinger and J G Richter. From about 1760 there was a large output of Meissen-type figures, under the direction of the chief modeler from 1747–1784, J J Niedermayer. The bases of these assist in their dating, beginning as a mound with a little scrollwork, before becoming more like a flat slab and finally adopting a Neo Classical high base with vertical edging with molded and gilt designs.

The factory was again in difficulties in 1784, when a successful wool merchant, Konrad von Sorgenthal, took over as manager. The restoration of its fortunes which he brought about lasted well into the 19th century, and it did not close until 1866.

In the Sorgenthal period, neo-Classicism asserted itself, as the pieces tried to recapture the forms of classical antiquity in much the same way as Wedgwood did in England, though sometimes the decoration could become too elaborate.

A useful guide to dating post 1783 Vienna is that, in addition to the impressed shield, two or three numbers are also impressed as date marks, eg. 89 = 1789, 808 = 1808.

A 'Vienna' puce ground plate, the center painted with a scantily draped nymph standing beside a flaming altar, imitation blue beehive mark, circa 1880, 25.5cm. diam. (Christie's London) $750

A pair of Vienna vases and covers, decorated with groups of classical figures in oval panels, signed *Cauffmann*, 32cm. (Lawrence Fine Arts) $600

A Vienna style rectangular porcelain plaque with 'Fruhling' painted by Bauer, with two maidens accompanied by children, with blue beehive mark and inscription, circa 1880, 11 x 8½in. (Christie's S. Ken) $1,000

A Vienna style vase, the claret lustrous ground reserved with a shaped panel of two maidens in a garden, signed *Legles*, 14¾in. high. (Christie's S. Ken) $600

A Vienna figure of a pretzel seller standing beside a tree stump, a wicker basket slung over his left arm, holding a pretzel, circa 1760, 19.5cm. high. (Christie's London) $3,600

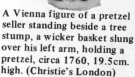

A 'Vienna' circular dish, painted by Falera with the head and shoulders of a young woman, inscribed *Coquetterie*, imitation blue beehive mark, circa 1900, 34cm. diam. (Christie's London) $800

VINCENNES

Vincennes may be said to be the birthplace of the famous Sèvres factory, whither it was removed in 1756 on the orders of King Louis XV.

The entire operation began however at Vincennes between 1738–40, when two financiers, Orry de Vignory and Orry de Fulvy were granted a permit by Louis to use the chateau there for experiments in porcelain manufacture. Their first managers, the brothers Dubois, proved unreliable and were sacked in 1741. Their assistant, François Gravant, took over and his efforts were more successful.

In 1745, with the king increasingly interested, a group of prominent figures was brought together to run the factory with the Orrys and Gravant, its capital was greatly increased, it received a 'privilege' from the king, and the period of its true greatness really began. Vincennes was something of an anachronism in that it set out only to produce soft paste porcelain. Perhaps its backers were wedded to the French traditions that had served well enough at Rouen, Chantilly and Mennecy, or perhaps it just lacked adequate supplies of kaolin, but the result was that it remained hampered by a process that was both costly and increasingly obsolete.

No such conservatism was seen in its decoration however. A new range of colors were developed, with an original range of forms and much use of gilding. Vincennes set out to compete with Meissen, but unlike Meissen pieces, the colors in the Vincennes palette were absorbed into the glaze, which on the usual white ground gave a wonderfully jewel like effect. By 1753 colored grounds were becoming increasingly popular and this led to many

A Vincennes miniature campana vase, painted in colors with sprays of heartsease, gilt rims, 6cm., interlaced L's marks. (Phillips) $650

A Vincennes circular baluster sugar-bowl and cover painted with sprays of flowers including pink roses, date letter for 1754, 8cm. diameter. (Christie's) $750

A Vincennes bleu celeste teacup and saucer (gobelet Hébert) with gilt entwined branch handle, painted with trailing flowers from cornucopia-shaped bleu celeste borders, date letter B for 1754. (Christie's) $4,000

A Vincennes bleu celeste vase duplessis of flared trumpet shape, painted in puce camaieu with Cupid among clouds within gilt scroll and flower cartouches beneath a gilt dentil rim, date letter C for 1755, 19.5cm. high. (Christie's) $10,000

A Vincennes blue celeste sugar-bowl and cover (pot à sucre du roy) painted with figures walking by buildings in wooded landscapes, date letter B for 1754, 8.5cm. diameter. (Christie's) $5,000

A Vincennes bleu lapis coffee-cup and saucer (gobelet à la reine) with loop handle, each side of the cup and the center of the saucer painted with two birds. (Christie's) $2,500

VINCENNES

pieces being covered in lapis blue, jonquil yellow and apple green. These grounds were often supplied with white reserves, which were embellished with superb miniature paintings of landscapes, dallying couples, birds, and an abundance of floral motifs. Gilding was lavish, sometimes enhanced with engraving or, in some cases, two tones of gold were used to give an even richer effect.

While much of the production consisted of tableware, Vincennes, being so closely involved with the Crown, had to maintain French international prestige, and many highly ornamental pieces, vases, urns, jardinières etc. were also produced and these were often used as Royal gifts.

Vincennes also set out to rival Meissen's figure production, and some wonderfully refined sculptures were made. Most were left in the white, but what made the essential difference was a decision in 1749 not to glaze them. The resulting biscuit had a texture akin to the finest marble and immediately became immensely popular.

After the death of the Orrys in the early 1750s, some reorganisation was urgently necessary. The King more or less took over and decreed in 1754 that the factory should remove to Sèvres. It did so in 1756, bringing the Vincennes period to a close.

Dating early Vincennes is extremely difficult. Some pieces are unmarked, others carry only crossed *Ls*. From 1753 an alphabetical date code was introduced with *A* for 1753 and so on. These dates were usually placed within the crossed *Ls*.

A Vincennes goblet litron, 7 cm. high, crossed LL mark in blue enamel.   **$700**

A Vincennes blue lapis teacup and saucer (gobelet calabre) with indented loop handle painted in puce camaieu with Cupid holding a torch and a putto with a bunch of grapes and a spear, date letter A for 1753. (Christie's)   **$4,000**

One of a pair of Vincennes two-handled small seaux in the Meissen style, blue interlaced L marks enclosing dots, circa 1752, 13.5cm. wide.   **$15,000**

A Vincennes bleu lapis conical teapot, blue interlaced L marks and painter's mark of Thevenet, circa 1753, 11cm. high.   **$1,850**

A Vincennes circular bowl, blue crowned interlaced Ls enclosing the Bourbon fleur-de-lys, circa 1752, 32.5cm. diam.   **$12,000**

A Vincennes partly glazed white biscuit figure of a sleeping putto resting on a bale of hay, circa 1753, 11cm. high.   **$1,500**

VYSE

Charles Vyse was an English sculptor and potter who studied at Hanley Art School before moving to London where he opened his studio in Chelsea in 1919. With his wife Nell, he experimented with wood ash glazes on stoneware, and also during the 1920s successfully reproduced Chinese Sung vases.

His figure groups, realistically modeled and sometimes colored, are very sought after. His work is usually marked with initials or a signature. Charles Vyse died in 1968.

A Charles Vyse figure of a Shire horse, on rectangular base, 28.5cm. high. $450

A Charles Vyse figure of a ribbon seller on a square plinth, circa 1925, 30.5cm. high, including plinth. $1,000

A Charles Vyse pottery figure of The Piccadilly Rose Woman, modeled as a plump lady, 10in. high. $800

A stoneware oviform jar by Charles Vyse, 1928, 17cm. high. (Christie's) $250

A Charles Vyse group in the form of Pan kneeling on the ground with lambs in his arms, his companion leapfrogging over his shoulders, 33cm. (Bearne's) $950

A stoneware globular vase by Charles Vyse, covered in a lustrous mottled khaki and brown glaze with areas of crimson, incised *CV 1933*, 13cm. high. (Christie's London) $750

'Fantasy', a Charles Vyse pottery group, of a woman seated cross-legged on a grassy base, scantily clad with a turquoise and mauve robe, 21.50cm. high. (Phillips) $500

A Charles Vyse oviform, stoneware vase decorated with tenmoku-brown and yellow-green tree forms, 29cm. high. (Phillips) $250

WAIN

Louis Wain (1860–1931) was an English illustrator and designer who is best remembered for his illustrations of cats engaged in human pursuits. In the early 1900s he designed series of postcards, the A-Mewsing Write-away Series, on this theme for Raphael Tuck. Between 1910–20 he also designed pottery figures of cats in the Cubist style and brightly colored in eg. green, orange and black. His work became increasingly eccentric, however, and he died in an asylum in 1931.

A Louis Wain porcelain Bull-dog vase, decorated in cream, yellow, green, russet and black enamels, 14.5cm. long. (Christie's) $1,350

A Louis Wain porcelain vase, decorated in blue, green, yellow and russet enamels, with painted marks Louis Wain, Made in England, 14.5cm. high. (Christie's)
$500

A Louis Wain porcelain lion vase, decorated in black, yellow, green and russet enamels, 11.8cm. high. (Christie's) $1,350

A Louis Wain porcelain animal vase, the stylised figure of a dog bearing a shield, with shaped aperture on its back, 14.2cm. high. (Christie's) $1,500

A large Louis Wain pottery vase, modeled as a seated cat, 25.4cm. high. $1,850

A Louis Wain ceramic animal model of a stylised dog with squared geometric features, coloured in green, red, black and blue, 13cm. high. (Phillips London) $675

A Louis Wain porcelain cat vase, decorated in white, green, russet and black enamels, with impressed and painted marks, 15.5cm. high. (Christie's) $2,250

A Louis Wain porcelain pig vase, decorated in green, yellow, russet and black enamels, with impressed and painted marks, 12.4cm. high. (Christie's) $2,250

WEDGWOOD

Josiah Wedgwood founded his pottery at Burslem in 1759. It operated there until 1774, by which time he had already opened his Etruria factory, and the business continues in the family until the present day.

Wedgwood products were noted from the first for their high quality, and the company was always in the forefront of pioneering new techniques. One of their early successes, achieved as early as 1761, was the cream colored earthenware, durable and reasonably priced, which was known as creamware. In 1765 came a commission to supply a 60-piece tea service to Queen Charlotte, and this met with such royal satisfaction, that Wedgwood was allowed to call his recent invention Queensware, which name it has borne ever since.

In response to a call for a whiter earthenware, Wedgwood set to work again to develop pearlware, which contained more white clay and flint and was fired at a higher temperature to give a bluish white body. This again proved hugely popular and sold in great quantities between 1790-1820. Production continued until 1846.

Bone porcelain production was attempted from 1812 and successfully resumed in 1878. With Copeland and Minton, Wedgwood was in the vanguard of parian production and parian ware, notably portrait busts, were being produced from 1848 onwards.

Majolica was produced between 1860–1910 for such items as umbrella stands, plaques, comports etc., often using émaux ombrants for decoration. Tiles were also made, and usually transfer printed.

In the 1870s came other developments, such as

A Wedgwood Fairyland luster malfrey pot and cover designed by Daisy Makeig-Jones and decorated with pixies and elves, 1920's, 22cm. diam. (Christie's) $8,250

19th century blue and white Jasperware Stilton cheese dish and cover, possibly Wedgwood. (G. A. Key) $175

'Sun & Wind', a Wedgwood green and white Jasper plaque designed by Anna Katrina Zinkeisen, 12.5cm. diam. (Phillips) $450

A pair of mid 19th century Wedgwood black basalt triton candlesticks of conventional type, 28cm. high. (Christie's) $1,350

A Wedgwood creamware punch pot and cover, transfer printed in black with two oval panels of Aurora in chariots representing day and night, 25cm. (Phillips London) $1,500

A Wedgwood flame Fairyland luster tapering oviform vase with flared neck designed by Daisy Makeig-Jones, 1920's, 30cm. high. (Christie's) $1,500

WEDGWOOD

Victoria ware, with a body midway between bone porcelain and Queensware. From 1880, decoration with printed and painted landscapes and commemorative wares, often at first for the American market, began.

Jasperware had been in Wedgwood's range from the beginning. In the early years of the 20th century it began to be relief decorated not only now in lilac and green but also olive, crimson, buff, black and turquoise. At this time too luster ware production began, notably the Dragon and Fairyland luster series designed by Daisy Makeig-Jones.

Traditional designs continued – particularly at the end of the 19th century there was much harking back to earlier styles – but innovations were, at the same time, constantly being introduced. In 1940 the factory moved to Barlaston.

Marks include *Wedgwood* and from 1891 *Made in England*. Bone porcelain from 1878 is marked with a replica of the Portland Vase. Various designers also signed their works.

A rare Wedgwood creamware teapot and cover, depicting on one side the Jeremiah Meyer portrait of George III reversed with the Thomas Frye portrait of Queen Charlotte, height 4½in. (Bonhams)   **$6,500**

A good Wedgwood Fairyland luster bowl, decorated with numerous figures on a waterside, printed mark in brown, circa 1920, 8¾in. diam. (Tennants)   **$1,800**

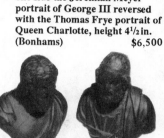

Two Wedgwood black basalt miniature busts of Homer and Aristophanes, circa 1785, 11cm. and 10cm. high. (Christie's)   **$2,000**

A rare Ralph Wedgwood & Co. creamware ovoid jug, printed in black with the full arms of the Cordwainers Company, 18cm. (Phillips London)   **$475**

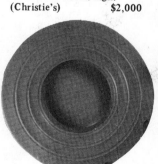

A Wedgwood creamware oval sauce tureen, cover and pierced stand, painted in the manner of James Bakewell, circa 1770, the stand 26.5cm. wide. (Christie's)   **$3,350**

A Wedgwood pottery charger designed by Keith Murray, covered in a matt straw yellow glaze, printed facsimile signature *Keith Murray,* and *Wedgwood, Made in England,* 35.5cm. diam. (Christie's London)   **$750**

A Wedgwood Boat Race cup designed by Eric Ravilious, decorated with three oval colored panels showing scenes associated with the Boat Race, 25.5cm. high. (Phillips London)   **$3,500**

WEDGWOOD & BENTLEY

In around 1770 Josiah Wedgwood arranged with Thomas Bentley for the latter to open a workshop in Cheyne Row Chelsea, where painters would be engaged in decorating creamware. Their partnership lasted for a number of years, and their catalog of 1779 shows that they were producing biscuit ware, jasperware and pearlware.

A Wedgwood & Bentley black basalt teapot and cover of globular shape with a curved collar and reeded handle, 21.5cm. wide. (Phillips London) $1,800

A Wedgwood & Bentley black basalt cylindrical ink-well, circa 1775, 7.5cm. diam. (Christie's) $450

A Wedgwood & Bentley black basalt encaustic-decorated circular sugar bowl and cover, circa 1775, 11.5cm. diam. (Christie's) $2,500

A pair of Wedgwood & Bentley black basalt griffin candlesticks, seated on their haunches, their wings raised towards the fluted nozzles, circa 1775, 33cm. high. (Christie's) $6,750

A Wedgwood & Bentley cream-ware large flower pot and stand, circa 1775, the stand 27cm. diam. (Christie's) $1,500

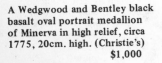

A Wedgwood and Bentley black basalt oval portrait medallion of Minerva in high relief, circa 1775, 20cm. high. (Christie's) $1,000

A Wedgwood & Bentley black basalt oval portrait medal-lion of Oldenbarneveld in high relief, circa 1780, 7cm. high. (Christie's London) $275

A Wedgwood & Bentley black basalt oval portrait medallion of Solon in high relief, circa 1775, 16cm. high. (Christie's) $475

WEDGWOOD WHIELDON

Thomas Whieldon (1719-95) was perhaps the last and greatest of the traditional Staffordshire potters using traditional potting methods. He also had an eye for talent and in 1754 took as his apprentice and then partner Josiah Wedgwood. Together they developed earthenware figures characterised by their dripping colored glazes. Whieldon is particularly associated with a tortoiseshell glaze, made by the use of a limited range of high temperature oxides. The partnership lasted until 1759, when Wedgwood struck out on his own.

A Wedgwood/Whieldon teapot and cover, with crabstock handle, circa 1765, 6in. high.
$2,750

A Wedgwood/Whieldon hexagonal teapot and cover in chinoiserie style, 16cm. high. $2,250

A mid-18th century Wedgwood Wheildon type cauliflower molded coffee pot and cover, 24.5cm. high. (Spencer's) $2,250

A Wedgwood/Whieldon cauliflower teapot and cover in shaded green colors. (A. J. Cobern) $1,100

A Wedgwood/Whieldon cauliflower molded coffee pot and domed cover, of pear shape, 25.5cm. (Phillips London) $2,250

A Wedgwood/Whieldon cauliflower teapot and cover, 11.6cm. high. $900

A creamware double rectangular tea caddy of Wedgwood/Whieldon type, circa 1760, 14.5cm. wide. (Christie's) $2,500

A Wedgwood/Whieldon lobed hexagonal teapot and cover with scrolling handle, in green with ocher streaks, 12cm. (Phillips London) $2,700

233

WEMYSS

Wemyss Ware is the most distinctive product of the Scottish potteries. Its trademarks are free flowing designs on white of roses, cherries and apples.

The pottery of Robert Heron & Sons was based at Kirkcaldy in Fife and its fame really began when a young Bohemian decorator called Karl Nekola joined the staff in 1883. He became Art Director and by the time he died in 1915 he had made Wemyss Ware famous. The name was taken from nearby Wemyss Castle, the home of the Grosvenor family who did much to popularise the pottery with their upper class friends in London. Thomas Goode and Co, the Mayfair china shop, became the sole outlet for Wemyss Ware in London and sent up special orders for individual customers.

Nekola trained other artists and also his own two sons in the work of ceramic decoration and though no pieces were signed, it is possible to identify different artists by their style. Wemyss was produced in a vast range of shapes and sizes from buttons to garden seats and the washstand sets were particularly well designed, especially the squat jug with its generous mouth.

A Wemyss character jug modeled as the Fair Maid of Perth and painted with a floral sprigged yellow dress, 21.5cm. (Phillips London) $600

Wemyss ware plant pot decorated with branches of cherries, green borders, spiral fluted body, 8½in. x 7in. (Barbers Auctions) $600

An attractive Wemyss (Bovey Tracey) model of a pig in the usual squatting pose, with ears pricked, painted all over the back and ears with sprays of flowering clover, 46cm. (Phillips) $3,000

A Wemyss vase of paneled baluster form, the shoulders with eight pierced circular panels, 38cm. (Lawrence Fine Arts) $1,250

A Wemyss Plichta cat signed *Nekola*. (R.K. Lucas) $900

A rare signed Karel Nekola Wemyss comb tray, painted with mallards and ducks by reed pond, 29.5cm. long. (Phillips) $4,000

A Wemyss sauce boat or flower holder modeled as a goose, with green neck, yellow beak, purple and blue breast. (Phillips London) $1,100

WESTERWALD

The Westerwald was one of the great stoneware centers of Germany, though little of value is recorded until the late 16th century. Jugs and Krugs were made in great numbers, often with initials and small decorations such as rosettes, lion masks and angel heads until the late 17th century. Thereafter, greater use was made of incised and combed lines which acted as barriers to contain the cobalt blue and manganese purple colors. Production of these wares continues to the present day.

A German Westerwald stoneware jug, circa 1750, 22cm. high. $5,750

Late 17th century Westerwald stoneware square flask, 22.5cm. high. (Christie's) $650

Early 18th century Westerwald oviform tankard (Birnkrug) painted in blue and manganese on the gray body, 24cm. high. (Christie's) $500

A Westerwald stoneware inverted baluster kanne molded allover with relief rosettes on a blue-ground, 32cm. high. (Christie's) $500

A German Westerwald stoneware baluster jug with horizontally ribbed neck and pewter cover and mount, 17th century, 8in. high. (Christie's S. Ken) $600

A Westerwald tankard of cylindrical shape, the body with two bands of square panels incised and molded in relief with floral motifs, 19.5cm. (Phillips London) $500

A Westerwald stoneware Sternkanne, the oviform body impressed with a starburst enclosing a heart within a circular cartouche, circa 1700, 30cm. high. (Christie's) $1,350

A Westerwald buff stoneware jug of large globular shape with cylindrical grooved neck and loop handle, circa 1700, 22cm. high. (Christie's London) $750

WHIELDON

Thomas Whieldon (1719–95) was an English potter working out of Fenton Low, or Little Fenton, in Staffordshire. He gave his name to the distinctive earthenware which he produced and which is notable for its range of colors. He was in partnership with Josiah Wedgwood from 1754–79.

No marks were used.

A 7in. 18th century Whieldon pottery study of a ram on naturalistic base. (Riddetts) $1,850

A Whieldon style teapot and cover, the portrait of Flora molded on either side with flowing hair, 14cm. high. (Bearne's) $6,500

A creamware cauliflower-molded baluster coffee-pot and cover of Whieldon type, the upper part with cream florettes and the lower part with crisply molded overlapping green leaves, circa 1765, 24.5cm. high. (Christie's) $6,750

A pair of creamware Arbour figures of Whieldon type, modeled as a musician playing the fiddle in streaked gray topcoat and yellow waistcoat, his companion in a green splashed crinoline and holding a pug dog on her lap, circa 1750, 15cm. high. (Christie's) $59,000

A Staffordshire creamware tea caddy of Whieldon type, the molded paneled sides framed by ropetwist pattern, circa 1760, 9.5cm. high. (Christie's) $750

A Whieldon cauliflower molded teapot and cover with green scrolling handle, the oviform body naturalistically modeled with green glazed leaves, 11cm. (Phillips) $1,500

A Whieldon green-ground cornucopia wall-pocket of spirally molded form, circa 1750, 26.5cm. high. $1,500

A rare and small Whieldon 'pear' teapot and cover, 8.5cm. high. (Phillips) $10,000

WOOD

The Wood family of Burslem are famous to collectors because of their high quality pottery figures made by two, if not by three, generations of Ralph Woods. Ralph Wood Senior, who died in 1772, and his brother Aaron developed an individual style for their productions which they passed onto their respective sons. Ralph's son, also named Ralph, lived between 1748 and 1795, and worked as a potter of model figures in Burslem with his cousin Enoch (died 1840). Their products were particularly noted for delicate coloring. Ralph Wood III succeeded his father Ralph but died at the early age of 27 in 1801. Some earthenware figures that bear the name mark *Ra Wood* may have been his handiwork as may also be porcelain examples. Enoch Wood started his own factory in 1784 and in 1790 went into partnership with James Caldwell, making tableware marked *Wood & Caldwell* which was shipped to America in vast quantities.

An Enoch Wood model of a lion painted in shades of dark brown with his forepaw resting on a ball, 12in. wide. (Christie's) $1,000

A Ralph Wood figure of a harvester, circa 1775, 20cm. high. (Christie's) $2,750

A pair of creamware figures of Ralph Wood type, each modeled as a youth in translucent blue, yellow and manganese clothes, circa 1780, 12.5cm. and 12cm. high. (Christie's) $650

A Ralph Wood white pearlware group of Roman Charity, the veiled woman suckling a child at her breast, circa 1790, 20cm. high. (Christie's) $900

A Ralph Wood pearlware figure of St. Peter standing holding a crucifix and a Bible under his right arm, wearing puce-lined green robe and turquoise trousers, circa 1800, 36cm. high. (Christie's) $1,100

A creamware model of a fox of Ralph Wood type, naturally modeled to the right with brown coat, a bird beneath his right forepaw, circa 1780, 9.5cm. high. (Christie's) $2,500

A Staffordshire pearlware figure of a gentleman of Ralph Wood type, wearing a black hat, his gray-lined pale-green cloak tied with a blue ribbon, circa 1785, 25cm. high. (Christie's) $2,100

WORCESTER

The history of porcelain making in Worcester is a complex one, involving a number of principal factories. The process began around 1751, when the Worcester Tonquin Manufactory was set up by a consortium of 15 local businessmen. The leading figures in the group were a local surgeon, John Wall, and an apothecary, William Davis. During this earliest, or 'Dr Wall' period, a soaprock body was perfected from experiments at Bristol. The wares were decorated both in blue and white and a colorful polychrome, in a manner which amalgamated both oriental and European influences to form a highly distinctive style of their own. The shapes of these were graceful and the painting very fine.

During the ten years from 1755, decoration became increasingly subtle, derived mainly from Meissen or Chinese ideas, and while oriental figure painting was fairly naive, flower painting reached surprising heights of sophistication.

No factory marks were used until after 1765. Between then and 1776, which is generally seen as the end of the First Period, there was an enormous output of all the standard forms in a huge range of patterns. Both potting and painting continued to be of a high standard.

Between 1757-76 transfer printing in overglaze jet black became common and took the form of either European scenes or commemorative prints, of which the most common is Frederick of Prussia. Most were engraved by Robert Hancock.

Wall retired in 1775, and Davis struggled to keep the factory going in the face of increasing competition, in particular from the Caughley

A Worcester blue-scale porcelain lobed circular plate, circa 1770, 19.5cm. diam. (Christie's) $1,250

A Worcester yellow ground armorial baluster mug with grooved loop handle, circa 1770, 12cm. high. (Christie's London) $12,500

A wide trophy-shaped vase, on a fluted circular base, the body painted with yellow and white roses, signed *J. Lander*, 19cm., date code for 1909. (Phillips) $800

A Worcester vase, painted with two Highland cattle on a misty mountainside, signed *H. Stinton*, 16.5cm., date code for 1911. (Phillips London) $1,000

A very rare Worcester wine funnel, painted in famille-rose enamels with flowering paeony branches, 9.8cm., 1753–1755. (Phillips) $22,000

A Worcester porcelain scalloped shallow dish, the center painted with sprays of flowers, 8¼in. wide. (From the Marchioness of Huntly service) circa 1770. (Dacre, Son & Hartley) $675

WORCESTER

factory, which, under Thomas Turner, had by then more or less cornered the market for blue and white.

In 1783, Davis was joined by John Flight, and after that they managed to produce some blue and white to compete with Caughley, but most was by now of an inferior quality. By the time a further new partner, Martin Barr, joined in 1793, blue and white production had ceased.

The factory had received a further blow in 1787, when Turner had persuaded Flight's chief decorators, Robert and Humphrey Chamberlain, to set up on their own as painters and decorators. The partners now decided to concentrate their efforts of producing high quality, though not always very expensive pieces, for the top end of the market. Flight improved the soaprock body with the result that tea services were now of unsurpassed thinness and translucence. They also rediscovered fine gilding.

By 1790 Chamberlain's had severed their links with the Caughley factory and were now making their own products. Because of their common backgrounds perhaps, the products which they and Flight's turned out over the next decade were very similar. Both, for example produced tea services in spiral, fluted shapes, decorated in underglaze blue with gold, or simple gold sprigs. Flight's however continued to play more for the upper end of the market, and their quality was unsurpassed.

They did, however, have to find new painters. Of these, John Pennington was the only one capable of reproducing the cabinet pieces of Sèvres. Zachariah Boreman and Joseph Hill specialised in landscapes. Between 1808–13, William

An ovoid vase, the body well painted with two Highland cattle, signed H. Stinton, 21cm. high, shape no. 1762, date code for 1910. (Phillips) **$900**

A Barr, Flight & Barr inkwell painted with a shell attributed to Samuel Smith, painted with a whelk-type shell and seaweed, 7cm.
(Phillips) **$4,500**

An early Worcester fluted coffee cup with scrolling handle, painted in famille-rose palette with trailing flower sprays, 5cm.
(Phillips) **$2,250**

A Worcester porcelain two handled pot pourri vase and cover, painted with a horizontal band of landscape within molded bands of beads, 5½in. high. (Christie's S. Ken) **$250**

A Worcester large bulbous mug printed with three flowers and four butterflies, 6in. high. (G.A.Property Services) **$450**

A Worcester blue and white baluster flaring vase painted with two tall Chinese maidens, circa 1765, 8in. high. (Christie's S. Ken) **$450**

WORCESTER

Billingsley, the greatest flower painter of the age, also worked for Flight before leaving for Swansea and Nantgarw.

By now a third Worcester factory had been opened by Thomas Grainger, who had been a manager at Chamberlains. For the next 80 years Graingers were to rival the two main factories, for while their wares were generally cheaper and aimed at the more modest end of the market, at their best they could produce pieces quite equal in quality to Flights and Chamberlains.

After the Neo-Classical period of the early 1800s, the 1820s and 30s saw a revival of a fussier, almost neo-rococo taste. Richness and extravagance were called for both in terms of shapes and decoration. Graingers and Chamberlains both answered this demand with hundreds of different, complicated designs, with each fancy border available in a selection of coordinating colors. Flights, however, failed to adjust and this failure ended in their near bankruptcy and merger with Chamberlains in 1840, when the company became known as Chamberlain & Co.

Times were getting harder for everyone, however, and the new company was failing to compete with the bigger Staffordshire factories. It was bought by Kerr & Binns in 1851 and became the Worcester Royal Porcelain Co in 1862.

The popularity of parian had prompted a renewed interest in figure making, and Worcester became the most important maker of colored figures when these became popular in the 1870s and 80s. Their success was due in no small measure to the modeling skills of James Hadley, who though largely untutored, was able to design

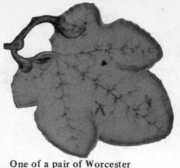

One of a pair of Worcester leaf dishes with green stalk handles, circa 1760, approx. 18cm. wide.(Christie's)
$3,000

A Dr. Wall Worcester quart mug with strap handle, circa 1770, 6.1/8in. high. (Skinner Inc.)
$250

A remarkable globular pot-pourri vase and cover with scroll handles, painted with brilliant specimens of Easter cacti, signed *W Hale*, 20.5cm., date code for 1905. (Phillips)
$2,500

A Worcester partridge-tureen and cover, the bird on an oval nest to the right, its plumage enriched in shades of brown, the edge of the cover with stylised entwined straw, circa 1765, 17.5cm. long. (Christie's)
$12,000

A Worcester flared cylindrical mug with strap handle, painted in a typical famille rose palette with The Beckoning Chinaman Pattern, circa 1758, 11.5cm. high. (Christie's London)
$1,000

A Worcester hunting jug, painted in the manner of John Wood, with two dogs stalking a capercaillie, a horseman approaching, 18.7cm. (Phillips London)
$1,250

240

and model in any required style. Also very popular at the time were ivory carvings which were being brought over from Japan and India. Most porcelain factories tried to reproduce these tones, but Worcester was by far the most successful with their 'Old Ivory' and 'Blush Ivory' bodies, which were widely copied and used on most of Hadley's figures, as well as vases and teawares.

After the death of their director R W Binns in 1900 and Hadley in 1903, the Worcester factory, which had bought out Graingers in 1889, continued to rely on the popularity of their designs, and little new or very exciting was produced for the next twenty years.

During the later first period a crescent or square mark was used on pieces decorated with underglaze blue, then incised *B* marks were used from 1792 till 1800. Thereafter the name of the factory usually appears, with date codes below the factory mark from 1862.

A Worcester finger bowl stand, painted in colors with sprays of flowers, 14.5cm., and a saucer en suite, 13cm.
(Phillips)   (Two) $900

A Worcester blue and white faceted baluster cream jug, painted with The Root Pattern, circa 1758, 9cm. high.
(Christie's) $1,250

A pair of Kerr and Binns reticulated perfume bottles and stoppers with jeweled panels, 16cm., 1862. (Phillips London) $1,100

A very fine large Worcester mug of bell shape with a plain handle, painted in bright Chinese style enamels with the 'Beckoning Chinaman' pattern, 14cm., circa 1754–56.
(Phillips) $7,800

A Kerr & Binns vase in Limoges enamel style, by Thomas Bott Snr., signed and dated 1862, 24cm., shield mark and signature. (Phillips London) $400

A Worcester leaf dish with a butterfly hovering above flowering branches, circa 1758, 18.5cm. wide. (Christie's) $800

A small Worcester vase, painted with festoons of pink and yellow roses, signed *Chair*, below the fine arabesque piercing by George Owen, 10.8cm.
(Phillips London) $3,000

ZSOLNAY

The Zsolnay earthenware pottery was established in 1862 at Pécs in Hungary by Vilmos Zsolnay, with the aim of shaping a characteristic national style.

Most of the output consisted of practical ware for everyday use, though some ornamental pieces were produced, often with Persian inspired motifs. Vases and bowls were made in Art Nouveau style with boldly colored glazes and luster decoration. These were the achievements of an experimental workshop under the direction of Vinsce Wartha which was operational around the turn of the century. Around that time too, vases with painted decoration designed by Josef Rippl-Rónai, also in Art Nouveau style, were produced.

The marks consist of versions of five churches with *Zsolnay*, and sometimes also with *Pécs*.

A Zsolnay ceramic jug, the handle formed as an Art Nouveau maiden with flowing hair and dress, 22.8cm. high. (Christie's) $350

A Zsolnay Pecs green luster jug, the handle modeled as a nude maiden gazing over rim, 16in. high.
(Christie's S. Ken) $1,000

A Zsolnay Pecs luster group, modeled as two polar bears on a large rock in a green and blue golden luster, 4½in. high. (Christie's) $375

A large Zsolnay luster vase covered with a violet/plum luster glaze with random spots of gold/green/amber hues, 45.5cm. high. (Phillips London) $1,000

A small Zsolnay figural luster vase decorated on the shoulders with the partially clad Orpheus with his lyre beside him and an amorous mermaid, 13cm. high. (Phillips) $1,000

A large Zsolnay luster group, of two men possibly Cain and Abel, one lying prostrate on a domed rocky base with the other towering above him, 37.5cm. high. (Phillips) $800

A Zsolnay luster figural ewer possibly designed by Lajos Mack molded around its circumference with three sinuous Art Nouveau maidens, 35cm. high. (Phillips) $550

ZURICH

The Zurich porcelain factory was begun by a group of business men in 1763, under the direction of Adam Spengler, a skilled faiencier. At first, soft paste porcelain was produced, but later production changed to hard paste, using clays from near Limoges.

The early years were very productive, with a thriving export trade. Small individual pieces of tableware were made, as well as great services. From about 1780 vases in the Sèvres style were produced in simple forms with painted rural scenes, often inspired by Nilson engravings.

1775–9 saw the finest period of figure production. Many of these were by Johann Valentin Sonnenschein, whose work followed German models, depicting peasants, soldiers etc. in contemporary dress. Towards the end of his career he also designed some larger table centerpieces. Spengler's son, John James, also spent a short while making figures at Zürich before going to Derby.

The smoky brown hue of Zürich porcelain can often look rather like Ludwigsburg, and there was little originality of form. The best known painter at the factory was the poet Salomon Gessner, who signed his work, and specialised in rather tedious Swiss landscapes.

After Spengler's death in 1790 porcelain production ceased, and faience only was produced thereafter.

The usual mark is a Z with a stroke through it, in underglaze blue.

A Zurich figure of a shepherd modeled by J. J. Meyer, 20cm. high, incised mark N I. (Phillips) $6,500

A Zurich figure of a young girl feeding chickens, her long skirt with alternating bands of cornflowers and berried foliage, circa 1775, 11.5cm. high. (Christie's London) $1,500

A Zurich ornithological teapot and a cover of bullet shape, painted in colors, one side with an owl and a woodpecker, the other with an eagle and a snipe, circa 1770, 17cm. wide. (Christie's Geneva) $3,000

Zurich sugar bowl and cover with gilt fruit knop and floral decoration, circa 1765, 10cm. high. $2,250

A Zurich oval dish with pierced border, painted in colors with a parrot perching on a branch, incised Z, blue Z and two dots, circa 1770, 12.3cm. wide. (Christie's Geneva) $3,750

A Zurich figure of a sportswoman, a duck in her left hand, a rifle in her right, with a spaniel at her side, circa 1770, 20.5cm. high. (Christie's Geneva) $1,500

CHROMIUM PLATE

Chromium plate is a thin sheet of chromium which is electrolytically deposited on metal to increase its resistance to corrosion. It further imparts a brilliant silver sheen.

From its invention it was used for a wide variety of quality goods, such as car lamps and wristwatches. It also found favor with Modernist designers during the 1930s after its use for furniture was pioneered by such as Le Corbusier, Mies van der Rohe and Marcel Breuer in the 20s.

Chrome and wood cigarette box, 1930s.
(Muir Hewitt) $45

Chrome yacht ash tray, 7in. high, 1930s.
(Muir Hewitt) $40

Stepped chrome vase, 1930s.
(Muir Hewitt) $40

Shell wall light of glass with chrome mount.
(Muir Hewitt) $60

1950s chrome and plastic soda syphon.
(Muir Hewitt) $40

Chrome ashtray with female figure, 1930s.
(Muir Hewitt) $45

Chrome ashtray with stylized birds.
(Muir Hewitt) $40

Chromium plated table gong, 1930s, 7in. high.
(Muir Hewitt) $70

Chrome Angel figure table bell, 1930s. (Muir Hewitt) $25

Stylized chrome animal, 1950s. (Muir Hewitt) $20

Cocktail nibbles dish in chrome and plastic, 1930s. (Muir Hewitt) $30

Chrome cigarette case, 1930s, 6½ in. long. (Muir Hewitt) $30

1950s Piquot ware tea set on matching tray. (Muir Hewitt) $100

Chrome companion set with Elizabethan figure support. (Muir Hewitt) $75

Chrome cake stand with stylized female support. (Muir Hewitt) $40

Chrome and glass tray, 1930s. (Muir Hewitt) $55

1950s chrome and plastic coffee percolator. (Muir Hewitt) $40

Pair of chromed metal candle-sticks, early 20th century, possibly Chicago, 3in. high. (Skinner) **$80**

Cocktail shaker, 1950s, complete with instructions, 7in. high. (Muir Hewitt) **$30**

Beldray chrome plated vases with Art Nouveau decoration. (Muir Hewitt) **$70**

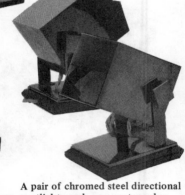

A pair of chromed steel and acid textured glass wall lights, circa 1940, 36.5cm. high. (Christie's) **$900**

Chrome and bakelite smoking stand, Brooklyn, New York, circa 1930, with chrome topped ash-tray and supports, 20¾in. high. (Skinner) **$175**

A pair of chromed steel directional spotlights each on a rectangular base supporting a box shade, stamp-ed Desney, 15.8cm. high. (Christie's) **$2,500**

One of a pair of silver col-oured metal frames, each swivel mounted in angled open supports, 31cm. high, 1930's. **$300**

Pair of chromed metal candlesticks by Salvador Dali, impressed signa-ture, 14in. high. (Skinner) **$800**

A Modernist glass and chrome metal fish tank, with polished copper column supports at each corner, on polished steel rectangular base inset with amber-tinted glass, 130.5cm. high. (Christie's) **$7,000**

CHROMIUM PLATE

Chrome cigarette lighter in the form of a bottle and two glasses. (Muir Hewitt) $55

Pussycat chromium cast money bank, with key, circa 1935. (Auction Team Koeln) $30

Chrome gong with stylized female figure, 1930s. (Muir Hewitt) $60

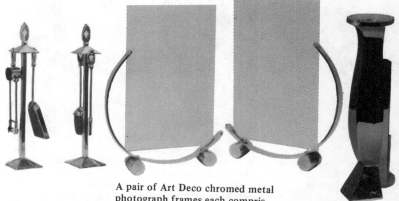

Chrome companion sets with shovel, tongs, brush and poker. (Muir Hewitt) $75

A pair of Art Deco chromed metal photograph frames each comprising a semi circular bar mounted at an angle, 17in. high. (Christie's) $450

W.M.F. chrome and glass vase, 1930s, 9in. high. (Muir Hewitt) $75

Chrome picture frame with picture of 1930's acrobats. (Muir Hewitt) $10

Chrome cake stand with two female figures support, 1930s. (Muir Hewitt) $45

Chrome frame complete with film star photograph. (Muir Hewitt) $25

Also known as a tavern or coaching clock, these large English wall clocks date from the early 18th century and were incorrectly named after an Act of 1797–8 whereby a tax was levied on clocks and timepieces. The dial is usually either round or shaped, and very prominent, often about 30in. diameter and both dial and case are often lacquered or painted. Alternatively the dial can be painted white within a mahogany case. They are weight driven, and usually non-striking.

An Act of Parliament timepiece, signed beneath the dial Thomas Fenton, London. $1,850

A mahogany Act of Parliament clock, the 22in. dial signed Thos. De La Salle, London. $5,000

A mid-Georgian black japanned Act of Parliament clock signed *Willm. Calvert, Bury* on the shaped 28in. dial with Roman and Arabic gold painted chapters, 6in. high. (Christie's) $2,250

A George III 'Act of Parliament' clock signed *Justin Vulliamy, London*, the timepiece movement with tapered rectangular plates, spring suspended pendulum to anchor escapement, last quarter 18th century, 58in. high. (Christie's) $8,000

A George III scarlet japanned Act of Parliament clock signed *Owen Jackson Cranbrook*, on the shaped 26in. green repainted dial with Roman and Arabic chapters, 58in. high. (Christie's) $1,750

A late 19th century black japanned Act of Parliament clock, the circular dial with gilt Roman numerals and Arabic minutes, 60in. high. (Spencer's) $4,500

A George III black lacquered and chinoiserie decorated tavern wall timepiece, signed Frans. Perigal, London, 1.44m. high. $2,250

A Georgian black lacquered tavern wall timepiece, the shield-shaped dial with gilt chapter, the weight driven movement with anchor escapement, 5ft.2½in. high. (Phillips) $5,000

George III black-painted
Act of Parliament wall
timepiece, dial signed
Henry Riddle, London,
5ft.2in. high. $3,500

A mahogany tavern time-
piece with five pillar
movement, 43½in. $1,500

Black japanned and gilt
decorated 'Act of Parlia-
ment' tavern clock by
John Wilson, Peterborough.
$5,000

A mid Georgian black
japanned tavern or Act of
Parliament clock signed
Robert Allam, London, on
the shaped 30in. dial, 59in.
high. $9,000

A mid Georgian black japanned
longcase Act of Parliament
clock, 31in. dial signed Will.
Threlkeld, London, 6ft. 10in.
high. $3,000

A George II black lacquered
striking Act of Parliament clock,
the dial of typical cartouche
outline with ogee-molded
frame surmounted by two giltwood flambeau finials, 61in.
high. (Christie's) $13,000

A Georgian tavern clock
signed Will[m]Murrell Horsham,
4ft.8½in. high.(Phillips)
$3,600

A lacquered tavern time-
piece, with 25in. cream
painted wooden dial, the
case inscribed J. Bartho-
lomew, 57in. high. $6,500

An 18th century striking Act
of Parliament clock, signed
Ino. Wilson, Peterborough,
56½in. high. $2,250

AUTOMATON CLOCKS

These are clocks and watches with animated figures or objects, which are set in motion by the going or striking train. The earliest examples date from the 17th century, and were usually to be found on public buildings, with the figures emerging and perhaps enacting a small drama when the clock struck. It was a type particularly beloved of German and French clockmakers, who adapted the principle to smaller timepieces. Negroes and animals were popular subjects, as was the Crucifixion, which was favored by German and French clockmakers of the 17th century.

'Monkey Cobbler', automaton with papier-mâché head, glass eyes, and articulated jaw, seated on a box.
(Phillips) $1,000

A mid 17th century South German negro automaton clock, 11½in. high. $9,000

Napoléon III bronze and ormolu mantel clock with automaton rocking ship, the case of naturalistic form with the ormolu figure of Neptune, 21in. high.
(Christie's) $1,750

A Black Forest clock automaton, the brightly painted limewood figure of a clockmaker moves his head and whistles a tune, while carrying under his arm a small Black Forest clock with pendulum and key, circa 1950.
(Auction Team Köln) $1,000

A Napoléon III bronze and ormolu singing bird mantel clock, the glazed case applied with trailing foliage and with acanthus leaf moldings, 16½in. high.
(Christie's) $4,000

Mid 19th century Swiss musical automaton of singing birds, on oval base, 60cm. high. (Christie's) $2,000

A three-dimensional wood model picture clock showing a French Chateau, under glass dome, 21½in. high.
                      $2,750

A singing bird automaton with clock, Swiss, probably by Jacquet Droz, circa 1785, 20in. high. (Christie's)
                      $45,000

Late 18th century gilt metal musical automaton clock for the Oriental market, 19¾in. high. $35,000

A cast iron blinking eye timepiece, 'Sambo', America, circa 1860, 16in. high. $2,100

Mid 19th century Swiss musical automaton of singing birds, 38in. high. $1,500

A 19th century French ormolu mantel clock with automaton, the circular case raised above a glazed base housing a singing bird, 1ft. 4½in. (Phillips) $3,500

A Louis XVI ormolu-mounted Paris porcelain musical automaton clock, playing a selection of six tunes through ten organ pipes, cam-and-rod drive through a composition tree to an automaton bird atop flapping its wings, rotating and opening and shutting its beak, 26¼in. high. (Christie's) $17,500

A late 19th century South German automaton quarter striking bracket clock, the stained wooden case in the style of a church with onion spire finial and belfry, 30in. high. (Christie's S. Ken) $1,850

A 19th century mechanical organ automaton with clock, 26in. high. $18,750

A Swiss automaton mantel clock, 9in. high. $3,750

An automaton clock in the form of a ship's bridge, 12½in. high. $4,500

BRACKET CLOCKS

That the first 'bracket' clocks were designed to stand on tables as often as against a wall is indicated by the fact that they often have elaborately engraved backplates and a glazed back door. Also, they had handles on the top, so that they could be carried from room to room. As they became mass produced and hence cheaper, however, these details were often omitted. The earliest bracket clocks, dating from the 17th century also had a 'cock' fixed to the backplate to conceal the suspension of the pendulum.

The bracket clocks with which we are more familiar today, in wooden cases, appeared in the second half of the 17th century before the longcase clock became popular. They were generally rather squat in form, and quite plain, with a flat or portico top and had a verge escapement. They quickly became more elaborate, however, but, although the anchor escapement was introduced in 1675 it was not generally adopted for bracket clocks until midway through Queen Anne's reign. The longer, heavy disk pendulum usually associated with anchor escapement took longer to find favor, due to the obvious disadvantages such a feature would have when the timepiece was being carried about.

From the first, brackets clocks were usually fitted with a striking train sounding the hours, while some also struck the quarters. At the end of the 17th century the basket top was introduced while in the 18th century luxury versions with musical mechanisms became popular with those who could afford them. Decoration also became more elaborate in the early part of the century and clocks acquired ormolu or silver mountings and finials. The arched dial found favor at this time too. Towards the end of the century, however, styles became plainer, and broken arch, arch top, lancet and balloon tops were introduced.

An 18th century Italian quarter-striking bracket clock, 25in. high. $2,750

An olivewood bracket clock, the 8in. dial signed Joseph Knibb, 14½in. high. $52,000

Late 18th century George III gilt and cut glass mounted floral painted quarter-chiming musical bracket clock for the Turkish market, signed Benj. Barber, London, 37½in. high. $67,500

A small ebony silver-mounted striking bracket clock, circa 1708, the 4³/₄ x 5¹/₄in. dial signed *Tho: Tompion & Edw: Banger London,* 9in. high. (Christie's) $1,012,440

A George III satinwood 'balloon' bracket clock, the enamel dial signed Webster London, 24in. high. $9,000

A George III bracket clock with enamel dial, by Robt. Henderson, 15½in. high. $15,000

EBONISED

Late 18th century ebonised striking bracket clock, signed A. Van Eeden, Haarlem, 20in. high. $2,500

A late Victorian ebonised chiming bracket clock, inscribed Thompson, Ashford, 24in., with later wall bracket. $1,850

A mid-Georgian ebonised striking bracket clock, the dial signed John Fladgate London, 18½in. high. $3,500

An Austrian ebonised grande sonnerie bracket clock, the bell top case with crowned cherub carrying handle and winged paw feet, mid 18th century, 23½in. high. (Christie's New York) $2,750

Josephus Pryor, a Charles II ebony striking bracket clock of large size, the plinth shaped case with gilt carrying handle to cushion molded top, glazed sides, the 10in. square skeletonised dial with silvered chapter ring. (Christie's) $17,500

Dan: Quare London 62 (Graham No. 550), a George I ebonised striking bracket clock of small size, the case with large giltmetal handle to cushion molded top, circa 1715, 11⁷/₈in. high. (Christie's) $104,000

A Regency ebonised striking miniature bracket clock, the border engraved backplate signed Kenth. Maclennan London, behind the bell, 10½in. high. (Christie's) $2,000

A small and very fine veneered ebony quarter repeating bracket clock, the 6in. dial signed Tho. Tompion Londini fecit, 12½in. high. $82,500

A William III ebony striking bracket clock, circa 1700, the 7¹/₄ x 8in. dial signed *Tho: Tompion Londini fecit,* 15¹/₂in. high. (Christie's) $115,000

INLAID

An inlaid balloon bracket clock, signed J. Leroux, London, 18¾in. high. **$1,500**

A 19th century mahogany and brass inlaid bracket timepiece, the circular case surmounted by a flame finial, 2ft. ½in. high. (Phillips) **$750**

A George III satinwood bracket clock, the movement signed Tregent, Strand, London, 21in. high. **$6,000**

A Regency brass inlaid mahogany bracket clock, signed *Thos. Halder, Arundel*, the twin fusee movement with anchor escapement, striking the hour on bell, circa 1820, 19³/₄in. high. (Christie's) **$1,500**

An Edwardian inlaid mahogany mantel or bracket clock, with silvered dial, 16¾in. high. **$500**

A 19th century mahogany and brass inlaid bracket clock, signed Wand & Hills, Rochester, the twin fusee movement with anchor escapement, 1ft. 11in. high. (Phillips) **$750**

Regency mahogany cased bracket clock with brass inlay and mounts, the striking movement inscribed *E Watson, King Street, Cheapside*, 18in. tall. (G. A. Key) **$1,350**

A late 19th century mahogany bracket clock, the circular painted dial signed *Camerer Cuss & Co., London*, the twin fusée movement with anchor escapement, 1ft. 6in. high. (Phillips) **$1,000**

A George IV brass inlaid mahogany bracket clock with hour striking movement and painted dial, 19¾in. high. (Tennants) **$1,500**

LACQUERED

A George II brown japanned bracket clock, dial signed Jn. Cotton London, 16¼in. high.
$2,250

A mid Georgian scarlet japanned quarter striking, musical and automaton bracket clock in the style of G. Grendey, 37in. high.
$110,000

A scarlet lacquer striking bracket clock, the brass dial signed Jas. Smith, London, 20in. high.
$2,500

A George III black lacquer striking bracket clock with alarm, 6³/₄in. dial signed in the silvered aperture *Ralph Goat, London*, on cast bracket feet, 21in. high.
(Bonhams)
$3,000

An 18th century C. European red lacquered quarter chiming bracket clock, the backplate signed Iohan Maurer in Prag, 57cm. high.
$11,000

A George III scarlet japanned musical bracket clock for the Turkish market by Wm. Kipling London, the bekk-top case decorated overall with gilt chinoiseries, 25in. high
(Christies)
$42,500

An early George III dark japanned musical chiming bracket clock for the Turkish market, dial signed Edward Pistor, London, 23½in. high.
$7,500

Dutch japanned bracket clock, c. 1750, red laquered case, enamelled dial and calendar dial inscribed Ellicot London, 24in. high.
(Skinner Inc)
$1,750

19th century bracket clock with silvered brass dial, the black lacquered case decorated with a polychrome chinoiserie pattern, 14in. high.
(G. A. Key)
$500

ROSEWOOD

Victorian rosewood cased
bracket clock, inlaid with
brass floral decoration.
$2,500

A rosewood bracket clock
with movement by Yonge
& Son of the Strand, 11in.
high. $5,000

A rosewood bracket time-
piece, signed Wm. Speakman,
London, 20½in. high. $750

A 19th century rosewood
and inlaid bracket timepiece,
32cm. high. $1,250

A French 18th century gilt
brass mounted and inlaid
rosewood bracket clock,
signed Jean Tolly a Paris,
36in. high. $2,250

A Regency period bracket
clock, the brass inlaid lancet
case of Egyptian styling, circa
1810, 20in. high. $3,000

A Regency rosewood and
brass inlaid mantel timepiece,
the silvered dial signed
Carpenter, London, 9½in.
high. $4,500

A rosewood bracket clock, the
twin fusee movement with
domed plates, anchor escapement and bell striking, signed
Wilson, Stamford, 32.5cm.
(Lawrence Fine Arts) $1,500

A Regency rosewood bracket
clock, the case with gadrooned
top, the shaped silvered dial
signed G.Searle, London, the
twin fusee movement with
anchor escapement. 1ft. 4in.
high. (Phillips) $2,000

A gilt brass mounted walnut quarter chiming bracket clock, 32¾in. high. $1,500

An 18th century bracket clock in burr walnut case, with eight-day movement by Jos. Kirk, 16in. high. $4,000

A walnut quarter repeating bracket clock with 7½in. brass dial, backplate signed Jacob Massy, London, 17in. high. $4,500

A substantial late 19th century walnut quarter chiming bracket clock, signed *John Carter*, the triple fusee movement chiming on eight bells, 75cm. high. (Phillips) $1,500

A walnut chiming bracket clock, by Viner London, No. 2208, 22in. high, and a walnut bracket, 8in. high. $1,500

A walnut bracket clock with verge escapement and pull quarter repeating on two bells, the florally engraved backplate signed in a cartouche Johannes Fromanteel Londini Fecit, 12½in. high. (Phillips) $5,000

A Regency walnut cased bracket clock with silvered dial, maker Raw Bros., London. $1,000

A walnut chiming bracket clock, the three train fusee movement striking quarter hours on 8 bells or four.gongs, 15in. high. $3,000

A Victorian English walnut veneer chiming bracket clock, white painted dial signed *F. Dent, 61 Strand, London*, triple fusée, signed anchor movement chiming on eight bells, 31in. (Bonhams) $1,350

BAMBOO

The carriage clock, as its name suggests, was originally designed, with its spring driven movement, for use whilst traveling. It was a French innovation, probably derived from the pendule d'officier pioneered by Abraham Louis Breguet of Paris in the 18th century. Essentially, it has a rectangular case, 3–12in. high, with a carrying handle and often incorporated such complex refinements as repeat and date mechanisms and sometimes even a dial showing the phases of the moon. Early examples usually had silvered dials, and were housed in ormolu cases, often embellished with Corinthian columns. The type became particularly popular in the course of the 19th century when examples typically had fine cast brass cases with thick beveled glass windows resting on grooves in the frame. Later the glass at the top became smaller and was let into a metal plate. Carrying handles were usually round, tapering towards the ends, and because there was often a repeat button on the top front edge, the handles folded backwards only. French clockmakers began to produce the clocks en masse, with production also beginning from circa 1820 in England, America and Austria.

A 19th century French brass and enamel mounted carriage clock, bearing the Drocourt trademark, in a bamboo case, 7½in. high. (Phillips) $2,000

A French porcelain panelled 'bamboo' carriage clock, 7in. high. $3,250

A late 19th century French carriage clock in gilt 'bamboo' chinoiserie case, inscribed John Bennett, Paris, 8in. high. $2,750

A brass miniature carriage timepiece, with gilt chapter ring signed Wm. Drummond & Sons Melbourne, bamboo case, 3½in. high. (Christie's) $2,500

BAROMETER

A 19th century French gilt brass and champleve enamel carriage timepiece and barometer, centered by a thermometer, 15cm. high. (Phillips) $1,100

A grande sonnerie calendar carriage clock cum barometer, the barometer inscribed R. W. Inglis 1897, 6½in. high. $4,500

A clock/barometer desk set, with white enamel dials, in beveled-glazed brass-framed oval case, surmounted by a folding scroll loop handle, 5in. high. (Christie's) $700

CARRIAGE CLOCKS

DECORATED FACE

French glass and brass carriage timepiece, dial signed Mappin & Webb Ltd., Paris, circa 1900, 6½in. high. $400

An English carriage clock, enamel dial signed Dent London, 8¾in. high. $9,000

Late 19th century American brass and glass carriage timepiece with eight-day movement, 9.1/8in. high. $450

A miniature French 19th century brass and enamel carriage timepiece, bearing the mark of Auguste Margaine, in an anglaise case, 10cm. high. (Phillips) $1,350

A late 19th century French carriage clock, 2in. silvered annular chapter ring, set within a pierced bird and foliate and polished gilt background, signed *EGLG Paris*, 6¼in. (Bonhams) $600

A 19th century French gilt brass carriage clock, the lever movement striking on a bell and signed on the backplate Ch. Frodsham Paris, 6in. high. (Phillips) $1,100

A gilt metal striking carriage clock with silvered lever platform, the gilt chapter ring signed Leroy Paris, 6¼in. high. $1,100

An English chronometer carriage timepiece, by Dent, London, with mahogany carrying case, 8½in. high. $15,000

A 19th century French gilt brass carriage clock, the backplate bearing the Drocourt trademark, 6½in high. $2,250

OVAL CASE

An oval engraved gilt brass grande sonnerie carriage clock, 7½in. high. **$3,750**

A gilt metal grande sonnerie oval carriage clock with enamel dial, 6.1/8in. high. **$3,600**

Aneroid barometer of carriage clock form, signed R. & J. Beck, London, 3¼in. high. **$675**

A French 19th century gilt brass carriage clock, the movement with replaced lever platform, the case with curved side panels, 7½in. high. (Phillips) **$800**

A fine and rare brass grande sonnerie and minute repeating alarm carriage clock in oval Corinthian case, signed by the retailer *Bailey, Banks & Biddle Co., Philadelphia*, 4³/₄in. high. (Christie's S. Ken) **$6,250**

A miniature French oval gilt brass and porcelain paneled carriage timepiece, with lever platform escapement, the porcelain dial decorated with a young girl and boy, 4in. high. (Phillips) **$2,500**

A 19th century French oval gilt brass carriage clock, the enamel dial signed for *Mercier & Fils, Genève*, in an oval case, 17cm. high. (Phillips) **$1,200**

Gilt metal grande sonnerie oval carriage clock in engraved case with scrolling handle, 6in. high. **$2,250**

A gilt brass oval striking carriage clock with strike/repeat on gong, enamel dial with Breguet style hands, 4½in. high. (Christie's) **$1,000**

Porcelain mounted carriage clock, dial signed J. W. Benson, London, 8½in. high, backplate stamped Drocourt.
$15,000

A 19th century French gilt brass and porcelain mounted carriage clock, 18cm. high.
$4,500

A gilt brass porcelain mounted striking carriage clock, the dial and side panels painted in the Sevres style, 5½in. high.
$6,750

Gilt brass porcelain mounted miniature carriage timepiece with bi-metallic balance to lever platform, the blue porcelain dial with Roman chapter ring and pierced gilt hands, 3in. high. (Christie's)
$2,500

A gilt brass porcelain mounted striking giant carriage clock, the porcelain dial and sides painted with genre scenes of carousing cavaliers, signed H. Desprez, 8¹/₂in. high. (Christie's)
$7,500

A French gilt brass and porcelain paneled carriage clock, with replaced lever platform escapement, alarm, push repeat and striking on a gong, 7¹/₂in. high. (Phillips)
$1,800

A French gilt brass carriage clock, the dial and side panels decorated with scenes of young couples, 7in. high.
$1,850

A 19th century French brass carriage clock, the lever movement striking on a gong with alarm and push repeat, 7½in. high.
$3,000

A porcelain mounted carriage clock, the repeating lever movement stamped Maurice et Cie, 5½in. high.
$2,000

ROUND FACE

An alarm carriage clock, the enamel dial signed James Muirhead & Son, Glasgow, 6¾in. high. $3,600

Chronometer carriage clock by Dent, London, dial signed, 7in. high. $18,500

French gilt brass and glass repeating carriage clock, circa 1900, 7¼in. high. $1,850

A gilt brass quarter striking carriage clock with cut bimetallic balance to lever platform, dial signed in Cyrillic *Pavel Buhre*, blued spade hands, within gilt mask, 6¼in. high. (Christie's) $1,000

A 19th century bronze and gilt brass carriage timepiece, the circular movement with going barrel and lever platform escapement, 13.5cm. high. (Phillips) $800

A good English gilt brass carriage clock, the twin fusee movement with lever platform escapement, signed Chas Frodsham, London, 8in. high. (Phillips) $7,500

Large carriage clock with enamel dial, movement stamped Drocourt, 8½in. high. $5,000

A gilt metal striking carriage clock, inscribed Examined by Dent and with presentation inscription dated 1877, 7in. high. $1,100

A quarter-striking carriage clock, the enamel dial signed Dent 33 Cockspur Street, London, 6in. high. $3,500

An unusual miniature carriage timepiece, late 19th century, the movement with platform lever escapement, signed Bigelow, Kennard & Co., Boston. (Christie's) $1,500

A grande sonnerie alarm carriage clock, the movement stamped Fumey, 7½in. high. $3,000

A gilt brass miniature carriage timepiece with uncut bimetallic balance to silvered lever platform, the caryatid case with harpies to the angles, 2¾in. high. (Christie's) $1,500

An unusual 19th century French gilt bronze and porcelain mounted carriage clock, bearing the Drocourt trademark on the backplate, in an ornate rococo case, 9in. high. (Phillips) $6,500

A rare chased gilt carriage clock with singing bird automaton, signed *Japy Freres & Cie.*, surmounted by glazed virtrine with rising handle displaying the bird perched within realistic silk and feather foliage, circa 1860, 12¾in. high. (Christie's) $16,000

A fine chased gilt grande sonnerie carriage clock with moon phase, calendar, thermometer and winding indicator, the movement stamped *H.L.* in lozenge punch, circa 1860, 8in. high. (Christie's New York) $17,500

A French gilt brass carriage clock, the repeating movement with lever escapement, gong striking and signed John P. Cross, Paris, 6½in. (Lawrence Fine Arts) $2,000

An ornate gilt repeating carriage clock, signed Bolviller a Paris, 6¼in. high. $1,500

An unusual 19th century gilt brass French carriage clock, the movement with lever platform escapement, push repeat and alarm, signed *Lucien, A. Paris*, 9½in. high. (Phillips) $5,000

The cartel clock is a French wall clock dating from circa 1750. The casing, of wood or brass, is usually highly ornamental, even flamboyant, with frequent ormolu or vernis Martin embellishment. Common motifs include wings, laurel leaves, cupids and mythological figures. English examples are more often of wood, while French clocks are more often of bronze and gilt or cast brass. Cartel clocks were also made in Holland and Scandinavia.

Late 18th/early 19th century French giltwood cartel clock, 28in. high. $1,500

Louis XVI ormolu cartel clock, dial signed Imbert, 36½in. high. $2,250

A late 18th century French cartel clock, urn shaped and festooned with laurels, with a female face above the dial and pineapple finial, the white enamel face signed *Hartingue, Paris.* (Finarte) $4,000

An Austrian parcel-gilt cartel clock, the circular enamel dial signed *Toban Vellauer a Vienne*, the shaped case surmounted by a vase flanked by seahorses, 30in. high. (Christie's) $2,250

A Louis XVI ormolu cartel clock with circular enamel dial signed *Baret A Breuvanne*, in a cartouche-shaped case surmounted by a flaming urn, 29in. high. (Christie's) $5,750

A French cartel clock with eight day movement, 9½in. high. $400

An 18th century Continental carved giltwood cartel clock, 64cm. high. $1,850

A wall clock, by Sewill (maker to the Royal Navy), Liverpool, 40in. high. $600

CUCKOO CLOCKS

German Black Forest carved cuckoo clock. **$75**

A 19th century Black Forest Trumpeter wall clock, the carved case decorated with a stag's head and a door below opening to reveal two trumpeters, 2ft. 10in. high. (Phillips) **$3,600**

A finely carved Black Forest cuckoo clock decorated with a stag and dead game. **$1,000**

A fine Black Forest clock with two train movement striking in a wire gong and with cuckoo, 48in. high. **$2,500**

A Black Forest carved wood striking cuckoo clock of standard form, the dial with Roman chapter ring, pierced bone hands, a cuckoo and seated boy appearing on the hour behind shutters, 30in. high. (Christie's) **$1,350**

A small 1950's decorated carved wood clock with two cuckoos and a weight driven movement. **$60**

Black Forest shelf mounted German cuckoo clock with spring driven movement, striking on a gong and cuckoos. **$450**

Combined cuckoo and weather clock, complete with thermometer. **$60**

A small 1980's Black Forest cuckoo clock with weight driven movement. **$50**

A gilt brass timepiece table compendium, with trade label of John Cockburn, Richmond, base 9in. wide. $6,750

1950s round Cartier desk clock, with lapis and gold face and gold and green enamel hands, signed *Cartier nn 8364–5728.* (Finarte) $7,000

A late 19th century French timepiece with 3½in. plain glass dial, 9½in. high. $675

A Bulle Clockette electric desk clock in red-brown bakelite case, the silvered dial behind arched glass door, 21cm. high, 1910/20.
(Auction Team Köln) $150

A chromium plated and gilt desk timepiece modeled as an Edwardian tourer, 8½in. high. (Christie's) $675

A finely decorated and cast gilt French desk clock with hand painted porcelain inlay, the 8 day non striking movement signed *Japy Freres, France*, 45cm. diameter, circa 1890.
(Auction Team Köln) $250

A brass digital desk clock with calendar attachment, the American movement signed *The Plato Clock*, 15cm. high, circa 1900.
(Auction Team Köln) $210

A Seth Thomas American desk clock, the 8-day movement striking on a gong, in walnut case with galleried pediment, the painted metal dial with Roman numerals, circa 1880/90.
(Auction Team Köln) $240

A German oak and walnut cased desk clock with calendar automaton, the 8-day movement with half hour striking on a gong, circa 1890, 51cm. high.
(Auction Team Köln) $2,400

DESK CLOCKS

German cast metal desk clock with a hunter and his bag, German 1-day movement, silvered dial, 30cm. high, circa 1930.
(Auction Team Köln) $150

A Swiss hexagonal silver 8-day desk clock, enameled in blue, signed on box *St. Pauls Lodge num. 43, Ladies Night 1928*, 9cm. high.
(Duran) $350

A hardstone and enamel timepiece, unmarked, circa 1900, 16.5 cm. high.
$5,000

A brass desk timepiece with barometer and thermometer, the rectangular case surmounted by a handle with compass below, 8in. high.
(Phillips) $650

An unusual presentation deskwatch with battery operated winding in mottled green enameled brass case with applied Rolex name and crest and the words Timed to the second, 90mm.diam.
(Christies) $5,000

A guilloche enamel desk clock, the split seed-pearl bezel enclosing a white enamel dial with black Arabic chapters, white metal, marked Faberge, 1899-1908, 5in. high. (Christie's)
$20,000

A gilt timepiece and barometer desk set in oval case surmounted by a carrying handle, with timepiece movement and platform escapement, 6¾in. high.
(Christie's) $500

Late 19th century circular silver mounted hardstone desk clock by Faberge, St. Petersburg, 12.3cm.
$2,500

A Viennese enamel desk clock, mid 19th century, the whole supported by Hercules, decorated with polychrome classical scenes over a pink ground, 8in. high.
(Skinner Inc.) $1,350

LANTERN CLOCKS

The lantern clock, often erroneously called the Cromwellian clock, was introduced in England in the early 17th century and continued in production for about a hundred years. All the earliest examples were weight driven with a balance wheel escapement. As they quickly became popular, the movements began to be encased in brass, and brass soon replaced iron for the various wheels. The case was formed by a pillar at each corner with plates between, these plates often being finely engraved. Another common adornment was fretwork, particularly at the top of the front and side to conceal the space between the top of the case and the bell, which would be surmounted by a single finial. The frets can be a useful guide to determining the age of the clock. A shield and mantling design was among the earliest to be used, while scrolling and monsters' heads became common in the first half of the 17th century. The crossed dolphin design evolved from the monsters' heads after 1640 and remained the favorite until the clocks went out of fashion.

During the late 17th and early 18th century the diameter of the dial increased, without any corresponding enlargement of the case, so the former would protrude noticeably on each side.

Lantern clocks could be fitted with alarms, and those that were can be identified by a small dial behind the hand of the hour numbers in Arabic figures. From around 1670 the pendulum came to replace the balance wheel and a cord spring in a barrel and the key-wound fusée began to replace the traditional cord and weight drive. A thirty hour movement is general and was never exceeded, while some of the earliest examples might run for 12 or 15 hours.

Lantern clocks have been widely copied to the present day.

A late 17th century brass "winged" lantern clock with pierced dolphin fret above the Roman chapter ring, 14½in. high. (Christie's) **$1,600**

Midlands Clockmaking, a small and rare alarm lantern timepiece, 8½in. high. **$11,000**

An early 18th century brass lantern clock of typical form, the engraved centerfield inscribed Humphrey Marsh, Highworth, fecit, number 105, with a single steel hand, 16in. high. (Christie's S. Ken.) **$2,000**

An interesting late 17th century English brass lantern clock with pierced and engraved decoration of entwined dolphins and foliage, 34cm. high. (Henry Spencer) **$1,500**

A brass lantern clock of typical form, the rectangular case with turned pillars at the corners, 15½in. high. (Christie's S. Ken.) **$1,000**

Late 17th century small alarm lantern timepiece, dial signed Joseph Knibb Londini, 6½in. high. **$6,750**

A brass lantern clock with alarm, unsigned, 17th century, with restorations, 14½in. high. $3,750

A French brass lantern clock, the circular chased dial with enamel numerals, 41cm. high. $1,400

Lantern clock, dial signed Nicholas Coxeter, London, circa 1680, 16½in. high. $4,500

A brass lantern clock, the dial with brass chapter signed Wilmshurst, Odiham, 1ft.3in. high, together with an oak wall bracket. $2,250

Lantern clock, late 17th century, by Nicholas Coxeter at the Three Chaires in Lothbury, London, 15in. high.
(Brian Loomes) $3,750

A brass lantern clock, the dial with brass chapter and engraved centre signed *Tho Muddle, Rotherfield*, 1ft 3½in. high.
(Phillips) $1,100

Brass lantern clock by J. Windmills, London, with silvered chapter ring, Roman numerals and anchor escapement, early 18th century, 36cm. high.
(Auktionsverket) $400

A rare quarter chiming lantern clock, the going train with verge escapement and later pendulum suspension, signed *D. Lesturgeon, London*, circa 1700, 7in. wide.
(Christie's New York) $2,000

A Chares II brass striking lantern clock, with original verge escapement and bob pendulum, the florally engraved dial signed *Tho. Wintworth, Sarum Fecit*, 14¾in. high.
(Christie's) $4,250

The longcase clock, often referred to as the grandfather clock, emerged shortly after the invention of the pendulum and of the anchor escapement in 1670, since the narrow arc of swing of this escapement made it possible to enclose the weights and pendulum in a narrow trunk.

The type derives from the lantern clock, probably as a means of protecting the weights and pendulums, which had hitherto swung free on the wall. The earliest examples were slender, and were rarely more than 7ft. tall. They usually had square hoods, often with barley twist capitals and stable-looking base sections. As luxury items they boasted carcases of oak veneered first in ebony and later in yew, walnut, kingwood or laburnum. Later in the 17th century Dutch floral marquetry became fashionable.

A boulle month calendar longcase clock, dial signed Daniel Quare, 7ft. 5in. high.
$37,500

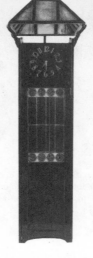

An Arts and Crafts black painted oak electric longcase clock, with a stained and leaded glass door, 76in. high.
(Christie's) $600

An olivewood long-case clock, dial signed ned Joseph Knibb, 6ft.4in. high.
$42,500

Height and style continued to vary with fashion – as higher ceilings came in, the clocks became taller, often by the addition of a flattened dome, or 'cushion top' above the hood, which in turn was often adorned with brass finials. Some too have fret cut friezes at the top of the hood to allow the chimes to be clearly heard. These appeared after 1696, when Edward Barlow introduced the first chiming mechanism. In 1710, Tompion

An unusual Art Deco ebonised and chromium plated cocktail cabinet, fashioned as a longcase clock, having a 'Temco' electric timepiece, 170cm. high.   (Phillips) $2,000

An unusual weight driven calendar clock with astronomical indications, signed *G. Croenen Inu. & Fecit, anno 1813*, 19th century, 65in. high excluding dome.
(Christie's) $24,000

An eight day long case clock, the silvered and brass square dial inscribed *John Nethercott, Chipping Norton*, 7ft. 5in. high.
(Tennants) $750

introduced the arched dial, and by 1720 this was in widespread use. Early faces were made of brass adorned with floral and scroll engraving. By the 1680s, these had increased to 10in. square, while from the beginning of the 18th century, 12in. dials were common, following the introduction of the arch. The earliest spandrels, or ornamental corner pieces on the dial, were of cupids' heads between curved wings. Later, scrollwork became popular, and by 1700 this often incorporated a female mask.

Later in the 18th century, clock cases became plainer, as bracket clocks superseded the longcase in popularity. By 1750, however, the widespread use of mahogany, and the wonderful designs of, for example, Sheraton and Chippendale, had restored the longcase to popularity.

While height has little to do with the value of a clock, slender examples have always been more favored. Better clocks tend to have at least eight day movements, and some will run for months or even a year. Country made examples, on the other hand, often had thirty hour movements, which were well within the scope of the local blacksmith, who would produce them for locally made carcases. After 1790, as quantity took over from quality in many cases, the painted wood or iron dial was introduced.

There are some interesting features to look for, which though by no means infallible, can be useful for dating a clock. The fleur de lys, for example, used to mark the half hours, was seldom employed after the 1740s, the same period that larger Arabic numerals replaced the Roman as minute markers. After 1750, an engraved brass or silvered face without a chapter ring was often used and, from 1775 a cast brass pre-enameled copper face was introduced.

An ebony veneered month longcase clock, the 10in. dial signed Joseph Knibb, 6ft.7in. high. $45,000

A 1930's longcase clock, movement engraved 'Johnston Crawford Production No. 1', 176.5cm. high. $2,250

Federal birch inlaid tall case clock, New England, circa 1780, 90in. high. $4,500

A celebrated Queen Anne astronomical longcase clock of long duration signed Edward Cockey, Warminster, in an ebonised, parcel-gilt and silvered case, 10ft.2in. high. (Christie's) $100,000

Queen Anne maple tall clock, Benjamin Cheney, East Hartford, Connecticut, circa 1760, 89¹/₂in. high. (Skinner) $15,000

A 30 hour longcase clock, the 10in. square brass dial signed at the base Thomas Tompion Londini, with winged cherub's head spandrels and silvered chapter ring, 7ft 8in. high. (Phillips) $12,000

BALLOON CASE

A 19th century mahogany mantel timepiece, of balloon form, the circular painted dial signed Daldorph, Croydon, the fusee movement with anchor escapement. (Phillips) $350

Fine Regency period satinwood balloon cased mantel clock with sunburst inlay, and pineapple finial, 17in. high.
(G. A. Key) $1,350

A Scottish Regency mahogany balloon mantel regulator of large size, with handles to sides and on brass ball feet, the backplate signed *Ian. Dalgleish Edinburgh*, 25^{1}/$_{2}$in. high.
(Christie's) $2,000

BAROMETER CLOCKS

A gilt brass combination timepiece aneroid barometer and thermometer, the timepiece with platform lever escapement, 11in. high.
(Lawrence Fine Art) $650

A 19th century brass double-dialed barometer and timepiece in the form of a ship's wheel surmounted by a gimbaled compass, signed *La Fontaine Opticien*, 11^{1}/$_{2}$in. high.
(Christie's S. Ken) $1,850

A French boudoir combined timepiece, barometer and thermometer with cream enamel dials and silvered-metal scale, 12in. high.
(Bearne's) $450

CAST IRON

Cast iron mantel clock with painted dial and eight-day time and strike movement, America, circa 1860, 20in. high. $450

A cast iron front mantel clock, polychrome painted, America, circa 1890, 11¾in. high. $150

A cast iron and mother-of-pearl shelf clock by Terry & Andrews, with painted dial, circa 1855, 15¾in. high. $300

FIGURAL

An Empire ormolu mantel clock, the dial signed F. B. Adams, London, 17in. high.
$2,000

A 19th century English ormolu and bronze mantel timepiece, the fusee movement with anchor escapement, signed on a cartouche *Baetens, 23 Gerrard Street, Soho, London*, 11³/₄in. high.
(Phillips) $2,750

Late 19th century bronze and ormolu figural mantel clock, France, 28½in. high.
$3,250

A French Directoire ormolu and marble mantel clock, the case depicting 'La Lecture', the female figure seated before a draped table with a lamp, 1ft. 1in. high.
(Phillips) $3,250

A French 19th century bronze ormolu and red marble mantel clock, the enamel dial signed Guibal A Paris, 57cm. high. $3,500

A 19th century ormolu and white marble mantel clock, the circular case decorated to the side with a winged putto reading and with foliage and a globe, signed *Mannheim à Paris*, 12½in. high.
(Phillips) $1,100

Charles X gilt-bronze figural clock, circa 1830, the engine-turned circular clock face within an ivy frame set in a rectangular case surmounted by a ewer, 14³/14³/₄in. high.
(Butterfield & Butterfield)$1,200

A Second Empire yellow marble, ormolu and bronze striking mantel clock, the case with ormolu foliate mounts and surmounted by a bronze lion, 15in. high.
(Christie's) $800

A gilt and ormolu French mantel clock, with a female figure leaning on a rocky mound, the dial with Roman numerals and signed *Bioula a Amien*, mid 19th century.
(Herholdt Jensen) $500

FOUR GLASS

Late 19th century champleve, glass and brass mantel clock, France, 10¾in. high. $1,200

A French late 19th century champleve, bronze and glass mantel clock, 15½in. high. $1,850

An oval four-glass lacquered brass 8-day striking mantel clock with enamel dial, 9½in. tall. $575

A 19th century French gilt brass mantel clock, of four glass form, the circular enamel dial signed Callier, Horloger de la Marine Imperiale, 22 Bould Montmarte 22, 14in. high. (Phillips) $1,000

An early Victorian four-glass mantel timepiece, engraved silvered dial signed W. Davis & Sons, the four pillar single chain fusee movement with anchor escapement, 8¾in. high. (Christie's) $1,300

A 19th century French bronze and glass mantel clock, 8 day Paris movement sounding the half hours on a bell and with Brocot escapement, 30cm. high. (Duran) $600

A rosewood four glass mantel timepiece, silvered chapter ring signed Vulliamy London, chain fusee movement, 7¼in. high. (Christie's) $8,000

A French four glass and gilt brass mantel clock, the two-train movement with Brocot suspension, 14¼in. high. $1,000

A 19th century French ormolu and enamel four glass mantel clock, decorated Corinthian columns, 12in. high. (Phillips) $1,350

FOUR PILLAR

A French Empire gilt bronze mounted black marble mantel clock, 16in.   **$600**

A French Siena marble and ormolu mounted mantel clock, the drum-shaped case with lyre finial, 15½in. high. (Christie's)   **$450**

A Louis XVI ormolu mounted marble pendule a cercle tournant, signed Ant. Coliau a Paris, 15½in. high.   **$6,750**

French mahogany hall clock with four columns on a rectangular base, the enamel face in a palmetto surround, circa 1830, 44cm. high. (Kunsthaus am Museum)   **$1,000**

A French ormolu mounted gray and white marble mantel clock, the white enamel dial with Roman numerals, pierced gilt hands and signed *Chopin a Paris*, 24½in. high. (Lawrence Fine Art)   **$900**

A French mahogany portico clock, the gilt dial with Roman numerals and engine-turned centerfield signed *Bernard et fils, Bordeaux*, the eight-day movement with outside countwheel strike on a bell, 18½in. high. (Christie's S. Ken)   **$750**

An Empire mahogany and ormolu pendulum mantel clock of architectural design, the circular dial with Roman numerals on a white enamel face, 53cm. wide (Finarte)   **$3,000**

A Louis XVI white marble and ormolu mantel clock, the enamel dial inscribed A Paris, 1ft.10½in. high.   **$2,250**

A white marble and ormolu portico clock, circa 1830, the white enamel annular dial signed Leroy a Paris, 19½in. high.   **$1,850**

LALIQUE

A Lalique opalescent glass clock, 12.5cm., 1930's. $1,000

Moineaux, a Lalique frosted glass clock of domed outline, the central dial enclosed by nestling sparrows. (Phillips) $1,500

A Lalique clear glass clock of flat square form, 'Inseparables', 4¼in. square. $1,250

'Inseparables', a Lalique opalescent clock, the clear and opalescent glass molded with two pairs of budgerigars among prunus blossom, 11.2cm. high. (Christie's) $3,000

'Deux Figurines', a Lalique molded and engraved glass clock, of arched form, the clear and satin-finished glass molded in intaglio with two scantily clad maidens, 38.7cm. high. (Christie's) $26,000

'Sirènes', a Lalique frosted opalescent glass desk clock, the square frame molded in relief with sea sprites, 11.5cm. high. (Christie's) $2,000

Cinq Hirondelles, a Lalique glass timepiece, molded with five swallows in flight amid branches of blossom, 15cm. high. (Phillips) $2,400

A Lalique clock, the satin-finished glass molded with two pairs of love-birds in blossoming branches, with brown stained decoration, 21.8cm. wide. (Christie's) $1,350

René Lalique Deux Figurines clock, with recessed molded design of two women in diaphanous gowns, 14in. high. (Skinner Inc.) $8,350

LIBERTY

A Liberty & Co. 'Cymric', copper, mother-of-pearl and lapis clock, Birmingham 1903. $12,000

A Liberty & Co. pewter and enamel clock, with scrolling decoration and four turquoise enameled hearts, the circular face with Arabic chapters, 10.3cm. high.
(Christie's) $350

Liberty & Co., an "English Pewter" plain arch mantel timepiece with enameled dial.
(David Lay) $250

A Liberty & Co. oak and enamel mantel clock designed by Archibald Knox, the circular dial with a red scrolling design on a mottled blue and green ground, 29.3cm. high. (Christie's) $2,000

A Liberty & Co. lightly hammered silver mantel clock, with panels of repoussé decoration, the circular clock face with Arabic chapters, stamped L&Co with Birmingham hallmarks for 1911, 14.5cm. high, 760 grams gross.
(Christie's) $1,500

A Liberty and Co. hammered pewter clock, the body decorated with stylised tree and foliate panels, the copper clock face with black enamel Roman chapters and turquoise enamel center, 18.2cm high.
(Christie's) $1,000

A Liberty & Co. Tudric pewter clock designed by Archibald Knox, decorated with rectangular panels of abalone, circular dial with Roman chapters, circa 1902, 16.7cm. high.
(Christie's) $2,250

A Liberty & Co. pewter and enamel clock of domed rectangular outline, the circular dial centered in blue and turquoise enamels, 18cm. high, factory marks and '01156' to base.
(Phillips) $800

A Liberty & Co. 'Cymric' silver and enameled timepiece, embellished with a tree motif against a ground of colored enamels, Birmingham marks for 1903, 11.5cm. high.
(Phillips) $7,750

LYRE CLOCKS

The lyre clock was a wall or shelf clock which first appeared in France in the late 18th century. It is named from its lyre shaped frame, often of bronze or ormolu mounted marble, which could be decorated with enamel or diamanté. The dial was mounted in the lower part, with the gridiron pendulum suspended above to simulate lyre strings. The bob was connected to the escapement and sometimes formed a ring set with paste brilliants around the dial.

An 8 day version was also produced in America by firms in Massachusetts between circa 1820–40.

A Regency rosewood striking mantel clock of lyre form, circular 3in. white enamel dial signed *Thwaites & Reed, London*, 8in. high.
(Bonhams) $1,800

A 19th century French white marble and ormolu mounted lyre clock, 1ft.4in. high.
$2,000

Louis XVI style gilt-bronze mounted white alabaster lyre clock, Japy Frères, late 19th century, the white enameled dial painted with floral festoons, 24in. high.
(Butterfield & Butterfield) $1,800

A 19th century Viennese enamel and silver-mounted timepiece of lyre shape, painted with scenes of Omphale, Queen of Lydia, with Hercules spinning yarn, 11½in. high, overall.
(Christie's S. Ken) $4,000

A 19th century French mahogany and ormolu mounted mantel clock of lyre shape, the twin train movement striking on a bell, 19½in. high.
(Christie's) $2,000

An Empire ormolu and bronze mantel clock of lyre shape supported upon seated griffins, 10½in. high.
$2,250

A 19th century French ormolu mantel clock, the case in the form of a lyre, 38cm. high, on an oval ebonised stand under a glass shade.
$1,350

Louis XVI style marble and ormolu mantel clock, France, 19th century, lyre form frame on stepped oval base (key missing), 48cm. high.
(Skinner Inc.) $1,850

MAHOGANY

A 19th century mahogany and brass inlaid mantel clock, the circular painted dial signed Condliff, Liverpool, 35cm.high. **$1,500**

A Regency mahogany mantel timepiece signed Weeks Museum, Coventry St., on the enamel dial, 12in. high. **$2,250**

A Regency mahogany and brass inlaid mantel timepiece with circular enamel dial (damaged), 9½in. high. **$600**

A Victorian mahogany mantel clock with stepped chamfered top, inscribed Yonge and Son, Strand, London, the twin fusee movement with shaped plates and engraved border, 18½in. high. (Christie's) **$1,650**

A George III mahogany striking clock, the case on gilt brass ball feet with fish-scale sound frets to sides and front door, chapter disc signed *Gravel & Son, London*, 16¾in. high. (Christie's) **$1,350**

A 19th century mahogany nightwatchman's timepiece, the silvered dial with outer recording ring and with plunger above, the fusee movement with anchor escapement. (Phillips) **$525**

An early 19th century mahogany mantel regulator, the 7¼in. silvered dial signed Reid & Auld Edinr., 17in. high. **$5,000**

A late 19th century mahogany night watchman's clock, 5in. engraved silvered dial inscribed *H. H. Plante*, 15in. high. (Bonhams) **$600**

A 19th century mahogany and brass inlaid clock, with anchor escapement chiming the quarters on two bells, 1ft.10in. high. (Phillips) **$1,250**

MARBLE

A Regency white marble and gilt bronze mantel timepiece, the gilt dial signed Viner, London, 8in. high. **$1,000**

A French ormolu and porcelain paneled mantel clock, signed on the dial *Le Roy & Fils, Palais Royal, a Paris, Rue Montpellier*, the eight-day movement with outside countwheel strike on a bell, 12in. high. (Christie's S. Ken) **$825**

Late 19th century red and black marble mantel clock with strike. (British Antique Exporters) **$100**

A late 18th century French white marble and ormolu mantel clock, the case surmounted by a twin handled urn flanked by columns wrapped with leaves, 15¹⁄₂in. high. (Phillips) **$750**

A fin-de-siècle pink marble and ormolu small mantel timepiece, signed *Le Roy & Fils 57 New Bond Strt. Made in France Palais Royal Paris* with pierced gilt hands, the going barrel movement with lever escapement, 6¹⁄₄in. high. (Christie's) **$1,200**

A Regency ormolu and marble mantel timepiece, the case on milled bun feet supporting the rectangular white marble base applied with a ribbon-tied fruiting swag, signed *Webster London*, 8in. high. (Christie's) **$2,000**

Louis XVI bronze and white marble mantel clock, early 19th century, urn finials and circular dial, 25in. high. (Skinner Inc.) **$1,850**

A good black marble and bronze mounted mantel timepiece in Egyptian style, single fusee movement signed on the backplate *Vulliamy, London*, 9in. high. (Christie's S. Ken) **$40,000**

A 19th century French gilt brass and white marble mantel timepiece, the rectangular case surmounted by a rooster, 7½in. high. (Phillips) **$700**

OAK CASED

A late Victorian three-train oak mantel clock, the fusée anchor movement with silvered dial, the case with break-arch top, circa 1880, 20in. high.
(Tennants) $750

Victorian pollard oak cased mantel clock with eight day Continental movement.
(British Antique Exporters) $200

A Hiller talking clock, with single-train timepiece movement connected to the speaking movement, in oak case with full-height dial, 16½in. high, circa 1911.
(Christie's) $4,500

A Gustav Stickley oak mantel clock, early 20th century, the door with faceted cut-out framing brass dial, Seth Thomas movement, 13¾in. high.
(Skinner Inc.) $2,500

An oak cased railway station clock, the white 14in. dial with black Roman numerals, initialed *B.R. W*, 23in. high.
(Bonhams) $375

Carved oak cased chiming mantel clock, German movement, square dial with brass spandrels, 17½in. high.
(G. A. Key) $375

Gustav Stickley mantel clock, circa 1902, overhanging top above single door with copper hardware, Seth Thomas works, 21in. high
(Skinner) $6,500

A Westminster chime Admiral's hat mantel clock in an oak case, circa 1930. $45

L. & J. G. Stickley mantel clock, Fayetteville, New York, circa 1910, designed by Peter Heinrich Hansen, signed with Handcraft decal, 22in. high.
(Skinner Inc.) $7,000

ORMOLU & PORCELAIN

A 19th century French ormolu and porcelain mounted mantel clock, the dial signed E. W. Streeter, 11in. high. **$1,100**

A 19th century French ormolu and porcelain mounted mantel clock, the case surmounted by a gilt urn with ram's head supports, 14¹/₂in. high. (Phillips) **$900**

A Paris (Jacob Petit) clock-case and stand of scroll out-line, blue JP marks, circa 1835, 37cm. high overall. **$1,850**

An ormolu and dark blue ground Sevres pattern porce-lain mantel clock, signed *Lister & Sons S F 20 Paris,* late 19th century, 20in. high. (Christie's) **$3,350**

A Second Empire porcelain mounted ormolu mantel clock, the Sèvres style dial with Roman chapters, backplate with the stamp of *Brocot,* set with a further porcelain panel of Cupid, 13in. high. (Christie's) **$900**

An ormolu and dark blue ground porcelain mantel clock, the shapèd dial centered with a maritime scene above a cartouche painted with a har-bor scene 17in. high. (Christie's) **$1,250**

Victorian gilded spelter mantel clock, with pink and white polychrome decorated reserve panels and face, early 19th century, 15in. high. (G.A. Key) **$500**

A Charles X ormolu and por-celain clock, the movement signed Leroy , Paris 1102, 16in. high. **$1,500**

A French 19th century ormolu and porcelain mounted clock, painted dial with Roman chapter, bell striking movement, signed *R. and C.,* 14¹/₂in. (Bonhams) **$1,000**

PORCELAIN

Late 19th century Dresden clock group, 66.5cm. high. **$1,500**

A Louis XVI ormolu and terracotta mantel clock, the dial signed Sotiau A Paris, with figures of Minerva and attendants, 18in. wide. **$5,000**

Ansonia porcelain mantel clock with Roman numerals. **$450**

A 19th century Continental porcelain mantel clock, the Meissen case decorated with four putti representing the Seasons, the associated movement stamped *Hy Marc Paris*, 1ft. 6in. high. (Phillips) **$4,750**

An unusual 19th century Austrian miniature porcelain timepiece, the shaped case decorated with flowers on paw feet, signed *Doker, in Wien*, 55mm. high. (Phillips) **$700**

A Martin Brothers stoneware mantel clock, the base decorated to each corner with fierce griffin-like heads, the arched pediment raised off twin griffin supports with applied lizard above, 31.5cm. high. (Phillips) **$1,750**

A 19th century French porcelain mantel clock with eight-day striking movement, inscribed Raingo Freres, Paris, 15in. high. **$500**

Weller Dickensware art pottery mantel clock, housed in elaborated pottery frame decorated with yellow pansies, 10in. high. (Skinner Inc.) **$400**

A Meissen clock case of shaped outline, circa 1880, the eight-day striking movement with enamel dial, 41.5cm. high. **$2,250**

A Viennese picture clock, depicting an inland river scene, the Roman enamel dial set into the clock tower, the going barrel movement with pierced-out plates and lever escapement, 29 x 24½in.
(Christie's) $1,500

A Viennese quarter striking picture clock depicting carousing cavaliers at a tavern with lakeland views and castle, with silk suspended pendulum in carved giltwood frame, circa 1850, 39½ x 29in.
(Christie's) $5,000

A musical picture clock with figures on a river bank with the clock face in church tower, in a carved gilded frame, 29½ x 34½in. overall, circa 1850. $2,250

A Big Ben musical picture clock in black wooden case, the melody playing every quarter, or on pulling the cord, 70cm. high.
(Auction Team Köln) $450

A Viennese picture clock depicting sportsmen and their dogs, twin going barrel movement stamped *Villenense* with recoil escapement and strike on gong, 28¼ x 23in.
(Christie's) $2,500

A German framed automaton windmill novelty timepiece, the printed landscape depicting a windmill with automaton sails, dated *1892* above the doorway, 20¼in. high.
(Christie's) $1,850

A musical clock set into the frame of a Bavarian landscape picture, with Roman numerals and playing two melodies.
(Herholdt Jensen) $650

A rare French automaton clock picture, Napoléon III, Paris, circa 1851, depicting the Crystal Palace, Hyde Park, with two rows of automated figures, 122cm. wide.
(Sotheby's) $11,000

A Viennese quarter striking picture clock, the painting on copper depicting a harvest scene with the sea and mountains in the background, circa 1860, 35¼ x 36½in.
(Christie's) $3,350

This name is given to one of the most attractive of American shelf clocks, having delicate feet, slender pillars, one at each side and one in the center, with a broken arch or double scroll at the top. They are sometimes also called Terry clocks, as Eli Terry, a Connecticut clockmaker and businessman, was the first to produce them in large numbers around 1816. They continued in production until the 1830s, and other notable manufacturers were Seth Thomas and Silas Hoadley, also of Connecticut.

Federal mahogany pillar and scroll clock, by Ephraim Downes, Conn., circa 1825, 31in. high. $1,250

A Federal mahogany pillar and scroll clock, by E. Terry & Sons, circa 1835, 31in. high. $1,500

A late Federal mahogany pillar and scroll shelf clock, Seth Thomas, Plymouth, Connecticut, circa 1820, with a glazed cupboard door flanked by colonettes and enclosing a white dial with Arabic chapter ring, 31in. high.
(Christie's) $1,350

A Federal mahogany shelf clock, labeled Seth Thomas, Plymouth, Connecticut, first quarter 19th century, the swan neck pediment above a rectangular case with double glazed door, 29in. high.
(Christie's) $1,300

A Federal pillar and scroll shelf clock by Seth Thomas, Plymouth, Connecticut, circa 1805, the swan's-neck pediment centering three brass urn finials, 31in. high.
(Christie's) $3,500

A Federal mahogany pillar and scroll clock, by E. Terry & Sons, Conn., circa 1820, 29in. high. $2,250

Federal mahogany pillar and scroll clock, by Ephraim Downs for G. Mitchell, Conn., circa 1820, 31in. high. $1,350

Federal mahogany pillar and scroll clock, E. Terry & Sons, Conn., circa 1825, 31in. high. $1,000

SHELF CLOCKS

The shelf clock, either weight or spring powered, was designed, as its name suggests, to stand on a shelf, and is the first truly indigenous American clock. It became the best known and most typical American clock because it was adopted and developed by the infant manufacturing industry in Connecticut. Eli Terry's first production model was in a box case with a plain glass door, on the inside of which were painted the hour numerals and simple corner spandrel decorations. The wooden movement could be seen through the glass, with an hour bell below, a pendulum in front, and a weight on each side.

Victorian 'ginger bread' framed shelf clock with an Ansonia Clock Co. striking movement. $200

Round Gothic shelf clock, probably by Brewster & Ingraham, circa 1845. 20in. high. $1,000

An Empire carved mahogany shelf clock, by M. Leavenworth & Son, Conn., 30in. high. $2,250

A hammered copper shelf clock, by Tiffany & Co., New York, early 20th century, on rectangular brass platform base, 11in. high. (Skinner Inc.) $1,000

Empire mahogany carved shelf clock, by Eli Terry & Son, Conn., circa 1825, 31in. high. $1,350

Federal mahogany shelf clock, by Aaron Willard, Mass., circa 1825, 34in. high. $11,500

An Empire carved mahogany shelf clock, by Riley Whiting, Conn., circa 1825, 29½in. high. $600

A Federal mahogany shelf clock, by Reuben Tower, Massa., 1836, 34½in. high. $12,750

The skeleton clock first became popular in France in the second half of the eighteenth century, not finding favor with the English for almost a hundred years. The wheels of the movement pivoted not in a solid plate but in an open, usually brass, framework, which would be mounted on a wooden or marble base and covered by a glass dome. The dial was often a plain silvered ring fixed to the front frame. The later Victorian examples show clear Gothic influence, being often in the shape of a cathedral, say Westminster Abbey, or even the Brighton pavilion. These are elaborate works of art and sell for correspondingly high prices.

A 19th century brass skeleton clock, on an oval rosewood base, under a glass shade, 1ft. 11in. high. $3,750

A skeleton clock of Lichfield Cathedral type, dated 1851, 17½in. high. $1,500

A Victorian helical-geared small skeleton timepiece, the silvered frame with double-screwed pillars, single chain fusée with helical gearing to the anchor escapement, 10in. high. (Christie's) $2,250

A brass chiming skeleton clock, on oval oak base with glass dome, English, circa 1900, 24in. high including dome. $8,250

A 19th century brass striking skeleton clock, the pierced shaped and waisted plates with six turned screwed pillars, on oval ebonised base, with glass dome, 13in. high. (Christie's S. Ken.) $2,250

A Victorian brass skeleton clock, 12½in. high, with glass dome. $4,750

An unusual English skeleton clock, the movement placed between two C-scrolls, anchor escapement, based on the famous model by William Strutt, 29cm. high. (Duran) $800

A 19th century French brass skeleton alarm timepiece, with engraved A plates, 10¼in. high. (Phillips) $650

The table clock is a small metal cased clock with a horizontal dial, designed to be placed on a table and viewed from above. They were mostly made in Germany and date from the late 16th to early 18th centuries. The earliest are also known as drum clocks in which the iron movement is typically of skeleton form with balance, in a gilt brass case with silver chapter ring.

Table clock is also a more accurate description of many particularly English clocks dating from 1675–1800 termed mantel or bracket clocks.

An early Anglo-Flemish weight driven clock, circa 1600, 19cm. high. $1,500

An enameled silver grande sonnerie world time table clock, signed Patek Philippe & Co., Geneve, 7½in. diam. $40,000

A French 19th century white marble and bronze table clock, trumpet playing winged putto carrying a drum incorporating an eight day cylinder movement, signed *Falconnet*, 9in. (Bonhams) $750

An early electric Eureka table clock in glazed mahogany case, the signed white enamel dial with Roman numerals and subsidiary seconds, dated 1906, 13¼in. high. (Christie's) $1,100

An ormolu and bronze table clock of Louis XVI design, the terrestrial globe case supported by three putti on shaped base edged with scrolls, 30in. high. (Christie's) $5,000

An important silver mounted gilt table clock, the movement signed *D. Buschman [Augsburg]*, raised on four paw feet each chased with winged mask, circa 1660, 6in. high. (Christie's) $8,000

A 19th century Japanese table clock in glazed shitan wood case, with chain fusee going and spring barrel striking train with outside countwheel, 7½in. (Christie's) $5,000

A Germanic late Renaissance quarter-striking hexagonal table clock signed Michael Fabian Thorn, the movement with baluster pillars, steel great wheels, chain fusee for the going, 6in. diam. (Christie's) $7,000

A 17th century German quarter striking table clock, decorated with the figure of a hound with automated eyes and tail, the dial to the side with silvered chapter and center alarm set, 8in. high.
(Phillips) $8,000

A 16th century gilt metal drum clock, 6cm. diam., together with an alarm mechanism of drum form.
$3,500

A gilt quarter striking table clock with alarm by *Johann Gottlieb Thÿm à Thorn*, on four silvered lion feet, the sides with conforming glazed panels, early 18th century, 5¹⁄₂in. wide.
(Christie's) $7,000

A mahogany Steeple table clock, the American 8 day movement by the Gilbert Clock Co. Winsted CT, striking on a gong, the painted metal dial with Roman numerals, 43cm. high, circa 1850.
(Auction Team Köln) $200

A Biedermeier ormolu mounted walnut and parquetry automaton table clock with organ, the front with an automaton representing a garden grotto with rotating glass rods simulating water jets spouting into the mouths of dolphins, 22¹⁄₄in. high.
(Christie's) $20,000

An interesting 19th century Japanese table clock in pierced cast gilt brass drum case glazed to the top, the white enamel chapter-ring with Japanese numerals, 4³⁄₄in. high.
(Christie's S. Ken) $3,750

A 17th century gilt brass table clock, the rectangular case surmounted by a bell, 17cm. high. $4,750

An early 18th century gilt brass Continental table clock, the square case with glazed apertures to the sides and winged paw feet, 13cm. square.
(Phillips) $3,000

A mid 17th century French gilt brass table clock with minute hand, calendar and alarm, signed G. Estienne A Caen, 12in. high. $250,000

CARS 1900–1909
BING

Ignaz and Adolf Bing opened their Gebrüder Bing works in Nuremberg in 1863, and they went on to become one of the 'Big Three' German toy manufacturers of the later 19th century, the others being Märklin and Lehmann.

They produced a wide range of clockwork toys, boats, steam-driven models, trains and cars and their work was characterised from the first by the solidity of its construction and by a meticulous attention to detail. The best of their cars were hand painted, had opening doors and beveled glass.

Up to 1918, Bing products were marked *GBN* (Gebrüder Bing Nuremberg), whereas after 1919 they were marked *BW* (Bing Werke).

BUB

The Karl Bub Company was founded as far back as 1851 in Nuremberg and is most famous for its range of clockwork and electric model trains. It took over the Bing company in 1933, and after the Second World War had a factory in England, although their products are not generally well-known over here. The company ceased trading in 1967.

CARETTE

The Carette company was founded in Nuremberg in 1886 by Georges Carette, and came to be regarded as one of the top toy manufacturers of the period. Quality was paramount and many toys, such as large scale cars, boats and trains, were hand-enameled. There was also great attention to detail and early Carette cars are unique in having folding windscreens and hand brakes.

Carette closed in 1917 and did not start up again until after the First World War. Their trademarks are *GC* or *GC & Cie.*

A rare 'De Dion', hand enameled tinplate car, by Bing, circa 1904, finished in white, with maroon seats, black interior, 7¾in. long. (Christie's) $3,500

Carette, a clockwork four seater Torpedo, hand painted in cream with green lining, lacking lamps, windscreen and two tires, 32cm. long. (Phillips) $6,300

Lehmann, No. 686 clockwork open tourer with hood 'Berolina' finished in blue with gold lining and yellow fabric hood, 10.5cm.   (Phillips) $1,500

"Hessmobile", a lithographed and painted tinplate two seater car, with a hand-cranked flywheel mechanism, by Hess, circa 1908, 8¾in. long. $600

A rare Marklin clockwork four-seat Tourer, German, circa 1909, 9¼in. long.   **$9,000**

An unusual Marklin small limousine, German, circa 1900, 8¼in. long.   **$4,000**

A Carette lithographed tinplate and clockwork rear entrance four-seater Tonneau automobile, 12¼in. long, German, circa 1907.   **$3,750**

A Bing hand-painted open-cab limousine with beveled glass windows, German, circa 1908, 10½in. long.   **$4,000**

A live-steam spirit-fired, hand enameled model of a horseless carriage, probably by Bing, circa 1902, 9in. long.   **$2,250**

A Carette tinplate Open Tourer, German, circa 1906, 8in. long, together with original cardboard box.   **$6,000**

A Bing hand-enameled tinplate model of a De Dion runabout motor car, circa 1905, 7½in. long.   **$1,100**

A German hand-painted Bing limousine, circa 1908, 8in.   **$2,250**

CARS 1910–1919

GUNTHERMANN

Siegfried Gunthermann
founded his toymaking firm
in Nuremberg in 1877. He
died in 1890 and his widow
remarried Adolf Wiegel,
whose initials were
incorporated in Gunthermann
toys until 1919, after which
time *SG* was used.

Gunthermann are famous
for their tinplate horse-drawn
vehicles, fire engines and
aeroplanes, all of which were
of very high quality, while
their clockwork cars, dating
from the 1930s and 40s, are
now among the most
collectable of the period.

MÄRKLIN

The firm of Gebrüder
Märklin was established in
1859 in Göppingen, in
Bavaria. It produced toys that
were mainly for the export
market, and manufactured
trains etc. in styles and
liveries according to the taste
of the importing country, also
altering the names on ships
accordingly.

They have remained
preeminent in the field of toy
production up to the present
day.

MOKO

The Moko trademark is that
of Moses Kohnstam who set
up as a toy distributor and
wholesaler in Furth,
Germany, in 1875. He was
used by many local toy
manufacturers to market their
toys, which often carried the
Kohnstam trademark.

In the 1930s the
Kohnstams fled the Nazis
and came to England, where
Moses' grandson Richard
continued to manufacture and
also to wholesale the
products of small London
companies such as Benbros
and Lesney. There is also a
small range of interesting
diecast toys by unknown
manufacturers which bear the
Kohnstam mark.

A hand painted limousine, by Carette, circa 1912,
complete with clockwork mechanism driving rear
axle, operating brake (lacks chauffeur and headlamps),
10½in. long. (Christie's)   **$1,500**

An early hand-enameled four seater open tourer,
No. 3358/21, by Carette, circa 1911, with clockwork
mechanism driving rear axle, composition painted
chauffeur (very slightly chipped), 21cm. long.
(Christie's)   **$4,500**

A Carette lithographed tinplate clockwork model of
a four seater tonneau, with rubber tired spoked
wheels, handbrake, and side lamps, 33cm. long.
(Henry Spencer)   **$3,000**

A repainted tinplate limousine, with clockwork mech-
ansim driving rear axle, possibly by H. Fischer & Co.,
circa 1912, 13in. long. (Christie's S. Ken)   **$375**

A Carette hand-painted four-seat Open Tourer, German, circa 1910, 12½in. long, together with original cardboard box. $11,250

A Moko clockwork six-cylinder saloon, 9½in. long, German, circa 1918-20. $750

A Bing tinplate De Dion vehicle, the clockwork mechanism driving the rear axle, 6in. long, German, circa 1910. $1,100

A printed tinplate model of a limousine, by Carette, circa 1910, 15½in. long. $2,500

A Carette tinplate and clockwork limousine, circa 1910. $3,000

A Carette lithograph limousine, with clockwork mechanism, German, circa 1911, 8½in. long. $1,850

A Gunthermann tinplate four-seat open tourer and passengers, German, circa 1910, 7½in. long. $4,500

A Carette lithographed limousine, complete with driver, German, circa 1910, 8½in. long. $3,000

CARS 1920–1929

C I J

This, the Compagnie Industrielle du Jouet, was a French company founded in the 1920s and based in Paris. They produced high quality, large scale clockwork cars, such as the Alfa Romeo P2, which was almost 22 inches long.

Their products are very sought after, and mint boxed examples of this particular model have fetched over £2,000 at auction.

J E P

JEP (Jouets de Paris) was a subsidiary of the Société Industrielle de Ferblanterie (SIF), which was established in France in 1899. The JEP trademark was used between 1932 and 1965, when the company went out of business.

MARX ·

Louis Marx established his toy company in New York in 1920.

His products were often aimed at the lower end of the market, being popular, amusing and cheap. A factory was opened in South Wales in the 1930s, but following the Second World War most products were manufactured in the Far East.

TIPP & CO

Tipp & Carstans established a toy manufactory in 1912 in Nuremberg, to which by 1919 Philipp Ullmann had succeeded as sole owner. During the 1930s the company turned out a fine range of large-scale tinplate cars and planes.

The rise of Nazism meant that by 1934 Ullmann was forced to leave Germany. He came to the UK and settled in South Wales, where the company continued to manufacture tinplate toys until 1971.

Their trademark is an intertwined *T.Co* or *Tippco*.

A rare Fischer lithographed and painted tinplate limousine, with clockwork mechanism driving rear axle, German, circa 1927 (roof chipped, slightly damaged), 12½in. long. (Christie's) $800

A fine Distler printed and painted tinplate limousine No. 525, with chauffeur in front compartment, finished in tan over black, German, circa 1927, 6½in. long. (Christie's) $350

Automobile mechanique Andre Citroen, a large clockwork four door saloon, finished in two tone blue with black roof, 53.5cm., 1920's. (Phillips) $2,500

A rare hand painted tinplate four seater open tourer steam car by Doll & Co., circa 1924. (Christie's) $4,500

A printed tinplate model of a limousine, by Tipp, circa 1920, 15in. long.
$600

An early Bing hand-painted open four-seat Tourer, German, circa 1920, 12¼in. long.
$5,000

A Bub tinplate and clockwork roadster, with tinplate driver, 36cm. long overall.　　**$2,250**

The Buddy 'L', a painted metal push-along model T Ford Coupe, 10½in. long, U.S.A., circa 1924.　　**$600**

A printed and painted tinplate model of a four-door limousine with clockwork mechanism, by Tipp & Co., circa 1928, 8¼in. long.　　**$900**

Gunthermann Fire Car, German, circa 1925, 6¾in. long.　　**$1,000**

A J.E.P. tinplate Renault Open Tourer, French, circa 1929, 13¼in. long.　　**$1,500**

Turner steel four door sedan, circa 1924, 26½in. long.　　**$1,275**

CARS 1930–1939

METTOY

The Mettoy Company was set up by Philipp Ullmann (of Tipp fame) and one of his erstwhile collaborators in Germany, Arthur Katz, after both men were forced to flee the Nazis in 1934. They took factory space with a firm of Northampton based engineers, where they developed a range of tinplate toys and finally opened their own factory in 1936, launching the Mettoy company in the same year. The first catalog showed a range of tinplate and pressed metal toys very similar to those which had been made by Tipp. Many had clockwork mechanisms. Among the most sought after examples from this period are the large racing car in red and white and the medium size car and caravan.

After 1942 the factory switched to making armaments and production was not resumed until 1946, when a new catalog was brought out, featuring many of the prewar lines, with slight variations.

In 1948 they launched a new range of heavy cast metal toys produced exclusively for Marks & Spencer. These were more robust than previous examples, and included coaches, a racing car, a fire engine, a lorry, van and saloons. The 830 racer even featured a clockwork engine, brake lever and steering control. This Heavy Car Mechanical Toys range was in production until 1951.

In 1949 the company opened a new factory in Swansea and it was here that the famous Corgi range of diecast models was made in the 1950s. Pressed tin toys continued to be made until 1960, when production switched entirely to the diecast Corgi products.

A printed and painted saloon, with clockwork mechanism driving rear axle, lady driver with hat and scarf, by Falk, circa 1933, 18in. long. (Christie's) $1,100

J.E.P., large painted tinplate Rolls Royce open tourer finished in cream with red mudguards, lithographed 'wooden' running boards, 51cm., repainted, No. 7395 fatigue to driving shaft.   (Phillips) $1,500

Marx spring action two door saloon finished in red, black and brown, 19.5cm.   (Phillips) $75

The American National Company, painted steel model of a Packard finished in red with red and yellow lining, 73cm. long.   (Phillips) $1,800

296

A Lehmann 'Gala' tinplate limousine, German, circa 1930, 12½in. $1,100

A Marx Charlie McCarthy & Mortimer Snerd auto, 1939, lithographed tin, 16in. long. $825

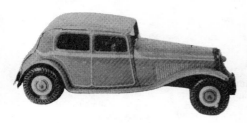

A Bing lithographed open tourer, the clockwork mechanism driving the rear axle, 12½in. long, German, circa 1930. $475

A Daimler Sedanca motor car, in the original box. $600

Mettoy, a large four-door Saloon finished in bright lime-green with cream lining, the interior with chaffeur at the wheel, in box, 35cm. long. $150

Painted and lithographed tin wind-up sedan, circa 1930, 11½in. long. $675

Fischer tinplate saloon finished in red and black, German, circa 1935, 12½in. long. $1,100

A large and impressive Karl Bub tinplate and clockwork limousine, circa 1932, German, 50cm. long. $1,850

CARS 1940–1970

CHAD VALLEY

By the 1930s and 40s British companies were working hard to compete with Continental tinplate toys. One of the most successful was the Chad Valley Co., which produced many diverse items from rag dolls to board games, but who also at this time produced a range of cars, ships and aeroplanes which were very much cheaper than their German counterparts. Their cars were mainly of the clockwork type, and in the 1930s their racing cars enjoyed a huge success. They are becoming increasingly sought after today.

CORGI

The 'Golden Age' of British toys, in the 1950s, saw the rise of a number of well-known companies. Corgi Toys was founded in 1956 and produced model cars etc. which were both innovative and represented excellent value for money. Their Chipperfield's Circus Gift Set in original box is now worth several hundred pounds. They also skilfully judged the market by launching models based on current crazes, the James Bond 'Goldfinger' Aston Martin DB5, for example, or Chitty Chitty Bang Bang, or even the Avengers Gift Set. Sadly, they too succumbed to flood of cheap imports from the Far East and went out of business in the 1970s.

ICHIKO

The Ichiko Company set up in post war Japan and produced tin toys, with cars as a speciality. Some have since been reissued, for example a 1960s large scale Mercedes Benz 300 SE was replicated in the 1980s. Collectors should therefore be careful as to the exact dating of any example.

A Distler gray battery-operated tinplate Porsche Electromatic 7500, with instructions, in original box.
(Christie's S. Ken) $900

A Wells printed and painted tinplate Rolls-Royce 'Coupe de Ville' limousine, with clockwork mechanism, 8¾ in. long, British, circa 1950. (Christie's) $275

Britains set 1321, large armored car with swiveling gun, khaki finish with white rubber treaded tires in original box (E-G, box G)1937. (Phillips) $425

Dinky, a rare half dozen trade pack of 106 'The Prisoner' mini-mokes, in original boxes and original cellophane wrapping. (Christie's S. Ken) $1,000

ALPS battery operated Mystery car finished in two tone red and cream, the interior with lithographed detail, 30cm. (Phillips) $800

Schuco 5300 Ingenico, the open top saloon car finished in bright red, the interior lithographed in green and checkered seats, 22cm. (Phillips) $500

CARS 1940–1970
MATCHBOX

From 1953 the Lesney Company in Essex produced the Matchbox range of contemporary vehicles, their size, as the name suggests, being generally smaller than the average Dinky type. From 1956, they added the Model of Yesteryear Range. Models dating up to 1962 are generally sought after, but prices decline sharply thereafter. The company is still in existence today.

In 1982 Matchbox Toys was formed to replace Lesney products which had sold out to David Yeh of Universal Toys. In 1987 Matchbox purchased the Dinky name and launched a new range of Dinky products. Manufacturing is now done in the Far East, though the research and development departments are based in Enfield.

SOLIDO

Solido is a post war French company making diecast models, the earliest of which date from the early 60s. They are still in business today, but as is the case with Dinky, are no longer the same company, having been subject to a number of takeovers.

SPOT-ON

The Triang Company countered the success of Dinky with their Spot-on range, which were produced between 1959 and 1967. These models were beautifully detailed, with proper suspension and numerous features. The average mint boxed car fetches around £50 while the Bedford 'S' Shell-BP Tanker fetches upwards of £700 and the LT Routemaster Bus almost £500. Many consider them now to be underpriced, so they could be looked on, with caution, as a reasonably good buy. Spot-On closed in 1967, and the dies were shipped overseas.

Corgi, 262, Lincoln Continental, in rare color scheme, blue/tan. (Phillips West Two) $225

Distler Electro Matic 7500, lithographed and painted battery operated Porsche car, with telesteering control, in original box, circa 1955, 9¾in. long. (Christie's S. Ken) $575

A Schuco Mercedes 190SL Elektro-Phänomenal 5503, with accessories and instructions, in original box, circa 1959. (Christie's S. Ken) $400

A Spot On Ford Zodiac No.100, original factory box. (Hobbs & Chambers) $75

KKK battery operated open top saloon car finished in red with cream interior and working head lights, 21.5cm., boxed. (Phillips) $110

Schuco, clockwork Radio Car 5000 finished in maroon and cream, complete with key and instructions, boxed. (Phillips) $2,750

DIRKS

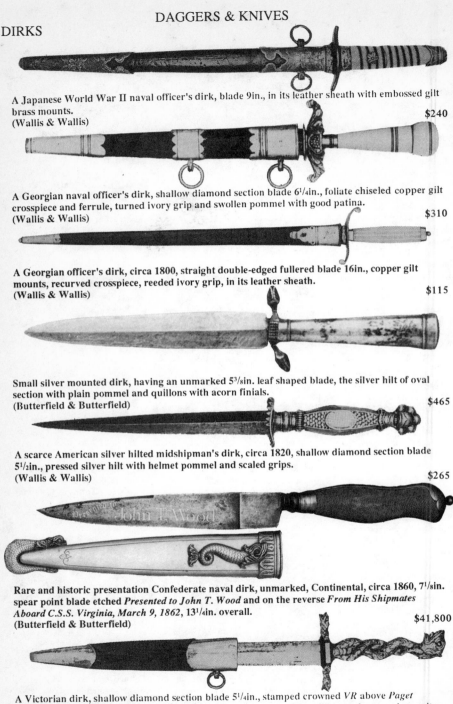

A Japanese World War II naval officer's dirk, blade 9in., in its leather sheath with embossed gilt brass mounts.
(Wallis & Wallis) $240

A Georgian naval officer's dirk, shallow diamond section blade 6¼in., foliate chiseled copper gilt crosspiece and ferrule, turned ivory grip and swollen pommel with good patina.
(Wallis & Wallis) $310

A Georgian officer's dirk, circa 1800, straight double-edged fullered blade 16in., copper gilt mounts, recurved crosspiece, reeded ivory grip, in its leather sheath.
(Wallis & Wallis) $115

Small silver mounted dirk, having an unmarked 5³⁄₈in. leaf shaped blade, the silver hilt of oval section with plain pommel and quillons with acorn finials.
(Butterfield & Butterfield) $465

A scarce American silver hilted midshipman's dirk, circa 1820, shallow diamond section blade 5¹⁄₂in., pressed silver hilt with helmet pommel and scaled grips.
(Wallis & Wallis) $265

Rare and historic presentation Confederate naval dirk, unmarked, Continental, circa 1860, 7¹⁄₈in. spear point blade etched *Presented to John T. Wood* and on the reverse *From His Shipmates Aboard C.S.S. Virginia, March 9, 1862*, 13¹⁄₄in. overall.
(Butterfield & Butterfield) $41,800

A Victorian dirk, shallow diamond section blade 5¼in., stamped crowned *VR* above *Paget* London, copper gilt hilt in the form of entwined sea monster with quillons and pommel en-suite.
(Wallis & Wallis) $185

HUNTING KNIVES

Bowie or hunting knife by John Coe, Sheffield, circa 1860, 15¹³/₁₆in. clip point blade, German silver hilt with ivory and horn grip scales, 21¹/₂in. overall.
(Butterfield & Butterfield) **$3,800**

Bowie or hunting knife by Joseph Rogers, Sheffield, circa 1890, 10³/₄in. spear point blade, stag horn grip and nickel silver mounted leather sheath, 14¹/₂in. overall.
(Butterfield & Butterfield) **$2,100**

Elaborate French hunting knife, circa 1850, 11⁵/₈in. spear point blade, profusely floral etched on ricasso and towards tip, marked *L. Chobert-Arquer à Paris*, the stag handle flanked by an iron guard and pommel cap, 17¹/₄in. overall.
(Butterfield & Butterfield) **$7,150**

A Victorian hunting knife, broad tapered single edged polished blade 8¹/₂in., molded horn octagonal grip with silver bands in the form of buckled straps, in its leather sheath.
(Wallis & Wallis) **$285**

An Imperial Russian hunting dagger from the Zlatoust Arsenal, double-edged blade 6³/₄in. etched with rabbits, flowers, foliage and *Zlatoust* in Cyrillic within fuller.
(Wallis & Wallis) **$345**

KNIFE PISTOLS

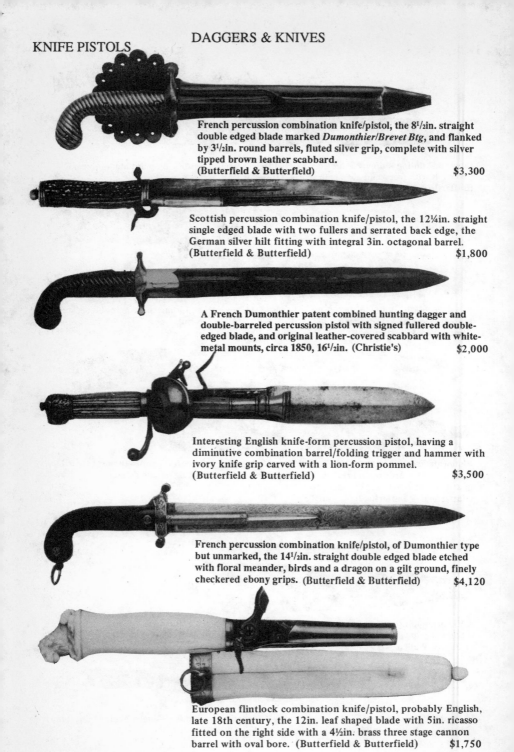

French percussion combination knife/pistol, the 8¹/₂in. straight double edged blade marked *Dumonthier/Brevet Btg*, and flanked by 3¹/₂in. round barrels, fluted silver grip, complete with silver tipped brown leather scabbard.
(Butterfield & Butterfield) $3,300

Scottish percussion combination knife/pistol, the 12¼in. straight single edged blade with two fullers and serrated back edge, the German silver hilt fitting with integral 3in. octagonal barrel.
(Butterfield & Butterfield) $1,800

A French Dumonthier patent combined hunting dagger and double-barreled percussion pistol with signed fullered double-edged blade, and original leather-covered scabbard with white-metal mounts, circa 1850, 16¹/₂in. (Christie's) $2,000

Interesting English knife-form percussion pistol, having a diminutive combination barrel/folding trigger and hammer with ivory knife grip carved with a lion-form pommel.
(Butterfield & Butterfield) $3,500

French percussion combination knife/pistol, of Dumonthier type but unmarked, the 14¹/₂in. straight double edged blade etched with floral meander, birds and a dragon on a gilt ground, finely checkered ebony grips. (Butterfield & Butterfield) $4,120

European flintlock combination knife/pistol, probably English, late 18th century, the 12in. leaf shaped blade with 5in. ricasso fitted on the right side with a 4½in. brass three stage cannon barrel with oval bore. (Butterfield & Butterfield) $1,750

A rare German Hauswehr with heavy single-edged blade curving up to meet the decoratively notched point, struck at the base on one face with two orb and cross marks, iron handle conforming to the shape of the tang and comprising deep rectangular ferrule, early 16th century, 16½in. long.
(Christie's) $2,700

An Ngombe tribal war knife Welo from Ubangi Province of Zaire, circa 1900, pierced swollen blade 19½in. with geometric tooled ribs and 2 copper inlays, brass and copper wound wooden hilt with leather covered pommel.
(Wallis & Wallis) $65

A South American silver mounted Gaucho knife, spear point blade 8½in., scallop top edge, etched with mounted huntsmen chasing stag, birds in foliage, South American embossed silver hilt decorated with bull's heads, patterns, Gorgon's head, and engraved with small armorial crest.
(Wallis & Wallis) $65

An early 19th century Afghan khyber knife, "T" section blade 27in. with narrow fullers, faceted steel ferrules with gold damascened flowers and foliage, gripstrap gold damascened with Persian inscriptions, large 2-piece ivory grips.
(Wallis & Wallis) $160

Rare elaborate California dress knife by M. Price, San Francisco, circa 1860, 7in. spear point blade, the ivory hilt ensconced in intricately etched coin silver, the ivory surface fitted with ten gold studs, 12in. overall.
(Butterfield & Butterfield) $52,800

An Ottoman sheath-knife with slightly curved single-edged blade inlaid with silver stars, with reinforced back-edged point and narrow fuller along the back on each face, and beaked handle with rounded wooden grip-scales, first half of the 17th century, 11¾in.
(Christie's) $5,800

PUSH DAGGERS

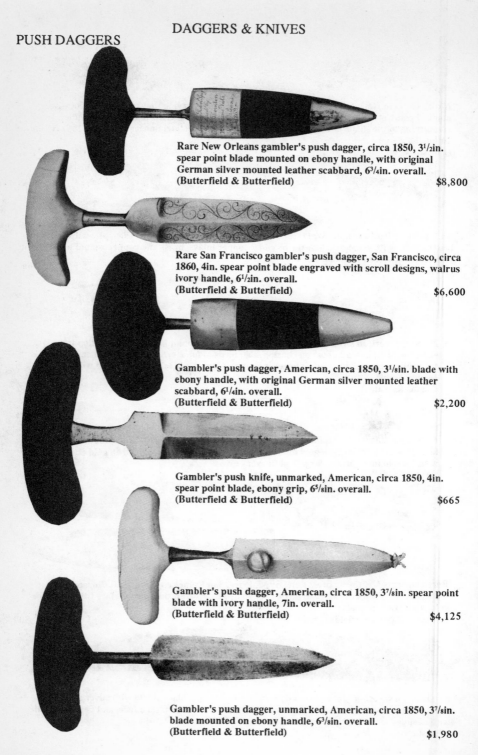

Rare New Orleans gambler's push dagger, circa 1850, 3^1/$_2$in. spear point blade mounted on ebony handle, with original German silver mounted leather scabbard, 6^3/$_4$in. overall.
(Butterfield & Butterfield) $8,800

Rare San Francisco gambler's push dagger, San Francisco, circa 1860, 4in. spear point blade engraved with scroll designs, walrus ivory handle, 6^1/$_2$in. overall.
(Butterfield & Butterfield) $6,600

Gambler's push dagger, American, circa 1850, 3^1/$_8$in. blade with ebony handle, with original German silver mounted leather scabbard, 6^1/$_4$in. overall.
(Butterfield & Butterfield) $2,200

Gambler's push knife, unmarked, American, circa 1850, 4in. spear point blade, ebony grip, 6^5/$_8$in. overall.
(Butterfield & Butterfield) $665

Gambler's push dagger, American, circa 1850, 3^7/$_8$in. spear point blade with ivory handle, 7in. overall.
(Butterfield & Butterfield) $4,125

Gambler's push dagger, unmarked, American, circa 1850, 3^7/$_8$in. blade mounted on ebony handle, 6^3/$_8$in. overall.
(Butterfield & Butterfield) $1,980

Cased Highland regimental dirk, the 10³/₄in. blade marked *Sanderson & Co./Edinburgh* and etched on one side *The Queen's Own Cameron Highlanders* with battle honors and sphinx badge, the obverse with crowned *VR*, highland motifs and the regimental number *79* within laurels. (Butterfield & Butterfield)
$1,430

An officer's dirk of the 93rd Sutherland Highlanders with 10¹/₄in. notched back fullered blade, cairngorm pommel and white metal mounted black leather covered scabbard. (Christie's)
$1,450

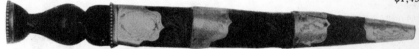

A Victorian Scottish dirk set, plain blade 11¹/₂in. with single fuller, part carved wooden hilt with thistle decoration, GS mirror pommel and base mount with beaded decoration, in its patent leather covered wooden sheath. (Wallis & Wallis)
$295

A Scottish officer's dirk set, scallop back plain blade 10¹/₂in. by Hamilton Crighton & Co Edinburgh, retaining much original polish, copper gilt mounted hilt, corded wood hilt mounted with gilt studs, thistle decoration to base mount, contained in a leather covered purple velvet lined fitted case. (Wallis & Wallis)
$1,450

A silver mounted Scottish dress dirk with signed partly hollow ground single edged blade, stamped *McLeod,* circa 1830, and a silver mounted sgian dubh, with fullered single edged blade, early 19th century, 17in. and 8¹/₂in. (Christie's S. Ken)
$1,000

A good Victorian Scottish officer's dirk set of the Seaforth Highlanders, scallop back blade 10in., with broad and narrow fullers, retaining all original polish, etched with crown, *V.R.* Thistles, foliage, crown, *"L"*, Elephant "Assaye" and *"Cuidich'n Righ"*. (Wallis & Wallis)
$2,000

BRU DOLLS

The doll making factory of
Bru Jne & Cie was
established in 1866 by
Casimer Bru. He remained
with the company until 1883.
It then passed through a
series of directorships before
amalgamating with a number
of other French firms to form
the Société Française de
Fabrication de Bébés et
Jouets (SFBJ) in 1899.
Bru dolls, though less costly
than their Jumeau
counterparts, were luxury
items, with bisque heads and
composition, wood or kid
bodies. Casimer was a great
experimenter, and he
invented many mechanical
devices.

His designs were many and
varied and included crying
dolls, feeding dolls and two-
faced dolls, which showed a
happy and a crying or
sleeping face.

With regard to bodies, Bru
designed types in jointed
wood, gusseted and jointed
kid and combinations of
composition and kid. Early
models had bisque shoulder-
heads or swivel heads
mounted on gusseted kid
bodies, and were often adult
in shape. These Bru lady
dolls tend to have smiling
faces with strikingly upturned
mouths. The eyes are usually
of glass, fringed by long,
densely painted lashes.

In 1872 the Bébé Bru line
was introduced often with
open molded mouths
revealing teeth and tongue.

Like other manufacturers
of the time, Bru made dolls
representing different
nationalities. Wigs were
made of various materials,
not only the conventional
mohair on canvas, but also
from lambswool or animal
fur on the original skin
backing. Bébé Bru models
continued to be made until
the 1950s.

The most common Bru
mark is *Bru Jne R*.

A bisque headed clockwork
walking, talking bebe petit
pas, marked BRU Jne R 11,
24in. high. $3,750

French Bru Jeune bisque
doll in original silk dress
and bonnet, 16½in. high,
circa 1875. $6,000

A bisque swivel-headed
fashionable doll, with closed
smiling mouth, narrow gray eyes
and kid body in contemporary
cream trained dress and
underclothes, 12in. high,
impressed *B*, probably by Bru.
(Christie's S. Ken) $2,250

A fine bisque swivel-headed
bébé, with closed mouth, fixed
brown yeux fibres outlined in
black with pink shaded lids,
20in. high, impressed *BRU Jne 7*,
circa 1880.
(Christie's S. Ken) $18,000

A 'walking/crying' Bru Jeune R
bisque doll, French, circa 1895,
24½in. high, in original Bebe Bru
Marchant No. 9 box. $5,000

A bisque headed bébé, with
brown yeux fibres, pierced ears,
fair mohair wig and jointed
wood and composition body,
28in. high, impressed *1907 13*.
(Christie's S. Ken) $1,250

DEAN'S DOLLS

Samuel Dean launched his toy making enterprise in 1903 with the laudably realistic purpose of making playthings for children who 'wear their food and eat their clothes'.

Soft toys were introduced shortly after rag books in the same year. The company produced comparatively few designs but those they had were durable and the same figures were still being issued as late as 1936. The first were in sheet form. From 1906 clothes were sometimes included on the sheet, and separate costume sheets were introduced in 1925.

After the First World War the True to Life range was introduced. These could be either molded or flat printed, and included a range of character dolls, including Charlie Chaplin and Popeye. Dean's worked hard to keep ahead of German and US rivals. Their A1 label was introduced in 1923, and under this they marketed some beautifully dressed dolls, including a Two faced Bo-peep.

Velvet faced dolls with glass eyes were launched in 1926, some very like those designed by Norah Wellings, and Dancing Dolls followed in 1928.

'Minnie Mouse', stuffed toy by Dean's Rag Book Ltd., circa 1930, 7in. high. $450

A painted cloth doll made for Oxo Ltd. by Deans Ragbook Co. Ltd., 17in. high. $450

Betty Oxo, a cloth doll with painted features, blue side-glancing eyes, smiling mouth and blonde mohair wig, 17in. high, marked with Dean's Rag Book label, especially made for Oxo Ltd. (Christie's S. Ken) $750

A gollywog, with cloth face, hands and shoes, comical eyes and mohair hair, with Deans Rag Book Co. stamp on bottom of foot, 13½in. high. (Christie's S. Ken) $275

A painted cloth character doll with blue shaded eyes, ginger wool wig and jointed legs, 18in. high, with Deans Rag Book Co. Ltd. circa 1926. $300

Mickey Mouse, stuffed toy by Dean's Rag Book Ltd., circa 1930, 6¼in. high. $500

English cloth character doll, by Dean's Rag Book Co. Ltd., of Lupino Lane, 13in. high. $300

307

GAULTIER DOLLS

Fernand Gaultier was a French manufacturer of porcelain dolls' heads and dolls who won a silver medal at the Paris Exposition of 1878. Other medals followed, and in 1889 the company became Gaultier Frères when he went into partnership with his brother François.

Gaultier products vary widely in quality, though the basic modeling was generally well done. Their heads are often found on bodies by other manufacturers, including Jumeau, and are marked *FG*. There have, however been many reproductions and forgeries of these.

Gaultier's fame as a doll manufacturer lay mainly in the manufacture of lady dolls in the Parisienne style, but they also made some very attractive child dolls with huge eyes and rather petulant expressions. There are much rarer than the lady dolls, and attract very much higher prices.

In 1899, Gaultier was one of those who amalgamated to become the SFBJ, in an attempt of counter the threat posed to the French doll making industry from German manufacturers.

A François Gaultier bisque shoulder head marotte with fixed blue glass eyes, pierced ears and closed mouth, 7in., marked *FIG*. (Phillips) $300

French FG bisque fashion doll in original blue dress, 16in. high circa 1875. $1,500

Pair of French bisque shell dolls, probably by F. Gaultier, circa 1875, 10½in. high. $3,000

A bisque swivel shoulder-headed Parisienne, with blue eyes, feathered brows, pierced ears, the stuffed body with kid arms and individually stitched fingers, 11in. high, probably by Gaultier. (Christie's S. Ken) $625

French bisque lady doll, Ferdinand Gaultier's Parisienne with Gesland stockinette body, circa 1870, 23in. high.
$3,000

Pair of French bisque adult dolls by Ferdinand Gaultier circa 1890, 13in. high.
$1,500

A bisque swivel headed Parisienne, with closed mouth, pale blue bulbous eyes and rigid kid body, by Gaultier, 11in. high. (Christie's S. Ken) $675

GEBRÜDER HEUBACH DOLLS

Gebrüder Heubach opened in 1840 as a porcelain factory in Lichte, near Wallendorf, Thuringia, and later in Sonneberg. They are principally noted for the superb quality of their heads, and they produced an astonishing range of character examples. These are fashioned with great sympathy for the subject and are characterised by their intaglio eyes, which were incised in the molding before being painted and highlighted. The faces have well defined features, and lightly molded hair is also common.

Unfortunately, the company tended to mount these on very inferior composition bodies. Many examples were made for export, and Heubach produced heads for many other companies, perhaps even for Jumeau.

Gebrüder Heubach used two marks. The earlier was a rising sun design, registered in 1882, while the later square mark is much more common.

German bisque character doll by Heubach, circa 1915, 9in. high, with 'googly eyes'. $675

A bisque figure of a seated fat baby, marked 95 and the Heubach square mark, stamped in green 68, 5in. high, together with two child dolls. $150

Trio, German all bisque miniatures, by Gebruder Heubach, circa 1900, each about 5in. high. $900

A bisque-headed whistling doll, marked with the square Heubach mark, 11½in. high. $775

A Gebruder Heubach bisque socket head baby boy doll, with molded hair line, painted features and composition body, 36.5cm. tall.
(Spencer's) $700

German bisque character doll with papier-mache body, 8in. high, by Heubach, circa 1915. $300

A bisque laughing walking doll with the walking talking mechanism concealed under original outfit of blue and cream lace, 9in. high, marked with Gebruder Heubach Square.
(Christie's) $375

PIERRE JUMEAU DOLLS

Pierre Jumeau opened his family doll making enterprise in Paris in 1842. They had a factory complex at Montreuil-sous-Bois where they made not only the wood and kid bodies, but also the clothes, and in 1873 kilns were opened, enabling the manufacture of heads as well. The company continued until 1899, when it became part of the SFBJ. After that time the SFBJ continued to produce Jumeau dolls, reissuing them as late as the 1950s.

Initially, Jumeau used heads by other manufacturers, such as Simon & Halbig. Original bodies were shaped kid or jointed wood, but after 1870 these were made also of composition, and it was then too that bébé-type dolls began to be made. (Though bébé refers to representations of children from babyhood to about 6 years, most Jumeau examples are of the older type.)

Jumeau dolls were very much at the top end of the quality scale, and won many international awards in the 1880s and 90s. The eyes are often particularly fine, while other characteristics include rather heavily drawn eyebrows and somewhat chunky bodies.

In addition to lady and child dolls, many character dolls were produced, perhaps modeled on real children. Two-faced dolls and those representing other nationalities were also made, together with a few mechanical types.

Jumeau were very skilful at marketing their dolls, which were displayed with accessories in the Paris showroom. Exhibitions specially devoted to them were also held at venues as far flung as Melbourne, London and New York.

A bisque headed bébé, with closed mouth, fixed blue eyes, blonde wig, and composition body, 14in. high, stamped in red, *Déposé Tête Jumeau Bte.* (Christie's S. Ken) $4,000

A bisque-headed bébé, with closed mouth, fixed brown eyes, blonde mohair wig and fixed wrist, wood and papier mâché body, 12in. high, impressed *DEPOSE E 4 J* and the shoes marked *E. JUMEAU MED. OR 1878 PARIS.* (Christie's S. Ken) $6,500

French bisque child doll by Emile Jumeau, France, circa 1880, 15in. high. $3,750

A bisque headed bebe with fixed blue yeux fibres and pierced ears, 15in. high, impressed 6 body stamped Jumeau Medaille d'or Paris. $1,850

A long-faced bisque headed bebe with closed mouth, pierced and applied ears, blue paperweight eyes, 19½in. high, head impressed 9, body marked with blue Jumeau Medaille d'Or stamp. (Christie's) $12,500

Jumeau phonograph bisque doll in original dress and straw bonnet, circa 1895, 24in. high. $4,500

KÄMMER & REINHARDT DOLLS

The firm of Kämmer & Reinhardt was established at Waltershausen in 1886 by a designer and modeler, Ernst Kämmer, and a business man Franz Reinhardt. They did not actually manufacture dolls, but organised the assembly of components brought in from a number of other sources. They were, however, responsible for the design of a great number of their end products, and held the relevant copyrights and patents.

Until 1909 they copyrighted several dolls, such as Mein Liebling, The Flirt, Der Schelm, and others. In that year, however they launched a completely new concept in doll production when they produced their first Charakterpuppe, and thus gave these dolls the generic name they have borne ever since.

The original Charakter-puppe, no. 100, represents a baby of about six weeks, and succeeding molds were numbered on from there, representing children of varying ages and expressions. These were all named, and among the most famous are Hans or Gretchen, no. 114, (the sex depending on the wig which was supplied) which was widely exported, and Max & Moritz (113 and 114) two naughty boys who were much copied by other manufacturers.

Many Kämmer & Reinhardt designs were produced in bisque by Simon & Halbig and in celluloid by the Rheinische Celluloid und Gummi Fabrik. They also produced dolls in rubber, wood, wax and felt and, in addition to the character dolls, made normal pretty-faced dolls, mechanical dolls and dolls representing various occupations.

German bisque character baby by Kammer & Reinhardt, circa 1915, 12in. high. $500

A bisque-headed character doll, with closed mouth, dressed as a boy in smock and breeches, 18in. high, impressed K*R. (Christie's) $3,750

A pair of bisque-headed baby dolls, with open/closed mouths, gray painted eyes and baby's bodies, 15in. high, impressed 36 K*R 100. (Christie's S. Ken) $1,500

A bisque headed character doll with closed mouth, blue painted eyes, blonde wig and jointed composition body, 18in. high, marked K*R 114.46. $3,750

German bisque character doll, by Kammer & Rein-hardt, circa 1915, 8½in. high. $2,250

German bisque child doll with brown head and body, by Kammer & Reinhardt, circa 1915, 22in. high. $1,500

KESTNER DOLLS

One of the earliest and most prolific of 'modern' German doll manufacturers was the firm of Kestner, which was established as early as 1805 in Waltershausen by Johannes Daniel Kestner and turned out papier-mâché heads and wooden bodies. These were known as Täuflinge (a Taufling is a child to be presented for baptism). These bodies were carved and painted but the name has come to refer to all dolls made at Waltershausen. By the middle of the century bodies of kid, fabric, and wax over composition heads were also being made.

In 1860 the company, under the direction of Johannes Daniel Kestner Jr., acquired a porcelain factory at Ohrdruf, and began to make china and bisque heads. The production of these continued until the late 1930s. Kestner are known for the fine quality of their bisque and in fact dolls with a bisque head and shoulders over a leather body are often known as 'Kestners'.

Kestner's output included lady, toddler and child dolls, and character dolls with a very wide range of expressions. Celluloid dolls with heads by Rheinische Gummi were also produced, as were all-bisque and dolls' house-size dolls.

The Kestner mark was registered in 1896 as a crown with streamers, though later the simple initials *JDK* were used.

Kestner executed many commissions, particularly for American designers. For Borgfeldt in particular they made bisque versions of such well-known dolls as Kewpie, Bye-lo Baby and the Natural Baby. They also produced versions of popular cartoon characters of the day.

A bisque headed character baby doll, 9in. high, marked 142 2/0 by Kestner. $300

A bisque headed character baby doll with open closed mouth, marked 211 J.D.K., 17in. high. $575

A pair of all bisque character dolls modeled as Max and Moritz, with painted black and ginger hair, by J. D. Kestner, 5in. high. (Christie's S. Ken) $2,000

A Kestner 'Googly' eyed bisque head character doll, with large blue eyes, on a jointed wood and composition toddler body, 17in., marked *Made in Germany*. (Phillips) $4,500

A bisque-headed child doll, with blue sleeping eyes, and fixed wrist jointed composition body dressed as Little Red Riding Hood, 13in. high, impressed *192 2*, by Kestner. (Christie's S. Ken) $700

An all bisque googlie eyed doll, with blue painted eyes glancing to the left, closed watermelon mouth and molded blue socks and black shoes, by Kestner, 5½in. high. (Christie's S. Ken) $500

KÄTHE KRUSE DOLLS

The dolls created by Käthe Kruse were the result of her dissatisfaction with the products available for her own children in the early years of this century. The wife of the sculptor Max Kruse, she decided to create her own, more realistic, dolls made of cloth. These designs were based on real people and given their names, and by 1910, Frau Kruse was making then for other people also, with hand painted, reverse treated muslin heads and stockinet bodies.

Her baby dolls were extremely realistic. They were sometimes even made to the actual size and weighted with sand to feel like a real baby, and were complete in every detail, even down to a lump for the tummy button! Perhaps such a degree of realism was too much for some tastes, for it was her toddler types which proved the most popular.

Her company, situated between Nürnberg and Munich, still produces dolls today in the original style, though modern examples have vinyl heads. New ranges have also been introduced, including an inexpensive terry toweling type.

Kathe Kruse boy doll, Germany, in original clothes, circa 1920, 17.3/8in. high. $2,250

German composition character doll by Kathe Kruse, circa 1920, 36in. high. $3,750

Early 20th century German character doll by Kathe Kruse, 17in. high. $450

A Kathe Kruse fabric boy doll with short wig, dressed in red cotton shorts, white shirt and raincoat, 20in. high. (Phillips) $850

A cloth character doll, the head in five sections, 16in. high, by Kathe Kruse, and The Katy Kruse dolly book, published 1927. $1,500

A painted cloth doll with brown painted hair, the stuffed body jointed at hip and shoulder, by Kathe Kruse, 17in. high. $600

An early Kathe Kruse cloth doll with swivel joints at hips, German, circa 1911, 17in. high. $1,400

LENCI DOLLS

Lenci is the tradename of a Turin based company founded in 1920, and it comes from the nickname of the wife of the proprietor, Enrico Scavini.

A remarkable range of figures was produced, from a 'Mozart' to a 'Madonna and Child', and it was claimed that each doll was studio designed by an Italian artist, and painted by hand.

Lenci dolls are made of felt, individually modeled on real children, and are often known as 'art' dolls. The faces were pressed in molds, and had no disfiguring seam. All the bodies were articulated, and small dolls were given real hair. The eyes are painted, with highlights, glancing to the side, and the facial expression is often sulky. A further characteristic of Lenci dolls is the fact that the middle fingers of each hand are joined.

Great attention was paid to detail and also to costume, and these dolls are much in demand today. The Lenci company is still in business, and from time to time produces re-issues of their popular 1920s and 30s designs.

Italian cloth character doll by Lenci, 1927, 22in. high. $3,750

William, a felt headed character doll, with side glancing eyes, fair mohair wig, the felt body dressed as a boy, Lenci 300 Series, circa 1930, 16in. high. (Christie's S. Ken) $2,000

A painted felt child doll, with blue eyes, blonde wig and original green and white frilled organdie dress, marked on the soles *Lenci,* circa 1930, 14in. high. (Christie's S. Ken) $875

A painted felt doll, wearing original organdie frock decorated with felt flowers, 17½in. high, 300 Series by Lenci.
(Christie's S. Ken) $625

A painted head doll with blue eyes, the felt body in original, clothes, 16in. high, marked Lenci, circa 1930. $250

Italian Lenci cloth character doll, by Madame di Scavini, circa 1925, 17in. high. $475

Italian Lenci cloth character doll, by Madame di Scavini, 13in. high. $250

ARMAND MARSEILLE DOLLS

Despite the undeniably French ring of the name, the firm of Armand Marseille was in fact founded in 1885 in Köppelsdorf in Thuringia, where they became one of the largest manufacturers of bisque dolls' heads.

Marseille created all sorts of dolls, the majority being of the straightforward pretty variety, with happy smiling faces, as these proved to be the best sellers. However, they also produced character dolls, and the marks sometimes vary to denote this. The usual mark is *AM* together with the Company's name and *Germany* or *Made in Germany*, and the mold no. *390*. This mold represented a pretty, socket head, which was made between c. 1900–c. 1938.

Another variation introduced in 1925 was the word *Ellar*, and mold *355* for an oriental type bisque head, and other mold numbers around this figure represent variations on this type, while *Fany* was used on a rather chubby child's head, issued with either molded hair or a wig.

Marseille created many dolls for other companies and to specific designs, some of which were requested by US importers such as Borgfeldt, Wolf and Amberg. Armand Marseille made their own technological advances and were, moreover, quick to take advantage of new techniques pioneered by others, such as sleeping, flirty or intaglio eyes, national dolls and dolls with a variety of bodies, composition, kid or celluloid, together with the occasional use of rubber for hands. Marseille produced dolls in a wide quality range, with some designed to be within the reach of the poorest child.

A bisque headed doll with jointed composition body, marked Armand Marseille, Germany A9M, 24in. high. $300

A bisque headed doll with moving eyes, marked on head A.M. 4DEP, Made in Germany, 19in. high. $300

A bisque-headed googlie-eyed doll, with brown sleeping side-glancing eyes, smiling closed mouth and composition baby's body, 8½in. high, impressed *323 A 5/0 M*.
(Christie's S. Ken) $675

An Armand Marseille 'Googly'-eyed bisque head character doll with light brown mohair wig, 13½in., marked *Germany 323 AOM*.
(Phillips) $1,000

Bisque headed character doll by Armand Marseille, circa 1920, 12in. high, in excellent condition. $1,100

German bisque character doll with five-piece papier mache body, by Armand Marseille, circa 1925, 7in. high. $425

PAPIER MÂCHÉ DOLLS

Papier mâché dolls began to be made in the 18th century, and became really popular in the Regency period, when hairstyles lent themselves to a molded treatment. A few, however, do have hair wigs, and these are particularly rare and sought after.

Most models were made by pressing pulp into metal or plaster molds, and the rough cast result then covered by an even layer of gesso or plaster to provide a sound base for painting.

The shoulder heads were glued on to fabric, leather or wood bodies which were filled with sawdust and stiffened by wire.

In the 19th century German papier mâché head manufacturers were paramount, though French bodies were generally used.

Later in the century design improved, with simple, everyday hairstyles and these were the forerunners of attempts to create childlike figures.

Throughout the later part of the 19th century experiments were being carried out to find an alternative substance which was both strong and could be successfully molded. As a result of these experiments later papier mâché heads are of a much denser mixture, with so much plaster that they can be very easily scraped away. This type or debased papier mâché came to be known as 'composition'.

From about 1855, therefore, the era of true papier mâché had passed and even the later sales literature referred to the debased mixture as being 'similar to china', by which, with wax, it was finally superseded. The painting was usually skilfully done and the finished face then lightly varnished.

A papier-mache shoulder-headed doll, Sonneburg, circa 1840, 25in. high.
$825

A papier-mache headed autoperipatetikos with brown painted eyes, 10in. high.　**$500**

A papier-mache headed doll with molded ringlets, the stuffed body with wooden limbs, 11in. high, circa 1840. (Christie's)　**$450**

A papier mache headed doll, the molded black hair arranged in a loose bun at the nape, 9in. high, circa 1840. (Christie's)　**$200**

A Biedermeier shoulder-papier-mache doll with painted face, circa 1825, 10½in. high.　**$500**

19th century miniature papier-mache doll with kid body, circa 1850, 7½in. high.　**$375**

PEDLAR DOLLS

Pedlar dolls are usually considered as a purely English phenomenon though some are featured in German catalogs dating from the turn of the century, and wax street vendors were made until quite recently in Mexico. The real thing, however, dates principally from the Regency and early Victorian periods. Pedlar dolls were not made as playthings, but as ornaments for adults, many having glass shades which not only protected them from dust but also from prying little fingers.

Fake pedlar dolls abound, and great care must be taken. Fakes are most often of the wooden type, though battered wax dolls can also be equipped with spurious items such as knitted gloves, hats and purses (these knitted on dressmaker's pins), eked out with some bits and pieces from old dolls' houses. Sprayed with dust, they can look quite effective, and potential buyers should look carefully for fading and warping.

It is dolls dating from the early 19th century which are the most sought after, and the pins used to hold the wares in place, or even those on sale, can provide useful clues to age and authenticity. In the early 19th century the Tudor method of making a pin from two pieces of brass wire, one coiled into a brass head, was still being used. This was superseded by a one-piece construction, retaining the coiled head. Then in 1830 solid headed pins began to be made by Taylor & Co. Reels of cotton would also be out of place on a genuine doll of the period, since at that time thread would still have been sold in hanks. The genuine article usually has a very 'settled' appearance, acquired over a hundred years or so.

A 19th century pedlar doll standing beside a table cluttered with her wares.
$2,000

A wax over composition headed pedlar doll, 12in. wide, under glass dome.
$1,000

A papier mâché shoulder-headed pedlar doll, with painted features, brown wig and stuffed body, wearing a flower-sprigged dress, red cloak and brown bonnet, circa 1840, 12in. high. (Christie's) $1,250

A china-headed pedlar doll, dressed in original striped and printed cotton frock, 10in. high, late 19th century, under dome. (Christie's S. Ken) $800

A good Edwardian pedlar doll on ebonised stand under glass dome, the wax covered boy sailor standing on his one leg. (David Lay) $400

An English mid 19th century vendor doll of wood and cloth, under glass dome with turned walnut base, 16in. high. (Skinner Inc.) $3,250

BRUNO SCHMIDT DOLLS

The firm of Bruno Schmidt was one of those active in Waltershausen where it was established in 1900. They produced bisque, composition and celluloid dolls in varying designs which included baby, oriental and character varieties. Schmidt acquired Bähr and Pröschild's porcelain factory at Ohrdruf in 1918.

Their main trademark was based on a heart shape.

SCHOENAU & HOFFMEISTER DOLLS

It is often possible for the novice to confuse dolls made by Schoenau and Hoffmeister with Simon & Halbig, since the initials are of course the same. The Schoenau & Hoffmeister mark is SPBH with the initials PB (Porzellanfabrik Burggrub) enclosed in a five-pointed star.

In general, although some of their products display great delicacy of feature, they are inferior to their Simon & Halbig counterparts. Among the best models turned out by Schoenau & Hoffmeister are their Oriental girl doll and some of their closed mouth bébés. They also made baby heads marked only Porzellanfabrik Burggrub. These are often untinted, and there is a tradition that some of these dolls were intended as clowns, to have their faces decorated by the purchaser. Some still bear traces of commercial spray-on paint color.

Many Schoenau & Hoffmeister dolls carry numbers on the back of their heads which seem to be the year of production, such as 1909, but the same models continued to be used for many years. The much rarer shoulder heads are marked with an 1800 sequence.

Rare late 19th century Bruno Schmidt bisque Oriental doll, Germany, 16in. high, in original dress. $2,250

Rare Jumeau 19th century Bruno Schmidt bisque Oriental doll, Germany, 16in. high, in original dress. $3,000

A Schoenau & Hoffmeister shoulder-bisque Marotte doll, German, circa 1900, 15in. high. $500

Schoenau and Hoffmeister 'Princess Elizabeth' bisque headed doll impressed Porzellanfabrik Burggrub Princess Elizabeth 6½ Made in Germany, 23in. high. (Hobbs & Chambers) $725

A Schoenau & Hoffmeister 'Princess Elizabeth' bisque doll, circa 1938, 16in. high. $1,500

Schoenau and Hoffmeister doll with blue eyes, 26in. tall, circa 1909. $450

SCHOENHUT DOLLS

Names are nothing to go by when guessing the nationality of doll makers and Schoenhut is no exception. The company was established in Philadelphia in 1872 and made all-wood dolls and toys, such as the Humpty Dumpty Circus. The wooden dolls all had carved heads with molded hair and their bodies were fully jointed. They could moreover be easily positioned, for the joints were metal springs and the feet drilled with holes to fit onto a small stand.

Wooden character doll by Schoenhut, Philadelphia, 12in. high, circa 1915. $350

American wooden character doll by Albert Schoenhut, circa 1915, 18in. high. $450

American wooden character doll with intaglio brown eyes, by Schoenhut of Philadelphia, circa 1911, 15in. high. $375

American carved wooden doll and animal, 'Milkmaid and Cow', by Schoenhut of Philadelphia, each 8in. $625

A wooden character doll with carved and painted features, in pink velvet and organza dress and original underwear, 14½in. high, by Schoenhut. (Christie's) $625

American wooden character doll by Schoenhut, circa 1911, 16in. high. $1,150

American carved wooden character doll with brown intaglio eyes, by Schoenhut of Philadelphia, circa 1911, 15in. high. $450

American wooden character doll, by Schoenhut of Philadelphia, circa 1911, 16in. high. $675

S.F.B.J. DOLLS

The Société Française de Fabrication de Bébés et Jouets was set up in 1899 to assist French makers in their struggle to compete with the increasing flood of German imports, many of which were of better quality and less expensive than their French counterparts. About ten companies amalgamated under the association, which ironically came under the leadership of Saloman Fleischmann of Fleischmann & Bloedel. Each of these donated the rights to one of its designs, usually of the bébé type, and those companies which had porcelain manufactories leased them for head production.

In addition to this bank of existing designs, SFBJ also launched many new ones, and produced a wide range of different dolls. Their initials were adopted as their trademark in 1905. Reissues of popular lines, such as Bébé Bru and Bébé Jumeau occurred at intervals right up to the 1950s.

SFBJ products could vary enormously in quality. The better ones are very good indeed, but there are many which are poorly modeled and badly decorated.

A bisque headed character baby doll, 27in. high, marked SFBJ252 Paris 12. $2,250

French bisque character doll by SFBJ, Paris, circa 1915, 19in. high. $1,100

French bisque child doll by SFBJ, Paris, circa 1915, 30in. high. $2,500

A bisque headed child doll, marked SFBJ Paris 14, 32in. high, original box marked Bebe Francais. $1,250

An SFBJ bisque character boy doll, impressed 237 8, with jointed composition body in navy sailor suit, French, circa 1910, 23in. high. $2,000

French bisque character doll, SFBJ, circa 1915, 12in. high. $3,500

A bisque-headed character baby doll, with open/closed mouth, blue sleeping eyes and baby's body, 18½in. high, impressed *R S. F.B.J. 236 PARIS 10*. (Christie's S. Ken) $950

SIMON & HALBIG DOLLS

The Simon & Halbig porcelain factory was established at Ohrdruf, Gräfenhain, in 1869 and made many other products apart from dolls' heads. Their head output, however, was exceeded only perhaps by Marseille and they made for many other companies, both French and German. They appear to have made heads specifically to order, for each head is marked with a mold number and each number was used by only one company.

In particular, Simon and Halbig worked closely with Kämmer & Reinhardt on their 100 series of character dolls. They in fact became part of K & R in 1920, and thus part of the Bing empire, which had taken over K & R some two years before.

The quality of Simon & Halbig's bisque was excellent and they were also expert modelers and painters. They produced baby, child and lady dolls. Their lady dolls were often of the double-jointed type, very delicately constructed and most attractive. Their open-mouth types were not generally so pleasant as the sweeter-faced closed-mouth examples. They also produced many large-size dolls, which often seem to make more money on the size alone.

Colored and oriental dolls were produced, sometimes from the same molds, and simply in a different colored bisque, though they did have some special molds for these which allowed for greater accuracy or representation.

Simon & Halbig trademarks vary; early examples generally only have the initials *SH*, which was revised to *S&H* in 1905. Sometimes the name is written in full, and the mold numbers are usually included.

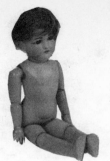

A Simon & Halbig bisque headed doll with composition ball jointed body, 24in. high. **$500**

Very rare late 19th century black bisque doll, impressed 7 1302 Dep S & H, 19½in. high. **$9,000**

A bisque-headed character doll, modeled as an Oriental, with sleeping slanting brown eyes, and yellow jointed wood and composition body, 15in. high, impressed *S H 1199 DEP 6¹/₂*. (Christie's S. Ken) **$2,000**

Simon and Halbig bisque headed doll, having brown sleeping eyes, open mouth with two molded upper teeth, 23½in. high. (Hobbs & Chambers) **$450**

A bisque-headed child doll, with blue lashed sleeping eyes, pierced ears and blonde mohair wig, 21in. high, marked *Simon & Halbig K*R 53*. (Christie's S. Ken) **$1,000**

A bisque-headed character child doll, 23in. high, marked K*R Simon and Halbig 117n58, and a boy doll, 22in. high. **$1,500**

STEINER DOLLS

The firm of Jules Nicholas Steiner was established in France in 1855. They produced all kinds of dolls, from the bébé variety to lady dolls, but are perhaps best known for their mechanical examples, which could often both walk and talk and in addition were most elegantly dressed.

The molding of the head is usually very fine, and many early examples have a double row of teeth, cast in the molded head. Steiner also produced colored dolls of different races, and some representing different occupations, such as clowns.

A bisque headed bebe, marked J. Steiner Paris, SreA.3, 11in. high. $1,250

A Steiner Motschmann-type bisque doll, France, circa 1860, with fixed glass eyes, 12¾in. high. $2,000

A bisque swivel shoulder-headed doll, with blue yeux fibres, feathered brows, upper and lower teeth, 15in. high, by Jules Nicholas Steiner, circa 1880. (Christie's S. Ken) $1,850

A bisque headed bebe with jointed composition and wood body, by Steiner, 12in. high. $1,750

A bisque headed bébé, with blue lever-operated sleeping eyes, pierced ears, two rows of teeth, blonde skin wig and jointed wood composition body, 17in. high, marked STe A 1, Steiner, circa 1880. (Christie's S. Ken) $4,500

French bisque automaton by Jules Nicholas Steiner, circa 1890, 20in. high. $2,250

A bisque headed bebe with papier mache jointed body, marked 12 by Steiner, 29in. high. $3,750

Steiner bisque head girl doll with five-piece composition body, Paris, circa 1890, 9in. high. $750

WAX DOLLS

Wax composition dolls first became really popular in the Regency period. The composition substance which formed the core of the heads was similar to papier mâché, and the heads were made in two molds which were then joined with glue and applied with pink watercolor after being dipped in wax.

Eyes could be fixed or sleeping, and the dolls were sometimes given wigs. Bodies were usually of strong cotton, often with leather 'gloves', and filled with sawdust.

A later development was the poured wax doll, which was made by pouring a delicately tinted wax into a mold and allowing it to cool before adding another layer. After removing the mold the eye sockets were cut out and glass eyes inserted. The complexion was then powdered to render it less glossy and hectic. Hair was inserted laboriously into the head, usually by means of a metal gouge and a heated roller to seal.

The major doll-making families in London in the late 19th century were the Pierottis, the Montanaris and Lucy Peck. The Pierottis made dolls which tended to be slimmer and more shapely than those produced by the Montanari. The latter's offerings, on the other hand, were very lifelike, and characterised by plump, short necks, with a roll of fat at the front, and attractive violet eyes. They were made for only a short time, and are comparatively rare.

Lucy Peck was another maker of wax dolls at the turn of the century, and she obligingly stamped her dolls with an oval or rectangle on the stomach. She specialised in little girls with thick bodies and limbs, and would insert the owner-to-be's own hair on demand.

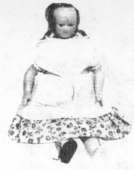

A poured-wax child doll with lace edged underclothes, circa 1851, 13in. high. (Christie's) $475

A wax over composition headed doll with smiling painted face, circa 1878, 7in. high. $200

A wax over composition headed doll, with fixed blue eyes and blonde ringlets, carrying a banner embroidered with the message *Forget me not,* mid 19th century, 12in. high, in glazed case. (Christie's S. Ken) $575

A beeswax headed figure of a woman, with bead eyes, cloth body and wax hands, in original embroidered muslin dress decorated with metal braid and blue and white silk tasseled fringe, 11in. high, 1795. (Christie's S. Ken) $1,500

A poured wax headed doll, with blonde mohair wig, the stuffed body with wax limbs, dressed in contemporary red frock, 21in. high. (Christie's S. Ken) $300

A waxed shoulder-composition doll, circa 1880, 21½in. high, slight cracking to face. $350

WOODEN DOLLS

Wood has been used as a doll making medium since earliest times, as the Paddle dolls of ancient Egypt testify. Nowadays, however, most collectors will be looking for jointed wooden dolls dating from the 18th century at the earliest, which are often referred to as Queen Anne dolls. Good examples have ball joints and well-carved hands, while cheaper ones might have only the body carved of wood. An eighteenth century development was the application of a molded mask or brotteig to the plain turned head core.

These continued to be made throughout the 19th century alongside the new Grödnertals. These cheap little wooden figures, characterised by frequent use of combs in their hair, came from the area of that name in Bavaria. The classical Grödner type, slim waisted and high busted, reached its production peak in 1820, after which time the style became much more stolid.

Folk type dolls, some of which were known as penny woodens, were also made throughout this period, but these were seldom of high quality.

Towards the end of the century it was American manufacturers who were producing the finest wooden dolls. Joel Ellis of Springfield, Vt., is generally accredited with having produced the first peg-jointed wooden doll on a commercial basis at his Vermont Novelty Works. His products were very much lady dolls from only one mold, which was adapted by painting in different styles. The tradition was carried on by Mason & Taylor and later by the Schoenhut Company, who produced different models almost every year.

A William and Mary wooden doll with a wisp of real auburn hair and nailed-on stitched linen wig, English, circa 1690, 16¾in. high. $27,500

A George II wooden doll with blonde real hair nailed-on wig, English, circa 1750, 16in. high. $16,500

A pair of carved and painted wooden nodding figures, with moving lower jaws, 8in. high, probably South German, circa 1850. (Christie's) $300

A George I wooden doll, the gesso-covered head with finely painted blushed cheeks, English, circa 1725, 16in. high. $18,500

An English William and Mary wood doll, circa 1690, 14½in. high. (Sotheby's) $112,000

A very rare carved and painted Charles II wood doll, with bright pink rouged cheeks, 13in. high, circa 1680. (Christie's) $125,000

DOLL'S HOUSES

The earliest English dolls' houses date from the early 18th century, though in Germany they appeared some two centuries earlier. They were not children's toys, but were usually commissioned by rich noblemen either for themselves or as gifts, beautifully made and lavishly appointed, with miniature furniture which was exquisite in its detail.

By the 19th century the average dolls' house had become less grand, and represented rather a middle class suburban villa. Genuine antique dolls' houses are quite rare and many collectors have turned to buying good reproductions, and then filling them with genuine old furniture.

A painted wooden doll's box-type town house of three bays and three storeys, 25in. high. **$750**

Victorian wooden doll's house, cottage style, with working door with brass knob at front, circa 1890. **$1,850**

An early 20th century two-storeyed doll's house, facade 20 x 18in., depth 12in. **$600**

A wooden doll's house painted to simulate stonework of two bays and two storeys, circa 1850, 57in. approx. **$600**

An early 20th century doll's house, paper covered to simulate brickwork, 88cm. high. **$600**

Belgian doll's house, modeled as a detached town villa with three bays, 1870's. **$4,250**

A 19th century wooden kitchen, maker unknown, several pieces marked Germany, 26 x 15 x 15in. **$2,250**

Late 19th century yellow Victorian doll's house and furniture, 26¾in. wide. **$450**

DOLL'S HOUSES

A wooden doll's house, opening at the front to reveal six rooms, hall and staircase, the kitchen with dresser and fire surround, with Christian Hacker stamp on the base, 33in. high. (Christie's S. Ken) $875

A model of a Georgian house with portico entrance and large bay, two storeys with basement, the case 19in. wide. (Christie's) $900

A painted wooden doll's house modeled as a Swiss chalet, opening to reveal three rooms with original lace curtains, floor and wall papers, furnished, German, circa 1920, 21in. wide. (Christie's S. Ken) $900

A wooden doll's house, of three bays and two storeys, opening at the front to reveal four rooms with staircase and landing, interior doors and fire surrounds, by G. and J. Lines, circa 1910, 37in. high. (Christie's S. Ken) $2,000

A painted wooden doll's house, of five bays and four storeys, opening to reveal ten rooms with hall, staircase and landings, interior doors, bathroom fittings, four side windows and contemporary wall and floor papers, 50in. wide. (Christie's S. Ken)
$16,500

A painted wood and printed brick paper on wood doll's house, opening at the front to reveal four rooms with original kitchen paper, dresser and fire surrounds, 28in. high, (Christie's S. Ken) $350

A painted wooden dolls' house, simulating stone with brick quoining and window and door surrounds, 37in. wide, late 19th century. (Christie's) $750

A late Georgian wooden carpenter made doll's house, painted to simulate brickwork, circa 1830, 4ft. long, 45in. high. (Christie's S. Ken)
$3,350

A wooden doll's house, painted to simulate brickwork with gray roof with scalloped eaves, opening to reveal four fully furnished rooms, circa 1900, 50in. high. (Christie's S. Ken)
$3,750

A 19th century English wooden dolls' house, the deep red brick painted exterior having four gables, 64in. high, circa 1880. (Phillips) $2,750

A model house and garden in a boxed scene, with balconies and balustrading to the first floor and simulated slate roof, circa 1850, 19in. wide. (Christie's S. Ken.) $625

A painted wooden dolls' house, simulating brickwork with slate roof, the base with shaped apron, furnished, 41in. high. (Christie's S. Ken) $1,000

A George III three storey painted wooden baby house, of three bays, with pedimented dentil cornice, 37½in. wide. (Christie's S. Ken) $4,000

A painted wooden doll's house of late Georgian style, opening in three hinged sections to reveal seven rooms, the staircase rising from the front hall to the first floor with separate treads, early Victorian, 46in. wide. (Christie's S. Ken) $2,250

A carpenter made wooden dolls' house with white painted gothic details and brass pediment, 23in. high. (Christie's) $1,500

An early 20th century English dolls' house, the wooden superstructure with nine windows to the façade, 30in. high, probably G. & J. Lines, circa 1900–1910. (Phillips) $750

A wooden box-type dolls' house, of four bays and two storeys painted on upper storey to simulate brickwork, 28in. wide, third quarter of the 19th century, English. (Christie's S. Ken) $1,000

An English wooden doll's house, the cream painted and simulated brick papered facade with eight windows, 51in. high, 1910, probably G. and J. Lines Bros. (Phillips) $1,000

It is sometimes hard to remember that many of the domestic gadgets which we take for granted today have really only been in existence for a few decades. Technological advances have been so rapid that early examples of hairdriers, vacuum cleaners and the like are now almost unrecognisable as such, and this gives them an exoticism which makes them eminently collectable.

Aluminium and metal butterfly electric fire, 1930s. (Muir Hewitt) $300

A Mitrella toaster with bakelite base, 1935. (Auction Team Koeln) $45

A very early AEG table fan, circa 1925. (Auction Team Koeln) $40

A French desk telephone by Ch. Ventroux Paris, wooden base and stand, receiver and extra receiver marked P. Jacquesson Paris, circa 1920. (Auction Team Koeln) $225

A fully automatic Morison's wooden washing machine, complete with tub, Belgian, circa 1900. (Auction Team Koeln) $185

A W. Feldmeyer spirit iron, with transverse tank and wooden handle, 1905. (Auction Team Koeln) $75

A nickel plated Friho-Sol hand held hairdrier of contemporary angular form, circa 1920. (Auction Team Koeln) $40

An Omega chromium toaster, circa 1935. (Auction Team Koeln) $45

A molded bakelite Siemens hand held hairdrier, circa 1930. (Auction Team Koeln) $25

An American Crown pleating iron by the American Machine Co., Philadelphia, with table clamp and brass rollers, 1880. (Auction Team Köln) $220

PhiliShave 6 dry electric razor by Philips, Holland, with bakelite case and plug in original box, circa 1938. (Auction Team Köln) $50

Wooden 12 litre butter churner, the 'New style white cedar', almost unused. (Auction Team Köln) $85

Cast iron American 'Sensible Press' winepress, complete with seive, by N. R. Streeter & Co., Rochester, New York, 42cm. high, circa 1920. (Auction Team Köln) $54

Ericsson skeleton desk telephone with magneto and enclosed mouth-piece, circa 1910. (Auction Team Köln) $1,543

Graeztor electric fire, black enamel with copper housing, 30 x 50cm., circa 1930. (Auction Team Köln) $150

A curious vacuum cleaner blower attachment with heating coil, in bakelite casing, circa 1935. (Auction Team Koeln) $30

Libelle fan with green hammer finish bakelite propeller, by Schoeller & Co Frankfurt, circa 1955. (Auction Team Köln) $75

German Bing No. 2 type bar typewriter, 1925. (Auction Team Koeln) $175

A heavy duty iron with replaceable wooden handle, circa 1920. (Auction Team Koeln) $20

An Ozonomat wall hanging air purifier, circa 1955. (Auction Team Koeln) $45

A wooden coffee grinder with colored tinplate sides and harvest thanksgiving motif, circa 1900. (Auction Team Koeln) $225

An early Kadus hairdrier, on cased movable stand, circa 1930. (Auction Team Koeln) $500

Prometheus Model WRS 4 toaster, 4 slice parallel tip mechanism, adjustable for 2–4 slices with control light and bakelite base, chrome, circa 1955.
(Auction Team Köln) $160

Katalyt 'Sun in Winter' paraffin heater, circa 1930.
(Auction Team Köln) $100

1950s "Frost" electric fan with green base.
(Muir Hewitt) $125

Nilfisk vacuum cleaner, an early industrial cleaner in original box with tools, circa 1935.
(Auction Team Köln) $75

An Alexanderwerk bread cutting machine, circa 1910. (Auction Team Koeln) $70

An Art Nouveau nickel plated cast iron stapler, circa 1890. (Aution Team Koeln) $65

A Dual dynamo pocket lamp, aluminium cased, circa 1940. (Auction Team Koeln) $20

An OBM Mokkadomat coffee machine, circa 1920. (Auction Team Koeln) $275

A Rolls Patent razor in plated case, circa 1910. (Auction Team Koeln) $25

A World Patented Mechanical Darner beard cutter, with adjustable levels and bakelite housing, English, circa 1930. (Auction Team Koeln) $25

A patented American cast iron Enterprise coffee grinder on wooden base, US patent dated *21 October 1873*, 32cm. high. (Auction Team Köln) $275

An early American flat iron No. 3, of unusual rounded shape, cast iron with wooden handle, 18cm. long, circa 1870. (Auction Team Köln) $540

An original Miele mangel with wooden rollers, restored, circa 1910. (Auction Team Koeln) $75

Sitting monkey doorstop, cast in full round, 23cm. high. (Auction Team Köln) **$85**

Two Scotties doorstop, cast in the half round, black, 15cm. high. (Auction Team Köln) **$69**

Girl in red dress doorstop, hand-colored, half-round model, 16cm. high. (Auction Team Köln) **$54**

Seated cat with glass eyes, doorstop, cast in the half round and colored, 25.5cm. high. (Auction Team Köln) **$123**

A doorstop shaped as a flower basket with poppies and cast in the half round, hand coloring, 18cm. high. (Auction Team Köln) **$69**

Decolleté lady doorstop, half round, colored, 26cm. high. (Auction Team Köln) **$93**

White lady with basket of flowers doorstop, half-round, hand-colored, 20cm. high. (Auction Team Köln) **$93**

A doorstop in the form of a duck, cast in the half round with fine detail and original decoration, 12cm. high. (Auction Team Köln) **$130**

Young lady with straw hat doorstop, one piece model cast in full round, colored, 21cm. high. (Auction Team Köln) **$69**

Mr. Punch doorstop cast in the half round, sitting on books and holding a pen, with the dog Toby, 31cm. high.
(Auction Team Köln)
$271

Blushing lady doorstop, half round, colored, 16 x 29cm.
(Auction Team Köln) $85

Dwarf with lantern and bunch of keys doorstop, cast in full round and colored, 25cm. high.
(Auction Team Köln) $69

A Hubley No. 25 flowerbasket doorstop, cast in the half round with original enameling and color, 19.5cm. high.
(Auction Team Köln) $69

A two-part hand-colored doorstop in the form of a white horse with blue markings, 20cm. high.
(Auction Team Köln) $93

Traffic policeman baby with dog doorstop, half round, painted, 20cm. high.
(Auction Team Köln) $50

Aunt Jemima, an original Hubley figure, two part full-round model in original enameled condition, 30cm. high.
(Auction Team Köln)
$216

Farmhouse doorstop cast in the half round and colored, 20 x 14cm.
(Auction Team Köln) $98

Black Butler doorstop, half round, hand-colored, 21.5cm. high.
(Auction Team Köln) $65

BELT PISTOLS

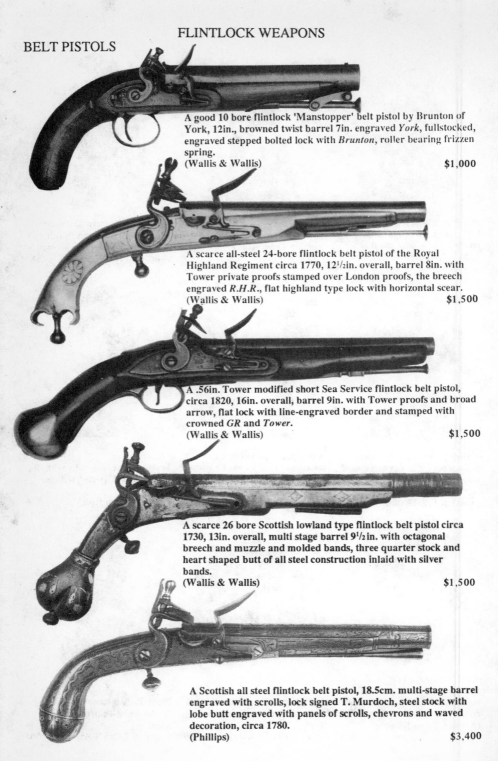

A good 10 bore flintlock 'Manstopper' belt pistol by Brunton of York, 12in., browned twist barrel 7in. engraved *York*, fullstocked, engraved stepped bolted lock with *Brunton*, roller bearing frizzen spring.
(Wallis & Wallis) $1,000

A scarce all-steel 24-bore flintlock belt pistol of the Royal Highland Regiment circa 1770, 12$^{1}/_{2}$in. overall, barrel 8in. with Tower private proofs stamped over London proofs, the breech engraved *R.H.R.*, flat highland type lock with horizontal scear.
(Wallis & Wallis) $1,500

A .56in. Tower modified short Sea Service flintlock belt pistol, circa 1820, 16in. overall, barrel 9in. with Tower proofs and broad arrow, flat lock with line-engraved border and stamped with crowned *GR* and *Tower*.
(Wallis & Wallis) $1,500

A scarce 26 bore Scottish lowland type flintlock belt pistol circa 1730, 13in. overall, multi stage barrel 9$^{1}/_{2}$in. with octagonal breech and muzzle and molded bands, three quarter stock and heart shaped butt of all steel construction inlaid with silver bands.
(Wallis & Wallis) $1,500

A Scottish all steel flintlock belt pistol, 18.5cm. multi-stage barrel engraved with scrolls, lock signed T. Murdoch, steel stock with lobe butt engraved with panels of scrolls, chevrons and waved decoration, circa 1780.
(Phillips) $3,400

BLUNDERBUSS PISTOLS

A brass barreled flintlock blunderbuss pistol, 20cm. three-stage barrel with ringed muzzle, engraved Liverpool, border engraved brass lock signed J. Parr. (Phillips) **$1,250**

A good brass framed brass barreled boxlock flintlock blunderbuss pistol with bayonet by Waters circa 1790, of the type favored by Naval officers, 13in., swollen barrel 7in. with reinforced muzzle, Tower proved. (Wallis & Wallis) **$1,700**

A steel barreled flintlock blunderbuss pistol circa 1820, 12in. overall, swamped barrel 7in. with B'ham proofs and stamped 'London' at breech, trade quality flat lock with swan neck cock and unbridled frizzen. (Wallis & Wallis) **$700**

A brass barreled French flintlock blunderbuss pistol with spring bayonet circa 1800, of the type favored by Naval officers, 12in., swollen barrel 6^1/2in. with turned reinforced muzzle, border engraved frame with military trophies of arms. (Wallis & Wallis) **$1,100**

A brass mounted Turkish flintlock blunderbuss pistol, circa 1800, 18^3/4in., flared steel barrel 11in. extensively silver inlaid overall, small brass maker's cartouche at breech, fullstocked. (Wallis & Wallis) **$635**

DUELING PISTOLS

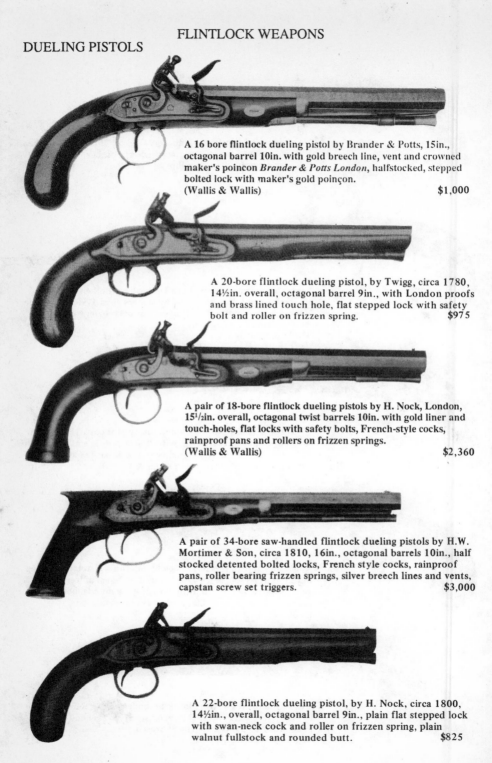

A 16 bore flintlock dueling pistol by Brander & Potts, 15in.,
octagonal barrel 10in. with gold breech line, vent and crowned
maker's poincon *Brander & Potts London*, halfstocked, stepped
bolted lock with maker's gold poinçon.
(Wallis & Wallis) $1,000

A 20-bore flintlock dueling pistol, by Twigg, circa 1780,
14½in. overall, octagonal barrel 9in., with London proofs
and brass lined touch hole, flat stepped lock with safety
bolt and roller on frizzen spring. $975

A pair of 18-bore flintlock dueling pistols by H. Nock, London,
15¹/₂in. overall, octagonal twist barrels 10in. with gold liner and
touch-holes, flat locks with safety bolts, French-style cocks,
rainproof pans and rollers on frizzen springs.
(Wallis & Wallis) $2,360

A pair of 34-bore saw-handled flintlock dueling pistols by H.W.
Mortimer & Son, circa 1810, 16in., octagonal barrels 10in., half
stocked detented bolted locks, French style cocks, rainproof
pans, roller bearing frizzen springs, silver breech lines and vents,
capstan screw set triggers. $3,000

A 22-bore flintlock dueling pistol, by H. Nock, circa 1800,
14½in., overall, octagonal barrel 9in., plain flat stepped lock
with swan-neck cock and roller on frizzen spring, plain
walnut fullstock and rounded butt. $825

HOLSTER PISTOLS

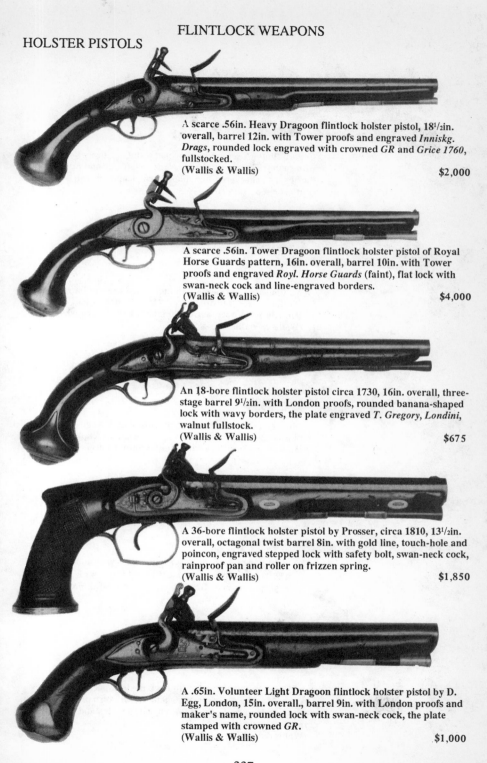

A scarce .56in. Heavy Dragoon flintlock holster pistol, 18½in. overall, barrel 12in. with Tower proofs and engraved *Inniskg. Drags*, rounded lock engraved with crowned *GR* and *Grice 1760*, fullstocked.
(Wallis & Wallis)   **$2,000**

A scarce .56in. Tower Dragoon flintlock holster pistol of Royal Horse Guards pattern, 16in. overall, barrel 10in. with Tower proofs and engraved *Royl. Horse Guards* (faint), flat lock with swan-neck cock and line-engraved borders.
(Wallis & Wallis)   **$4,000**

An 18-bore flintlock holster pistol circa 1730, 16in. overall, three-stage barrel 9½in. with London proofs, rounded banana-shaped lock with wavy borders, the plate engraved *T. Gregory, Londini*, walnut fullstock.
(Wallis & Wallis)   **$675**

A 36-bore flintlock holster pistol by Prosser, circa 1810, 13½in. overall, octagonal twist barrel 8in. with gold line, touch-hole and poincon, engraved stepped lock with safety bolt, swan-neck cock, rainproof pan and roller on frizzen spring.
(Wallis & Wallis)   **$1,850**

A .65in. Volunteer Light Dragoon flintlock holster pistol by D. Egg, London, 15in. overall., barrel 9in. with London proofs and maker's name, rounded lock with swan-neck cock, the plate stamped with crowned *GR*.
(Wallis & Wallis)   **$1,000**

POCKET PISTOLS

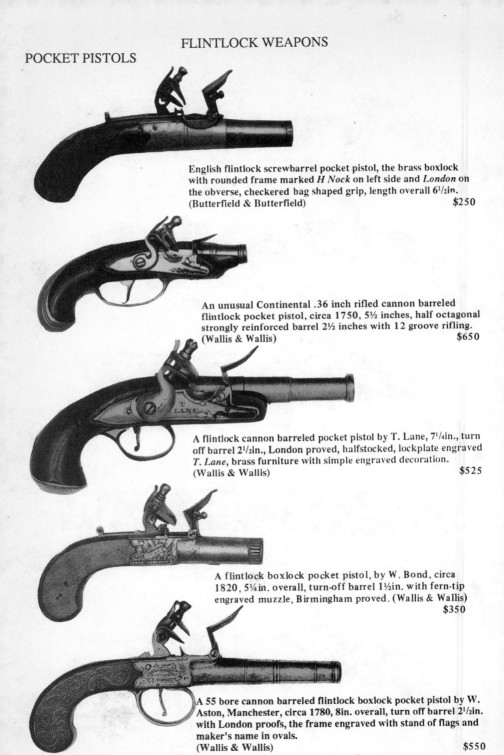

English flintlock screwbarrel pocket pistol, the brass boxlock with rounded frame marked *H Nock* on left side and *London* on the obverse, checkered bag shaped grip, length overall 6¹/₂in. (Butterfield & Butterfield) $250

An unusual Continental .36 inch rifled cannon barreled flintlock pocket pistol, circa 1750, 5½ inches, half octagonal strongly reinforced barrel 2½ inches with 12 groove rifling. (Wallis & Wallis) $650

A flintlock cannon barreled pocket pistol by T. Lane, 7¹/₄in., turn off barrel 2¹/₂in., London proved, halfstocked, lockplate engraved *T. Lane*, brass furniture with simple engraved decoration. (Wallis & Wallis) $525

A flintlock boxlock pocket pistol, by W. Bond, circa 1820, 5¼in. overall, turn-off barrel 1½in. with fern-tip engraved muzzle, Birmingham proved. (Wallis & Wallis) $350

A 55 bore cannon barreled flintlock boxlock pocket pistol by W. Aston, Manchester, circa 1780, 8in. overall, turn off barrel 2¹/₂in. with London proofs, the frame engraved with stand of flags and maker's name in ovals. (Wallis & Wallis) $550

TRAVELING PISTOLS

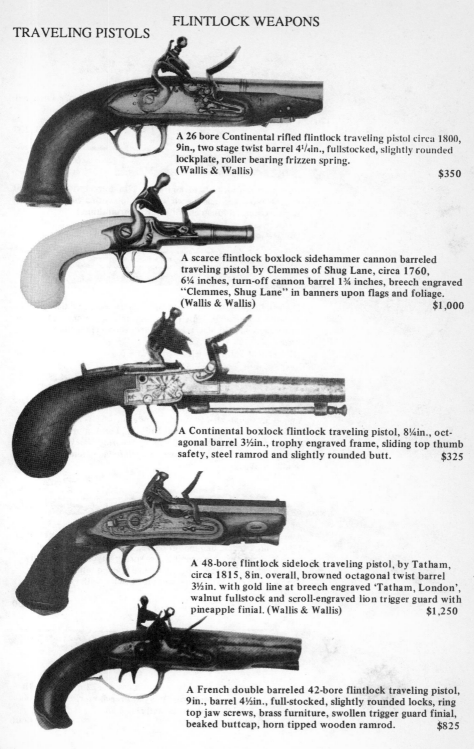

A 26 bore Continental rifled flintlock traveling pistol circa 1800, 9in., two stage twist barrel 4¼in., fullstocked, slightly rounded lockplate, roller bearing frizzen spring.
(Wallis & Wallis) $350

A scarce flintlock boxlock sidehammer cannon barreled traveling pistol by Clemmes of Shug Lane, circa 1760, 6¼ inches, turn-off cannon barrel 1¾ inches, breech engraved "Clemmes, Shug Lane" in banners upon flags and foliage.
(Wallis & Wallis) $1,000

A Continental boxlock flintlock traveling pistol, 8¼in., octagonal barrel 3½in., trophy engraved frame, sliding top thumb safety, steel ramrod and slightly rounded butt. $325

A 48-bore flintlock sidelock traveling pistol, by Tatham, circa 1815, 8in. overall, browned octagonal twist barrel 3½in. with gold line at breech engraved 'Tatham, London', walnut fullstock and scroll-engraved lion trigger guard with pineapple finial. (Wallis & Wallis) $1,250

A French double barreled 42-bore flintlock traveling pistol, 9in., barrel 4½in., full-stocked, slightly rounded locks, ring top jaw screws, brass furniture, swollen trigger guard finial, beaked buttcap, horn tipped wooden ramrod. $825

BLUNDERBUSS

English flintlock blunderbuss, 14in. brass cannon barrel marked *London* with proofs, engraved lock marked *Wilkinson*, brass buttplate, trigger guard and ramrod thimbles.
(Butterfield & Butterfield)   **$1,200**

European flintlock blunderbuss, the 17in. barrel with flared oval muzzle and octagonal breech fitted on top with a 14in. spring bayonet, pinned fullstock with iron ramrod thimbles, triggerguard and buttplate.
(Butterfield & Butterfield)   **$1,100**

English flintlock blunderbuss, the 14in. round brass barrel with flared muzzle and mounted with 13in. triangular spring bayonet, brass ramrod thimbles, trigger guard, counterplate and buttplate.
(Butterfield & Butterfield)   **$2,000**

A good brass barreled flintlock blunderbuss by Wilson circa 1785, 33in., stepped flared barrel 16¹/₂in., London proved, engraved *Mrs. Lee, Minories London, Totteridge Park*, fullstocked, border engraved military style lock with foliage on tail.
(Wallis & Wallis)   **$2,000**

A brass barreled flintlock blunderbuss with spring bayonet circa 1790, 30in. overall, bell mouth barrel 14¹/₂in. with octagonal breech, Tower private proofs, 13in. spring bayonet released by thumb catch on barrel tang, unbridled trade quality lock with simple engraved decoration, walnut fullstock with checkered wrist.
(Wallis & Wallis)   **$1,300**

Italian flintlock 'poacher's' blunderbuss, the 22in. barrel with flared oval muzzle and brass inlay at breech marked *L Lazarino*, the brass inlaid lockplate marked *D Donati*.
(Butterfield & Butterfield)   **$600**

A fine and rare Baker's 13 bore 1822 pattern flintlock carbine, 37in., barrel 21in., Birmingham proved with Ezekiel Baker's private proofs, and engraved *Ezekiel Baker & Son Gunmakers to His Majesty London.*
(Wallis & Wallis)
            $2,000

A .65in. India pattern Sergeant's flintlock carbine of 1807, 52in., barrel 37in., military proofs, fullstocked, lock engraved *Tower* with crowned *GR* and inspector's stamp, regulation brass mounts, buttcap spur engraved *5.*
(Wallis & Wallis)
            $1,200

A rare 22 bore turnover 'Wender' flintlock carbine by Harman Barne circa 1660, 31in., part octagonal barrels 15³/₄in., screw on pan and frizzen units both engraved *H. Barne.*
(Wallis & Wallis)
            $2,500

A rare .65in. Elliotts patent flintlock carbine, 43¹/₂in., barrel 28in., Tower military proofs, fullstocked, regulation lock with crowned *GR* and *Tower*, regulation brass mounts, steel saddle bar and lanyard ring.
(Wallis & Wallis)
            $1,350

A scarce 10 bore Nock's patent enclosed lock flintlock carbine, 41in., barrel 26in., Tower military proved, fullstocked, regulation lock engraved *H. Nock* with inspector's stamp, raised pan shield engraved crowned *GR* cypher.
(Wallis & Wallis)
            $3,550

A .65in. Paget flintlock carbine, 31in., barrel 16in., Tower military proofs with government sale marks, fullstocked, stepped bolted lock engraved crowned *GR* with Tower and inspector's stamp.
(Wallis & Wallis)
            $1,350

FLINTLOCK WEAPONS

Kentucky flintlock rifle, the 48in. part-round/part-octagon barrel engraved on top flat *D. Christ*, the lock marked *T./Ketland/& Co.*, the full stock with incised lines framing the ramrod trough and relief carved scrolls framing the bottom thimble.
(Butterfield & Butterfield) $14,500

French flintlock coach gun, the 25¹/₂in. two stage barrel slightly flared at muzzle and mounted on the underside with a 12in. spring bayonet, the half-stock with iron fittings.
(Butterfield & Butterfield) $700

A .62in. Baker's Volunteer flintlock rifle, 49in., barrel 30in., Tower proved, 2 leaf rearsight, bayonet bar to muzzle, fullstocked, regulation lock stamped *W. Ketland* with crowned *GR*.
(Wallis & Wallis) $2,250

Fine flintlock Indian trade gun, having a 36in part-round/part-octagon barrel marked *H.E. Leman Lancaster, Pa.* with proof marks, plain pinned full stock with brass dragon sideplate.
(Butterfield & Butterfield) $7,700

A .62in. Baker flintlock rifle, 46in., barrel 30in., fullstocked, lock engraved with crowned *GR* with inspector's stamp, regulation brass mounts, buttcap spur stamped *G/65*.
(Wallis & Wallis) $1,750

A German flintlock wall-piece, with earlier heavy two-stage sighted barrel dated *1612* at the breech and struck with two indistinct marks, earlier plain rounded lock, molded figured walnut half-stock carved with foliage in relief behind the barrel tang, early 18th century, 58³/₄in. barrel.
(Christie's) $3,300

A 60 bore Kentucky flintlock rifle, 56¹/₂in., octagonal barrel 40¹/₄in., fullstocked, adjustable double set triggers, brass furniture comprising trigger guard with finger rest, hinged patchbox, engraved buttcap spur.
(Wallis & Wallis) $885

FLINTLOCK WEAPONS

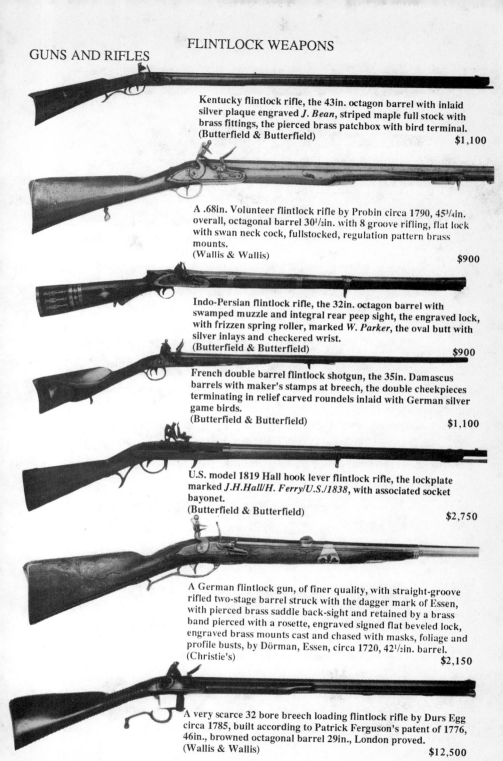

Kentucky flintlock rifle, the 43in. octagon barrel with inlaid silver plaque engraved *J. Bean*, striped maple full stock with brass fittings, the pierced brass patchbox with bird terminal.
(Butterfield & Butterfield) **$1,100**

A .68in. Volunteer flintlock rifle by Probin circa 1790, 45³/₄in. overall, octagonal barrel 30¹/₂in. with 8 groove rifling, flat lock with swan neck cock, fullstocked, regulation pattern brass mounts.
(Wallis & Wallis) **$900**

Indo-Persian flintlock rifle, the 32in. octagon barrel with swamped muzzle and integral rear peep sight, the engraved lock, with frizzen spring roller, marked *W. Parker*, the oval butt with silver inlays and checkered wrist.
(Butterfield & Butterfield) **$900**

French double barrel flintlock shotgun, the 35in. Damascus barrels with maker's stamps at breech, the double cheekpieces terminating in relief carved roundels inlaid with German silver game birds.
(Butterfield & Butterfield) **$1,100**

U.S. model 1819 Hall hook lever flintlock rifle, the lockplate marked *J.H.Hall/H. Ferry/U.S./1838*, with associated socket bayonet.
(Butterfield & Butterfield) **$2,750**

A German flintlock gun, of finer quality, with straight-groove rifled two-stage barrel struck with the dagger mark of Essen, with pierced brass saddle back-sight and retained by a brass band pierced with a rosette, engraved signed flat beveled lock, engraved brass mounts cast and chased with masks, foliage and profile busts, by Dörman, Essen, circa 1720, 42¹/₂in. barrel.
(Christie's) **$2,150**

A very scarce 32 bore breech loading flintlock rifle by Durs Egg circa 1785, built according to Patrick Ferguson's patent of 1776, 46in., browned octagonal barrel 29in., London proved.
(Wallis & Wallis) **$12,500**

A 14ct. gold engine turned Swan pen with vacumatic filling, inserted ball clip and original No.2 nib, circa 1920.
(Christie's S. Ken) $880

A shagreen Parker desk set with two lapis blue Parker Duofold pens with vulcanite tapers and gold Duofold nibs.
(Christie's S. Ken) $330

A 9ct. engine turned barleycorn design, lever filled Waterman's pen, with ball clip, circa 1920–29.
(Christie's S. Ken) $770

A gold colored Parker 51 with gray nib section, the cap inscribed 18K., in an original retailers box.
(Christie's S. Ken) $375

A lapis blue streamlined Parker Duofold junior pen with two cap bands and ball clip, circa 1927–28.
(Christie's S. Ken) $200

A dark green vacumatic filling Parker 51 with 'Icicle' pink and gold caps inscribed 14K and a matching propeling pencil, circa 1944.
(Christie's S. Ken) $1,450

A mandarin yellow hard rubber Parker Duofold Lucky Curve Senior pen with two narrow cap bands and ball clip, circa 1928–29.
(Christie's S. Ken) $880

A gold filled Hick's 'Detachable' pen, with telescopic barrel fitting into barleycorn decorated casing with ribbon ring, in original box with instructions in the base.
(Christie's S. Ken) $135

Dunhill-Namiki: a Taka Maki-E lacquer pen, decorated with three carp swimming amongst green aquatic plants, signed by the lever, circa 1937.
(Bonhams) $2,250

FOUNTAIN PENS

A 9ct. 'barleycorn' panel and spotted patterned engine turned overlaid Waterman's Ideal lever filled pen, circa 1915–29.
(Christie's S. Ken) $700

A sterling silver 'Gothic' design overlaid Waterman's lever filled pen, circa 1926.
(Christie's S. Ken)
                                                                                        $285

An emerald pearl Parker vacumatic standard pen and pencil set with three narrow cap bands and original Canadian arrow nib, circa 1933–36.
(Christie's S. Ken) $310

A heavily chased and scrolled sterling silver eyedropper Swan over fed pen, in original presentation box with red velvet lining, circa 1900–1908.
(Christie's S. Ken) $1,210

A sterling silver 'filigree' design overlay eyedropper Waterman's 12 pen, circa 1900–03.
(Christie's S. Ken)
                                                                                        $575

A gold filled scrolled and twisted design overlay eyedropper Swan pen with over/under feed nib, circa 1908–12.
(Christie's S. Ken) $1,100

A Pelican self feeding reservoir pen by Thomas de la Rue, hallmarked *London 1897*.
(Bonhams) $10,000

A fine lacquered Dunhill Namiki lever fill pen, with Maki-E design of a Japanese fisherman wearing large hat, carrying rod and bait basket on the barrel, with original Dunhill Namiki no. 20 nib.
(Christie's S. Ken) $4,850

Dunhill Namiki: a gold dust Maki-E lacquer pen, decorated with a small wood surrounding a lake with an erupting volcano in the distance, with 18ct. gold top.
(Bonhams) $1,450

345

GAMES

Anyone who was a child before the age of television still remembers evenings spent playing board games. The nostalgia element plays a large part in the collecting of games, of which many survive. Typical old favourites were Ludo, Snakes and Ladders and card games like Happy Families, while others, such as word games and general knowledge games, had a more educational bent. In the 1930s came Monopoly, the most famous of all board games, which was launched, ironically, at the height of the Depression.

It is interesting to note that the leading game and card manufacturers, Chad Valley, Waddington and Spear's, a company with strong German connections, are all still going strong today, and still producing many old favorites alongside constantly changing new ranges. When collecting vintage games, these should obviously be complete, and come with dice and shakers where applicable.

A set of six pottery carpet bowls, with a red, green or blue cross-hatched design, some glaze chipping.
(Bearne's) $325

Early 20th century tartan-ware whist marker. $10

Oscar, the Film Stars Rise to Fame. $20

Russian Novelty Clockwork Bus Track, circa 1960's.
$25

Bystander 'Fragments' Playing Cards by Chas. Goodall & Son Ltd. $45

American 'General Grant's marble game', circa 1870, diam. of marbles 1.1/8in.
$600

An Edwardian table racing game with folding mahogany board painted in green with a race track with baize center, and a mahogany box containing ten lead horses and riders, dice, tumblers and ivory markers, 60in. long. (Christie's London) $1,250

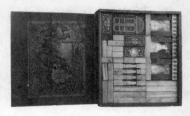

'The Game of Motoring', by Chad Valley, circa 1908, with original box. **$225**

Victorian wooden building game in a fine pictorial box. **$70**

'Steeplechase & Race Game'. **$100**

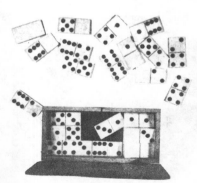

Victorian set of bone dominos in an oak box. **$75**

'The Portland Chess & Draughts Board', Robinson & Sons. **$8**

A Schuco-Varianto 3010 Motorway, in original box, US Zone W. Germany, circa 1955. $250

'Find the Car', by C. W. Faulkner, 1920. $8

A Schoenhut indoor golf game: 'set No. G/10, in original box with instructions, comprising: a 'Tommy Green' figure, a water hazard, and a putting green, etc. (Christie's) $700

Late 19th century parquetry folding cribbage board. $15

'James Bond, Secret Service Game', Spear's. $25

'The Popular Game of Halma', Squadron Edition. $15

'Wireless Whist, Score Cards', The Dainty Series, 1920's. $8

A scarce detached Scandinavian flintlock lock, circa 1650, 7 in. engraved with perched bird and foliage. (Wallis & Wallis) $400

A scarce English detached matchlock lock from a musket, circa 1680, slightly rounded lockplate. (Wallis & Wallis) $500

A rare detached snap matchlock lock, circa 1600, plate 8 in., struck with maker's initials "H.M." within rectangle. (Wallis & Wallis) $475

A rare Continental military style detached self priming pill lock from a musket, 6¼in., pill reservoir with screw on stopper. (Wallis & Wallis) $450

A detached Scandinavian flintlock lock, circa 1650, 7¾in., mainspring acts on toe of hammer. (Wallis & Wallis) $400

A detached Italian snaphaunce gun lock, circa 1675, 6¼in., plate chiseled with figure, scrollwork and stylised face on tail in relief. (Wallis & Wallis) $325

An unusual detached flintlock lock, probably provincial Italian, circa 1700, 6¾in., tail chiseled with animal's head, plate with reclining figure. (Wallis & Wallis) $375

A scarce detached English dog lock from a flintlock musket, circa 1650, 8½in. horizontally acting scear, swivel dog safety catch, (Wallis & Wallis) $425

An unusual detached double flintlock lock, for use on a gun with 2 charges in the same barrel, probably early 18th century. (Wallis & Wallis) $385

A good detached flintlock lock by Brooks, circa 1825 with patent enclosed pan, 4¾in. (Wallis & Wallis) $385

HAGENAUER

The Hagenauer workshop flourished in Vienna between 1898 and 1958. A definite house style began to emerge after the proprietor's son Karl joined the enterprise in 1919, and from the 1920s onward they produced figures, often either sporting or with a sporting motif, in metal and/or wood.

These were given a highly stylized, abstract, often whimsical interpretation, and their unique style makes them easily identifiable.

A Hagenauer wood and metal sail boat, circa 1920, 28.5cm. high.
$750

Hagenauer bronze vase, circa 1910, 11.5cm. high.
$750

A Hagenauer brass and copper bust of a woman, the stylised figure with lightly hammered surface, with applied beads to neck and curled and cut copper strips forming hair, 60.5cm. high. (Christie's) $9,000

'Man and Woman', a Hagenauer brass sculpture, of two stylised male and female figures, standing arm in arm, with curled strips at their feet in the form of grass, mounted on a triangular base, 98cm. high. (Christie's) $8,500

A Hagenauer brass twin branch candelabrum of interlaced form, the cylindrical sconces with gadrooned oval drip pans, decorated with a stylised dog, 35.5cm. high. (Christie's) $450

A gilt bronze and carved wood figure of a Spanish flamenco dancer cast and carved from a model by Hagenauer, 23.9cm. high. (Christie's) $1,000

Austrian Hagenauer chrome lady with ebony panther, 1930. $2,250

A Hagenauer carved wood and metal bust of a woman in profile, 12½in. high. (Christie's) $1,350

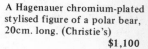

A Hagenauer bronze, modeled as a sleek horse's head and
neck, mounted on a rectangular
bronze base, 31.5cm. long.
(Phillips London) $1,350

A Hagenauer brass bowl, supported on a broad cylindrical
stem pierced with golfing
figures, 11cm. high. (Phillips)
                $525

A Hagenauer chromium-plated
stylised figure of a polar bear,
20cm. long. (Christie's)
                $1,100

A Hagenauer brass bust of a
young woman, lightly beaten
textured surface applied with
brass strips to form the flowing
hair and features, 47cm. high.
(Christie's) $7,250

A wood and bronze cockerel,
in the manner of Hagenauer,
the stylised form having a
wooden body and bronze face,
39.5cm. high. $700

A Hagenauer chromium plated
table mirror cast as a stylised
leaping deer, stamped monogram, 30.5cm. (Bonhams)
                $1,250

A pair of Hagenauer bronze
Tennis figures, each one
fashioned in sheet bronze as
male tennis players wearing
flannel trousers and adopting
athletic poses, 22.4cm. high
and 25.8cm. high respectively.
(Phillips London) $2,250

A pair of Hagenauer polished
steel and wood skiers, each
of stylised form, one in the
down hill position, the other
performing acrobatics, 33cm.
high. (Christie's) $2,000

A Hagenauer brass figure of a
tennis player, the stylised male
figure in serving position, stamped marks Hagenauer, Wien,
wHw, Made in Austria, 27.5cm.
high. (Christie's) $1,250

BALL TOPPED HELMETS

A Victorian officer's blue cloth ball topped helmet of The R. Artillery, gilt mounts, velvet backed chinchain and ear rosettes.
(Wallis & Wallis) $325

An officer's blue cloth helmet of the Royal Army Medical Corps by J. B. Johnstone, Sackville Street London.
(Christie's) $300

A post-1902 officer's blue cloth ball-topped helmet of The Royal Army Medical Corps. (Wallis & Wallis) $300

A Volunteer Artillery Officer's blue cloth ball topped helmet, silver plated mounts. (Wallis & Wallis) $250

Blue cloth ball-topped helmet, silver mounts and badge with scarlet backing, bearing title 'First London Artillery Volunteers'. $1,200

A post 1902 RAMC Captain's uniform, comprising blue cloth ball topped helmet, shoulder belt and pouch; full dress blue tunic, mess jacket with matching dull cherry waistcoat and pair breeches.
(Wallis & Wallis) $900

BEARSKINS

A good officer's bearskin of the Irish Guards, St. Patrick's blue feather plume, velvet backed graduated link gilt chinchain.
(Wallis & Wallis) $625

An officer's bearskin cap of the Royal Welsh Fusiliers with fine white metal mounted gilt grenade. (Christie's) $400

5th (Northumberland Fusiliers): officer's bearskin cap with regimental gilt grenade, inside is marked H.W. Archer, Esq., 5th Fusiliers. (Christie's) $600

A peaked burgonet, circa 1620, with high comb and hinged ear flaps embossed with rosettes, traces of later etched decoration overall, plume holder at base of comb. (Wallis & Wallis) **$1,275**

An unusual French closed burgonet of bright steel, with tall two-piece fluted skull of conical form with prominent ogival comb, circa 1630, 19in. high. (Christie's) **$11,250**

A German burgonet of bright steel, the one-piece skull with prominent comb and fixed fall pierced for a nasal secured by a wing screw, late 16th century, 11in. high. (Christie's) **$5,500**

A close burgonet, the heavy two-piece rounded skull with low rolled-over comb with iron plume-pipe at the base containing an iron candlestick nozzle, circa 1630, probably Dutch, 15in. high. (Christie's) **$2,000**

A closed burgonet, the rounded two-piece skull joined along the low finely roped comb with a rolled overlap, early 17th century, probably French, 12in. high. (Christie's) **$5,000**

A burgonet, the two-piece skull with roped comb, riveted pointed fall, single riveted neck-plate and deep hinged cheek-pieces, painted inside *SO 87*, mid-17th century, German or Dutch, 10¹/₂in. high. (Christie's) **$1,050**

A German closed burgonet from a black and white armor (polished bright), comprising one-piece skull with prominent roped comb, mid-16th century, 10¹/₂in. high. (Christie's S. Ken.) **$3,750**

A closed cuirassier's Savoyard type burgonet with raised comb and pointed peak. (Christie's) **$1,850**

A rare French burgonet, of blackened steel, the robust two-piece skull with high roped comb, third quarter of the 16th century, 11³/₄in. high. (Christie's S. Ken.) **$6,500**

CLOSE HELMETS

A French close-helmet, the one-piece skull with high roped comb, brass plume holder, pointed visor with single vision slit, circa 1570, 12in. high. (Christie's) $6,000

A Cuirassier's close helmet of light construction, the two-piece skull with low comb, the visor with small peak and attached bevor, 17th century. (Phillips) $1,000

A cuirassier close-helmet, the rounded two-piece skull joined along the low comb with a rolled overlap, English or Dutch, circa 1630, 13in. high. (Christie's) $4,000

A close-helmet, the rounded skull with low roped comb made in two pieces joined across the back of the neck, the main edges throughout bordered by pairs of engraved lines, English or Flemish, circa 1530–40, 13in. (Christie's S. Ken) $4,250

A visored bascinet (Hounskull) in 14th century style, the one-piece skull drawn up to a point to the rear of center and the edges bordered by holes for the lining and vervels for an aventail, 10^{1}/4in. high. (Christie's S. Ken) $5,500

A German foot-combat close-helmet with one-piece skull with low file-roped comb, brass plume-holder, bluntly pointed visor and upper and lower bevors pivoted at the same points on either side, circa 1630, 12^{1}/2in. high. (Christie's) $10,000

A cuirassier helmet with rounded one-piece skull and low file-roped comb, domed steel lining rivets throughout, circa 1600, probably Italian, 11in. high. (Christie's) $3,750

A composite German ('Maximilian') close helmet with one-piece globular fluted skull cut out at the back for one plain and two fluted neck-plates, early 16th century, 12in. high. (Christie's) $5,500

A cuirassier helmet, of bright steel, with fluted ovoidal two-piece skull rising to a ring finial on star-shaped rosette, early 17th century, probably German, 12in. high. (Christie's) $3,100

354

LANCE CAPS

An Edward VII officer's lance cap of The 12th (Prince of Wales's Royal) Lancers, with scarlet cloth sides and top. (Wallis & Wallis) **$4,200**

A Victorian officer's lance cap of the 16th (The Queen's) Lancers, black patent leather skull, blue cloth sides and top, embroidered peak, gilt lace trim and cords. (Wallis & Wallis) **$2,100**

A composite lance-cap (chapka) as for 16th Lancers with Q.V.C. white metal mounted gilt chapka-plate bearing honors to Aliwal and Sobraon. (Christie's S. Ken) **$2,000**

An extremely rare 1830–55 pattern Russian chapka of an officer of the 18th Serpoukhoff Regiment of Lancers with gilt numerals mounted on the white metal double-headed eagle plate. (Christie's S. Ken) **$6,750**

An Edward VII officer's lance-cap of The 12th (Prince of Wales's Royal) Lancers black patent leather skull and embroidered peak, gilt lace bands, scarlet cloth sides. (Wallis & Wallis) **$3,000**

A trooper's Victorian lance cap of the 9th (Queen's Royal) Lancers, of black patent leather with black/dark blue cloth sides. (Christie's S. Ken) **$500**

An officer's fine scarlet topped Victorian lance cap (chapka) of the 12th (Prince of Wales's Royal) Lancers, with scarlet feather plume with gilt socket. (Christie's S. Ken) **$3,000**

A Prussian NCO's lance cap of The 1st Guard Uhlan Regt. (Wallis & Wallis) **$1,000**

An officer's very rare lance-cap of the Bedfordshire Yeomanry with black cloth sides bearing ornamental gilt metal fittings. (Christie's) **$5,000**

LOBSTER TAIL HELMETS

HEADDRESS

A Cromwellian lobster tail helmet, ribbed skull with suspension loop, the peak with traces of armorer's mark and initial *F*, sliding nasal bar. (Wallis & Wallis) $1,000

A Cromwellian trooper's 'lobster tailed' helmet, two piece skull with low raised comb, pierced ear flaps, hinged visor with triple bar face guard. (Wallis & Wallis) $1,500

A Cromwellian period trooper's lobster tailed helmet "pot", one piece skull embossed with 6 radial flutes, small hanging ring finial. (Wallis & Wallis) $900

A lobster tailed pot, the one piece hemispherical ribbed skull with separate ring shaped finial, probably German, second quarter of the 17th century, 11in. high. (Christie's S. Ken) $900

An East European lobster-tailed pot (Zischägge) with one-piece fluted skull studded at the base of the flutes with brass rosettes and fitted at the rear with a brass plume-holder, third quarter of the 17th century, 12in. high. (Christie's S. Ken) $3,600

A Cromwellian trooper's lobster tail helmet, the skull formed in two halves with overlapping join, hinged peak stamped with initials *IH*. (Wallis & Wallis) $2,250

An East European lobster-tailed pot (Zischägge) with one-piece ribbed and fluted skull with separate ring-shaped finial on rosette-shaped washer, the peak formed as a separate piece, mid-17th century, 11¹/₂in. high. (Christie's) $2,500

An English lobster tailed Civil War period helmet, two piece siege weight skull, hinged visor with good quality triple bar face guard. (Wallis & Wallis) $1,350

A Cromwellian lobster tail steel helmet, the skull with six flutes, four piece articulated neck lames with large steel rivets. (Spencer's) $1,250

A good late 16th century Spanish morion, forged from one piece, of classic form with tall comb. (Wallis & Wallis) $1,350

A 17th century German black and white morion of Town Guard type, formed in two-pieces, plume holder. $750

A North Italian 'Spanish' morion, in one piece, with skull rising to a stalk, the base encircled by a row of brass lining rivets with rosette-shaped washers, late 16th century, 11½in. high. (Christie's) $8,000

A rare Saxon Electoral Guard comb-morion of one piece with roped comb and brim, the base of the skull encircled by sixteen gilt-brass lion-masks capping the lining rivets, struck on the brim with the Nuremberg mark, circa 1580, 11½in. high. (Christie's S. Ken) $13,000

An Italian 'Spanish Morion', of one piece, with tall pointed skull, etched throughout in the 'Pisan' manner with bands and borders of trophies, circa 1570, 10¾in. high. (Christie's S. Ken) $1,350

A Saxon Electoral Guard comb morion, of one piece, with roped comb and brim, the base of the skull encircled by sixteen gilt-brass lion-masks capping the lining rivets, the brim struck with the Nuremberg mark, circa 1580, 11¾in. high. (Christie's) $18,000

A good German late 16th century morion, made for a town guard, two piece skull with tall roped comb, turned over ribbed borders. (Wallis & Wallis) $875

An Italian 'Spanish morion' of one piece, with tall pointed skull surmounted by a stalk, encircled at the base by holes for lining rivets, circa 1580, 7½in. high. (Christie's) $1,750

A good morion circa 1580, formed in one piece, roped comb, retaining a few brass rosettes around base, roped edges. (Wallis & Wallis) $875

PICKELHAUBEN

A Prussian M.1915 Ersatz (Pressed Felt) O.R's Pickelhaube of a Pioneer Battalion. (Wallis & Wallis) $225

A fine Prussian General Staff officer's Pickelhaube, silvered Guard helmet plate, with enameled center to Guard star. (Wallis & Wallis) $1,800

A fine Prussian Telegraph Company officer's Pickelhaube, fine gilt helmet plate of Line Eagle. (Wallis & Wallis) $500

A fine Prussian General officer's Pickelhaube, gilt Guard Eagle helmet plate with silver and enameled Garde Star. (Wallis & Wallis) $1,500

A good, scarce 1842 pattern Prussian Reservist Infantry officer's Pickelhaube, gilt helmet plate with Landwehr cross. (Wallis & Wallis) $1,300

A fine Bavarian Chevauleger Reservist officer's Pickelhaube, fine gilt helmet plate, leather backed chinscales and mounts. (Wallis & Wallis) $875

A scarce Imperial German Wurttemburg General officer's Pickelhaube, gilt helmet plate with superimposed star and enameled center, gilt fluted spike. (Wallis & Wallis) $1,500

A Wurttemberg infantryman's ersatz (pressed tin) Pickelhaube gilt helmet plate, brass mounts with traces of gilt. (Wallis & Wallis) $400

An Imperial German Hesse Infantry officer's Pickelhaube, gilt helmet plate, leather backed chinscales and mounts, fluted spike, both cockades, leather and silk lining. (Wallis & Wallis) $700

PIKEMAN'S POTS

An English Civil War period pikeman's pot, two piece skull with raised comb, riveted border.
(Wallis & Wallis) $875

A 17th century pikeman's helmet "pot", two piece skull with shallow raised comb, turned over riveted brim, deeply struck with I.R. armorer's mark.
(Wallis & Wallis) $875

A mid 17th century pikeman's pot, the skull formed in two halves with raised comb and recessed border to brim.
(Wallis & Wallis) $1,800

PILL BOX HATS

A scarce floppy pill box hat of the Eton Volunteer Rifle Corps, Elcho gray cloth, triple lace headband, leather chinstrap.
(Wallis & Wallis) $150

An officer's pattern blue pillbox cap circa 1880 of the East Lothian Yeomanry Cavalry, and a scarlet jacket of the same.
(Christie's) $330

A good officer's pillbox hat of The Royal Artillery, gilt lace and braided top ornament, in its tin case.
(Wallis & Wallis) $200

SALLETS

A sallet of great weight, made from a single piece, the rounded skull with low keel-shaped comb pierced for a crest-holder, perhaps 15th century Italian, 9in. high.
(Christie's) $5,000

A very rare Milanese sallet, of one piece, the rounded skull arched over the face, with low-keel-shaped comb, short pointed tail and narrow outward turn along the lower edge, late 15th century, 10³/₄in. high.
(Christie's) $33,000

A German gothic sallet and bevor in late 15th century style, the sallet, of one piece, the bevor of two plates pivoted together.
(Christie's) $6,850

SHAKOS

U.S. Army dress shako, circa 1850, complete with cockade and light infantry plate. (Butterfield & Butterfield) $1,200

An interesting Italian Marines shako, circa 1910, black cloth, leather top, headband and peak, red plaited loop and braid trim. (Wallis & Wallis) $230

An Imperial German Prussian Landwehr OR's shako (re issued M 1866 pattern) oval metal badge in state colors with Landwehr cross. (Wallis & Wallis) $300

An Imperial Austrian army officer's shako, gilt Imperial eagle helmet plate, bullion cockade with *FJI* cypher, bullion cloth band. (Wallis & Wallis) $175

An officer's shako, circa 1855, of the 10th (The Prince of Wales's Own Royal) Light Dragoons (Hussars), black velvet body, black patent leather front peak. (Wallis & Wallis) $2,500

A good 1869 pattern officer's blue cloth shako of the 2nd Royal Cheshire Militia, patent leather peak, silver braid trim, velvet backed silver plated chinchain. (Wallis & Wallis) $675

A scarce officer's shako, circa 1850, of the Royal Dock Yard Battalion, black felt sides and top, silver lace top band. (Wallis & Wallis) $875

An officer's 1869 pattern shako of The 15th (York East Riding) Regt., two narrow gilt lace bands to top, one to headband, velvet backed gilt chinchain and ear rosettes. (Wallis & Wallis) $600

A Nazi Police officer's shako with bullion cockade and silk and leather lining. $500

An interesting Victorian officer's blue cloth spiked helmet of The Cheshire Regt., gilt mounts, velvet backed chinchain and ear rosettes. (Wallis & Wallis) $600

A Victorian officer's blue cloth spike helmet of The Bedfordshire Regt., gilt mounts, velvet backed chinchain and ear rosettes. (Wallis & Wallis) $500

An officer's Victorian blue cloth helmet of the Cheshire Regiment by Cater & Co., Pall Mall. (Christie's) $300

A scarce officer's 1878 pattern blue cloth spiked helmet of The 59th (2nd Nottinghamshire) Regiment. (Wallis & Wallis) $575

A very good post-1902 officer's blue cloth spiked helmet of The North Staffordshire Regiment, gilt mounts, velvet backed chinchain. (Wallis & Wallis) $750

A Victorian officer's blue cloth spiked helmet of the 5th Volunteer Battalion, The Royal Scots. (Wallis & Wallis) $1,000

A scarce officer's 1878 pattern blue cloth spiked helmet of The 108th (Madras Infantry) Regiment. (Wallis & Wallis) $500

A good Victorian officer's blue cloth spiked helmet of the 4th Volunteer Bn The Royal West Kent Regt, silver plated mounts. (Wallis & Wallis) $550

A very fine Victorian officer's blue cloth spiked helmet of the 1st Gloucester Volunteer Engineers, silver plated mounts. (Wallis & Wallis) $550

KATANA

A Mino Seki katana, Muromachi period (circa 1500), signed *(Orikaeshi-mei) Izumi (no) Kami Kanesada*, with longitudinal ridge line (shinogi-zukuri), tri-beveled back (mitsu-mune) and medium point (chu-kissaki); length (nagasa): 1 shaku, 4 sun, 4 bu (52.8cm.).
(Christie's) $3,000

An Osaka Tamba katana, Edo period (circa 1660), signed *Yamato (no) Kami Yoshimichi*, attributed to Yoshimichi II, with longitudinal ridge line (shinogi-zukuri), shallow peaked back (iori-mune) and medium point (chu-kissaki); length (nagasa): 2 shaku, 3 sun, 7 bu (72.1cm.).
(Christie's) $16,500

A Kaga katana, Muromachi period (early 16th century), inscribed *Kiyomitsu*, with longitudinal ridge line (shinogi-zukuri), shallow peaked back (iori-mune) and medium point (chu-kissaki); length 73.9cm.
(Christie's) $2,500

A Mino Seki katana, Muromachi period (circa 1530), signed *Kanenaga*, with longitudinal ridge line (shinogi-zukuri), shallow peaked back (iori-mune) and medium point (chu-kissaki); length 60.7cm.
(Christie's) $2,000

A Kaga Fujishima katana, Edo period (circa 1640), signed with three kin-zogan cutting attestations and kin-zogan-mei, *Kanemaki Saku*, with longitudinal ridge line (shinogi-zukuri), and medium point (chu-kissaki); length (nagasa): 2 shaku, 3 sun (69.9cm.); curvature (sori): koshi-zori of 1.3cm.; increase in width of blade (fumbari): 0.9cm..
(Christie's) $13,500

A Yamato katana, Edo period (circa 1675), signed *Fujiwara Kaneshige*, with longitudinal ridge line (shinogi-zukuri), shallow peaked back (iori-mune) and medium point (chu-kissaki); length (nagasa): 2 shaku, 3 sun, 4 bu (71.1cm.).
(Christie's) $4,500

TACHI

A Bizen Osafune tachi, dated *1960*, signed *Bizen (no) Kuni Osafune (no) ju Fujiwara Toshimitsu* [b. 1898] *Tsukuru*, with longitudinal ridge line (shinogi-zukuri), shallow peaked back (iori-mune) and medium point (chu-kissaki); length (nagasa): 2 shaku, 3 sun, 8.5 bu (72.6cm.).
(Christie's) $6,600

A Bizen tachi, Kamakura period (probably mid-13th century), signed *Yoshifusa*, with longitudinal ridge line (shinogi-zukuri), shallow peaked back (iori-mune) and small point (ko-kissaki); length (nagasa): 2 shaku, 4 sun, 1 bu (73.2cm).
(Christie's) $2,100

A Ko-Bizen tachi, Heian period (circa 1000), signed *Bizen (No) Kuni Tomonari Saku*, with longitudinal ridge line (shinogi-zukuri), shallow peaked back (iori-mune) and medium point (chu-kissaki); length (nagasa): 2 shaku, 3 sun, 6.5 bu (71.9cm.).
(Christie's) $33,000

A Chikuzen Kongo Byoe tachi, mid-Nambokucho period (circa 1350–1370), attributed to Reizen Sadamori, with longitudinal ridge line (shinogi-zukuri), shallow peaked back (iori-mune) and medium point (chu-kissaki); length (nagasa): 2 shaku, 2 sun, 5.5 bu (68.1cm.).
(Christie's) $41,800

A Bitchu Chu-aoe tachi, Nambokucho period, dated Jowa 3 (1347), signed *Bitchu (No) Kuni (No) ju Tsugunao saku*, with longitudinal ridge line (shinogi-zukuri), rounded back (maru-mune), and short, medium point (chu-kissaki); length (nagasa): 2 shaku, 9 sun, 6 bu (89.8cm.).
(Christie's) $154,000

A Bizen Osafune tachi, Nambokucho period (circa 1350), signed *Nagamitsu*, attributed to Nagamitsu III, with longitudinal ridge line (shinogi-zukuri), shallow peaked back (iori-mune) and small point (ko-kissaki); length (nagasa): 2 shaku, 1 sun, 6 bu (65.5cm.).
(Christie's)   £12,100

TANTO

A Shinshinto Edo Yamaura yoroi-doshi tanto after a 14th century example, Edo period, dated *Ansei 5* (1858), signed *Minamoto Masao*, of thick, flat, wedge section (hira-zukuri) with shallow peaked back (iori-mune); length (nagasa): 9 sun (27.4cm.); curvature (sori): none (muzori).
(Christie's) $11,000

An Osaka Gassan school tanto, dated *1960*, signed *Gokamei Motte Yotetsu Ryusen Sadatsugu Kore(o) Saku/Kotaishi Denka Goseikon Kinon*, of flat, wedge section (hira-zukuri) with tri-beveled back (mitsu-mune) and uchizori; length (nagasa): 7 sun, 5 bu (22.9cm.).
(Christie's) $6,750

A Showa tanto after Rai Kunitoshi, dated *1966*, signed *Utsushi Rai Kunitoshi Miyairi Shohei* (b. 1913), with longitudinal ridge line (shinogi-zukuri) with tri-beveled back (mitsu-mune); length (nagasa): 8 sun, 8 bu (26.7cm.); curvature (sori): uchizori of 0.2cm.
(Christie's) $8,250

A Bizen Osafune tanto after Bizen Kagemitsu, dated *1967*, signed *Bizen (no) Kuni Osafune (no) ju Toshimitsu* (b. 1898), of flat, wedge section (hira-zukuri) with shallow peaked back (iori-mune); length (nagasa): 8 sun, 6 bu (26cm.).
(Christie's) $6,750

A Bizen Osafune tanto, Muromachi period, dated *Bunan 6* (1449), signed *Bishu Osafune Sukemitsu*, of flat, wedge section (hira-zukuri) with shallow peaked back (iori-mune); length (nagasa): 9 sun, 4 bu (28.4cm.); curvature (sori): almost none (muzori); carving (horimono): inside (ura): a single bonji; outside (omote): Fudo Myo-o descending on a dragon.
(Christie's) $10,000

A tanto, dated *1980*, signed *Yoshindo* (b. 1942), of flat, wedge section (hira-zukuri), shallow peaked back (iori-mune); length (nagasa): 8 sun, 5 bu (25.6cm.); curvature (sori): uchizori of 0.1cm.
(Christie's) $6,000

WAKIZASHI

A later Soshu wakizashi, Muromachi period (circa 1470), signed *Soshu [No] Ju Hirotsugu Saku*, attributed to Hirotsugu I, with longitudinal ridge line (shinogi-zukuri), shallow peaked back (iori-mune) and medium point (chu-kissaki); length 55.3cm.
(Christie's)

$7,250

A Hizen Tadayoshi wakizashi, Edo period (circa 1665–70), signed *Omi Daijo Fujiwara Tadahiro* (Tadahiro II), with longitudinal ridge line (shinogi-zukuri), shallow peaked back (iori-mune) and medium point (chu-kissaki); length (nagasa): 1 shaku, 8 sun, 6 bu (56.5cm.).
(Christie's)

$8,250

A Hizen Tadayoshi wakizashi, Edo period (circa 1675), signed *Omi Daijo Fujiwara Tadahiro*, with longitudinal ridge line (shinogi-zukuri), shallow peaked back (iori-mune) and medium point (chu-kissaki); length (nagasa): 1 shaku, 8 sun, 1.5 bu (55cm.).
(Christie's)

$6,750

A Bizen Osafune wakizashi, Muromachi period, dated *Bunmei 9* (1477), signed *Bishu Osafune ?*, with longitudinal ridge line (shinogi-zukuri), shallow peaked back (iori-mune) and medium point (chu-kissaki); length 53.3cm.
(Christie's)

$2,750

A Hizen Tadayoshi wakizashi, Edo period (circa 1625), signed *Hizen (no) Kuni (no) ju Tosa (no) Kami Fujiwara Tadayoshi* (Tadayoshi II), with longitudinal ridge line (shinogi-zukuri), shallow peaked back (iori-mune) and long medium point (chu-kissaki); length (nagasa): 1 shaku, 3 sun, 3 bu (40.5cm.).
(Christie's)

$7,250

An Echizen Takai wakizashi, Edo period (circa 1675), signed *(Kiku-mon) Echizen (no) Kami Minamoto Nobuyoshi*, with longitudinal ridge line (shinogi-zukuri), shallow peaked back (iori-mune) and medium point (chu-kissaki); length (nagasa): 1 shaku, 4 sun, 8 bu (45.1cm.); curvature (sori): koshi-zori of 0.7cm.
(Christie's)

$3,850

LAMPS

Lamps have always provided an ideal medium for artistic expression, and the Art Nouveau/Deco periods were no exception. Some great generic types emerged at this time, such as the Tiffany lamp, and most great craftsmen in such varied media as sculpture, metalwork, art glass and ceramics produced characteristic forms. These ranged from the beauty of the cameo and acid-etched offerings of Daum and Gallé, through to the outré and whimsical products of Art Deco craftsmen such as Frank Clewett.

An Art Nouveau table lamp, beaten brass inset with coloured glass, on oval wooden base, 49cm. high. (Christie's) $650

Wrought iron lamp with mica shades, possibly England, early 20th century, cast leaf detail, unsigned, 17½in. high. (Skinner Inc.) $1,500

A figural bronze and glass table lamp, cast from a model by Pohl, with three young women wearing diaphanous robes, dancing around the central column, total height 52cm. (Phillips) $1,350

A Gabriel Argy-Rousseau pate-de-verre and wrought-iron veilleuse, the gray, blue and dark blue mottled glass molded with stylised leaves, 25.5cm. high. (Christie's) $3,350

'Pipistrello', a table lamp designed by Gae Aulenti, for Martinelli Luce, the telescopic stainless steel pedestal on a black enameled conical foot, 91cm. maximum height. (Christie's) $1,400

French cameo glass lamp, cut with Roman gladiators and Art Deco borders, supported on three arm metal fixture 19in. high. (Skinner Inc.) $1,600

'Batwomen', a large bronze and ivory table lamp by Roland Paris, the body modeled with three female figures gold patinated in bat-winged costume and ruffs, 94cm. high. (Christie's) $13,000

An Art Nouveau bronze oil lamp base with jeweled glass shade and glass funnel, cast after a model by G. Leleu, circa 1900, 57cm. without funnel. (Christie's) $900

A patinated bronze and ivory table lamp modeled as Pierrot seated on a bench beneath a tree, 19in. high.
(Christie's S. Ken) $1,250

'Nymph among the bullrushes', a bronze table lamp cast after a model by Louis Convers, 28.1cm. high. (Christie's) $775

Late 19th century Webb & Sons Fairy lamp, the plain shade and clear liner fitting into a decorated ruffle, 10in. high. $1,125

An Almeric Walter pate-de-verre and wrought-iron lamp, the amber glass plaque molded with a blue and amber mottled peacock, 27cm. high. (Christie's) $3,350

A German Art Nouveau silvered pewter nautilus shell desk lamp, stamped M H 20, 27cm. high. (Christie's) $2,800

A Gabriel Argy-Rousseau pate-de-verre and wrought-iron veilleuse, 17.5cm. high. (Christie's) $4,500

'Rudolph', a robot light fitting designed by Frank Clewett, the head formed by spherical glass shade, the adjustable arms with light bulbs forming the hands, 149cm. high. (Christie's) $1,450

Art Deco Daum style table lamp, on rectangular silvered base, the club shaped frosted glass shades sitting on outstretched arms, circa 1925, 29cm. high. (Kunsthaus am Museum) $900

A Durand art glass lamp, with domed shade and baluster base, fitted with two socket lighting, 15in. high. (Skinner Inc.) $1,000

DAUM

Auguste (1853–1909) and Antonin (1864–1930) Daum were French glass craftsmen who were much influenced by Gallé and became members of the Ecole de Nancy. They made great use of cameo glass enameling and later also worked in pâte de verre. Acid etched pieces are also common. Their lamps are highly characteristic for their frequent use of the mushroom shade. Stems are also of glass, and these are decorated to form a uniform whole with the shade.

A Daum cameo glass table lamp with conical shade, 51cm. high, signed. (Phillips) $4,500

A Daum Art Deco table lamp, frosted glass with wrought iron, engraved with cross of Lorraine, circa 1925, 46cm. high. (Christie's) $5,000

A Daum cameo table lamp with wrought-iron, three-branch neck mount, 44.1cm. high. (Christie's) $9,000

A Daum acid etched, carved and enameled landscape table lamp, of acid textured and cased polychrome glass, enameled with a Dutch village in a snowy wooded landscape, 39cm. high. (Christie's) $20,000

A Daum overlaid and acid-etched table lamp with wrought-iron mount, 60cm. high. (Christie's) $12,000

A Daum enameled and acid etched landscape table lamp with wrought-iron mounts, 48.5cm. high. (Christie's) $4,750

A Daum Art Deco glass table lamp with geometric panels enclosing stylised foliage and berries, supported on three chromed arms, 53.5cm. high. (Phillips) $9,500

A Daum carved and acid-etched double-overlay lamp, the shade of stepped conical form, with yellow ground overlaid in red and burgundy with a wooded river landscape, 32cm. high. (Christie's) $10,000

EMILE GALLÉ

Emile Gallé was born in 1846 and started his career as a ceramicist. In 1874 he established a small workshop in Nancy, where during 1890s he was to become the inspiration for what became known as the Ecole de Nancy, a group of French Art Nouveau artists who followed his techniques and decorating style. He made earthenware and later also experimented with stoneware and porcelain. His pieces were decorated with heraldic motifs and plant designs, and featured flowing, opaque glazes.

His forms were for the most part simple, sometimes even a little clumsy, though some of his shapes were borrowed by the Rookwood pottery in the USA, who acknowledged their debt to him.

In the early 1870s he also started experimenting with glass, and this is the medium with which he is now most associated. In fact, he revolutionised its manufacture by going completely against the traditional ideal of crystalline purity and aimed instead for an opaque, iridescent effect. He experimented with the addition of metal oxides to the glass melt, coloring glass in imitation of semi-precious stones, and also even exploited the impurities to give glass the quality of a fabric or the suggestion of mist or rain.

Gallé was much influenced by Japanese and Chinese arts and his close friendship with a Japanese botanist who was studying at the Ecole Forestière in Nancy further accentuated this. Such influence is particularly noticeable in his cameo glass pieces.

Gallé pâte de verre and

A Gallé carved and acid-etched lamp, with bronze mount, cast from a model by Pondany, the glass shade of mushroom-cap form with undulating rim, 53.5cm. high. (Christie's) $7,000

A Galle double overlay and wheel-carved glass table lamp, the matt-yellow ground overlaid in brown, blue and purple, circa 1900, 52.5cm. high. (Christie's) $10,000

A Galle blowout lamp, varying shades of red on an amber ground, signed, circa 1900, 44.5cm. high. (Christie's) $65,000

A tall Galle cameo table lamp, the domed shade and stem overlaid with claret-colored glass, 63.5cm. high. (Christie's) $13,000

A Galle cameo and bronze mounted 'Veilleuse', the globular frosted glass shade with bronze dragonfly finial, resting within a mount of three further dragonflies, 18cm. high. (Phillips) $5,250

A Galle triple overlay cameo glass lamp, blue and green over a pale amber ground, circa 1900, 61cm. high. (Christie's) $15,000

GALLE

clair de lune glass had a wonderful translucent glow like moonlight, and he was also notable for having developed the technique of marquêterie de verre, in which colored pieces were pressed into semi-molten glass before it was cooled. His most complicated vases were made up of several separately colored layers of glass, which were wheel engraved to different depths, to reveal each layer below. These would then be finished with marquetry and patination. He also used acid to bite into the glass surface, to create delicate bark or web like effects.

From the mid 1880s Gallé had further diversified into furniture design. His creations show restrained lines with the inevitable naturalistic ornamentation. Here again there was much use of plant motifs and the use of marquetry on flat surfaces.

It was around 1900 that Emile Gallé began the decorative application of glass to lighting, when he began producing lamps in the form of flowers, the bulbs being shaded by the half open petals. He used all the immense range of techniques which he had mastered in producing his lamps, and cameo, carved and acid-etched examples abound. He favored the mushroom shades which were so to influence the Daum brothers, and the thematic and decorative integration of base and shade.

Gallé signed all his creations, and after his death in 1904 a star was added to the signature. His factory continued in operation until 1931 under his friend and assistant Victor Prouve.

A Gallé carved and acid-etched double-overlay lamp, the milky-white glass overlaid with orange and yellow nasturtium, supported by a bronze naturalistic base, 38.5cm. high. (Christie's) $14,000

A Gallé cameo glass lamp, the broad bullet-shaped shade of salmon-pink tone overlaid with reddish-orange and reddish-brown glass, 44cm. high. (Phillips) $14,500

A Galle triple-overlay cameo glass and Emile Guillaume gilt-bronze table lamp, the pale acid-textured glass of compressed form, 70cm. high. (Christie's) $60,000

A Gallé carved and acid-etched, double-overlay table lamp, the yellow glass overlaid in royal blue and purple with harebells, the base and shade with carved signatures *Gallé*, 61cm. high. (Christie's) $65,000

A Galle double overlay cameo glass lamp, circa 1900, 32.4cm. high. (Christie's) $11,500

Austrian bronze lamp with Gallé Cameo glass shade, base after Friedrich Gornick, late 19th century, with stag and doe beneath trees, signed, 23$^{1}/_{2}$in. high. (Skinner Inc.) $5,500

LALIQUE

René Lalique's work is characterised by the use of milky opalescent glass and also glass so richly colored as to give the impression of precious stones. He used both of these in his lamp production, together with his favourite decorative motifs, dragonflies and female faces and forms. Later, he also made lamps of circular or semi-circular sheets of glass.

LE VERRE FRANÇAIS

Charles Schneider (1881–1962) opened his Cristallerie Schneider at Epiny-sur-Seine in 1913, and it is here that Le Verre Français is now recognised as having been produced. This was Art Deco glassware, cameo cut with stylized flowers, fruit and insects, chiefly in rich tones of crimson, orange, ultramarine and purple. It was produced between 1920–33, mainly for sale in large stores. Principal products were vases, bowls and lamp bases, sometimes with shade en suite. These usually consisted of a marbled glass core, with a superimposed layer of thin clear, or sometimes speckled glass.

LEGRAS

The Legras glasshouse was established in 1864 by Auguste Legras at St Denis, near Paris. It is noted for its Art Nouveau style ornamental ware, often featuring cameo snowscapes or autumn scenes. Later, Art Deco cameo glass was also produced. In 1920 the company merged with the Pantin glasshouse to become Verreries et Cristalleries de St Denis et de Pantin Réunies.

A Lalique blue stained table lamp, the shade molded with six dancing maidens wearing classical dresses, 23.5cm. width of shade. (Christie's London) $12,000

A Lalique glass and metal table lamp, the frosted pyramidal shade molded on the inside with stepped bands of beads, 51cm. high. (Phillips) $2,000

A Le Verre Francais acid etched table lamp with three-pronged wrought-iron mount, 42.2cm. high. (Christie's) $2,500

A Le Verre Francais acid etched cameo table lamp, the milky white acid textured glass overlaid with amber fruiting vines, 46cm. high. (Christie's London) $6,600

A Legras etched and enamelled glass table lamp with mushroom shaped shade, 50.6cm. high. (Christie's) $2,500

A Legras glass table lamp having a domed shade, painted in colored enamels with a pair of budgerigars and foliage, 36.5cm. high. (Phillips London) $1,250

LOETZ

It was the firm of Loetz, founded at Klostermühle in Austria in 1836, which became one of the leading manufacturers of Jugendstil glass in the last years of the 19th century. Particularly striking was their iridescent glass and of all his European imitators, it was Loetz who succeeded in reproducing most closely the Favrile glass of Tiffany. Many Loetz products were in fact exported to the US,

Bronze and cameo glass lamp by Loetz, 44cm. high, circa 1900. $6,000

A Loetz glass and gilt metal table lamp. $12,000

A Loetz iridescent glass table lamp, with bronze base formed as two Art Nouveau maidens standing amid flowers, 51cm. high.
(Phillips) $1,350

MULLER FRERES

The brothers Henri and Desiré Muller, who were active during the first third of the 20th century, trained under Gallé at Nancy, before setting up their own businesses in Luneville and Croismare in 1895. Their vases and lamps, which often combine up to seven layers of glass, are usually beautifully carved. They also developed the technique of fluorogravure, using hydrofluoric acid to bite into glass painted with deep colored or iridescent enamels. They made much use of landscape and floral motifs and sometimes applied glass cabochons.

A bronze lamp base with a Loetz shade cast from a model by M. Csadek, the base modeled as two lions seated by a tree trunk, the hemispherical shade with iridescent mother-of-pearl finish, 46cm.high. (Christie's)
$2,250

A brass table lamp with a Loetz glass shade, the lightly iridescent green glass shade applied with trailed amethyst bands, 38cm. high. (Christie's) $700

Muller Freres cameo glass illuminated column table lamp and mushroom shaped shade, 23in. high. $3,750

A Muller Frères carved and acid-etched cameo landscape table lamp, the orange and white glass overlaid in dark amber with a wooded river landscape and deer, 48cm. high.
(Christie's) $13,000

ROYAL DOULTON

Royal Doulton figural lamp bases set out purely as figures, and were later mounted and modified. This was done by Doulton themselves, and their catalogs from the 1930s, for example, show pages of 'Modern Decorative Electric Lamps of Royal Doulton' showing various figures beneath an assortment of shades.

A table lamp with the Royal Doulton figure Genevieve on the base, H.N. 1962, total height 44.5cm. $400

Royal Doulton figure of 'Janet', mounted as a table lamp, issued 1936, 35cm. high. $375

A Doulton Flambe figure by Noke, modeled as a seated Buddha, mounted as a lamp, circa 1930, 57.5cm. high. (Christie's) $1,250

Royal Doulton table lamp featuring 'Hinged Parasol', issued 1933, height of figure 6½in. $575

A Royal Doulton group entitled 'The Flower Seller's Children', H.N.1206, withdrawn 1949, mounted as a table lamp. (Bearne's) $675

SABINO

Marius Ernest Sabino or Sabino-Marino, was a French glass artist who flourished in the 1920s and 30s. He produced Lalique inspired pieces, composed of units of pressed glass molded on an invisible foundation and also made lampshades and vases in smoky-colored glass.

His mark is Sabino, Paris, engraved or molded.

One of a set of four Sabino wall lights, with molded decoration, 38cm. high. (Christie's)
Four $2,000

A Sabino frosted glass table lamp, the shade formed as a triple cascade of water supported on three metal arms, 19.5cm. high. (Phillips London) $400

A post 1902 heavy gilt crown Household Cavalry standard top, 4¼in., with base screw stud.
(Wallis & Wallis) $120

A late 18th century model of a bronze barreled field gun, 21in. overall, bronze barrel 9in. with turned reinforces, swollen muzzle and cascabel.
(Wallis & Wallis) $650

Civil War Ketcham hand grenade, marked *Patented Aug. 20, 1861*, mounted on a wood plaque.
(Butterfield & Butterfield) $450

A German cartridge-holder, comprising wooden body drilled for five cartridges and inlaid on either side, blackened iron frame with bright lines, circa 1570, 4¼in. high.
(Christie's) $1,500

The embroidered devices from an early Victorian Household Cavalry trumpet banner, double sided, laid down on pink damask, with original gilt cords and tassels, 26 x 24in.
(Wallis & Wallis) $50

A massive brass shell case, 16 x 31in., engraved *Jokobynessen Battery (Deutschland)* headstamped *Polte Magdeburg X–17–1679*.
(Wallis & Wallis) $375

A leather, brass & steel MacArthur & Prain 1905 patent 'Gannochy rapid load' cartridge-dispenser, for one hundred 12-bore cartridges.
(Christie's) $800

A silver bugle of the London Rifle Brigade, engraved with Regimental Badge, and, around the mouth, *Presented by Captain G. R. Reeve, M.C., and Lieutenant R. R. Reeve 6th May 1935*.
(Wallis & Wallis) $675

A rare Accles Positive feed magazine, for the Model 1883 Gatling gun, the hollow drum with internal spiral guides and rotating cartridge propeller.
(Christie's) $1,000

A massive brass shell case, 48in. in length, engraved *Knocke Battery (Kaiser Wilhelm II)* on wooden stand.
(Wallis & Wallis) **$635**

A good .56in. Colt bullet mould for the percussion revolving rifle, 8in., for ball and bullet, body stamped *.56 S*, cut off stamped *Colts Patent*.
(Wallis & Wallis) **$300**

A scarce Victorian embroidered buff silk pipe banner of the 1st Bn The Seaforth Highlanders, gilt tasseled border.
(Wallis & Wallis) **$450**

A remarkable 1890 halfpenny coin, the obverse stamped *Oakley*, the edge deformed by shot or bullet strike.
(Christie's) **$2,125**

An Imperial Chemical Industries Eley & Kynoch cartridge-board with metallic and paper dummy-cartridges and components arranged radially around an *I.C.I* medallion, 31 x 25in. overall.
(Christie's) **$2,600**

An interesting 18th century turned wood ramrod head, for a 32pr gun, diameter 6in., stamped on rear flat *32*.
(Wallis & Wallis) **$180**

A large, well produced Italian Fascist Party calendar for 1933 bearing a portrait of Mussolini, in unused state.
(Wallis & Wallis) **$210**

A rare Imperial German Leib Gendarmerie helmet Parade Eagle, gilt finish, screw-nut attachment, 7in. high.
(Wallis & Wallis) **$1,100**

An interesting 18th century gunpowder barrel, height 21in., diameter 18in., bound with four copper bands and remains of split willow binding.
(Wallis & Wallis) **$80**

A lacquer katana stand for a daisho, Meiji period (circa 1900), raised on two rolled feet, and decorated with gilt lacquer on the leading edges of the supports, width 59cm. (Christie's) $4,180

A pair of R.A.F. goggles, Mk. VIII, with spare reflective pattern lenses, dated *1940*, in their original cardboard carton.
(Wallis & Wallis) $100

The shabraque of an officer of the Long Melford Troop of the Suffolk Yeomanry Cavalry of dark blue cloth with scarlet cloth borders.
(Christie's) $1,000

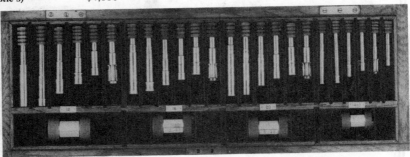

A rare set of gunmaker's master pattern chamber-gauges, for 2⁹/₁₆in. chambers, 28 gauges in total, possibly made by Charles Osborne & Co., in their oak velvet-lined and fitted case. (Christie's) $1,125

A miniature armor in the Maximilian style, the helmet with one-piece fluted skull and bellows visor, mounted on a wood stand, 68cm. high, 19th century. (Phillips) $2,000

A good pair of officer's gilt chain link shoulder scales of the East Lothian Yeomanry, on scarlet cloth with gilt embroidered edging.
(Wallis & Wallis) $75

A lacquer tachi stand, Meiji period (late 19th century), on a rectangular base with indented corners, fitted with shaped neck terminating in a leaf-form upper support, 62.5cm. high.
(Christie's) $4,625

A lacquer katana stand, Meiji period (late 19th century), raised on two rolled feet and fitted with three vertical supports and a cross-bar, width 66.3cm.
(Christie's) $5,300

A pair of World War II WD dispatch rider's goggles in original issue packet and tin dated *1944*.
(Wallis & Wallis) $50

A large heavy dark green velour table cover 64 x 68in., bearing the richly embroidered ornaments from one side of an officer's shabraque of the 14th Light Dragoons.
(Christie's) $580

A good 18 cavity brass gang mold c. 1800 for casting graduated balls from 120 bore to 12 bore.
(Wallis & Wallis) $125

A well made 19th century miniature copy of a full suit of 16th century Maximilian armor, comprising fluted breast and backplate, helmet with fluted and pierced visor, overall height 23in.
(Wallis & Wallis) $2,000

A rare World War I R.A.F. part chamois lined leather enclosed flying helmet, original printed linen label *Adastra. Supplied by Geo. H. Leavey 1918.*
(Wallis & Wallis) $200

A pair of pre 1855 officer's gilt shoulder scales of the Bengal Artillery, padded scarlet cloth backing and original lace ties.
(Wallis & Wallis) $285

An officer's full dress waistbelt of the 6th (Inniskilling) Dragoons, gilt regimental lace on red morocco.
(Wallis & Wallis) $250

A pair of officer's gilt greatcoat shoulder scales of The Royal Regt of Artillery 1840–55, bearing silver plated crown/ Bath star/badge.
(Wallis & Wallis) $410

MODEL AIRCRAFT

The first toy planes made by the Dinky Toy Company were launched on the market in 1934 and given the identification Number 60. The scale used was roughly 1/200. Planes were issued in boxes of six to be sold boxed or singly. Production continued until 1939 when it slowed down and by 1941 came to a standstill because of the lack of raw materials which were needed for the war effort. The original models were made of lead alloy but before 1939 this was replaced by a substitute called Mazak which was an alloy containing aluminium, copper, zinc and some magnesium. Sometimes trace elements that were present made the alloy brittle and cracks appeared. Examine any Dinky toys well because cracks will only get worse. Always store in a cool, dry place out of direct sunlight. The most common model plane produced was the Percival Gull which was produced in many colors but after 1940 the planes were always camouflaged and Spitfires, Hurricanes, Blenheims, Fairey Battles, Armstrong Whitworth Whitleys, Ensigns, Leopard Moths and Vickers Jockys joined the range. Because they were only produced for a short time they are rare and valuable. Boxed sets which are available are The R.A.F. Presentation Set, The Camouflaged Set and The Presentation Set. After the war, Dinky planes were back in production and new ranges were produced in 1946 and in the 50s. Probably the most sought after model to any Dinky collector is number 992 Avro Vulcan. This model of the most famous of the R.A.F. V-Bombers, was produced between 1955 and 1956. The model is quite large and finished in silver.

JU89 Heavy Bomber, 67A, 1940-41, German markings, boxed. $300

Nimrod Dinky Comet (Conversion). $185

Dinky F-4 U.S.A.F. Phantom, U.S. Market only. $150

Shetland Flying Boat No. 701, 1947-49, boxed. $900

Camouflaged Whitworth Ensign Liner No. 68A, 1940-41. $300

Dinky Hurricane, ME109. $70

Dinky Diamond Jubilee Spitfire, boxed. $150

Pre-war Frog Penguin, unmade in kits. $35

378

MODEL AIRCRAFT

Bristol Britannia No. 998, 1959-65, boxed.
$275

A large scale model of the British airship
R100-G-FAAV, 10ft. long, with tower, 4ft.
$2,600

Meccano No. 2 special model aeroplane constructor outfit complete and good order, play damage to paintwork, pilot missing, circa 1939.
(James of Norwich) $325

Atlantic Flying Boat, boxed. $450

Lockheed Constellation No. 60C, produced by Meccano France, 1957-63, boxed. $210

Camouflaged Frobisher Air Liner. $330

A rare printed and painted tri-engine cabin biplane, with red and blue lining and RAF roundels, by Wells, circa 1936, 21¼in.
(Christie's) $675

Hindenburg, a rare printed and painted tin-plate airship, with clockwork mechanism, in original paintwork with swastikas, German, 10in. long. (Christie's S. Ken) $725

Armstrong Whitworth Whitley No. 62T, Silver, 1937-41, boxed. **$225**

Frog Hawker Hart Mark II Day Bomber, with accessories and instruction book, in original box, with Hamley's retail label, circa 1935.
(Christie's S. Ken) **$1,500**

A pre-war Frog de Havilland 80A 'Puss Moth' in original box with winding key, accessories. (Christie's) **$500**

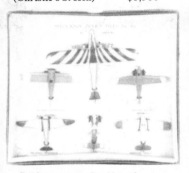

Dinky pre-war Set No. 60 Aeroplanes (2nd Issue), including Imperial Airway Liner, D. H. Leopard Moth, Percival Gull, Low Wing Monoplane, General 'Monospar' and Cierva Autogiro, in original box, circa 1934. (Christie's) **$6,250**

Flying Fortress No. 62G, 1939-41, boxed. **$250**

Douglas Air Liner No. 60T, (supposed to be a DC3 by many, but is probably a DC2) boxed. **$250**

A Meccano No. 1 Aeroplane Constructor Outfit, assembled as a light biplane, silver plates, R.A.F. roundels, circa 1931. (Chrsitie's) **$300**

Armstrong Whitworth Ensign Air Liner No. 62P, 1938-41, boxed. **$175**

A detailed model of the Focke-Wulf FW 190-A6 single-seater fighter, serial No. 1-5 with considerable external detailing, finished in camouflage, 6 x 15½in. (Christie's) **$400**

MODEL AIRCRAFT

A well detailed ⅛th scale flying model of the Hawker Typhoon 1B Serial letters RB222, built by D. Banham, 65in.
(Christie's) $1,250

Mayo Composite Aircraft No. 63, 1939-41, boxed.
          $500

A modern painted tinplate Fairey Swordfish torpedo bomber, by Tin Pot Toy Co., 14in. long.
(Christie's) $325

Dinky pre-war set No. 60 Aeroplanes (2nd Issue), with markings and instructions, in original box. (Christie's S. Ken) $750

The first Dinky boxed set, No. 60, issued in 1934 to 1940. $1,500

Kings Aeroplane (Envoy) No. 62K, 1938-41, boxed. $300

A pre-war Empire Flying Boat No. 60R, 1937, boxed. $275

Britains rare set 1431 Army Co-operation Autogiro with pilot, in original box, 1937.
(Phillips) $3,400

Frobisher Class Air Liner No. 62, 1939-41, boxed. $275

Large monoplane model, made by Charles R. Witteman, Staten Island, New York, circa 1912, 62in. long, wingspan 78in. **$1,900**

A model of a Bleriot-type (Morane) monoplane, with engine, wingspan 40½in. **$225**

A Lehmann Ikarus tinplate aeroplane, No. 653, German, 10½in. long. **$1,900**

Tipp Co., clockwork lithographed bomber bi-plane TC-1029, wing span 36.5cm., 25.5cm. long, key, lacking pilot, three bombs. **$625**

A Marklin monoplane in cream and green, fitted to a double bogie, plane 20cm. long. **$475**

A Britain's set No. 434, R.A.F. Monoplane, with two pilots and four R.A.F. personnel, in original box. **$2,400**

A 1:24th scale wood and metal model of the Royal Aircraft Factory SE5a, built by R. Walden, 1976. **$450**

Biplane No. 24, with clockwork mechanism, Deutsche Lufthansa markings, wingspan 20¼in. long, by Tipp, circa 1939. **$775**

French tinplate Paris-Tokio bi-plane, clock-work mechanism driving the wheels, circa 1935, 9in. long. $475

A J.D.N. clockwork tinplate model bi-plane, made circa 1928. $775

A Mettoy jet airliner, No. 2016/1, in original box with four mechanical sparking replace-ments, the box 20½in., English, circa 1935. $400

'Strato Clipper', a printed and painted tinplate four-engine airliner with battery mechanism, by Gama, circa 1956, wingspan 20in. $300

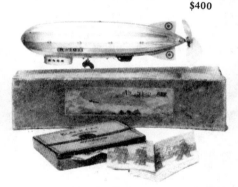

A pre-war Japanese R101 airship by GK, the aluminium body with tinplate gondolas and fins, 13in. long, together with newspaper cuttings, circa 1930. $950

A flying scale model of the Gloster Gladiator single seater fighter Serial No. K.8032 with external details, finished in silver with R.A.F. markings, wingspan 56in. $775

American Flyer Manufacturing Co., Model No. 560 spring-driven monoplane, 54cm. long, span 60cm., boxed. $475

An Exhibition Standard 1:30 scale model of the prototype Panavia Tornado F-2 Multi Role Combat Aircraft, wingspan 17½in. $4,125

Model ships can really be divided into two distinct types. The first consists of the craftsmen built or builder's model type, faithful scale models of the original and exact in every detail, designed to be set in glass cases and wondered at. Some of the earliest examples of these were manufactured by French prisoners of war during the Napoleonic period and sold by them to obtain money to eke out their rations. They were made from left over bones, string and straw, and embellished with scraps of wood, ivory or metal. These now fetch many thousands of pounds, as do the more conventionally built builders' models, the price reflecting the care and precision which has gone into the making. Beloved by collectors too are the ship in a bottle types, many of which have been lovingly made by old sailors.

Strictly speaking, however, these are not really toys, and it is to the tinplate manufacturers of the turn of the century that we must look for the earliest examples of the second type. While the first were accurate in every scale detail, the charm of the second type lies often in their bright colors and disproportionate sizes. The earliest were not even meant for the water, but had detachable wheels so that they could be 'sailed' on the carpet! Early examples, even in poor condition, are all likely to be of value, particularly the large (up to 36") German models with steam or clockwork mechanisms. Tinplate boats from the 1930s are also worth looking out for, and even those from the 1950s by German makers such as Arnold can fetch hundreds. The record is £125,000 paid in 1989 for an 1885 Märklin boat, the Imperator.

Ernst Plank, a large hand painted battleship with guns, handrails, finished in gray with red lining, 60cm. (Phillips West Two) $3,000

An early wood/composition base toy of a Dreadnought with three funnels, 12.5cm., circa 1905. (Phillips West Two) $85

A German painted tinplate steam riverboat, finished in red and white, blue and red lined, and yellow funnel with red star, circa 1905, 30cm. long. (Christie's S. Ken) $600

Ingap, clockwork lithographed twin funneled river boat, the main body finished in cream, on four silver spoked wheels, 15.5cm. (Phillips) $300

A Third Series painted tin-plate clockwork ocean liner, by Bing, circa 1925, complete with masts and rigging, the hull fitted with clockwork mechanism, 16in. long. (Christie's) $2,650

Carette, a lithographed tinplate flywheel driven carpet toy sailing vessel, with eccentric rocking action and lithographed card sail (lacks flywheel), circa 1905, 24cm. long. (Christie's S. Ken) $400

An Arnold four funnel ocean liner, with clockwork mechanism powering two three blade propellers, German, circa 1920 (some parts missing, flags missing, patches of rust, worn), 15½in. long. (Christie's) $450

Hornby Speed Boat No. 2 'Hawk', green and white, in original box, circa 1936, 9¼in. long. (Christie's S. Ken) $150

A shipbuilder's model of the schooner yacht 'America', American, circa 1850, 28in. long. **$5,500**

Mid 19th century English contemporary model of a sailing ship hull, 9in. long. **$325**

A 20th century carved and painted model of the paddle steamer 'City of Key West', American, in wooden and glass case, 38in. long. **$1,500**

Mid 19th century English model of the brig 'Vanda', probably sailor-made, 15in. long. **$2,000**

A restored and repainted early Marklin three-funnel tinplate battleship, German, circa 1910, 17in. long. **$1,100**

A 1:100 scale model of the three masted auxiliary schooner 'Cruz del Sur' built by W. M. Wilson, Silloth, 12 x 17½in. **$650**

A carved and painted model of ocean liner 'Liberte', executed for the Companie Generale Transatlantique, circa 1950, in wooden and plexi-glass case, 54in. long. **$6,000**

A builder's mirror back half model of a single screw cabin motor cruiser built by John I. Thorneycroft & Co. Ltd., London, 6 x 26in. (Christie's) **$2,250**

A finely engineered and detailed live steam, spirit fired model of the Passenger Tramp Steamer Belle Morss of London, 22$\frac{1}{2}$in. x 51$\frac{1}{2}$in. (Christie's) $2,500

A finely detailed electric powered radio controlled model of the paddle steamer Albion, 16in. x 52in. (Christie's) $2,500

A well detailed and presented fibreglass wood and metal electric powered, radio controlled model of the Lowestoft Herring Drifter Gull, Licence No. H241, built by W.A. Williams, London. 68in. x 35in. (Christie's) $3,350

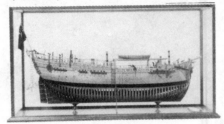

A boxwood, lime and walnut model of 'H.M.S. Endeavour', made by Brian Hinchcliffe, English, modern, 30in. long. $9,000

Cased, carved and painted ship model, America, late 19th/early 20th century, polychrome model of the steam ship City of New York, 35$\frac{1}{2}$in. wide. (Skinner Inc.) $1,500

An $\frac{1}{8}$th scale wooden display model of the German cruiser S.M.S. Viktoria Louise, the hull carved from the solid, masts and rigging and deck details including anchors, deck rails, bridge, stayed funnels, guns in turrets and other details, 29in. x 67$\frac{1}{2}$in. (Christie's) $750

A builder's 3/16in.:1ft. scale model of H.M.S. 'Transport Ferry No. 3016', built for the Royal Navy by R. & W. Hawthorn, Leslie & Co. Ltd., Hebburn-on-Tyne, 1945, 16 x 63$\frac{1}{2}$in. $5,500

A finely planked and pinned unrigged model of the ship rigged sloop Myridon of circa 1881, built by P. Danks, Leighton Buzzard, from plans supplied by the National Maritime Museum, 8in. x 32in. (Christie's) $2,250

A well presented fully planked and framed model of a 30ft. Royal Navy armed pinnace of circa 1877, built by P. Smith, Ealing, 15in. x 23.5in.
(Christie's)   **$750**

Early 20th century shipbuilder's model of the turret deck steamer 'Duffryn Manor', English, 44in. long, in glazed mahogany case.   **$3,750**

An extremely fine and detailed exhibition standard fiberglass wood and metal, electric powered radio controlled model of H.M.S. Warspite built by G. Edwards, Cheddington, 17¹/₂in. x 61in. (Christie's)   **$6,500**

A finely detailed and well researched fully planked and framed electric powered radio controlled model of a Thornycroft 55ft. coastal motor torpedo boat, built by R.R. Bullivant, Leighton Buzzard, 14¹/₂in. x 38in.
(Christie's)   **$1,500**

A well detailed and presented 1:150 scale static display model of the Spanish paddle/sail corvette San Ildefonso of circa 1840, built by W.M. Wilson, Carlisle, 10¹/₂in. x 19in.
(Christie's)   **$400**

A fine and detailed exhibition standard ¹/₇₅th scale model of the French 64-gun ship of-the-line Le Protecteur, built to drawings supplied by Le Musee de la Marine, Paris, 32¹/₂in. x 39in.
(Christie's)   **$3,350**

Early 20th century model of the Clyde steamer 'Duchess of Fife', made by N. S. Forbes, 54in. long.   **$5,500**

Early 20th century shipbuilder's model of the cargo vessel 'Nailsea Manor' built by Bartram & Sons Ltd. of Sunderland, 54in. long.   **$4,000**

MODEL TRAINS

Toy trains were being manufactured in France, Germany and England shortly after the introduction of the real thing, but it was to be another 50 years before they had any track to run on. Made of wood or tinplate, early examples were carpet toys designed to be pushed or pulled along.

Model steam locomotive, London Brighton & South Coast, 'Atlantic' class, 4-4-2, 3½in. gauge. (H.P.S.) $3,750

The earliest train sets in the form we know them today were produced by Märklin in the early 1890s, when they produced impressive figure-8 layouts for clockwork trains. Their beautifully painted accessories, in the form of railway stations etc. are all highly sought after today.

A (3-rail) electric model of the LNER 4-4-0 No. E220 special locomotive and tender No. 201 'Bramham Moor'.   (Christie's S. Ken) $1,500

Standardising scale in some way was a pressing necessity, and by the early 1900s two major gauges, 0 and 1, had been established. The larger no. 1 ran on a track 45mm wide, while the smaller 0 gauge was used for indoor displays.

In England, Wenham Bassett-Lowke, son of a Northamptonshire engineer, was determined to make near perfect scale models, and produced his famous gauge 1 Lady of the Lake in 1904. This and his first clockwork models formed a serious challenge to the German manufacturers.

The First World War brought building to a halt and had the further effect of inhibiting the hitherto fruitful cooperation between British and German firms. This proved to the advantage of Hornby, who began making model railways in the 1920s, and by the end of the decade could boast a full and comprehensive range of train sets and accessories. The value of Hornby sets often varies with their livery, Southern Railway engines, for example being quite rare. By and large this is true of all makes.

A Marklin tinplate 'Rocket' gauge 1 train set, German, circa 1909. $45,000

Hornby, 3.R.E. Princess Elizabeth and tender, boxed. $2,250

388

Model steam locomotive, London Brighton & South Coast, Brighton terrier class, 0-6-0, 5in. gauge. (H.P.S) $3,000

Rare Hornby-Dublo pre-war (3-rail) EDL7 S.R. 0-6-2 tank locomotive No. 2594, in original box, circa 1938. (Christie's S. Ken) $1,000

Painted and stenciled tin train, Stevens and Brown, Cromwell, Connecticut, 1868-1872, black, green and red engine inscribed *Thunderer*, engine 6in. long. (Skinner Inc.)
                    $4,000

A rare clockwork model of the SAR 0-4-0 No. 1 tank locomotive No. 7206, in original box, circa 1926. (Christie's S. Ken)
                    $475

A finely detailed exhibition standard 7¼in. gauge model of the GWR Class 1101. 0-4-0 Dock tank Sisyphus, originally built by the Avonside Engine Company, Bristol, 19 x 38½in. (Christie's S. Ken) $9,000

Model steam locomotive, London Midland & Scottish, shunting tank engine, 0-6-0, 5in. gauge. (H.P.S) $3,350

A rare (3-rail) electric model of the 0-4-0 No. LE220 locomotive No. 10655, finished in green livery with gray roof, circa 1934. (Christie's S. Ken) $2,250

A spirit fired 4-4-0 locomotive and 8 wheeled bogie tender, finished in black with red and gold detailing, circa 1909, slight chipping.
(Phillips) $6,350

A Märklin hand-painted bogie Midland Railway family saloon, with opening roof, detailed interior, opening doors and seated figures, circa 1907.
(Christie's S. Ken) $2,250

A clockwork 4-4-0 Paris-Lyon Mediterranee painted tinplate 'windcutter' locomotive and 6 wheeled tender CV 1022, finished in dark green with gold and red banding and lining, circa 1905.
(Phillips) $7,835

A 3-rail electric 20v 4-8-2 ME locomotive and 8 wheeler tender finished in pale green, dark green and red.
(Phillips) $6,750

Hornby control system: lever frame and 'Windsor' signal cabin, in original boxes, with adjustable No. 2 20in. control rail, two control points and nine rod guide brackets, circa 1925.
(Christie's S. Ken) $765

A Hornby Series 'Palethorpes' sausage van, in original box, circa 1939.
(Christie's S. Ken) $830

A 3-rail electric 4-4-2 NBR locomotive and tender No. CE 6513021, finished in brown with red, yellow and black lining, excellent condition, tender sticky.
(Phillips) $3,000

A 3-rail electric, 20v, 4-6-2 HS pantograph locomotive, finished in brown with orange lining and black roof, slight retouching.
(Phillips) $6,350

A spirit fired NBR 4-4-2 locomotive and 6 wheeled tender No. 4021, finished in brown with red, yellow and black lining.
(Phillips) $2,800

MODEL TRAINS

A rare Hornby Series E120 Special Electric FCS Argentinian tank locomotive, in lake, red and gold livery, circa 1938.
(Christie's S. Ken) $1,325

A well detailed 7in. gauge static display model of Stephenson's 'Rocket' of 1829, 22 x 31³/₄in.
(Christie's S. Ken) $3,250

A rare Märklin-bodied Bassett-Lowke clockwork Great Western 'King George V' and matching six wheel tender, circa 1936.
(Christie's S. Ken) $3,600

A rare Hornby Series FCS Argentinian refrigerator van, with open axle-guards, early hinged doors and handles, in original box with Argentinian label, circa 1927.
(Christie's S. Ken) $1,000

A Märklin hand painted and stamped station newspaper kiosk, with four-gable roof, pay windows, clocks and relief work, circa 1910, 5in. high.
(Christie's S. Ken) $5,400

A Hornby Series 'Crawford's' biscuit van with opening doors and white roof, in original box, circa 1927.
(Christie's S. Ken) $875

A 3-rail electric 0-4-4-0 steeple cab PO-E1 locomotive, with forward and reverse lever, finished in green with pale green and black detail, gold window frames, black roof.
(Phillips) $1,850

An extremely fine mid-19th century 5¹/₂in. gauge spirit-fired model of the Sheffield to Rotherham Railway Stephenson 2-4-0 locomotive and tender No. 45 'Albert', signed *Alfred Chadburn Maker 1855*, 14³/₄ x 36in.
(Christie's S. Ken) $25,000

A 3-rail electric, 20v, 4-0-4 Gotthard type locomotive No. S 64/13021, with forward and reverse action, finished in brown with orange lining.
(Phillips) $4,500

OPTICAL TOYS

The Victorians were fascinated by photography and viewing instruments, as the host of optical toys dating from the period bears witness. They have wonderful names, such as graphoscope, mutoscope, stereoscope, and enchanted adults and children alike. Perhaps most fun of all is the zoescope, or 'wheel of life' in which figures on the inside of a rotating cylinder are made visible through slots, providing an illusion of animated motion. The forerunner, in fact of modern cinematography.

A Magic Disc phenakisticope optical toy with 8 discs, each 7in. diam., a viewing disk, 9in. diam., and a Fantascope disc, 5in. diam. $1,000

A pressed and pierced metal magic lantern with fluted chimney and lens, 11¹/₂in. high. (Christie's S. Ken) $250

A 19th century box stereoscope, the case decorated with flowers on a black ground. (Michael Newman) $660

The 'Improved Phantasmagoria Lantern, by Carpenter & Westley, with patent argand solar lamp with a quantity of lantern slides. (Christie's) $400

Rosewood stereo viewer, table top, manufactured by Alex. Becker, N.Y., circa 1859. $550

A mohagany-body bi-unial magic lantern with a pair of two-draw brass bound lenses each with rack and pinion focusing, all in a fitted combined container. (Christie's S. Ken) $3,250

British projection lantern for max 19 x 19cm. slides, having wood and brass Petzval type optics with gear drive and red filter equipped for 21cm. diam. condensor, original gas burner. (Auction Team Köln) $435

A mahogany body table Achromatic Stereoscope by Smith, Beck and Beck, with a pair of focusing eyepieces and original mirror. (Christie's S. Ken) $925

A metal bodied Flickergraph optical toy with viewing lens, handle and one reel, printed paper labels *For use with the Animated Pictorial*. (Christie's S. Ken) $650

A burr walnut Brewster pattern stereoscope with rack and pinion focusing, shaped lens hood mounted on hinged lens section. (Christie's S. Ken)

$350

A molded black-plastic body OTHEO Stereo Viewer x5 with red illuminant button and a pair of focusing eyepieces by Ernst Leitz Canada Ltd., in maker's fitted box. (Christie's S. Ken) $1,000

A Brewster-pattern hand-held stereoscope with Japanese lacquer-work decoration depicting flying storks and trees. (Christie's S. Ken.) $700

A mahogany and brass-fitted biunial magic lantern with a wood-mounted snow effect mechanical slide with printed label *E.H. Wilkie*, in a fitted wooden box. (Christie's S. Ken) $1,800

A mahogany sliding box camera obscura front section with lens and turned wood lens cap, body stamped By His Majestys Special Appointment. Jones, (Artist.) London. (Christie's S. Ken) $650

Gaumont, Paris, a 45 x 107mm. mahogany bodied table stereoscope with internal mechanism and slide holders. (Christie's S. Ken) $550

A 20 x 14cm. Polyrama Panoptique viewer with diced-green paper covered body, brass fittings, and black leather bellows with thirteen day and night views. (Christie's S. Ken) $1,200

A mahogany-body pedestal Scott's Patent Stereoscope with rack and pinion focusing eyepiece section, with plaque *Negretti & Zambra*. (Christie's S. Ken) $1,100

Rowsell's parlor grapho-
scope, folding table model,
base 23 x 12in., circa 1875.
$300

A London Stereoscopic Co.
Brewster-pattern stereoscope
with brass mounted eye pieces,
in fitted rosewood box, 13in.
wide. (Christie's) $600

A Fantascope optical toy comprising a fitted mahogany box
with drawer containing fifteen
picture discs.
(Christie's) $7,500

A metal-body upright magic
lantern type 720 by Ernst
Planck, Germany, with giltmetal decoration lens, chimney
and illuminant.
(Christie's S. Ken) $400

A twelve inch diameter black
painted Zoetrope and a quantity of picture strips each with
a printed title and *'Entered
at Stationer's Hall'*.
(Christie's S. Ken) $575

A 'The Designoscope' kaleido-
scopic toy, contained in
maker's original box bearing
the legend *The Designoscope*.
*An endless source of artistic
pleasure*. (Christie's S. Ken)
$85

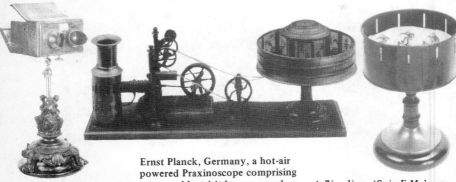

Negretti and Zambra, a
mahogany stereoscope with
focusing section, hinged top
lid and hinged rear reflector.
(Christie's) $1,500

Ernst Planck, Germany, a hot-air
powered Praxinoscope comprising
a removable spirit burner, condensing pistons and 6in. diameter praxinoscope drum with three picture
strips.
(Christie's) $5,750

A 7in. diam. 'Spin-E-Ma' zoetrope with three picture strips
each labeled *Kay. Made in
England. Copyright*. (Christie's
S. Ken) $400

A wood and brass magic lantern with brass bound lens and chimney with a slide holder and a small quantity of slides in wood box. **$350**

A mahogany-body Kinora viewer with inlaid-wood decoration and a picture reel no. 273 showing a white polar bear. (Christie's S. Ken) **$1,150**

A Le Praxinoscope optical toy with shade and ten picture strips, by Emile Reynaud, drum with seller's label. **$300**

A burr walnut pedestal stereoscope with focusing eye-pieces and internal mechanism. (Christie's) **$500**

An Ive's Kromskop color stereoscopic viewer, in wood carrying case. **$1,250**

A mutoscope in cast iron octagonal shaped case, electrically lit, 22in. high. **$1,250**

A 12-inch diameter black metal drum zoetrope mounted on a turned mahogany stand with 7½ inch diameter friction-drive wheel with handle. (Christie's S. Ken) **$1,500**

An upright cylinder lantern with red and gilt decoration on barrel with chimney by Ernst Planck, Nuremberg. (Christie's) **$1,000**

A cardboard-body New Patent Jewel Kaleidoscope by London Stereoscopic Co., with brown morocco-leather finish, and ball-socket mounting section. (Christie's S. Ken) **$1,550**

PEWTER

Pewter, an alloy of tin and other metals, usually copper or lead, has been used for domestic items since Roman times. During the medieval period it became the favored metal for tableware, as a relatively cheap substitute for silver, and in 1348 the Pewterers' Company was established to set standards of workmanship and register craftsmen. By 1503 all pewterers had to register their 'touches' with the company. These marks were impressed on the handles or rims of pieces, and the system continued to operate up to 1820.

About this time pewter fell from favor. As a material associated with the Middle Ages, however, it was ripe for revival when the Arts & Crafts movement came along to extol all things medieval.

Its use in Art Nouveau settings was perhaps first taken up by the German firm of Kayser Sohn, whose pewter wares or Kayserzinnwaren designed by Hugo Leven, were sold from 1896 in the Atelier Englebert Kayser in Cologne. His tea wares with their elegant flowing decoration were the counterpart of the Liberty Tudric range in the UK.

Pewter and enamel crumb tray with Art Nouveau design, circa 1910.
(Muir Hewitt) $100

One of a pair of Art Nouveau pewter candlesticks, 9in. high. $600

A Loetz pewter mounted two-handled iridescent glass vase, 8¾in. high.
(Christie's) $500

A 'Victoria' radio loud-speaker with cast white metal figure of a female piper, circa 1925, 21in. high. $525

A white metal and colored enamel dressing mirror in the Art Nouveau style, attributed to the March Bros., 50cm. high. $475

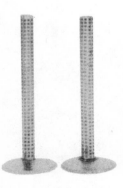

Two Argentor silvered metal candlesticks, after a design by Josef Hoffmann, circa 1910, 28cm. high. $1,500

A Jugenstil pewter mirror, with pierced frame, circa 1900, 53cm. $325

A Silberzinn pewter oil lamp, designed by Albin Muller, circa 1905, 24cm. high. $475

A Jugendstil polished pewter triptych mirror in the style of P. Huber, 32.2 x 53.4cm. (Christie's) $700

An Edelzinn pewter candelabrum, designed by J. Olbrich, 1902, 36cm. high. $5,000

A pewter mounted iridescent glass vase attributed to Loetz, circa 1900, 26.5cm. $750

A Wiener Werkstätte white-metal box, with hinged cover, decorated with a repoussé frieze of a stag and bird amid stylised trees, 8.8cm. long. (Christie's) $5,250

A Loetz white metal mounted baluster vase, the metallic orange glass with pulled loop metallic green and white decoration, 19.1cm. high. (Christie's) $1,000

One of a pair of pewter five-branch candelabra, probably Dutch, circa 1900, 45.5cm. high. $775

A glass jar with pewter cover and mounting, after a design by Peter Behrens, 6¼in. high (Skinner Inc.) $425

An Art Nouveau electroplated pewter candlestick, formed as a freestanding scantily clad maiden holding a curvilinear branch, on pierced floral base, 32cm. high. (Christie's) $475

A Swedish art pewter inkwell by Svenskt Tenn, Stockholm, 12.5cm. high. (David Lay) $70

A Continental Art Nouveau pewter plaque, with the bust head of pre-Raphaelite maiden, flanked by curved uprights, 21cm. wide. (Spencer's) $100

One of a pair of Art Nouveau silvered pewter vases, each cast Flora, with copper liners, 41.5cm. high. (Christie's) $1,500

Pewter claret jug decorated with embossed Art Nouveau designs, circa 1870. (Spencer's) $350

A Glasgow style pewter and enamel cigar box, with an enamel plaque of a maiden holding an apron of fruit, 8¾in. wide. (Christie's) $300

One of a set of three Art Nouveau pewter wall sconces, each with two light fittings. $600

A Palme Konig und Habel vase mounted in a pewter stand, with pierced mount formed by three Art Nouveau maidens on pierced tripartite stand, 24.3cm. high. (Christie's) $800

A pair of Argentor silvered metal vases, after a design by Josef Hoffman, circa 1920, 17cm. high. $850

One of a pair of Art Nouveau pewter three light candelabra, each with flowerhead sconces with foliate drip-pans, 25.5cm. high. (Phillips) Two $900

KAYSERZINN

The firm of Kayser Sohn was founded in 1885 at Krefeld-Bochum, near Dusseldorf, by Jean Kayser (1840–1911). From 1896 they manufactured Jugendstil, or Art Nouveau, items such as ashtrays, beakers, vases, lamps, etc, known as Kayserzinnwaren, or Kayser pewter wares. Their principal designer was Hugo Leven (b. 1874). Pieces were characterised by their flowing floral decoration and they were sold at the Atelier Englebert Kayser.

Pair of Art Nouveau polished pewter presentation cups attributed to Kayserzinn, 9¼in. high. **$450**

A Kayserzinn Art Nouveau pewter dish on four ball feet, 10½in. wide. **$325**

An electroplated pewter Jugendstil mirror frame, probably Kayserzinn, 46cm., circa 1900. **$1,100**

A Kayserzinn pewter teaset, the tray 18in. wide, all with stamped marks. (Christie's) **$350**

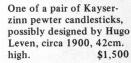

One of a pair of Kayserzinn pewter candlesticks, possibly designed by Hugo Leven, circa 1900, 42cm. high. **$1,500**

German pewter three-handled soup tureen with boar mount, by Kayserzinn, 15in. high. (Worsfolds) **$400**

Pair of Kayserzinn pewter candlesticks on three feet, circa 1900, 30.5cm. high. (Christie's) **$600**

A Kayserzinn pewter jardiniere, stamped Kayserzinn 4093, 29.8cm. high. (Christie's) **$400**

LIBERTY

In the 1890s in England, the Art Nouveau style was championed above all by Arthur Lazenby's Liberty store, so much so that in Italy, for example, it came to be known simply as 'il Stile Liberty'. In the late 1890s Liberty appointed the Manxman Archibald Knox as their chief metalwork designer, and he set to work on a range of silverware, 'Cymric', and pewterware, 'Tudric', which epitomised everything that was Art Nouveau and which continued to be produced until 1938.

Tudric ware is characterised by the combination of Celtic motifs with the stylized natural decoration which was the essence of Art Nouveau. The range included functional items such as tankards, spoons and plates, while applied decoration was often added to vases, trays, candlesticks and clocks. Sometimes, too, pieces were decorated with applied plaques of green or blue enamel, mother of pearl or copper, and some fruit bowls were pierced and lined with colored glass.

Liberty Tudric pewter dish, Archibald Knox design, 8in. diameter, circa 1900. (Muir Hewitt) $100

A Liberty & Co. pewter and enamel clock, circa 1905. $625

'For Old Times 'Sake', a pair of Liberty & Co. 'Tudric' twin-handled vases of cylindrical shape, 20cm. high, impressed 'Tudric and 010' to base. (Phillips) $450

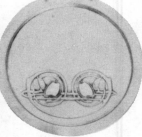

A Liberty & Co. Art Nouveau pewter circular tray designed by Archibald Knox, embellished in relief with entwined tendrils terminating with stylised honesty leaves, 25.2cm. diam. (Phillips London) $900

A pair of Liberty & Co. Tudric pewter twin-branched candelabra designed by Archibald Knox, with pierced decoration of leaves and berries on tendrils, on rectangular flat foot, 27.8cm. high. (Christie's) $2,750

A Liberty & Co. pewter and enamel cigarette box and cover, the rectangular form having a hinged cover inset with a rectangular enameled panel, by Varley, 17.20cm. long. (Phillips) $625

A Liberty pewter and Clutha glass bowl on stand, designed by Archibald Knox, stamped Tudric 0276, circa 1900, 16.3cm. high. (Christie's) $700

A Liberty pewter and green glass bowl, designed by A. Knox, stamped Tudric 0320 Rd, 426933, 20.3cm. diam. (Christie's) $600

Liberty's Tudric pewter beaker holder with green glass liner. (Muir Hewitt) $75

A Liberty Tudric two-handled rose bowl on raised circular foot, 24cm. diam. $625

A Liberty & Co. English pewter bowl, with Clutha glass liner, the mount pierced and embellished with plant forms, 16.5cm. high. (Phillips London) $1,500

Liberty's Tudric pewter three piece tea set, 1930s. (Muir Hewitt) $75

Liberty & Co. Tudric pewter two-handled motto cup, London, circa 1910, 7.7/8in. high. (Skinner Inc.) $185

A Liberty & Co. pewter rose bowl designed by Rex Silver, embellished in relief with heavy plant form motifs, set with glass studs, 15.6cm. high. (Phillips London) $525

One of a pair of Liberty & Co. 'Tudric' pewter and enamel candlesticks, circa 1905, 30cm. high. $1,100

A Liberty & Co. 'Tudric' pewter box and cover, designed by Archibald Knox, 11.9cm. high. (Christie's) $400

A Tudric planished pewter bowl raised upon four fluted cabriole supports terminating in trefoil feet, with cut card type terminals, 13in. wide over feet terminals.
(Spencer's) $250

A Liberty Tudric pewter biscuit box designed by Archibald Knox, of cuboid form stamped with a row of formalised flowers over a row of square leaves, 5in. high over handle.
(Spencer's) $500

A Liberty & Co. enameled pewter tray, decorated with organic patterns and central turquoise enamel reserve, stamped *English Pewter*, 31cm. long. (Christie's London)
                              $550

A Liberty Tudric pewter and Powell green glass decanter, circa 1900, 30cm. high. $575

A Liberty and Co. pewter four piece tea service designed by Archibald Knox, the teapot with compressed globular body, stamped Made in England, English Pewter. (Christie's) $800

A Liberty pewter and enamel table clock designed by Archibald Knox, circa 1900, 14.2cm. high.
(Christie's) $2,000

A Liberty & Co. 'Tudric' pewter timepiece, showing the influence of C.F.A. Voysey, in the form of a dwelling, 34cm. high.
(Phillips) $3,000

Tudric pewter dish with stylized floral decoration, circa 1900.
(Muir Hewitt) $100

One of a pair of Liberty Tudric mugs designed by A. Knox with original green glass liners by J. Powell & Son, circa 1900, 13cm. high. $400

WMF

These letters stand for the Württembergische Metallwarenfabrik (Württemberg Metalware Factory) which was situated at Geislingen, about 30 miles from Stuttgart. Here they produced Art Nouveau and Art Deco style tableware in a stainless steel alloy of their own manufacture known as Cromagen, and also in a type of German silver which they patented as Ikora metal.

With regard to decorative pieces, mirrors, candlesticks, decanters etc, under the direction of Carl Haegele and their chief designer Beyschlag, WMF pushed the curvilinear style of Art Nouveau metalwork to its extreme. It was described variously as the Whiplash style, the Spaghetti style or, as put by Charles Rennie Mackintosh, 'resembling melted margarine'! Art Nouveau flowing-haired and flowing-robed maidens are also very prevalent on WMF pieces. A combination of pewter and green glass was a favorite medium.

A glass studio was also attached to the factory in 1921, with teaching workshops for glass and gem cutting. This was under the direction of Wilhelm von Eiff.

Ikora glass was developed in 1925 and used to make usually heavy glass objects with airbubble decoration in organised patterns and encrustations in color. Some diatreta glass vases were also produced after 1932. This technique, which dates from Roman times, involves a double layered glass vessel with the outer layer cut away to form a delicate, intricate trellis over the lower layer, to which it remains attached by means of small decorated struts.

A WMF electroplated pewter sweetmeat dish, the trefoil scalloped form with handle formed by a freestanding Art Nouveau maiden, stamped with usual WMF marks, 31.3cm. long. (Christie's) $475

Large WMF twin-handled electroplated metal vase with Art Nouveau handles, circa 1900, 50cm. high. $750

A WMF electroplated pewter centerpiece, the trumpet form body with pierced panels of floral decoration and two buttress supports, 51cm. high. (Christie's London) $475

A WMF electroplated pewter drinking set with shaped rectangular tray, circa 1900, tray 48 x 34cm. (Christie's) $1,100

A WMF pewter coupe, the pierced oval body formed by two Art Nouveau butterfly-maidens, with shaped green glass liner, , 17.8cm. high. (Christie's) $450

A WMF silver plated pewter mounted green glass decanter, circa 1900, 38.5cm. high. (Christie's) $600

A WMF electroplated metal centerpiece of boat form, circa 1900, 46cm. wide. $1,100

A W M.F. pewter letter tray, of curvilinear form, cast in shallow relief with a naked maiden, 10in. long. (Christie's S. Ken) $350

A WMF pewter centerpiece, decorated with flowerheads and butterflies, with cobalt-blue shaped glass liner, 42.3cm. long. (Christie's) $1,150

A WMF electroplated pewter vase mount, modeled with a seated male figure holding up a rose to a scantily clad maiden, on four openwork feet, (liner missing) 40.4cm. high. (Christie's) $900

A WMF silvered pewter wall plaque cast in relief with three mermaids gazing up to a maiden picking fruit from a tree, 23in. wide. (Christie's) $700

One of a pair of WMF electroplated candlesticks, each cast as a young woman supporting a flower sprouting to form the four candleholders, 48cm. high, circa 1900. $3,250

A WFM pewter mounted glass claret jug with foliate handle and hinged cover, 13¾in. high. $475

Four W.M.F. glasses on spiral stems. (Muir Hewitt) $475

A WMF silvered pewter jardiniere cast as a conch shell with a salamander, 32cm. high. (Christie's) $750

A WMF pewter dish, of shaped oval section, in the form of a river, a frog playing the flute sitting on the bank, 23cm. long. (Christie's) $250

A WMF pewter centerpiece, cast as a young girl with flowing robe forming an irregular-shaped tray, 22.5cm. high. (Christie's) $675

A W.M.F. pewter letter tray of curvilinear form, modeled with a maiden reading a letter, stamped marks, 12½in. long. (Christie's S. Ken) $825

An electroplated pewter mirror frame attributed to WMF, circa 1900, 50cm. high. (Christie's) $700

A pair of pewter W.M.F. candelabra with nymphs entwined around tendrils which form the sconces, on spreading bases, 25cm. high. (Phillips) $1,350

A W. M. F. electroplated pewter lamp stand, modeled as an Art Nouveau maiden holding aloft a bulbous stand, 32.3cm. high. (Christie's) $700

One of a pair of Art Nouveau pewter vases, attributed to WMF, with glass liners, stamped A K & Cie, 36cm. high. (Christie's) $1,600

A WMF pewter centerpiece with rectangular clear glass tank, stamped marks, 55.5cm. wide, 31.4cm. high. (Christie's) $1,300

A WMF pewter mounted green glass decanter of flaring form on four leaf molded feet, 15in. high. (Christie's) $475

Choumoff (Paris), Autographed portrait of Claude Monet, circa 1910, warm-toned platinum print, 6³/₈ x 8¹/₄in., signed in red ink.
(Christie's) $2,556

Pedro Meyer, "Boda en Coyoacan" (Wedding in Coyoacan, 1983, gelatin silver print, 8 x 12in., signed and titled in pencil on verso, framed.
(Butterfield & Butterfield)
                               $467

Yousuf Karsh, "Jascha Heifetz", 1950s, gelatin silver print, 9⁶/₈ x 11³/₄in., signed in ink in the margin, framed.
(Butterfield & Butterfield)
                               $825

Julia Margaret Cameron, "Sappho", circa 1866, albumen print, 14¹/₂ x 11¹/₂in., signed and annotated *from life not enlarged* in ink.
(Butterfield & Butterfield)
                             $1,980

Roger Mayne, 'Ladbroke Grove – group watching car crash', 1958, printed circa 1960, gelatin silver print, 7¹/₄ x 9¹/₈in., photographer's ink copyright stamp and title on verso.
(Christie's) $456

Dorothy Wilding, HRH Princess Margaret, 1947, gelatin silver print, 18 x 14⁵/₈in., pencil border, mounted on tissue with photographer's printed signature.
(Christie's) $183

Alfred Ellis, two photographs: 'Mr. Oscar Wilde' and Oscar Wilde and friend, circa 1880s, albumen cabinet cards.
(Butterfield & Butterfield)
                               $550

Anon, Reclining nude (inspired by Ingres), 1850s, stereoscopic daguerreotype, hand-tinted, gilt highlights, paper-taped.
(Christie's) $14,960

Julia Margaret Cameron, 'Paul & Virginia', 1867–70, albumen print, 10¹/₂ x 8¹/₂in., mounted on card.
(Christie's) $4,862

Anon, Sleeping dog, mid 1850s, sixth-plate daguerreotype, gilt metal mount.
(Christie's) $469

Lewis Carroll, 'Irene at Elm Lodge', July 1863, oval albumen print, 6⁷/₈ x 8⁷/₈in.
(Christie's) $15,400

Alice Boughton, portrait of Robert Louis Stevenson, circa 1900, platinum print 6 x 8in.
(Butterfield & Butterfield) $3,300

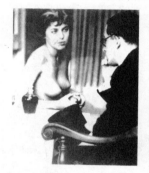

Edouard-Denis Baldus, Pavillon Turgot, Louvre, circa 1855, salt print, 17⁵/₈ x 13⁵/₈in., signed and numbered *E. Baldus No. 47* in the negative, mounted on card.
(Christie's) $2,009

Josef Britenbach, 'Dr. Riegler and J. Geno', 1933, printed later, photogravure, 12 x 9¹/₂in., the photographer's estate blindstamp.
(Butterfield & Butterfield) $660

Dorothy Wilding, The Duke and Duchess of Windsor, autographed portrait, 1944, gelatin silver print, 9¹/₈ x 6¹/₂in., mounted on tissue, signed by sitters and dated in ink.
(Christie's) $1,735

Alexander Rodchenko, "Portrait of Majakowski", 1924, printed 1989, gelatin silver print, 12 x 9³/₈in., titled and dated in pencil.
(Butterfield & Butterfield) $1,100

George Bernard Shaw (1856–1950), Alvin Langdon Coburn, July 1906, photogravure, 8³/₈ x 6³/₈in., on tissue, then card, matted.
(Christie's) $876

Cecil Beaton, "Lily Langtrey, Lady de Bathe", gelatin silver print, 10⁷/₈ x 8in., titled in white ink on image, signed in orange watercolor on mount.
(Butterfield & Butterfield) $550

Ansel Adams, 'Moonrise, Hernandez, New Mexico', circa 1942, printed circa 1976, gelatin silver print, 15¼ x 19⅜ in., signed in pencil on the mount. (Butterfield & Butterfield) $8,250

Frantisek Drtikol, Fat boy posing, 1925, gelatin silver print, 8⅞ x 6¾ in., photographer's blindstamp with date on recto. (Christie's) $1,122

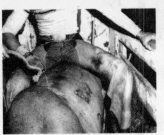

Susan Felter, 'Roy (red chaps) riding bull', 1978, Cibachrome, 13 x 16⅞ in., signed and dated in the margin, signed and dated in pencil on the reverse. (Butterfield & Butterfield) $522

Anon, Lady with large black dog, circa 1860, quarter-plate ambrotype, with gilt metal mount. (Christie's) $391

Henri Cartier-Bresson, 'Rue Mouffetard', 1954, printed later, 14 x 9⅜ in., signed in ink and the photographer's blindstamp in the margin. (Butterfield & Butterfield) $3,850

Willard Van Dyke, "Nehi", circa 1931, gelatin silver print, 9½ x 7½ in., signed, titled, dated. (Butterfield & Butterfield) $1,210

Roger Mayne, Boy with gun, 1956, gelatin silver print, 9⅞ x 7¼ in., photographer's ink copyright stamp on verso. (Christie's) $548

Photographer unknown, Album containing 24 photographs of The Paris Exposition Universelle, 1889, albumen prints, each measuring approximately 8¾ x 11¾ in. (Butterfield & Butterfield) $495

W. Eugene Smith, "Spanish spinner", 1951, printed 1977, gelatin silver print, 12¾ x 9 in., signed on the mount in ink. (Butterfield & Butterfield) $1,650

Duane Michals, "Magritte's room", 1965, printed later, gelatin silver print, 6³/₄ x 9⁷/₈in., signed.
(Butterfield & Butterfield)
$467

Andre Kertesz, "Circus", 1920, printed for "A Hungarian Memory" portfolio, gelatin silver print, 9³/₄ x 7³/₄in.
(Butterfield & Butterfield)
$1,320

Jacques Henri Lartigue, "Horse races at Montreuil", 1911, printed 1972, 6¹/₂ x 9in., signed in ink on the mount.
(Butterfield & Butterfield)
$440

R. Lowe (Cheltenham), Caroline Georgina Colledge and her brother John, circa 1855, a 5 x 4in. daguerreotype.
(Christie's)
$730

Andre Kertesz, "Wandering violinist", 1921, printed 1980 for "A Hungarian Memory" portfolio, gelatin silver print, 9³/₄ x 7¹/₂in., signed in pencil on verso.
(Butterfield & Butterfield)
$1,320

Frank Meadow Sutcliffe, 'His Son's Son', late 19th century, carbon print, image size 7⁷/₈ x 6in., numbered 31 with photographer's initials in the negative, matted.
(Christie's)
$548

Edward Steichen (1879–1973), Noel Coward, 1932, gelatin silver contact print, 10 x 8in.
(Christie's)
$1,369

Photographer unknown, 2 albums containing 133 photographs: Chinese landscapes, portraits and genre scenes, 1880s, albumen prints.
(Butterfield & Butterfield)
$2,200

Man Ray, 'Mrs Simpson', 1936, double exposure silver print, 8³/₈ x 6¹/₄in., matted, framed.
(Christie's)
$2,465

Howard Coster (1885–1959), T.E. Lawrence on his Brough Superior motorbike, 1925–26, gelatin silver print on textured card, 7³/₈ x 9¹/₄in. (Christie's) **$513**

Anon, Group portrait of girls, 1850s–60s, half-plate daguerreotype, lightly hand-tinted, gilt surround, in thermo-plastic union case with geometric and scroll design. (Christie's) **$1,540**

Roger Mayne (b. 1929), Brenda Sheakey (screaming child), Southam Street, 1956, printed mid/late 1960s, gelatin silver print, 7¹/₄ x 9¹/₄in. (Christie's) **$1,643**

Herb Ritts, 'Man holding shell', Australia 1986, gelatin silver print, image size 18⁵/₈ x 15¹/₄in., photographer's copyright blindstamp in margin. (Christie's) **$1,132**

Irving Penn (b. 1917), 'Two Thin New Guinea Women', New Guinea, 1970, printed 1984, multiple-printed and hand-coated platinum-palladium print, 13¹/₄ x 13¹/₈in. (Christie's) **$2,739**

Albert Watson (b. 1942), Untitled, (1970s), gelatin silver print, 39¹/₂ x 29¹/₂in., mounted on board, signed and numbered *34/35* in ink on verso, framed. (Christie's) **$365**

Greg Gorman, Dave Michelak, 1987, gelatin silver print, 30¹/₄ x 24³/₄in., signed and dated in ink with the photographer's copyright stamp. (Butterfield & Butterfield) **$1,278**

Izis (1911–1980), 'Jardin des Tuileries', Paris 1950, gelatin silver print, image size 11¹/₈ x 8⁵/₈in., titled and dated with photographer's credit stamp on verso. (Christie's) **$1,004**

Brassaï, 'Salvador Dali', 1932, printed later, gelatin silver print, 11³/₄ x 8¹/₂in., signed and numbered *11/30* in red ink in the margin. (Butterfield & Butterfield) **$1,100**

Anon, Family group portrait, circa 1895–97, mammoth carbon print, 29¹/₂ x 39¹/₂in., finely hand-tinted, contemporary gilt frame.
(Christie's) $694

Gustave Le Gray (1820–82), The Great Wave, Sète, 1856–59, albumen print from two negatives, 12³/₈ x 15¹/₂in.
(Christie's) $31,042

Jacques Henri Lartigue, Woman and dog, 1920s, printed 1972, 6¹/₂ x 9in., signed in ink on the mount.
(Butterfield & Butterfield) $660

Edouard-Denis Baldus, 'Paris Saint-Eustache', circa 1860, albumen print, 16³/₈ x 13in., signed in the negative, mounted on card.
(Christie's) $7,304

Auguste Belloc, Reclining nude, 1852–54, coated (possibly waxed) salt print, 6 x 7⁷/₈in., corners trimmed, mounted on card.
(Christie's) $7,304

Bert Hardy (b. 1913), 'Maidens in Waiting, Blackpool', 1951, printed later, gelatin silver print, image size 13 x 10in., signed in ink in margin, framed.
(Christie's) $730

Lotte Jacobi (1896–1990), 'Peter Lorre', 'Grock' and other portraits, (1940s–50s), printed late 1950s, six gelatin silver prints, 6¹/₂ x 4³/₄in., to 9¹/₂ x 7¹/₂in.
(Christie's) $584

Robert Howlett (1831–1858), Attempted launch of the "Great Eastern", November 28, 1857, printed early 1900s, gelatin silver print, 10 x 8¹/₂in., arched top, mounted on card.
(Christie's) $511

Yousuf Karsh (b. 1908), Pablo Picasso, 1954, printed later, gelatin silver print, 23¹/₂ x 19¹/₂in., mounted on card, signed in ink on mount, matted, framed.
(Christie's) $2,008

David Octavius Hill & Robert Adamson, John Henning, mid 1840s, calotype, 8 x 6in., matted and framed.
(Christie's) $1,402

William Klein, 'Three heiresses, Greece', 1963, printed later, gelatin silver print, 9 x 13¹/₂in., signed, titled and dated in pencil on verso.
(Butterfield & Butterfield) $550

Philippe Halsman, "Dali skull", 1951, printed 1970, gelatin silver print, 12¹/₂ x 10¹/₂in., signed, titled, and dated in pencil.
(Butterfield & Butterfield) $1,540

Man Ray (1890–1976), Robert Winthrop Chanler, 1929, toned gelatin silver print, 10⁷/₈ x 8¹/₈in., signed *Man Ray Paris* in red crayon.
(Christie's) $639

Edward Weston, "White Sands, New Mexico", 1940, gelatin silver print, 7⁵/₈ x 9⁵/₈in., initialed and dated.
(Butterfield & Butterfield) $12,100

Brian Griffin (b. 1948), George Melly', 1990, printed later, gelatin silver print, image size 14 x 14in., signed and dated in pencil on verso, framed.
(Christie's) $547

Yousuf Karsh, "Nikita Khrushchev", 1963, printed later, 19³/₄ x 15³/₄in., gelatin silver print, signed in ink on the mount.
(Butterfield & Butterfield) $990

Gisele Freund, "Andre Malraux, Paris", 1935, printed later, gelatin silver print, 11³/₄ x 9¹/₂in., signed and dated in ink in the margin.
(Butterfield & Butterfield) $302

Galerie Contemporaine series: Valery, "Victor Hugo", circa 1880, Woodbury type, 9 x 7¹/₂in., on the original letterpress mount.
(Butterfield & Butterfield) $412

Berenice Abbott, "Portrait of Orozco", early 1930s, gelatin silver print, 13³/₄ x 11⁵/₈in, signed in pencil on mount. (Butterfield & Butterfield) $825

Irving Penn (b. 1917), Pablo Picasso, Cannes, 1957, probably printed early 1960s, gelatin silver print, 22⁷/₈ x 22⁷/₈in., flush mounted on plywood. (Christie's) $2,191

Frederick Evans, Portrait of Aubrey Beardsley, circa 1894, photogravure, 5 x 4¹/₈in., credit printed in the margin. (Butterfield & Butterfield) $220

Bill Brandt (1906–1984), 'Hampstead, London 1953', printed later, gelatin silver print, 12³/₈ x 10³/₈in., singed in ink on verso, matted, framed. (Christie's) $766

Judy Dater, "Nehemiah", 1975, gelatin silver print, 10³/₈ x 13³/₈in., signed in pencil on the mount, framed. (Butterfield & Butterfield) $715

Gisèle Freund, 'Samuel Beckett', n.d., gelatin silver print, image size 12 x 7⁷/₈in., photographer's blindstamp on image, signed in ink in margin. (Christie's) $694

Philippe Halsman, "Marc Chagall", 1946, printed later, gelatin silver print, 13⁵/₈ x 10³/₄in., signed, titled, and dated in pencil. (Butterfield & Butterfield) $935

Irving Penn (b. 1917), Igor Stravinsky, 1948, printed 1970, multiple-printed and hand-coated platinum-palladium print, 19 x 13³/₄in., with aluminium backing, signed. (Christie's) $4,382

(?) Herman, Toulouse Lautrec seated at his easel, 1894, gelatin silver print, 7³/₄ x 6¹/₄in., mounted on card, signed and dated by the photographer, matted and framed. (Christie's) $1,461

S.L. Carleton, 'Young girl with King Charles spaniel', circa 1848, sixth-plate daguerreotype, folding morocco case.
(Christie's) $313

Jacques-Henri Lartigue, 'Avenue du Bois de Boulogne', 1911, printed later, gelatin silver print, image size 9⁵/₈ x 13⁷/₈in., signed in ink.
(Christie's) $2,349

Lewis Carroll (Charles Lutwidge Dodgson) (1832–98), Xie Kitchin, circa 1873, cabinet card, albumen print 5¹/₂ x 4in., numbered *2223* in ink in Carroll's hand on verso.
(Christie's) $2,349

Thomas Annan (1829–87), 'Close, No. 28 Saltmarket', 1868–77, carbon print, 11 x 9in., mounted on card, printed title and number *26* on mount.
(Christie's) $587

Herb Ritts, 'Men with Kelp', Paradise Cove, 1987, gelatin silver print, image size 19¹/₈ x 15¹/₄in., photographer's copyright blindstamp in margin, signed.
(Christie's) $587

G. Riebicke, 'Archer with borzoi', circa 1930, gelatin silver print, 6¹/₂ x 4³/₄in., photographer's ink credit stamp on verso, matted.
(Christie's) $783

Robert Doisneau, Pablo Picasso, 1952 printed 1989, gelatin silver print, image size 10³/₈ x 8¹/₈in., signed in ink in margin.
(Christie's) $1,174

Anon, Little girl holding puppy, mid 1850s, sixth-plate daguerreotype, lightly hand-tinted, gilt metal mount.
(Christie's) $332

Don McCullin (b. 1935), Melanesian portrait, 1983, gelatin silver print, image size 17 x 12in., matted, signed and dated in ink on mount.
(Christie's) $587

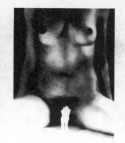

Robert Frank, "Paris, 1950", printed later, gelatin silver print, 8³/₄ x 13³/₈in., signed, titled, and dated in ink in margin.
(Butterfield & Butterfield)
$2,475

Frantisek Drtikol (1883–1961), Nude, 1933, toned gelatin silver print, 11¹/₂ x 9in.
(Christie's) $3,520

Aleksandr Rodchenko (1891–1956), Red Square (early 1930s), gelatin silver print, 7 x 9³/₈in., indistinct inscription in ink and pencil on verso.
(Christie's) $5,874

Horst P. Horst (b. 1906), The Mainbocher corset, Paris 1939 printed 1986–87, gelatin silver print, image size 16¹/₄ x 13in., signed in pencil in margin, matted, framed.
(Christie's) $4,699

Julia Margaret Cameron, Alfred, Lord Tennyson, 1860s printed 1875, carbon print, 13¹/₂ x 10in., printed by the Autotype Company, mounted on card.
(Christie's) $587

Richard Avedon (b. 1923), 'Robert Frank, photographer Mabou Mines, Nova Scotia', 1975, gelatin silver contact print, 10 x 8in., no. 29 of an edition of 50, signed in ink.
(Christie's) $2,545

Roger Mayne (b. 1929), Girl seated on steps, Southam Street, late 1950s, gelatin silver print, 14⁷/₈ x 10¹/₂in., mounted on card.
(Christie's) $1,468

Edward Weston (1886–1958), D.H. Lawrence, 1924, gelatin silver print, 9¹/₂ x 7¹/₂in., ink credit stamp *The Carmelite* and various pencil annotations on verso.
(Christie's) $587

Frank Meadow Sutcliffe (1853–1941), Portrait of a fisherman, 1880s, printed later, toned gelatin silver print, image size 8¹/₂ x 6in.
(Christie's) $352

BELT PISTOLS

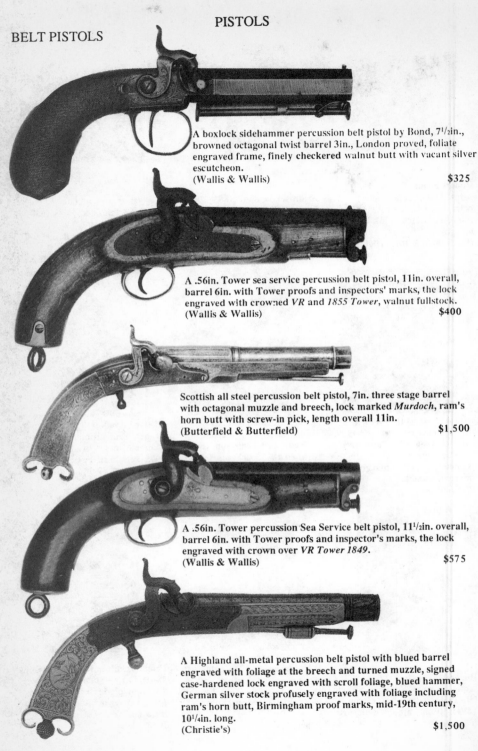

A boxlock sidehammer percussion belt pistol by Bond, 7½in.,
browned octagonal twist barrel 3in., London proved, foliate
engraved frame, finely checkered walnut butt with vacant silver
escutcheon.
(Wallis & Wallis) $325

A .56in. Tower sea service percussion belt pistol, 11in. overall,
barrel 6in. with Tower proofs and inspectors' marks, the lock
engraved with crowned *VR* and *1855 Tower*, walnut fullstock.
(Wallis & Wallis) $400

Scottish all steel percussion belt pistol, 7in. three stage barrel
with octagonal muzzle and breech, lock marked *Murdoch*, ram's
horn butt with screw-in pick, length overall 11in.
(Butterfield & Butterfield) $1,500

A .56in. Tower percussion Sea Service belt pistol, 11½in. overall,
barrel 6in. with Tower proofs and inspector's marks, the lock
engraved with crown over *VR Tower 1849*.
(Wallis & Wallis) $575

A Highland all-metal percussion belt pistol with blued barrel
engraved with foliage at the breech and turned muzzle, signed
case-hardened lock engraved with scroll foliage, blued hammer,
German silver stock profusely engraved with foliage including
ram's horn butt, Birmingham proof marks, mid-19th century,
10¼in. long.
(Christie's) $1,500

A .41in. rifled back action Derringer percussion pistol, 5$\frac{1}{2}$in., barrel 2$\frac{1}{2}$in., fullstocked, foliate engraved lock, stock of classic form with engraved white metal trigger guard, escutcheon and sideplate.
(Wallis & Wallis)   **$510**

Wm. M. Marston three barrel Derringer, serial No. 1978, .32 caliber, standard model.
(Butterfield & Butterfield)   **$725**

American percussion Derringer by Seaver, maker marked 3in. barrel with German silver bands at breech, the forend cap with ramrod, checkered grip.
(Butterfield & Butterfield)   **$675**

Remington Elliot Derringer, British proofed, serial No. 12295, .22 caliber, standard model with 3in. fluted barrel of five shot configuration, nickel plated finish.
(Butterfield & Butterfield)   **$1,200**

American percussion Derringer by Gillespie, 4$\frac{3}{8}$in. barrel with floral engraved breech marked *Gillespie*, engraved and maker marked lock, German silver mounts, checkered grip.
(Butterfield & Butterfield)   **$605**

HOLSTER PISTOLS

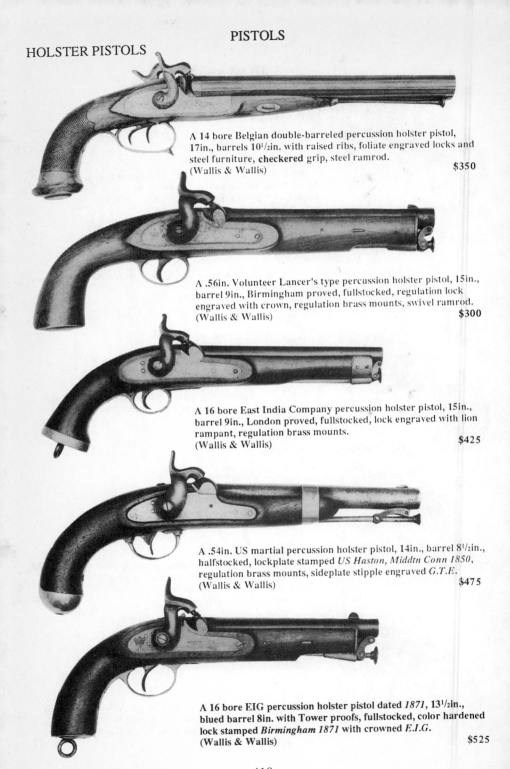

A 14 bore Belgian double-barreled percussion holster pistol,
17in., barrels 10½in. with raised ribs, foliate engraved locks and
steel furniture, **checkered** grip, steel ramrod.
(Wallis & Wallis) $350

A .56in. Volunteer Lancer's type percussion holster pistol, 15in.,
barrel 9in., Birmingham proved, fullstocked, regulation lock
engraved with crown, regulation brass mounts, swivel ramrod.
(Wallis & Wallis) $300

A 16 bore East India Company percussion holster pistol, 15in.,
barrel 9in., London proved, fullstocked, lock engraved with lion
rampant, regulation brass mounts.
(Wallis & Wallis) $425

A .54in. US martial percussion holster pistol, 14in., barrel 8½in.,
halfstocked, lockplate stamped *US Haston, Middtn Conn 1850*,
regulation brass mounts, sideplate stipple engraved *G.T.E.*
(Wallis & Wallis) $475

A 16 bore EIG percussion holster pistol dated *1871*, 13½in.,
blued barrel 8in. with Tower proofs, fullstocked, color hardened
lock stamped *Birmingham 1871* with crowned *E.I.G.*
(Wallis & Wallis) $525

POCKET PISTOLS

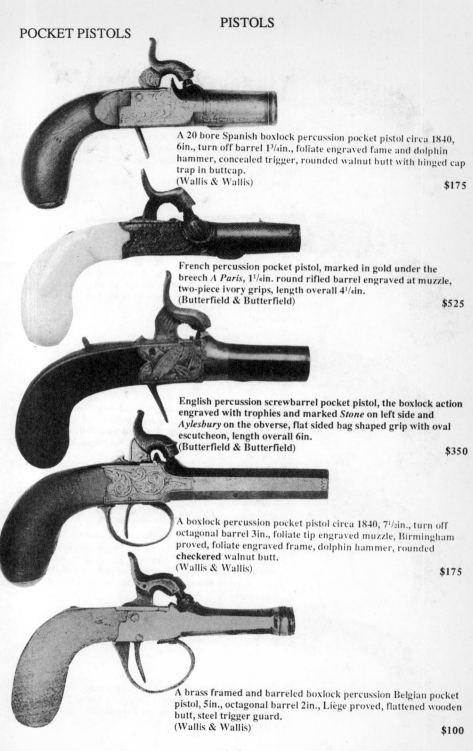

A 20 bore Spanish boxlock percussion pocket pistol circa 1840, 6in., turn off barrel 1³/₄in., foliate engraved fame and dolphin hammer, concealed trigger, rounded walnut butt with hinged cap trap in buttcap.
(Wallis & Wallis) $175

French percussion pocket pistol, marked in gold under the breech *A Paris*, 1¹/₄in. round rifled barrel engraved at muzzle, two-piece ivory grips, length overall 4¹/₄in.
(Butterfield & Butterfield) $525

English percussion screwbarrel pocket pistol, the boxlock action engraved with trophies and marked *Stone* on left side and *Aylesbury* on the obverse, flat sided bag shaped grip with oval escutcheon, length overall 6in.
(Butterfield & Butterfield) $350

A boxlock percussion pocket pistol circa 1840, 7¹/₂in., turn off octagonal barrel 3in., foliate tip engraved muzzle, Birmingham proved, foliate engraved frame, dolphin hammer, rounded **checkered** walnut butt.
(Wallis & Wallis) $175

A brass framed and barreled boxlock percussion Belgian pocket pistol, 5in., octagonal barrel 2in., Liège proved, flattened wooden butt, steel trigger guard.
(Wallis & Wallis) $100

TARGET PISTOLS

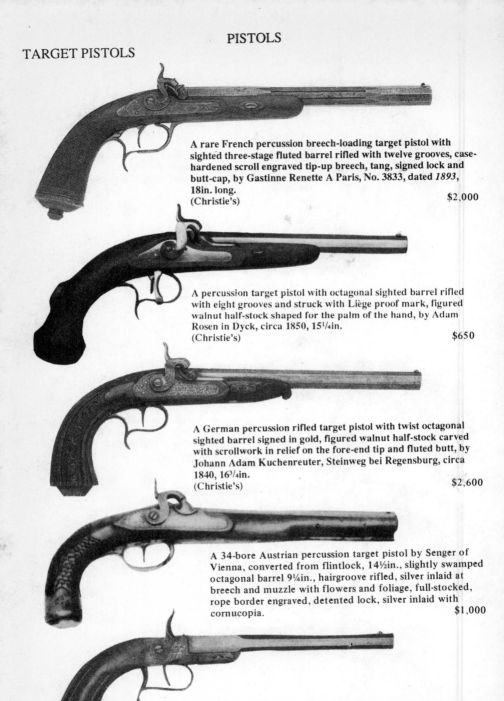

A rare French percussion breech-loading target pistol with
sighted three-stage fluted barrel rifled with twelve grooves, casehardened scroll engraved tip-up breech, tang, signed lock and
butt-cap, by Gastinne Renette A Paris, No. 3833, dated *1893*,
18in. long.
(Christie's) $2,000

A percussion target pistol with octagonal sighted barrel rifled
with eight grooves and struck with Liège proof mark, figured
walnut half-stock shaped for the palm of the hand, by Adam
Rosen in Dyck, circa 1850, 15¼in.
(Christie's) $650

A German percussion rifled target pistol with twist octagonal
sighted barrel signed in gold, figured walnut half-stock carved
with scrollwork in relief on the fore-end tip and fluted butt, by
Johann Adam Kuchenreuter, Steinweg bei Regensburg, circa
1840, 16¾in.
(Christie's) $2,600

A 34-bore Austrian percussion target pistol by Senger of
Vienna, converted from flintlock, 14½in., slightly swamped
octagonal barrel 9¼in., hairgroove rifled, silver inlaid at
breech and muzzle with flowers and foliage, full-stocked,
rope border engraved, detented lock, silver inlaid with
cornucopia. $1,000

A .15in. Continental enclosed action percussion target pistol,
12¾in., tip down smooth bore octagonal barrel 7½in., secured
by side lever and opening merely for capping, steel furniture
and fluted walnut butt. $650

420

TRAVELING PISTOLS

A good DB 80-bore side-by-side percussion boxlock side-hammer traveling pistol, 5½ inches overall, integral barrels 2 inches with B'ham proofs, the top rib engraved "E. Akrill, Beverley". (Wallis & Wallis) $700

A .36 double barreled American Bruce & Davis boxlock percussion travelling pistol, 7½in., round barrels 4¼in., top sighting channel, scroll foliate engraved round frame, single trigger, double long nosed hammers, two-piece bag-shaped wooden grips. $425

A good boxlock percussion traveling pistol by Whitfield & Sons, fitted with sprung bayonet, circa 1835, 8in., turn off barrel 3¼in. Birmingham proved, husk engraved muzzle, slab walnut butt. (Wallis & Wallis) $350

A 24 bore percussion traveling pistol by Wood of Worcester, well converted from flintlock, 9½in., octagonal barrel 5in., fullstocked, stepped bolted lock engraved with foliage and *Wood Worcester*, steel trigger guard. (Wallis & Wallis) $400

A 16 bore percussion traveling pistol by Tipping & Lawden, circa 1840, 8½in., octagonal barrel 4in., fullstocked, foliate engraved lock with *Tipping & Lawden*, rounded checkered grip. (Wallis & Wallis) $400

PLASTER

Plaster is a very versatile medium, and a number of interesting sculptures appeared during the Art Nouveau/Deco periods, some disguised, for example silvered, to make them look like something completely different. Richard Garbe produced many classical/Art Nouveau figures, of naked maidens with flowing hair and drapery.

An Art Deco silvered plaster figure of a naked female with a hoop, circa 1935, 11½in. high. $200

A late 19th century French plaster bust of 'L'Espiegle', signed on the shoulder J. B. Carpeaux, 51cm. high. (Christie's) $2,250

A Richard Garbe green-tinted plaster figure of a naked seated maiden, 1928, 104cm. high. (Christie's) $1,100

An English plaster panel, in oak frame carved 'Speed with the light-foot winds to run', 42.2 x 37.7cm. (Christie's) $200

A Richard Garbe plaster figure of a naked maiden, 1912, 99cm. high. (Christie's) $700

A Richard Garbe plaster figure of a naked kneeling maiden with streaming hair and flowing drapery, 102cm. high. (Christie's) $1,250

'Tete de femme', a plaster head of a woman by Moshe Ziffer, 28cm. high. $450

A James Woolford plaster figure modeled as a diving mermaid with a dolphin, circa 1930, 59cm. high. (Christie's) $375

PLASTIC

Plastics are the great revolutionary material of the 20th century. Celluloid came first, followed by bakelite and perspex. Much early plastic tended to be brittle, however, and it was not until the late 50's and 60's that such huge technological advances were made in terms of pliability and durability that there is now a plastic suitable for just about every purpose under the sun.

One of plastic's main attractions has always been its cheapness. As such, plastic items therefore appear an unlikely choice for collectables. However, many early plastic items are now being keenly collected, perhaps as much for their nostalgia value as anything.

"Teasmade" 1950s, in ivory plastic with chromium fittings.
(Muir Hewitt) $60

Perspex ice bucket, 1930s, in pale blue and ivory.
(Muir Hewitt) $35

Phenolic napkin ring in the form of a stylized elephant.
(Muir Hewitt) $15

Phenolic box, 1930s, depicting male and female dancers.
(Muir Hewitt) $35

Perspex lamp in pale blue and pink, 1940s, 8in. high.
(Muir Hewitt) $60

1950's green plastic perpetual calendar with Venetian scene.
$10

Perspex and chrome lamp in black and ivory, 1940s, 8in. high.
(Muir Hewitt) $35

1930s plastic powder bowl featuring a woman's head on the lid.
(Muir Hewitt) $20

A 17th century Continental flattened cow horn powder flask for a wheel-lock rifle, 11¼in., with shaped brass aprons.
(Wallis & Wallis) $400

A 17th/18th century Persian Circassian walnut powder flask, 6in., sprung steel lever charger with shaped top.
$550

A horn powder flask of flattened form, the body engraved with flowers and geometric patterns, 29.5cm. overall, 17th century.
(Phillips) $500

A German circular powder-flask, of wood with a horn-lined hole in the center, iron nozzle and tap, and two rings for suspension, 17th century, 5½in.
(Christie's) $1,600

A triangular musketeer's powder-flask with cloth-covered wooden body mounted in iron, the back with a pierced design, late 16th/early 17th century, probably German, 10in. high.
(Christie's) $1,850

A German circular powder-flask with turned wooden body encircled by a thin steel band carrying the nozzle, late 17th century, 5¾in. diameter.
(Christie's) $1,375

An Italian powder-flask, entirely of steel, with fluted triangular body of plano-convex section engraved with bands of running foliage, 17th century, 7¾in. high.
(Christie's) $1,000

An Italian all-steel powder-flask of curved faceted conical form with tapering two-stage nozzle octagonal at the base, curved into belt hook, early 17th century, 9¾in. long.
(Christie's) $1,100

An engraved bone Continental powder flask, circa 1600, 6¾in. tall. $650

A 17th century Italian fluted steel powder flask, 7in. overall. **$775**

An all-steel combined priming-flask and wheel-lock spanner with curved body flattened on one side, 17th century, probably German, 6³/₄in. long. (Christie's) **$1,100**

A 17th century Italian brass mounted steel powder flask, 7in. overall, with belt hook. **$800**

A German powder-flask in the manner of Johann Michael Maucher of Schwäbish-Gmünd, carved in high relief with two hounds attacking a boar, late 17th century, 4¹/₄in. diameter. (Christie's) **$14,700**

A 17th century staghorn powder flask, 8in., body engraved with a man and woman standing together in contemporary costume. (Wallis & Wallis) **$625**

A German circular powder-flask in the manner of Hans Schmidt of Ferlach, with turned rootwood body inlaid on the front with scenes of the chase in engraved silver sheet, third quarter of the 17th century, 5¹/₂in. diameter. (Christie's) **$7,700**

A German staghorn powder-flask with forked body of natural horn, the outer-face carved in low relief with the Temptation of Adam and Eve, 7³/₄in. (Christie's S. Ken) **$1,100**

A German powder-flask of flattened cow-horn incised on the front with three figures in a procession, and on the back with patterns of concentric circles and semi-circles, early 17th century, 12¹/₄in. (Christie's) **$775**

A German combined powder-flask, wheel-lock spanner and turnscrew, with tapering reeded horn body of circular section with wooden base-plate, second half of the 17th century, 8¹/₄in. (Christie's) **$920**

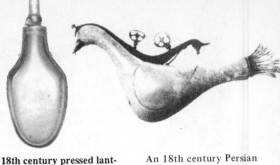

An 18th century Persian all steel powder flask, of swollen boat or swan form. $175

A late 18th century pressed lanthorn powder flask, 7¹/₂in., two piece translucent body with ribbed brass edges. (Wallis & Wallis) $175

An 18th century Persian priming powder flask, 5in. overall. $1,250

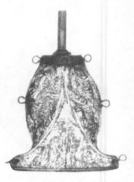

An 18th century staghorn powder flask, 7½in. overall, with small down turned nozzle and iron hanging loops. (Wallis & Wallis) $100

A Continental silver-mounted priming-flask, with brass mounts, and four rings for suspension, early 18th century, possibly Dutch, 4¹/₄in. long. (Christie's) $1,100

An 18th century engraved bone powder flask, 8¼in. overall, with six hanging rings. (Wallis & Wallis) $175

An early 18th century Arab silver mounted powder flask Barutdan, 8in., of iron in coiled horn form. $175

A Spanish 18th century powder flask, made from a section of Ibex or similar horn, 10½in. overall. (Wallis & Wallis) $150

An 18th century staghorn powder flask, 10½in. overall, with two horn hanging loops. (Wallis & Wallis) $210

19TH CENTURY

A copper bodied 3 way flask, 4³/₄in. overall, fixed nozzle, blued spring, hinged cover for balls, screw on base cap.
(Wallis & Wallis) $150

A brass mounted military gunner's priming horn circa 1820, 9¹/₂in., sprung brass charger with lever, brass end cap with unscrewable base for filling.
(Wallis & Wallis) $200

An embossed copper powder flask, 8¹/₄in., body embossed with woven design and foliage, common brass top with adjustable nozzle.
(Wallis & Wallis) $125

An embossed copper powder flask, 8¹/₄in., embossed with a design of hanging game above *James Dixon & Sons*.
(Wallis & Wallis) $180

A fine mid 19th century Afridi tribe powder horn from the North West Frontier, 9in. of polished horn. $400

An embossed copper powder flask, 8¹/₄in., embossed with dog and stag, patent top stamped *G&JW Hawksley Sheffield*.
(Wallis & Wallis) $200

A scarce embossed copper powder flask 8¹/₄in., embossed with foliage and geometric devices within flutes, with graduated nozzle.
(Wallis & Wallis) $210

A good white metal mounted scrimshaw engraved cow horn powder flask, circa 1840, 8¹/₂in. overall, nicely engraved with very early steam train, line engraved with adjustable nozzle.
(Wallis & Wallis) $225

A good bag shaped copper pistol flask, 5³/₄in., lacquered body and common brass top stamped *James Dixon & Sons*, unusually long nozzle.
(Wallis & Wallis) $275

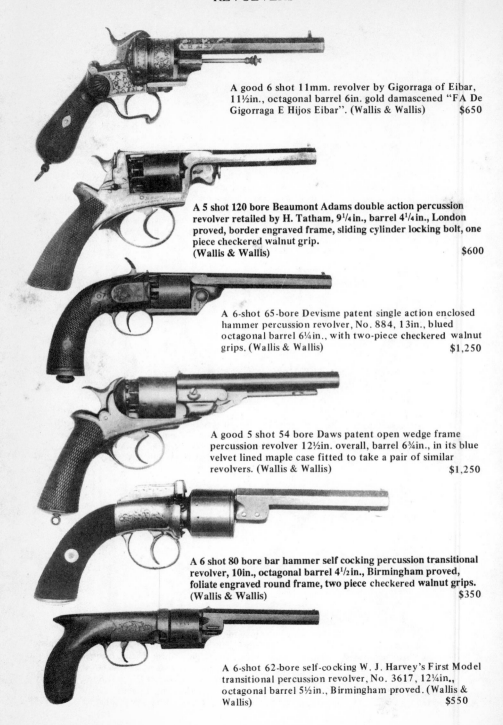

A good 6 shot 11mm. revolver by Gigorraga of Eibar, 11½in., octagonal barrel 6in. gold damascened "FA De Gigorraga E Hijos Eibar". (Wallis & Wallis) $650

A 5 shot 120 bore Beaumont Adams double action percussion revolver retailed by H. Tatham, 9¼in., barrel 4¼in., London proved, border engraved frame, sliding cylinder locking bolt, one piece checkered walnut grip. (Wallis & Wallis)   **$600**

A 6-shot 65-bore Devisme patent single action enclosed hammer percussion revolver, No. 884, 13in., blued octagonal barrel 6¼in., with two-piece checkered walnut grips. (Wallis & Wallis) $1,250

A good 5 shot 54 bore Daws patent open wedge frame percussion revolver 12½in. overall, barrel 6¾in., in its blue velvet lined maple case fitted to take a pair of similar revolvers. (Wallis & Wallis) $1,250

A 6 shot 80 bore bar hammer self cocking percussion transitional revolver, 10in., octagonal barrel 4½in., Birmingham proved, foliate engraved round frame, two piece checkered walnut grips. (Wallis & Wallis)   **$350**

A 6-shot 62-bore self-cocking W. J. Harvey's First Model transitional percussion revolver, No. 3617, 12¼in., octagonal barrel 5½in., Birmingham proved. (Wallis & Wallis) $550

ARMY REVOLVERS

A 6 shot .44in. Remington army single action percussion revolver No. 73082, 13½in., octagonal barrel 8in., underlever rammer, two piece wooden grips.
(Wallis & Wallis)   **$800**

Remington new model army percussion revolver, serial No. 6671, .44 caliber, standard model with government cartouche on left grip.
(Butterfield & Butterfield)   **$2,475**

A six-shot Starr army percussion revolver, 15.5cm. sighted barrel with rammer mounted beneath, plain cylinder, frame stamped Starr Arms & Co., New York.
                                                                    $600

Starr Arms Co. double action 1858 percussion army revolver, serial No. 17875, .44 caliber, standard model with government cartouche on either side of grip.
(Butterfield & Butterfield)   **$1,000**

A six-shot Remington army percussion revolver, 20cm. sighted octagonal barrel signed Patented Sept 14, 1858 E. Remington & Sons, Ilion, New York, U.S.A., New Model.
                                                                    $750

A 6-shot 12mm. Dumonthier Military double action pinfire revolver, 10½in., round barrel 6in., No. 5182, burl walnut bag-shaped grip with fitted lanyard ring, gate loading and rod ejection.
                                                                    $475

COLT REVOLVERS

Colt New Service double action revolver, serial no. 60432, .44-40 caliber, 5½in. barrel, blue finish, checkered hard rubber grips.
(Butterfield & Butterfield) $900

Colt model 1848 baby Dragoon revolver, serial no. 9031, .31 caliber, 6in. barrel with two line New York markings, cylinder with oval stop slots and Indian and Dragoon scene, ivory grips. (Butterfield & Butterfield) $2,300

Factory engraved Colt Sheriff's model 1878 Frontier double action revolver, serial no. 11337, .45 caliber, 4in. barrel, nickel finish, mother-of-pearl grips.
(Butterfield & Butterfield) $3,000

Colt Cloverleaf house model revolver, serial no. 1562, .41 caliber, 1½in. octagonal barrel, varnished walnut grips.
(Butterfield & Butterfield) $1,600

Factory engraved Colt Sheriff's model 1878 Frontier double action revolver, serial no. 5944, .45 caliber, 4in. barrel, lanyard ring at butt, checkered hard rubber grips.
(Butterfield & Butterfield) $1,000

Colt 1st model Dragoon revolver, serial no. 5485, .44 caliber, 7½in. barrel marked "Address Sam'l Colt New York City", frame marked "Colt's Patent US", oil finished grips.
(Butterfield & Butterfield) $4,000

COLT REVOLVERS

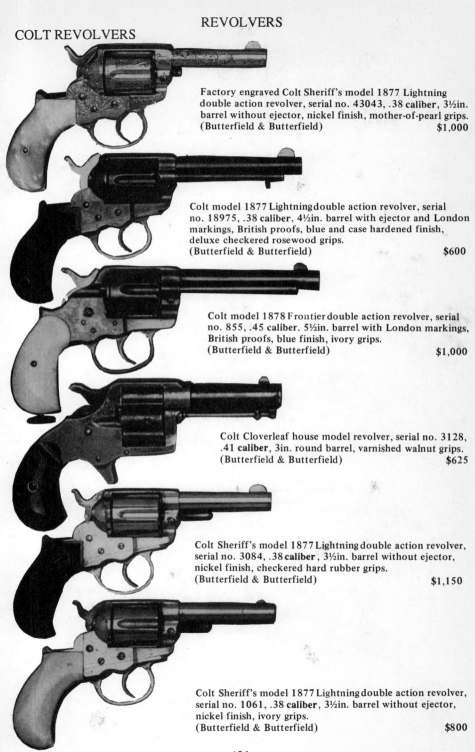

Factory engraved Colt Sheriff's model 1877 Lightning double action revolver, serial no. 43043, .38 caliber, 3½in. barrel without ejector, nickel finish, mother-of-pearl grips. (Butterfield & Butterfield) $1,000

Colt model 1877 Lightning double action revolver, serial no. 18975, .38 caliber, 4½in. barrel with ejector and London markings, British proofs, blue and case hardened finish, deluxe checkered rosewood grips. (Butterfield & Butterfield) $600

Colt model 1878 Frontier double action revolver, serial no. 855, .45 caliber. 5½in. barrel with London markings, British proofs, blue finish, ivory grips. (Butterfield & Butterfield) $1,000

Colt Cloverleaf house model revolver, serial no. 3128, .41 caliber, 3in. round barrel, varnished walnut grips. (Butterfield & Butterfield) $625

Colt Sheriff's model 1877 Lightning double action revolver, serial no. 3084, .38 caliber, 3½in. barrel without ejector, nickel finish, checkered hard rubber grips. (Butterfield & Butterfield) $1,150

Colt Sheriff's model 1877 Lightning double action revolver, serial no. 1061, .38 caliber, 3½in. barrel without ejector, nickel finish, ivory grips. (Butterfield & Butterfield) $800

COLT REVOLVERS

Colt deluxe factory engraved officer's model revolver, serial No. 515559, .38 **caliber**, 6in. barrel marked *Colt's Pt. F.A. Co. Hartford Ct. U.S.A. Pat'd Aug. 5 1884–July 4, 1905*, floral scroll engraved by Wilbur A. Glahn in Grade B pattern on barrel, frame, crane, gripstraps and cylinder.
(Butterfield & Butterfield)   **$14,250**

A 6 shot .357in. Magnum Colt Python 357 hand ejector target revolver, 11½in. overall, barrel 6in., Pachmayr soft **checkered** black rubber grips. (Wallis & Wallis)   **$475**

A 6 shot .31 inch Colt single action percussion pocket revolver No. 205952, 10 inches, octagonal barrel 5 inches engraved "Saml Colt" with foliage, foliate engraved underlever rammer. Foliate engraved frame stamped "Colts Patent". (Wallis & Wallis)   **$1,000**

Rare and unique cased Colt Paterson belt model percussion revolver, engraved and silver banded, .34 **caliber**, 4⁵/₈in. barrel marked *Patent Arms M'g Co. Paterson N.J. Colts Pt.*
(Butterfield & Butterfield)   **$770,000**

Historic Colt Whitneyville Walker model 1847 Dragoon percussion revolver, .44 **caliber**, 9in. half round octagon barrel marked *Address Sam'l Colt, New York City* and *U.S. 1847* over wedge.
(Butterfield & Butterfield)   **$275,000**

PEPPERBOX REVOLVERS

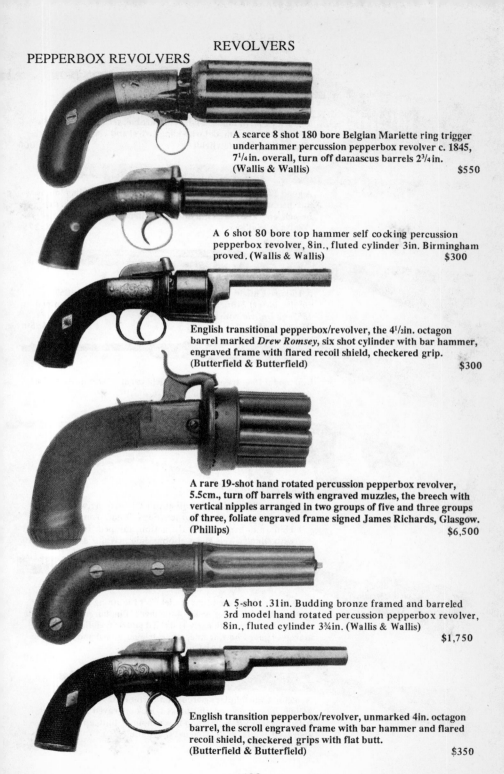

A scarce 8 shot 180 bore Belgian Mariette ring trigger underhammer percussion pepperbox revolver c. 1845, 7¼in. overall, turn off damascus barrels 2¾in. (Wallis & Wallis) $550

A 6 shot 80 bore top hammer self cocking percussion pepperbox revolver, 8in., fluted cylinder 3in. Birmingham proved. (Wallis & Wallis) $300

English transitional pepperbox/revolver, the 4½in. octagon barrel marked *Drew Romsey*, six shot cylinder with bar hammer, engraved frame with flared recoil shield, checkered grip. (Butterfield & Butterfield) $300

A rare 19-shot hand rotated percussion pepperbox revolver, 5.5cm., turn off barrels with engraved muzzles, the breech with vertical nipples arranged in two groups of five and three groups of three, foliate engraved frame signed James Richards, Glasgow. (Phillips) $6,500

A 5-shot .31in. Budding bronze framed and barreled 3rd model hand rotated percussion pepperbox revolver, 8in., fluted cylinder 3¾in. (Wallis & Wallis) $1,750

English transition pepperbox/revolver, unmarked 4in. octagon barrel, the scroll engraved frame with bar hammer and flared recoil shield, checkered grips with flat butt. (Butterfield & Butterfield) $350

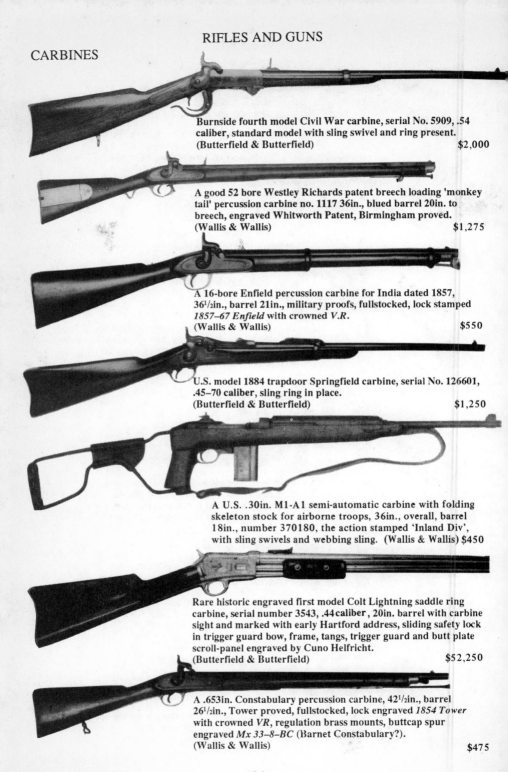

Burnside fourth model Civil War carbine, serial No. 5909, .54 caliber, standard model with sling swivel and ring present. (Butterfield & Butterfield) $2,000

A good 52 bore Westley Richards patent breech loading 'monkey tail' percussion carbine no. 1117 36in., blued barrel 20in. to breech, engraved Whitworth Patent, Birmingham proved. (Wallis & Wallis) $1,275

A 16-bore Enfield percussion carbine for India dated 1857, 36½in., barrel 21in., military proofs, fullstocked, lock stamped *1857–67 Enfield* with crowned *V.R.* (Wallis & Wallis) $550

U.S. model 1884 trapdoor Springfield carbine, serial No. 126601, .45–70 caliber, sling ring in place. (Butterfield & Butterfield) $1,250

A U.S. .30in. M1-A1 semi-automatic carbine with folding skeleton stock for airborne troops, 36in., overall, barrel 18in., number 370180, the action stamped 'Inland Div', with sling swivels and webbing sling. (Wallis & Wallis) $450

Rare historic engraved first model Colt Lightning saddle ring carbine, serial number 3543, .44 caliber, 20in. barrel with carbine sight and marked with early Hartford address, sliding safety lock in trigger guard bow, frame, tangs, trigger guard and butt plate scroll-panel engraved by Cuno Helfricht. (Butterfield & Butterfield) $52,250

A .653in. Constabulary percussion carbine, 42½in., barrel 26½in., Tower proved, fullstocked, lock engraved *1854 Tower* with crowned *VR*, regulation brass mounts, buttcap spur engraved *Mx 33–8–BC* (Barnet Constabulary?). (Wallis & Wallis) $475

HAMMER SHOTGUNS

American Arms Co. double barrel hammer shotgun, serial No. 176, 12 gauge, 27^1/2in. Damascus barrels, scroll engraved frame, trigger guard and hammers, checkered forend and pistol grip stock.
(Butterfield & Butterfield) $900

English double barrel hammer shotgun, serial No. 3835, .410 gauge, 28in. Damascus barrels with matte rib marked *Henry W. Egg No. 1 Picadilly London*, checkered forend and pistol grip stock.
(Butterfield & Butterfield) $1,000

Belgian double barrel percussion shotgun, 12 gauge, the 30in. Damascus barrels with central rib inlaid in gold with an arrow at the front sight and at the breech with gold lines and scrolling florals framing the inscription *Superior Laminated Steel.*
(Butterfield & Butterfield) $825

Gold inlaid Remington Exhibition rolling block shotgun, serial No. 1, 16 gauge, 30in. round barrel gold inlaid *E. Remington & Sons Ilion New York, U.S.A.* on the flat sighting ramp, gold filigree at breech and muzzle.
(Butterfield & Butterfield) $12,100

Austrian double barrel pinfire shotgun, the 28^1/2in. Damascus barrels with rib inlaid in gold *Joh. Springer in Wien*, gold lines and florals at breech, checkered straight stock.
(Butterfield & Butterfield) $550

Rare gold inlaid Exhibition Sharps model 1853 sporting shotgun, serial No. 18220., 28in. round barrel with brown finish and gold inlay at the breech with scrolling florals framing the Sharps name and address.
(Butterfield & Butterfield) $24,750

Colt model 1878 double barrel shotgun, serial No. 18253, 12 gauge, 30in. barrels, standard model with non-engraved frame and plain straight stock.
(Butterfield & Butterfield) $525

German double barrel percussion shotgun, the 32^1/2in. Damascus barrels inlaid with gold lines at breech and *P. Ebert & Sohne In Suhl* in gold on barrel rib, the half stock with finely carved wolf's head forend inlaid with ivory and ebony eyes.
(Butterfield & Butterfield) $1,450

HAMMERLESS SHOTGUNS

Ithaca double barrel hammerless shotgun, serial No. 270205, 20 gauge, 26in. barrels, checkered beavertail forend and pistol grip stock.
(Butterfield & Butterfield) $350

Lefever Arms Co. double barrel hammerless shotgun, serial No. 57677, 12 gauge, 30in. Damascus barrels with matte rib, checkered forend and pistol grip stock.
(Butterfield & Butterfield) $325

Parker VH grade double barrel hammerless shotgun, serial No. 154398, 16 gauge, 26in. barrels marked *Vulcan Steel*, checkered forend and pistol grip stock.
(Butterfield & Butterfield) $750

Parker D grade double barrel shotgun, serial No. 77172, 16 gauge, 30in. Damascus barrels with ivory front sight, scroll engraved frame with hunting dog and game scenes, checkered forend and pistol grip stock.
(Butterfield & Butterfield) $475

Winchester model 1887 lever action shotgun, serial No. 31187, 10 gauge, 32in. round barrel, blue and casehardened finish, varnish walnut stock.
(Butterfield & Butterfield) $5,500

English double barrel hammerless shotgun, 12 gauge, 30in. Damascus barrels, unmarked floral engraved frame, breeches and trigger guard, checkered forend and straight stock.
(Butterfield & Butterfield) $400

Gold inlaid and engraved Colt model 1883 hammerless shotgun, serial No. 7654, 12 gauge, 30in. and extra 28in. barrels marked *Colts Pt F A Mfg Co Hartford, Ct. U.S.A.* and gold banded at the breech and the breech fences, gold inlaid trigger guard marked *H.S. Kearny*.
(Butterfield & Butterfield) $22,000

L. C. Smith field grade double barrel hammerless shotgun, serial No. 110929, 12 gauge, 30in. barrels with matte rib and ivory front sight, checkered forend and pistol grip stock.
(Butterfield & Butterfield) $650

Kentucky percussion rifle, having an unmarked 42in. octagon barrel, the engraved lock marked *H. Elsell/Warranted*, the striped finish full stock with six German silver inlays, brass star inlay at cheekpiece and silver escutcheon at wrist.
(Butterfield & Butterfield) $3,000

Kentucky percussion rifle, the 39in. octagon barrel marked *J. Douglass*, the full stock, with striped finish and of delicate form, with brass fittings and pierced and engraved patchbox.
(Butterfield & Butterfield) $3,000

Kentucky percussion rifle, unmarked 29^{1}/4in. octagon barrel, the lock marked *Leman/Lancaster, Pa.*, full stock with striped finish and brass forend cap, ramrod thimbles, trigger guard, buttplate and small patchbox.
(Butterfield & Butterfield) $325

Kentucky percussion rifle, the 38in. octagon barrel with German silver front sight and German silver lines at breech, the striped finish full stock with semi-checkered wrist.
(Butterfield & Butterfield) $4,250

Kentucky half stock percussion rifle, the 30in. octagon barrel crudely engraved *Jonathan Dunmayer*, the lockplate marked *J D*, the striped maple stock with large pewter forend cap and numerous engraved silver inlays.
(Butterfield & Butterfield) $6,500

Kentucky percussion rifle, the 41in. octagon barrel stamped *A. McGilvray*, German silver blade sight, the full stock with brass forend cap, ramrod pipes, trigger guard, side plate, butt plate and pierced patchbox.
(Butterfield & Butterfield) $1,425

Kentucky percussion rifle, the 40in. octagon barrel marked *G. Fay*, the lockplate marked *Wm. H. Sowers/Warranted*, the full stock with striped finish, brass fittings and pierced and engraved patchbox.
(Butterfield & Butterfield) $1,000

Kentucky percussion rifle, the unmarked 38in. octagon barrel with brass blade sight, the lock marked *H. Elwell/Warranted*, the full stock with slight cheekpiece and brass fittings.
(Butterfield & Butterfield) $650

MARLIN RIFLES

Marlin model 1893 takedown rifle, serial No. 164578, .30–30 **caliber**, 25in. octagon barrel with full magazine, the barrel marked *Special Smokeless Steel.*
(Butterfield & Butterfield)   **$4,950**

Marlin model 1894 rifle, serial No. 214573, .38 **caliber**, 28in. round barrel with full magazine and Rocky Mountain sight, blue and casehardened finish, plain straight stock.
(Butterfield & Butterfield)   **$3,400**

Marlin model 1892 rifle, serial No. 365313, .25–20 **caliber**, 25in. octagon barrel with full magazine, blue finish with casehardened hammer and lever, plain straight stock.
(Butterfield & Butterfield)   **$1,325**

Marlin model 1897 lever action rifle, serial No. 241463, .22 **caliber**, 24in. octagon barrel with full magazine, blued and casehardened finish.
(Butterfield & Butterfield)   **$935**

Marlin model 1894 lever action rifle, serial No. 344789, .38–40 **caliber**, 24in. octagon barrel with full magazine, blue and casehardened finish, plain straight stock.
(Butterfield & Butterfield)   **$935**

Marlin model 1893 lever action rifle, serial No. 226044, .32–40 **caliber**, 26in. round barrel with full magazine, blue and casehardened finish, plain straight stock.
(Butterfield & Butterfield)   **$710**

Marlin model 1895 takedown lever action rifle, serial No. 150159, .45–90 **caliber**, 26in. octagon barrel with full magazine, blue and casehardened finish, plain straight stock.
(Butterfield & Butterfield)   **$2,000**

Rare factory engraved Marlin model 1881 rifle, serial No. 15585, .38–55 **caliber**, 28in. octagon barrel with full magazine and fitted with Rocky Mountain front sight, third type markings on barrel, the casehardened frame featuring a circular panel of a deer framed by scroll engraving on the left side and similar panel of a bear on the obverse.
(Butterfield & Butterfield)   **$110,000**

A .702in. pattern 1851 Minié percussion rifle-musket, 55in.,
barrel 39in., Tower military proved, ladder rearsight to 900
yards, fullstocked, lock engraved *1852 Enfield* with crowned *V.R.*
(Wallis & Wallis)   **$2,400**

Rare Winchester model 1892 musket, serial No. 793390, .44
caliber, 30in. round barrel secured by three barrel bands, blue
finish overall, plain straight stock, cleaning rod present in butt.
(Butterfield & Butterfield)   **$16,850**

Barnett percussion trade musket, the 36in. round barrel
octagonal at the breech, full stock with brass ramrod thimbles
and buttplate.
(Butterfield & Butterfield)   **$2,200**

A .76in. pattern 1839 percussion musket, 55in., barrel 39in.,
Tower military proof marks, fullstocked, regulation lock stamped
with crowned *V.R.*, and *Tower*, regulation brass mounts, steel
ramrod and sling swivels.
(Wallis & Wallis)   **$650**

A fine and very rare .753in. experimental Military percussion
musket and bayonet by Henry Wilkinson, circa 1850, 55in., blued
barrel 39in., London proved, fullstocked, color hardened lock
engraved *H. Wilkinson.*
(Wallis & Wallis)   **$3,000**

Rare Winchester model 1885 low wall takedown musket, serial
No. 107633, .22 Short **caliber**, 30in. No. 1 round barrel, type 44-A
rear sight, blue finish overall with casehardened lever, plain
straight stock.
(Butterfield & Butterfield)   **$11,500**

Rare Winchester single shot "high wall" musket, **caliber** 45-70,
30in. round barrel, blued finish with case hardened frame,
lever, butt plate and forecap, walnut stock with factory installed
entrenching tool released by button in butt plate, produced in
1893. (Butterfield & Butterfield)   **$11,000**

Winchester single shot "high wall" musket, 22RF short, 28in.
round barrel with single band, walnut stock with full forend
and two swivels, rare takedown feature, modified shotgun
style butt plate. (Butterfield & Butterfield)   **$2,600**

Stevens Favorite Variant model single shot rifle, serial No. 25691, .22 caliber, 22in. part round/part octagon barrel. (Butterfield & Butterfield) $360

Rare Colt double rifle, caliber 45–70, 28in. round side by side barrels, double trigger and double hammer, case hardened frame, hammers and butt plate with brown damascus finish on barrels, oil stained checkered walnut stock and forearm, blued trigger guard, lever and rear and front sight. (Butterfield & Butterfield) $18,500

Stevens Ideal single shot rifle, serial No. 80054, .25 caliber, 33½in. part round/part octagon barrel, straight stock with Schuetzen butt. (Butterfield & Butterfield) $350

A Dreyse 20-bore double-barreled needle-fire sporting rifle with browned sighted barrels rifled with seven grooves and signed in silver on the rib, blued folding back-sight, case-hardened chambers engraved with scrollwork, the barrels pivoting to the right for loading, and much original finish, by F. v. Dreyse, Sömmerda, circa 1870–80, 26¾in. barrels. (Christie's) $3,000

Remington model 1863 Zouave rifle, the lockplate and barrel dated 1863, with brass hilted sword bayonet and scabbard. (Butterfield & Butterfield) $3,200

A .577in. Volunteer 3 band Enfield percussion rifle, 54in., barrel 39in., ladder rearsight, fullstocked, lock engraved crowned VR with L.A.C° 1860, regulation brass mounts. (Wallis & Wallis) $830

Rare iron frame Henry rifle, caliber 44 RF, 24in. barrel with fifteen shot tubular magazine, cleaning rod in butt, blued finish, walnut stock, serial No. 192. (Butterfield & Butterfield) $34,100

WINCHESTER RIFLES

Ulrich engraved Winchester model 1866 rifle, serial No. 80361, .44 **caliber**, 24in. barrel with full magazine, scroll engraved with large panel scenes, the left side depicting a hunter firing into a herd of buffalo as his companion holds their horses.
(Butterfield & Butterfield)

$50,000

Engraved Winchester model 1873 rifle, British proofed, serial No. 6304, .44 caliber, late 1st model with thumbprint dust cover, 24in. round barrel with full magazine.
(Butterfield & Butterfield)

$5,650

A rare Winchester .44 W.C.F. 'Model 1873' lever-action repeating smoothbore rifle, the body of the stock inset with a steel presentation plaque inscribed *Presented by Annie Oakley to W.R.C. Clarke, 1891*, the blued round smoothbore barrel with full-length magazine and non-standard rear-and-fore-sights, 20in. barrel.
(Christie's)

$129,360

Winchester model 1886 extra lightweight takedown rifle, serial No. 136270, .33 W.C.F. **caliber**, 24in. Rapid Taper barrel with Lyman Hunting front sight and half magazine, blue finish with casehardened lever and hammer, deluxe wood and forend and pistol grip stock **checkered** in H pattern.
(Butterfield & Butterfield)

$5,000

Rare Ulrich engraved Winchester model 1873 One of One Thousand rifle, serial No. 35298, .44, first model with thumbprint dust cover, 26in. octagon barrel scroll engraved at breech and muzzle, and at breech with the legend *One of One Thousand*, platinum barrel bands.
(Butterfield & Butterfield)

$170,000

Winchester model 1885 high wall rifle, serial No. 97506, .32–40 **caliber**, 30in. No. 3 octagon barrel with Beach front sight, tang mounted Mid-Range Vernier peep sight, plain straight stock with crescent butt.
(Butterfield & Butterfield)

$1,800

Rare Winchester model 1873 One of One Thousand rifle, serial No. 18322, .44 caliber, 24in. octagon barrel with platinum lines and scroll engraving at muzzle and breech, the breech top flat engraved *One of One Thousand*.
(Butterfield & Butterfield)

$37,500

SPELTER

Spelter is another name for zinc, especially for impure zinc. It was smelted in England from around 1730, and was much in demand during the 19th century for cheap decorative items such as candlesticks, clock cases and statuettes. The terms lead spelter, aluminium spelter etc indicate alloys of zinc with these metals.

Stylized silvered spelter figure on marble base, holding blue glass clock, 20in. high, 1930s. (Muir Hewitt)　$675

1920s cold painted spelter figure of a dancer. (Muir Hewitt)　$450

Art Deco lamp with spelter figure. (Muir Hewitt)　$600

American spelter figure holding dish, 1930s, marked *Frankart*, 8in. high. (Muir Hewitt)　$275

1920s figure of lady fencer in cold painted spelter. (Muir Hewitt)　$650

Stylized 1920s spelter figure of a dancer, 9in. high. (Muir Hewitt)　$325

Stylized spelter figure on alabaster base, with mirror, 11¹/₂in. high, 1930s. (Muir Hewitt)　$325

Art Deco spelter figure lamp with stylized 1930s lady supporting crackle glass shade, 22in. high. (Muir Hewitt)　$750

Engineering model of an inclined compound surface paddle engine, 16½in. wide. $2,250

An early single vertical cylinder open crank gas engine, probably American, 24 x 9in. $350

A model Stuart triple expansion vertical reversing marine engine built by G. B. Houghton, Rochester, 7 x 8¾in. $1,150

A well presented approx. 1:20 scale model of the Weatherhill Pit Winding Engine of 1833, built by W. K. Walsam, Hayes, 19 x 14½in. $1,100

Late 19th century model of the three cylinder compound vertical surface condensing mill engine 'Asia', 16¼ x 13¼in. $3,000

An early 19th century small full size single cylinder six pillar beam engine, 31 x 34in. $1,600

A 1:20 scale brass model of the Fenton, Murray & Wood 6 N.H.P. underlever beam engine of 1806 built by G. L. Dimelow, Ashton-under-Lyne, 9¾ x 9¼in $1,100

An horizontal cylinder stationary steam engine, built by Negelin & Hubner, 28 x 64in. $1,000

A contemporary early 19th century brass and wrought iron single cylinder six pillar beam engine, built by Chadburn Bros., Sheffield, 19 x 19¼in. $3,400

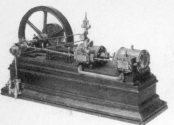

**A large well engineered horizontal twin cylinder steam plant driven by a separate boiler, the twin cylinders mounted in tandem, lacks boiler, overall 64cm. long.
(Phillips) $750**

A well engineered display model of a twin overhead camshaft, fuel injected V-8 car engine, finished in red, black and polished brightwork, 4¼ x 5½in. (Christie's) $500

A Marklin live steam spirit fired horizontal stationary steam engine, in original paintwork, circa 1921, 52in. high. (Christie's S. Ken) $1,250

A German spirit fired model of a horizontal steam engine, bearing the trademark M.G. & Cie, Wurtemberg, size of base 18½in x 20½in. (Lawrence Fine Arts) $1,750

A rare late nineteenth live steam, spirit fired, stationary steam set, with brass pot boiler and fretwork firebox, 8½in. high, possibly American. (Christie's) $300

A Schoenner live steam spirit fired tinplate overtype engine, with brass boiler and original fittings, 17½ x 15¾in., circa 1910. (Christie's) $1,500

A Marklin live steam, spirit fired horizontal stationary steam engine, with brass boiler and chimney, 13¼ x 11 x 16½in., German, circa 1920. (Christie's) $2,000

An extremely fine, mid-19th century brass, wrought and cast iron model of a four-pillar stationary steam engine and boiler, overall measurements: boiler, 22 x 30in., engine 23 x 12½in.
(Christie's S. Ken) $10,000

An early 19th century wrought iron and brass, single cylinder, four pillar overcrank model engine with cylinder approx. 2in. bore x 2in. stroke, 19 x 11¼in. (Christie's S. Ken) $400

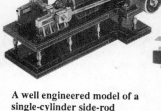

A well engineered and presented model stationary steam set built by D.J. Moir, 1976, overall, 24 x 30¼in.
(Christie's S. Ken) $1,500

A well engineered model of a single-cylinder side-rod horizontal mill engine built by G.B. Houghton, Rochester, 7¼ x 11in.
(Christie's S. Ken) $1,450

A finely engineered model of an early 19th century four column single cylinder beam pumping engine originally designed by D. E. Alban, 9½ x 9in. (Christie's S. Ken)
$900

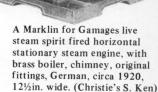

A well engineered Marklin horizontal steam plant having twin spirit-fired boilers served by single stack chimney, 46cm. x 38cm.
(Phillips) $3,400

Ducrette and Roger of Paris, a well detailed brass, vertical hot-air engine with glass enclosed piston driving flywheel, 39cm. high.
(Phillips) $600

A Marklin for Gamages live steam spirit fired horizontal stationary steam engine, with brass boiler, chimney, original fittings, German, circa 1920, 12½in. wide. (Christie's S. Ken)
$600

Doll et Cie spirit fired vertical steam engine, with lubricators, pressure gauge, whistle and taps, overall 41cm. high.
(Phillips) $525

A Märklin spirit-fired 'Three in One' convertible steam engine, single-cylinder over-type, in original box without lid, 1920's, 8in. long.
(Christie's S. Ken) $600

A finely engraved model Stuart No. 1 single-cylinder vertical reversing stationary engine built by A.L. Holloway, Sidcup, 14½ x 8¾in.
(Christie's S. Ken) $700

BROADSWORDS

An Italian broadsword with blade of flattened hexagonal section, hilt with double 'crab-claw' quillons and three concentric oval side-rings, ovoidal faceted pommel, and wire-bound wooden grip, circa 1620–30, probably Venetian, 28in. blade.
(Christie's) $1,375

An English basket hilted broadsword with tapering fullered double edged blade of flattened hexagonal section changing to diamond section towards the point, Irish basket hilt of blackened iron, circa 1610-20, 37¼in. blade. (Christie's S. Ken)
$1,850

An Italian broadsword with double-edged blade with shallow fuller on each face of the forte stamped with sickle and circle marks and twice with maker's mark, faceted globular pommel, and wire-bound wooden grip, circa 1630, probably Venetian, 29¼in. blade.
(Christie's) $2,500

A Scottish basket-hilted broadsword, the broad blade with three fullers on each face at the forte stamped 'Andrea Ferara' and with copper-inlaid orb and cross mark, the iron hilt comprising basket-guard of vertical slender bars framing S-shaped bars, second quarter of the 18th Century, 29½in. blade.
(Christie's S. Ken) $1,525

A good Scandinavian broadsword circa 1620 with Sinclair hilt, straight tapered double edged blade 32¼in., struck with maker's mark of a splayed foot cross.
(Wallis & Wallis) $1,100

A George V Scottish infantry officer's cruciform hilted broadsword, blade 32¼in. etched with crowned *GVR* cypher and Royal Arms amidst foliage, plated crosspiece and pommel.
(Wallis & Wallis) $200

DRESS SWORDS

A Life Guards officer's dress sword circa 1845, plain straight single edged blade 32in., brass hilt with traces of gilding, heart shaped guard, rounded knucklebow with large inner thumb ring, roped silver wire grip.
(Wallis & Wallis) **$1,100**

A scarce 2nd Life Guards officer's dress sword circa 1832, plain blade 40in., brass hilt, scrolled guard, flaming grenade to pommel and reverse of guard, brass wire bound grip, associated bullion dress knot, in its steel scabbard with brass suspension ring mounts. (Wallis & Wallis) **$1,000**

A US Army officer's dress sword, circa 1900, blade 29in. by Ridabock New York, retaining some original polish, etched with US eagle, military trophies and foliage, brass hilt with traces of gilding.
(Wallis & Wallis) **$175**

A rare Household Cavalry officer's 1814 pattern dress sword, straight, double fullered blade 34in., half basket copper gilt hilt, with crowned lion upon crown badge, circular pommel.
(Wallis & Wallis) **$3,000**

An EIIR RAF officer's dress sword, blade 32in., by Wilkinson Sword, retaining much original polish, etched with Royal Arms, blank scrolls and laurel sprays, gilt hilt, with royal cypher, eagle's head pommel, original bullion dress knot, gilt wire bound white fishskin covered grip.
(Wallis & Wallis) **$400**

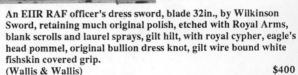

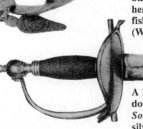

A 1796 heavy cavalry officer's dress sword, straight tapering double-edged blade 32in. signed in the short fullers *J.J. Runkel Solingen,* copper gilt hilt, boat shaped guard, ovoid pommel, silver wire bound grip.
(Wallis & Wallis) **$210**

EXECUTIONER'S SWORDS

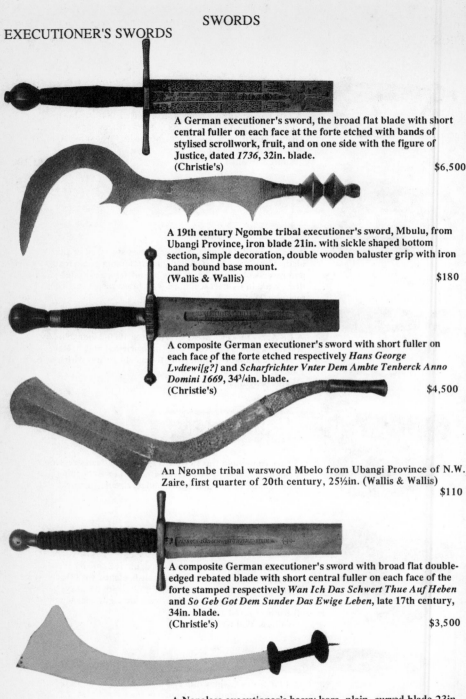

A German executioner's sword, the broad flat blade with short central fuller on each face at the forte etched with bands of stylised scrollwork, fruit, and on one side with the figure of Justice, dated *1736*, 32in. blade.
(Christie's) $6,500

A 19th century Ngombe tribal executioner's sword, Mbulu, from Ubangi Province, iron blade 21in. with sickle shaped bottom section, simple decoration, double wooden baluster grip with iron band bound base mount.
(Wallis & Wallis) $180

A composite German executioner's sword with short fuller on each face of the forte etched respectively *Hans George Lvdtewi[g?]* and *Scharfrichter Vnter Dem Ambte Tenberck Anno Domini 1669*, 34³/₄in. blade.
(Christie's) $4,500

An Ngombe tribal warsword Mbelo from Ubangi Province of N.W. Zaire, first quarter of 20th century, 25½in. (Wallis & Wallis)
                                                                                                $110

A composite German executioner's sword with broad flat double-edged rebated blade with short central fuller on each face of the forte stamped respectively *Wan Ich Das Schwert Thue Auf Heben* and *So Geb Got Dem Sunder Das Ewige Leben*, late 17th century, 34in. blade.
(Christie's) $3,500

A Nepalese executioner's heavy kora, plain, curved blade 23in., inlaid at top with brass geometric design, plain steel hilt, in its leather covered wooden scabbard. $250

SWORDS

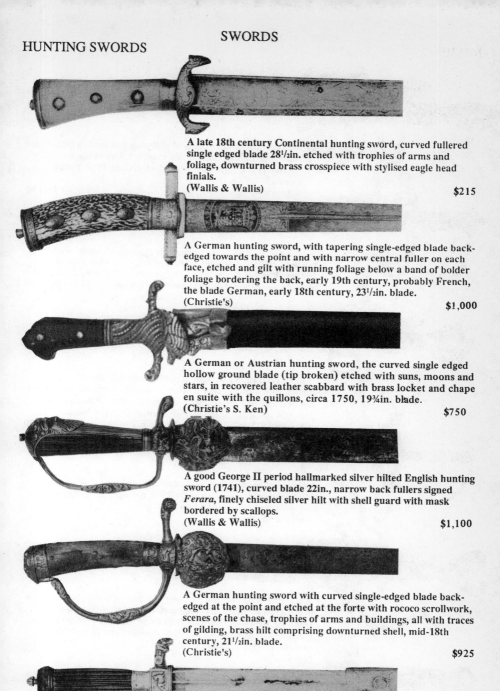

A late 18th century Continental hunting sword, curved fullered single edged blade 28¹/₂in. etched with trophies of arms and foliage, downturned brass crosspiece with stylised eagle head finials.
(Wallis & Wallis) $215

A German hunting sword, with tapering single-edged blade back-edged towards the point and with narrow central fuller on each face, etched and gilt with running foliage below a band of bolder foliage bordering the back, early 19th century, probably French, the blade German, early 18th century, 23¹/₂in. blade.
(Christie's) $1,000

A German or Austrian hunting sword, the curved single edged hollow ground blade (tip broken) etched with suns, moons and stars, in recovered leather scabbard with brass locket and chape en suite with the quillons, circa 1750, 19¾in. blade.
(Christie's S. Ken) $750

A good George II period hallmarked silver hilted English hunting sword (1741), curved blade 22in., narrow back fullers signed *Ferara*, finely chiseled silver hilt with shell guard with mask bordered by scallops.
(Wallis & Wallis) $1,100

A German hunting sword with curved single-edged blade back-edged at the point and etched at the forte with rococo scrollwork, scenes of the chase, trophies of arms and buildings, all with traces of gilding, brass hilt comprising downturned shell, mid-18th century, 21¹/₂in. blade.
(Christie's) $925

A French late 18th century silver mounted hunting sword, straight, double fullered, double-edged tapering blade 20in., crosspiece chiseled in the form of hounds' heads.
(Wallis & Wallis) $1,050

RAPIERS

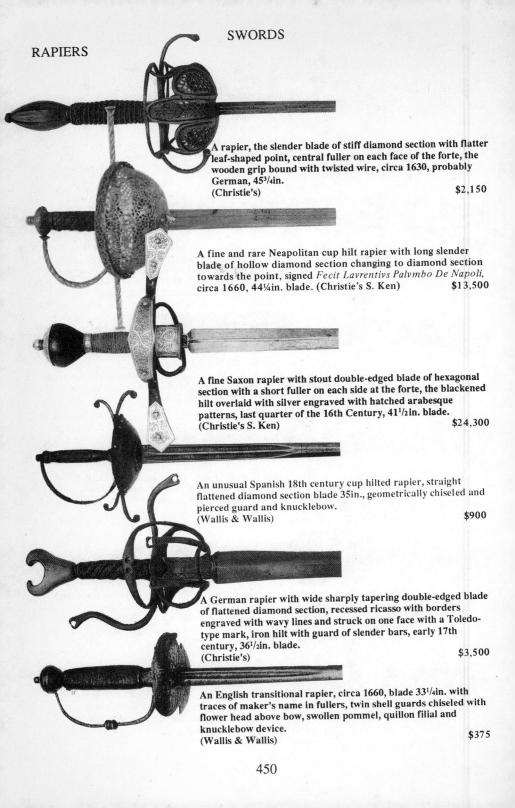

A rapier, the slender blade of stiff diamond section with flatter leaf-shaped point, central fuller on each face of the forte, the wooden grip bound with twisted wire, circa 1630, probably German, 45³/₄in.
(Christie's) $2,150

A fine and rare Neapolitan cup hilt rapier with long slender blade of hollow diamond section changing to diamond section towards the point, signed *Fecit Lavrentivs Palvmbo De Napoli,* circa 1660, 44¼in. blade. (Christie's S. Ken) $13,500

A fine Saxon rapier with stout double-edged blade of hexagonal section with a short fuller on each side at the forte, the blackened hilt overlaid with silver engraved with hatched arabesque patterns, last quarter of the 16th Century, 41¹/₂in. blade.
(Christie's S. Ken) $24,300

An unusual Spanish 18th century cup hilted rapier, straight flattened diamond section blade 35in., geometrically chiseled and pierced guard and knucklebow.
(Wallis & Wallis) $900

A German rapier with wide sharply tapering double-edged blade of flattened diamond section, recessed ricasso with borders engraved with wavy lines and struck on one face with a Toledo-type mark, iron hilt with guard of slender bars, early 17th century, 36¹/₂in. blade.
(Christie's) $3,500

An English transitional rapier, circa 1660, blade 33¹/₄in. with traces of maker's name in fullers, twin shell guards chiseled with flower head above bow, swollen pommel, quillon filial and knucklebow device.
(Wallis & Wallis) $375

SWORD PISTOLS

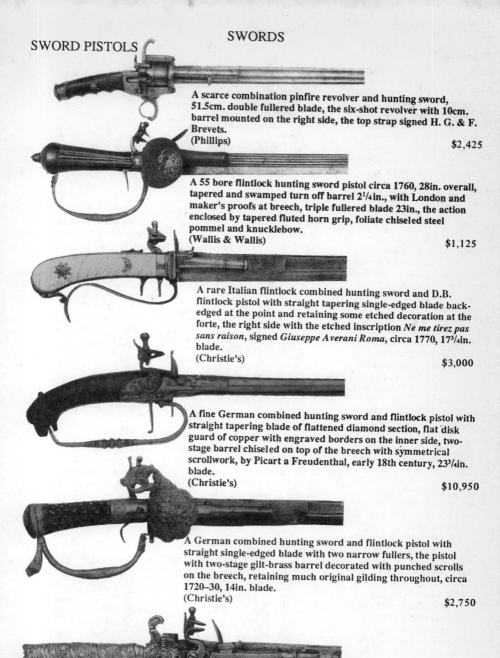

A scarce combination pinfire revolver and hunting sword, 51.5cm. double fullered blade, the six-shot revolver with 10cm. barrel mounted on the right side, the top strap signed H. G. & F. Brevets.
(Phillips) $2,425

A 55 bore flintlock hunting sword pistol circa 1760, 28in. overall, tapered and swamped turn off barrel 2¼in., with London and maker's proofs at breech, triple fullered blade 23in., the action enclosed by tapered fluted horn grip, foliate chiseled steel pommel and knucklebow.
(Wallis & Wallis) $1,125

A rare Italian flintlock combined hunting sword and D.B. flintlock pistol with straight tapering single-edged blade back-edged at the point and retaining some etched decoration at the forte, the right side with the etched inscription *Ne me tirez pas sans raison*, signed *Giuseppe Averani Roma*, circa 1770, 17¾in. blade.
(Christie's) $3,000

A fine German combined hunting sword and flintlock pistol with straight tapering blade of flattened diamond section, flat disk guard of copper with engraved borders on the inner side, two-stage barrel chiseled on top of the breech with symmetrical scrollwork, by Picart a Freudenthal, early 18th century, 23¾in. blade.
(Christie's) $10,950

A German combined hunting sword and flintlock pistol with straight single-edged blade with two narrow fullers, the pistol with two-stage gilt-brass barrel decorated with punched scrolls on the breech, retaining much original gilding throughout, circa 1720–30, 14in. blade.
(Christie's) $2,750

A rare German combined hunting sword and flintlock pistol reconverted from flintlock, with curved single-edged blade double-edged at the point and with one broad and one narrow fuller, the locket housing an iron ramrod, mid-18th century, 21¾in. blade.
(Christie's) $2,925

Most people are now familiar with the account of how the Teddy bear got its name. This tells how, while on a hunting trip in 1902, President Theodore Roosevelt could not bring himself to shoot a bear cub which had been conveniently tethered to a post by some well-meaning aide (the President having just shot its mother). Such fore'bear'ance on the part of the noted hunter appealed to the popular press, and the incident was captured in a cartoon of the day. Seeing this, one Morris Michtom, of the Ideal Toy Corp. who had created some toy bears, asked permission to call them after Theodore, so the Teddy bear came into being.

Roosevelt obviously felt the connection did no harm to the Presidential image, and when his daughter married in 1906, the wedding breakfast tables were decorated with tiny bears made by the Steiff toy company.

Margrete Steiff had been making felt animals at Geingen in Germany for some time and was joined in 1897 by her ambitious nephew Richard. They exhibited at the Leipzig Fair in 1903 and the popularity of their toys was so great that the factory simply could not keep up with demand.

Pre-1910 Steiff bears tend to be rather elongated for modern taste, with pointed snouts and humps. The Steiffs had the good marketing sense to put a characteristic button in each of their product's ears, thus making them instantly recognisable. They are now the most valuable bears for collectors.

Many firms in Britain too produced Teddy bears. Few, however are marked, and attribution is often impossible. Those by Merrythought now have quite a following among collectors.

A plush covered polar bear with button eyes, felt pads and joints at hips, 16in. long, with Steiff button, circa 1913. (Christie's) $600

Early white mohair teddy bear, Germany, circa 1906, 13½in. high. $1,125

A honey plush covered teddy bear with boot button eyes, wide apart ears, 13½in. high, with Steiff button in ear (one pad moth eaten). (Christie's) $700

A silver plush covered teddy bear with button eyes and felt pads, 14in. high, with Steiff button. (Christie's) $875

A plush covered bear on wheels with swivel head, boot button eyes, stitched nose and slight hump, with Steiff button in ear, 8¹/₂in. long. (Christie's S. Ken) $625

A long cinnamon plush cover, teddy bear with large button eyes, central face seam, wide set ears, 21in. high, circa 1905, probably Steiff. (Christie's) $2,300

STEIFF

A dark plush teddy bear with straw stuffed body and elongated arms, back hump and felt pads, probably by Steiff, 40cm. high. $1,100

A dark golden plush covered Roly Poly bear with boot button eyes, pronounced snout and wide apart ears by Steiff, circa 1909, 5¹/₂ in. high.
(Christie's S. Ken) $625

A Steiff Centennial teddy bear, for the German market, golden mohair, black button eyes and ear button, 17in. high, 1980. $550

A straw gold plush covered teddy bear with elongated limbs, pronounced snout, glass eyes, and Steiff button in ear, probably circa 1909, 24in. high. (Christie's S. Ken) $3,000

A plush covered pull-along bear mounted on a wheeled frame, 23in. long, with raised letters, Steiff button, circa 1920. (Christie's) $790

An early 20th century golden plush Steiff teddy bear, with Steiff metal button in the ear, swivel joints with felt pads, 51cm. high.
(Henry Spencer) $1,850

A light brown plush covered teddy bear with boot button eyes, 21in. high, by Steiff, circa 1905. (Christie's) $475

A cinammon plush covered bear with large black boot button eyes, 29in. long, Steiff button in ear, circa 1904. (Christie's) $2,800

A plush-covered teddy bear with round ears, button eyes, pronounced hump and long paws, probably by Steiff, 21in. high. $775

STEIFF

A cinnamon plush covered teddy bear, with boot button eyes, 24in. high, probably Steiff, circa 1908. (Christie's) $2,300

A Steiff gold mohair plush teddy bear with wide apart rounded ears, black boot button eyes, 16in., 1911. (Phillips) $1,600

An early 20th century Steiff blonde plush teddy bear. (Spencer's) $4,200

A white plush covered teddy bear with elongated limbs, pronounced snout, glass eyes, hump and Steiff button in ear, circa 1930's, 18in. high. (Christie's S. Ken) $1,600

A pale golden plush covered teddy bear with boot button eyes, wide apart ears, elongated limbs, hump, cut muzzle, stitched nose with four claws, felt pads and growler, with Steiff button in ear, circa 1911, 28in. high.(Christie's S. Ken.) $3,250

A beige plush covered teddy bear with felt pads, hump and squeeze growler, small blank Steiff button in ear, circa 1903-4, 10in. high. (Christie's S. Ken.) $1,000

A dark gold plush covered teddy bear with brown glass eyes, 19½in. high with Steiff button, circa 1920. (Christie's) $475

A long plush-covered teddy bear with black button eyes, with Steiff button in the ear, 25in. high. $3,000

A blonde plush covered teddy bear with boot button eyes, wide apart ears, 13in. high, Steiff button in ear. (Christie's) $1,000

STEIFF

German teddy bear by
Steiff of pale plush
color, renewed pads,
snout and nose, circa
1909. $2,250

A blonde plush covered teddy
bear with boot button eyes,
dressed as a sailor in blue
trousers, white jersey and blue
beret, by Steiff, 8¹/₂in. high.
(Christie's S. Ken) $575

A blonde plush covered teddy
bear with boot button eyes,
17in. high with Steiff button
in ear. (Christie's) $850

A Steiff gold plush teddy bear,
circa 1912, with black boot
button eyes, rounded pricked
ears, hump back, swivel joints,
and growl box, 68cm. long.
(Henry Spencer) $650

A strawberry blonde plush
covered teddy bear with boot
button eyes, 12in. high, with
plain Steiff button in ear,
circa 1903/1904. (Christie's)
                    $800

'Edward Bear', a blonde plush
covered teddy bear with boot
button eyes, cut muzzle ,
elongated limbs, with Steiff
button in ear, circa 1905, 10in.
high.
(Christie's S. Ken) $1,500

A Steiff blonde plush teddy
bear, with metal disc in left
ear, 17in. high. $2,750

A golden plush covered center
seam teddy bear with boot
button eyes, by Steiff, circa 1905,
20in. high (lacks stuffing in arms
from loss of front paw pads).
(Christie's S. Ken) $1,400

A golden plush covered teddy
bear with boot button eyes,
wide apart ears, and Steiff
button in ear, 16in. high.
(Christie's) $2,250

STEIFF

A Steiff pale plush teddy bear with black thread stitched nose and straw stuffed body, with button in left ear, 33cm. high.
$1,300

A golden plush covered teddy bear, the front unhooking to reveal a metal hot water bottle, by Steiff, 17in. high.
$2,750

A dark plush teddy bear with wide apart rounded ears, black button eyes and pointed snout, probably by Steiff, 34cm. high.
$1,000

A good early golden plush Steiff teddy bear, with black boot button eyes, pointed brown stitched snout, rounded pricked ears, back hump, swivel joints, felt pads and a growl box, 38.5cm. long.
(Henry Spencer) $4,000

An early golden plush covered teddy bear, with boot button eyes, hump, excelsior stuffing and elongated limbs, wearing tortoiseshell rimmed spectacles, with small blank Steiff button in ear, circa 1903/4, 20in. high.
(Christie's S. Ken) $625

Noel, a rare black plush covered teddy bear, with boot button eyes mounted on red felt, elongated limbs and wide apart ears, by Steiff, circa 1910, 20½in. high. (Christie's S. Ken) $4,500

A Steiff pale plush teddy bear with rounded wide-apart ears, black button eyes and large felt pads. (Phillips) $500

A dark golden plush covered teddy bear wearing a leather muzzle with lead, with Steiff button and white tag in ear, circa 1910, 12½in. high.
(Christie's S. Ken) $1,000

A gold plush teddy bear, with metal Steiff disc in left ear, German, circa 1907, 25in. high. $4,750

STEIFF

A cinnamon plush covered teddy bear, with boot button eyes, wide apart ears, elongated limbs, hump and cut muzzle, with Steiff button in ear, 13in. high. (Christie's S. Ken) $3,500

A dual-plush Steiff teddy bear, German, circa 1920. $82,500

A pale golden plush covered teddy bear with embroidered snout and slight hump, 15½in. high, with Steiff button. $2,500

A golden plush covered teddy bear with boot button eyes, cut muzzle, hump and elongated limbs, with Steiff button in left ear, 19in. high. $1,350

An early 20th century German blond plush large teddy bear, with black wooden eyes, stitched pointed snout, hump back and moving arms, 52cm. high, probably Steiff. (Spencer's) $1,850

A rare central seam golden plush covered teddy bear, with boot button eyes, wide apart ears, elongated limbs, hump and pronounced snout, by Steiff, circa 1905, 20in. high. (Christie's S. Ken) $1,500

An early golden plush covered teddy bear with boot button eyes, Steiff button in ear, 8½in. high. (Christie's) $1,000

A fine Steiff black mohair plush teddy bear with wide apart rounded ears, black boot button eyes, hump back and elongated felt pads, 19in, button in ear marked *Steiff*, 1912. (Phillips) $16,000

A honey plush covered teddy bear with boot button eyes, 14in. high, Steiff button in ear, circa 1903. (Christie's) $1,300

TERRACOTTA

Terracotta is a fired clay, principally associated with sculpture, and terracotta figures feature among the antiquities of China, Greece & Rome. The art was revived during the Renaissance, and in the 18th century France became a leading center of production. The popularity of the medium lasted well into the Art Nouveau period, and busts of typical flowing haired maidens were produced.

A late 19th century French terracotta bust of 'L'Esperance', signed J. B. Carpeaux 1874, 54cm. high. $1,500

A Belgian terracotta face mask by L. Nosbusch modeled as Rudolf Valentino, 14in. high. $350

A 19th century French terracotta bust of Mademoiselle Marguerite Bellanger, by Albert Carrier-Belleuse, 69cm. high, on a glazed terracotta socle. (Christie's) $13,000

A large pair of Italian terracotta busts of the rivers Reno and Zena shown as a god and goddess, by Andrea Ferreri, signed and dated, circa 1704, 35³/₄ and 37¹/₂in. high. (Christie's) $22,750

A 19th century French terracotta bust of Louise Brogniart, after Houdon, 50cm. high. (Christie's) $875

A terracotta bust of an Art Nouveau maiden, with long flowing hair, embellished with large trailing poppies in a green patination, 42cm. high. (Phillips) $650

Model for 'Gateway of Youth', plaster with terracotta colored painted finish, 22 x 18in. $350

Hellenistic terracotta figure of Dionysus, circa 300 B.C., depicted as the god of the vine, with long curly hair and beard and wearing a wreath of leaves on his head, 7³/₄in. high. (Butterfield & Butterfield) $3,000

A terracotta group of three amorini, adorned with fruiting vines, the base signed indistinctly, possibly Belgian, 20in. high. (Christie's S. Ken) $710

A pair of painted terracotta busts, in Arab costume. (Phillips) $1,320

French terracotta bust of a young woman, Charles Eugene Breton, dated 1916, smiling with long tresses bound at the back, 22in. high. (Skinner Inc.) $650

A 19th century French terra cotta bust of Rouget de l'Isle, by David d'Angers, signed and dated *David 1835,* 45.5cm. high. (Christie's London) $13,300

Pair of Empire terracotta urns, second quarter 19th century, campagna form, 20in. high. (Skinner Inc.) $1,200

A pair of terracotta chimney pots of Gothic design, the octagonal tops above cylindrical bodies, 43in. (Christie's) $1,100

A French terracotta group of 'Le Fleuve', after Jean-Jacques Caffiére, the bearded river-god shown seated, his left leg over an urn flowing with water, 19th century, 23½in. high. (Christie's) $2,810

A pair of Continental poly-chrome terracotta figures of Arab tribesmen, each robed and holding staffs, 18½in. high. (Christie's S. Ken) $775

A 19th century French terra-cotta group of a Bacchante, in the manner of Clodion, an infant satyr at her side, 15½in. high. (Christie's S. Ken) $1,150

A mid 17th century embroidered picture worked in silk and metal threads showing King Charles II and Catherine of Braganza, 27cm. x 37cm., English, circa 1660.
(Phillips) **$1,288**

A fine and large needlework picture, probably a firescreen banner, signed at the bottom *Mary Davidson, aged 13, 1706*, 27 x 19^1/$_2$in.
(Tennants) **$8,928**

An early George III silk picture, of a shepherdess and child with dogs, rabbits, birds and insects, walnut frame, 10^1/$_2$ x 13in.
(Tennants) **$3,720**

Beauvais tapestry pillow, 18th century, with one rounded side, sewn in shades of ocher, brown, tan, various shades of green and blue, crimson and burgundy, 19 x 18^1/$_2$in.
(Butterfield & Butterfield) **$1,100**

'Daffodil', a Morris & Co. curtain, designed by J.H. Dearle, printed cotton with braid border, repeating pattern of daffodils and wild flowers between waved stylised vines, 45 x 181cm.
(Christie's) **$689**

One of a pair of George II gros and petit point panels, worked in colored wools and heightened in silks, one with a gardener, the other with his companion, 19 x 22^3/$_4$in.
(Tennants)   (Two)
$1,953

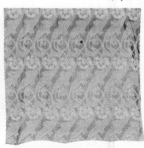

A George I panel, possibly from a large chair seat worked with a shepherdess beside a pond with swans, framed, 24in. square.
(Tennants) **$5,580**

A needlework picture, embroidered in colored silks and metal wire, with Bathsheba and her attendants, with King David watching from his castle, 12 x 17in., unfinished, mounted, English, mid 17th century.
(Christie's) **$4,478**

Fabric panel, attributed to C.F.A. Voysey, early 20th century, comprised of silk and cotton jacquard woven fabric in green and cream, 93 x 84in.
(Skinner Inc.) **$600**

A fine small Charles II silk needlework cushion, worked in a variety of stitches with the King and Queen beside a pool with fishes, 9¹/₂ x 6³/₄in.
(Tennants) $5,022

'Bird', two pairs of Morris & Co. curtains, woven wool, repeating pattern, pairs of birds amid foliage, with two tie backs, 223 x 84cm.
(Christie's) $4,725

A needlework picture, embroidered in colored silks with two figures by a well, possibly Rebecca and Eliezer, 8 x 10in., English, mid 17th century.
(Christie's) $5,257

A good Charles II needlework panel, worked with a group including a young man riding a camel watching a young woman being baptised by immersion, 9 x 7¹/₂in.
(Tennants) $2,604

A late 18th century needlework oval picture, of a kneeling girl playing a harp, 12¹/₄ x 9¹/₂in.
(Tennants) $521

'The Four Seasons', a wall hanging designed by Walter Crane, woven silk on cotton, repeating design of roundels enclosing classical figures, circa 1893, 216 x 111cm.
(Christie's) $6,695

An early 19th century embroidered picture portraying a classical archway with view to colonnades beyond and surrounding ruins, 33 x 45cm., English, circa 1810.
(Phillips) $221

A woven wool curtain, the design attributed to B.J. Talbert, repeating floral design, dark olive green ground with sage green, rust red and beige, 272cm. long x 125cm. wide.
(Christie's) $985

A needlework picture, worked in colored silks and metal threads, with a central medallion depicting Rebecca and Eliezer at the well, 16 x 21in., English, mid 17th century.
(Christie's) $12,850

A needlework purse, worked in the shape of a frog, the front and back embroidered in green and brown shades of silk, 1¹/₂in. long, early 17th century.
(Christie's S. Ken)
$2,972

A late 17th century petit point embroidered picture worked in wool and silk, portraying the coming of God's Angel to Abraham, 33cm. x 41cm., English, circa 1660.
(Phillips)
$1,196

A Queen Victoria souvenir beadwork purse, the gilt clasp marked *Victoria June 28th, 1838* with floral beadwork.
(Woolley & Wallis)
$144

A late 18th century chair back cover with colorful crewel work embroidery of a tree with bird and stylized peonies, roses and other flowers, 97cm. x 59cm.
(Phillips)
$930

A needlework casket, worked in colored silks against an ivory silk ground, depicting the story of Joseph, 5¹/₂in. x 14in. x 10in., with key and wooden case, English, 1660.
(Christie's S. Ken)
$159,225

A William Morris & Company embroidered wool portière designed by Henry Dearle, circa 1910, the central rectangular reserve embroidered with a flowering tree and song birds, 244 x 180.5cm.
(Christie's)
$71,610

A mid-17th century needlework picture, the ivory satin silk ground worked in silk threads, showing Charles II and Catherine of Braganza, 29.5cm. x 26cm., circa 1660.
(Phillips)
$1,112

Pair of Aubusson window surrounds, second half 19th century, floral bouquet with a pair of birds, 11ft. 10in. high.
(Skinner Inc.)
$5,100

A mid-17th century embroidered cushion worked in silk and metal threads on ivory satin silk ground, having a small tassel at each corner, English, 26.5cm. x 31cm., circa 1660.
(Phillips)
$1,112

A needlework panel, of natural linen, worked with a repeating pattern of grapes and vine leaves in black silk and gilt threads, 9in. x 13¹/₂in., English, late 16th century.
(Christie's S. Ken)
$3,185

'Core', a cotton wall hanging by Ruston Aust, screen printed pink ground with hand-written script and painted yellow stripes, signed bottom center *Ruston Aust*, 1989, 254 x 121cm.
(Christie's)
$1,494

Two cushions each of rectangular shape with tasseled ends, covered in Aubusson tapestry, one with a shepherd boy, the largest 21in. wide.
(Christie's)
$1,936

An early 18th century banner wall hanging of linen boldly embroidered with couched metal thread and colored silks, 1.35m. x 65cm., Italian, later red silk lining.
(Phillips)
$1,415

An early 19th century ivory silk handkerchief printed with Hackney Coach and Cabriolet Fares, Regulations and Acts of Parliament, 88 x 92cm., circa 1833.
(Phillips)
$221

A late 18th century oval silkwork picture, the ivory silk ground, designed with a romantic youth playing a flute, 17cm. long, English.
(Phillips)
$202

A late 18th century needlework embroidery of a hare and three leverets, executed in fine long and short stitch, possibly by Mary Linwood (1755–1845), English, 51cm. x 70cm.
(Phillips)
$5,055

A late 16th/early 17th century kid sweet bag embroidered with stylized Tudor roses, red, gold and black thread, approximately 6in. top to bottom.
(Woolley & Wallis)
$1,000

A late 18th century embroidered picture with charming harvest scene depicting laborers gathering sheaves of corn, English, 24.5 x 31.5cm., circa 1770.
(Phillips)
$1,380

CLOCKWORK

Clockwork toys have their illustrious origins in the ingenious automata which were made in the 17th and 18th centuries for the delight of aristocratic circles and in the 19th for a more general, but still largely adult, public. It was the Germans who first realised the potential for a juvenile market, especially as new inventions made mechanisms and production methods ever cheaper. By the turn of the century the market was flooded with cheap tinplate imports, and these are immensely popular with collectors today. Bing, Carette, Märklin, Günthermann and Lehmann are just some of the names to conjure with, and some of their best products dating from the first thirty years of this century can now fetch well into four figures. Their most popular models were cars, trains, aeroplanes, ships, stationary steam engines and figures as well, all of which were generally very finely painted or printed.

The British companies which entered into competition with these in the 1930s were Wells, Brimtoy and Chad Valley, and their products too are attracting quite a following today. The famous Tri-ang (Lines Bros.) company at this time launched their Minic range, small tinplate commercial vehicles with clockwork mechanisms. Their pre-war cars fitted with lead passengers are particularly rare today. Most early Minics had room for a battery which in turn powered the headlights, or, in the case of the breakdown lorry, the gears and winch of the crane unit.

By the 1950s the Japanese had entered the market and were producing clockwork and battery operated toys in tinplate and plastic which sold very cheaply.

A Lehmann Skirolf 781, a lithographed skier with sticks, 1930–41, 19cm. high. (Auktionsverket) $2,400

An early hand painted maid, standing at an ironing board, holding an iron and a winged collar, 8in. high, probably by Gunthermann, circa 1903. (Christie's) $900

Britains very rare set 1441, Mammoth Circus Flying Trapeze with clown, female trapeze artiste and original paper sunshade, in original box, 1937. (Phillips) $1,500

A Linemar Karl Alfred lithographed clockwork Popeye figure, moves forward on rollerskates swinging its arms, 1950s. (Auktionsverket) $600

A lithographed Penny Toy of a jigger dressed in red jacket, with yellow hat and trousers, on green box base, 9cm. (Phillips) $230

A rare humorous composition toy, modeled as a red faced man with startled eyes hanging on to a runaway donkey, 6½in. long, mid 19th century, German. (Christie's) $1,100

464

A clockwork wood and papier-mâché head-over-heels figure of a policeman, dressed in navy-blue felt uniform, 9½in. (Phillips) $200

A rare and early hand enameled tinplate woman pushing a cart, with caged goose, probably by Gunthermann, circa 1903, 7½in. long. (Christie's) $750

A Linemar battery-operated fabric and lithographed tinplate Mickey the Magician with disappearing chicken, in original box, 10½in. high. (Christie's) $735

A German lithographed Penny Toy of a pram and child within, on four spoked wheels, 6.5cm., some wear and rust. (Phillips) $175

A German post-war clockwork Boxing match, boxed (no lid). $200

Lithographed tin balloon man, triple animation, Germany, 1930, 6.5/8in. high. $650

A tinplate pool player, at a printed and painted tinplate pool table, with clockwork mechanism, 7¼in. long, stamped P.W., German, circa 1912. (Christie's) $600

A German clockwork Drummer Boy dressed as a soldier in busby, 28cm. high. $200

Nomura, a tinplate battery operated doll dressmaker seated at her sewing machine, 17cm. high. (Phillips) $150

CLOCKWORK

An early Japanese lithographed tinplate traveling boy, with clockwork mechanism, 1930's, 8in. high. (Christie's) $700

A Märklin signalman with moving arm, 1940s, in original packing. (Auktionsverket) $725

Linemar, battery operated Bubble Blowing Popeye. $475

A papier mâché headed political toy modeled as Churchill, with frowning expression, remains of cigar, small bowler hat, and red bow tie, 10$^{1}/_{2}$in. high, circa 1920s. (Christie's S. Ken) $150

Linemar battery operated Busy Secretary, the blond girl wearing spotty blouse and fluted skirt, 19cm. high., boxed. (Phillips) $225

A German lithographed clown dressed in yellow checkered trousers, blue jacket with a spinner above his head, 11cm. (Phillips) $60

A rare Schuco clockwork tinplate and fabric two-wheel 210 mousecart with two mice, circa 1932, 4in. wide. (Christie's) $545

A clockwork painted tinplate horse with seated gentleman rider finished with blue tailed jacket, 15.5cm. (Phillips) $400

Marx, clockwork Dagwoods aeroplane boxed. (Phillips) $350

CLOCKWORK TOYS

George W. Brown clockwork doll pushing hoop bell toy, Connecticut, 1872, 12in. long. **$4,500**

A Louis Marx 'Marx Merrymakers' tinplate mouse band, English, circa 1935, the lithographed figures sitting on and around a piano, 9in. long, some rust. (Sotheby's) **$875**

An English J.W.B. mechanical artist toy, contained in original box, circa 1900, 4½in. wide. **$1,500**

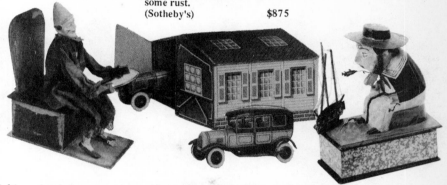

A bisque headed moving clown toy, the white face with painted hat and features, the wood and wire body with wooden hands and feet, the head impressed *1720*, German, late 19th century, 10in. high. (Christie's S. Ken) **$700**

A Bing tinplate garage and cars, German, 1920's, the double garage lithographed in gray and yellow with opening doors, the garage 8½in. wide. (Sotheby's) **$550**

A German papier-mâché sailor swallowing fish, the hand operated automaton with molded painted features, probably Sonneberg, late 19th century. (Phillips) **$1,350**

Late 19th century painted tin clockwork bowing man, 7½in. high. **$325**

Goodwin clockwork doll and carriage, doll with papier mache head, 11in. high, 9½in. long, 1868. **$1,250**

ALPS clockwork lithographed Little Shoemaker dressed in stripy T-shirt and checkered jacket, 15cm., boxed. (Phillips) **$120**

CLOCKWORK CYCLISTS

'Echo', EPL No. 725, a rare printed and painted tinplate motor cyclist, with clockwork mechanism, 8¾in. long, by Lehmann, circa 1910. (Christie's) $3,000

An Arnold army motorcyclist, lithographed tinplate, wind-up action with Firestone headlamp, lacking support, 1938–40. (Auction Team Köln) $435

Well's Big Chief mechanical motor cycle, with Indian Chief rider, clockwork mechanism, in original box, 1930s, 7½in. long. (Christie's S. Ken) $900.

Unique Art Manufacturing Co. clockwork 'Kiddy Cyclist', fair haired young boy on tricycle, the wheels with lithographed animals, 23cm. (Phillips) $380

'Mac 700', a printed and painted tinplate motorbike and rider with clockwork mechanism, causing the rider to hop on and off, 7¼in. long, by Arnold, W. Germany, circa 1955. $550

Kellermann, a lithographed freewheeling negro on a tricycle, dressed as a clown in stripy trousers, 10cm. long. (Phillips) $440

A. G. Vichy bisque-headed tri-cyclist automaton, French, circa 1880, 10½in. long $1,100

Ingap, clockwork lithographed motorcycle and rider finished in bright colors, 13cm. (Phillips) $475

An early French mechanical tricyclist, circa 1890, 8¼in. long. $1,300

A Japanese battery operated
tinplate pig farming wagon
'Pinkee' the farmer, 25cm.
(Phillips) $110

A 'Peter Rabbit' chickmobile,
hand car, No. 1103, circa
1935. $750

German clockwork automaton
of a Chinese mandarin pulling
a cart, circa 1900, man impressed Halbig. $2,000

A Gunda-Werke lithograph tinplate
motorcycle and sidecar with clockwork mechanism, 6½in. long, circa
1920, and a tinplate monkey
moneybox. $1,750

A Lehmann 'Naughty boy'
tinplate vis-à-vis, German, circa
1910, lithographed in cream
with blue trim, the driver in
brown the boy in blue, 5in. long.
(Sotheby's) $610

Ingap, clockwork lithographed
Dipsy car with young clown
rider finished in red, yellow and
pale blue, 12.5cm.
(Phillips) $230

A Bell-toy, with plush covered
monkey seated on a cloth
covered platform with three
fretwork metal wheels below,
8in.
(Phillips) $650

A Lehmann 'tut-tut' tinplate
mechanical car, German, circa
1920, lithographed in cream and
red, with handpainted driver.
(Sotheby's) $330

An early 20th century stock
tin plate clockwork four
wheel gocart, driven by a uni-
formed school boy, 12.75cm.
long. (Henry Spencer)
          $400

LEHMANN

The firm of Ernst Paul Lehmann was founded in 1881 in Brandenburg, away from the traditional centers of German toymaking, and they produced tinplate novelty toys which were very different from those turned out by Bing and Märklin, where quality was paramount. In contrast, Lehmann's toys were flimsily built and had a studied frivolity. Even the names were humorous – 'Toot toot' for example being the name of a car driven erratically by a driver blowing a hunting horn. Lehmann's products were cheap and cheerful, decorated with colored lithography, which was often, notwithstanding, of a very high standard, and parts were joined by tabs, rather than by soldering. Motors had pressed tinplate gears and spiral, rather than coil springs. Nevertheless, they were extremely attractive, and Lehmann is one of the most famous tinplate toymakers of the 1920s.

After the Second World War, Brandenburg found itself in East Germany, and Ernst Lehmann's cousin, Johann Richter, set up a new enterprise, the Lehmann Company, near Nuremberg.

Lehmann 'Zig-Zag' tin wind-up toy, 1910-45, 5in. long. $750

'Baker and Sweep', E.P.L. No. 450, by Lehmann, circa 1905, in original box. $3,000

Lehmann, Japanese coolie in conical hat pulling rickshaw, with spring-motor action operating woman's fan and spoked wheels, 1930's. (Christie's S. Ken) $2,000

Lehmann clockwork sailor dressed in white summer uniform discolored, 18.5cm. high, circa 1912. (Phillips) $350

A Lehmann tinplate 'Oh My', No. 690, the articulated figure holding the clockwork mechanism, circa 1920, 10½in. high. $800

A painted tinplate cat, 'Nina', EPL No. 790, by Lehmann, circa 1907, 11in. long. $1,750

An early Lehmann, EPL marque, 'Paddy riding his pig to market', with clockwork mechanism, circa 1910, 5½in. long. $625

LEHMANN

A Lehmann Performing Sea Lion, No. 445, in original cardboard box, German, circa 1900, 7½in. long. $300

A Lehmann tinplate Anxious Bride, No. 470, German, circa 1910. $1,250

A Lehmann Mikado Family, No. 350, German, circa 1898, 6½in. long. $1,100

'Dancing Sailor', a printed and painted tinplate sailor, in blue cloth uniform, 7½in. high, by Lehmann, circa 1912. (Christie's) $325

'Bulky Mule, The Stubborn Donkey', EPL No. 425, by Lehmann, circa 1910, 7½in. long. $400

Early 20th century Lehmann waltzing doll, head with EPL trademark, 9in. high. $1,000

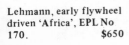

Lehmann, early flywheel driven 'Africa', EPL No 170. $650

'New Century Cycle', EPL 345, with clockwork mechanism, by Lehmann, circa 1910, 5in. long. $1,750

Kadi, a printed and painted teabox with two Chinese coolies, clockwork mechanism concealed in box, by Lehmann, circa 1910, 7in. long. (Christie's S. Ken) $1,000

MARTIN

Fernand Martin set up his toymaking business in Paris in 1878, and his tinplate clockwork toys came to rival their German counterparts in quality. Martin specialized in comical figures, often satirizing Paris society, and his toys were often dressed in fabrics, making them more realistic. He believed in having figures where the movement was amusing in its own right, such as a drunkard struggling to maintain his balance.

The firm was taken over by Victor Bonnet & Co. in the early 1920s. Martin's work was *FM* within a circle.

French 'Le Faucheur' scythe man by F. Martin, circa 1900, 7½in. high. $800

A painted tinplate toy of a cooper, by F. Martin, Paris, circa 1902, 7½in. long. $1,000

A German painted tinplate clockwork nursemaid, with rocking upper torso, umbrella, apron, cap and eccentric walking action, circa 1910, 6¹/₂in. high. (Christie's S. Ken) $975

F. Martin, clockwork L'Eminent Avocat, 22cm. high, boxed in excellent to mint condition, with Code Civil. (Phillips) $2,350

Fernand Martin, 'La Madelon casseuse d'assiettes', clockwork painted tinplate maid, dressed in blue with white apron and cap, circa 1913. (Christie's S. Ken) $825

A painted toy of a skater, with clockwork mechanism, by A. F. Martin, French, circa 1890, 8½in. high. $1,600

A painted tinplate parlor maid chasing a mouse with a broom, dressed in pale blue dress with white collar, 19cm., probably by Martin. (Phillips) $1,500

'Our New Clergyman', a stained and carved wood, metal and tinplate preacher, probably by F. Martin, circa 1890, 10½in. high. $2,600

Miniature cloth bear on wheels, circa 1900, 5 x 3in., with glass button eyes. **$250**

A 19th century circus wagon, 28in. overall, wagon 16 x 7½in. **$250**

Late 19th/early 20th century painted walking gait wooden horse toy, America, mounted on an iron frame, 28in. long. **$1,000**

A 19th century carved and painted wood horse pull toy, mounted on wooden base with wheels, 11in. high. **$650**

A skin covered horse on wheels with leather saddle and bridle, 16in. high, circa 1890. (Christie's) **$500**

A carved and painted pine horse pull toy, probably American, late 19th century, the stylized figure of a dappled gray horse with real horsehair mane and tail, 28½in. wide. (Sotheby's) **$1,750**

Early 20th century goatskin goat pull toy, baa's when head is pressed down, Germany, 16½in. high. **$1,000**

An M. J. tinplate pull-along train, French, circa 1905, 11in. wide. **$400**

A wooden pull-along horse, the painted dapple body with carved features, metal stud eyes and leather cloth saddle, 18in. high. (Phillips) **$400**

SCHUCO

The company making these toys was established in Germany in 1912 by H Mueller and H Schreyer. They traded as Schreyer & Co., but it is by their trademark Schuco that their products are best known. Schuco toys are very highly regarded, and some collectors consider them as being the most technically advanced of their type.

During the 20s and 30s they produced a range of novelty clockwork toys, which included animals that were wound up by an arm or leg rather than a key!

It was after the Second World War that Schuco started to produce an inexpensive range of clockwork tinplate cars. Some of these were amazingly complex, such as the Steerable Driving School car, which came complete with jack and tools to remove wheels.

Between the end of the war and 1951 Schuco toys were marked as having been made in the American Zone of Occupation, but thereafter were simply marked *Made in Germany*.

The company closed in 1977, but the brand name was bought by Gama.

Charlie Chaplin, with clockwork mechanism, in original clothing, walking stick and bowler hat, by Schuco, circa 1933, 6¾in. high. (Christie's S. Ken) $525

Schuco, felt and velvet rabbit, the orange creature with large ears, green trousers, dancing with its pink infant, 15.5cm. (Phillips) $250

Schuco tinplate Donald Duck, right foot fatigued, boxed, with label. (Phillips West Two) $725

Schuco clockwork felt covered fox dressed in red jacket, blue trousers and yellow tie, carrying a lithographed tinplate clockwork suitcase, 13cm. (Phillips) $225

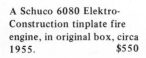

Donald Duck, a felt covered and painted tinplate toy, with clockwork mechanism, by Schuco, circa 1936, 6in. high. (Christie's S. Ken) $400

A Schuco 6080 Elektro-Construction tinplate fire engine, in original box, circa 1955. $550

Schuco, felt and velvet mouse drinking from a flagon, 11cm. (Phillips) $200

German plush pull toy of a baby elephant by Steiff, 14in. overall. $475

A Steiff golden velvet bulldog, with black stitched muzzle, orange felt tongue and glass eyes, 9.5cm. high. (Henry Spencer) $350

A plush covered lion cub, 9in. long, circa 1925 with Steiff button. $250

A Roly Poly blue and white rabbit with glass eyes and Steiff button in ear, 10½in. high with ears extended. (Christie's S. Ken) $1,350

A golden short plush covered lion on wheels, with curly plush blonde mane, by Steiff, circa 1913 (missing ears, growl inoperative). (Christie's S. Ken) $600

Mid 20th century life-size young donkey, probably Steiff, 39in. high, 39in. long. $375

A felt rooster with wire framed feet, yellow, red and green feathers with Steiff button and original white tag, 1117, circa 1905–26. (Christie's S. Ken) $1,000

A large Steiff rocking elephant, 45in. long, German, circa 1925. $1,100

A Steiff Mickey Mouse, the velvet covered head with felt ears and wide smiling mouth, 7in. (Phillips) $500

A tan leather Harrods gentleman's fitted dressing case, the interior finished in polished hide lined leather, 40 x 66cm.
(Onslow's) $285

A fine large leather Gladstone bag, with key and straps, initialed M.W.H., little used with foul weather cover.
(Onslow's) $360

A Louis Vuitton brown grained leather suitcase, interior finished in canvas with two straps, labeled *Louis Vuitton Paris, Nice, Lille, London,* 55 x 34 x 18cm.
(Onslow's) $1,000

A Louis Vuitton Johnny Walker whisky traveling drinks case, fitted for one bottle of whisky, two bottles of mineral water, one packet of cheese biscuits, two glasses and ice container.
(Onslow's) $3,600

A Louis Vuitton gentleman's cabin trunk, bound in brass and leather with leather carrying handle, on castors, 91 x 53 x 56cm.
(Onslow's) $1,500

A Louis Vuitton special order tan pigskin gentleman's fitted dressing case, accessories include silver tooth brush, soap and talc containers, 54 x 32cm., circa 1930.
(Onslow's) $4,500

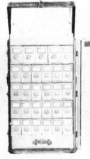

A Louis Vuitton shaped motor car trunk, covered in black material, interior with three matching fitted suitcases, 85 x 65 x 50cm.
(Onslow's) $6,265

A Louis Vuitton shoe secretaire, bound in leather and brass, fitted with twenty-nine shoe boxes with lids, one drawer and tray, 112 x 64 x 40cm.
(Onslow's) $7,700

A fine tan leather hat box by The Our Boys Clothing Company Oxford Street, with red velvet lining.
(Onslow's) $200

A Louis Vuitton yellow fabric covered motor car suitcase, brass bound, with nickel-plated padlock shaped lock, 59 x 39 x 17cm.
(Onslow's) $635

A Louis Vuitton cabin trunk, vermin proof for use in the tropics, covered in zinc and brass bound, interior finished in white cotton, 85 x 49 x 47cm.
(Onslow's) $4,000

A Malles Goyard cabin trunk, covered in Malles Goyard patterned material, bound in leather and brass, 85 x 49 x 47cm.
(Onslow's) $725

A Louis Vuitton suitcase, No 761119, with key and leather LV luggage label, 62 x 40 x 17cm.
(Onslow's) $3,000

A Louis Vuitton shoe secretaire, fitted with thirty shoe boxes with lids, two large drawers top and bottom and tray, 112 x 64 x 40cm.
(Onslow's) $6,200

A Louis Vuitton gentleman's cabin trunk on castors, covered in LV material, fitted with three trays, one with compartments, 90 x 51 x 48cm.
(Onslow's) $2,000

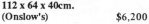

A Garrison black fabric covered picnic service for six persons, complete with yellow and gold crockery, 56 x 40 x 30cm.
(Onslow's) $725

A Louis Vuitton "Sac Chauffeur", the two circular halves covered in black material, the lower section watertight, 89cm diameter, circa 1905, designed to fit inside spare tires .
(Onslow's) $5,400

A matching white hide suitcase and hat box by John Pound, with chromium-plated locks and foul weather covers, the suitcase 56 x 36cm.
(Onslow's) $500

ARNOLD

A gold openface fusee lever watch, signed J. R. Arnold, Chas. Frodsham, London, 1853, 55mm. diam. $1,500

A gold pocket chronometer, the movement signed John Arnold & Son, 53mm. diam. $11,250

A silver cased pocket chronometer by John Arnold, London, 50mm. diam. $18,000

John Roger Arnold No. 1956, a rare 18ct. gold pocket chronometer in plain consular case, the white enamel dial with Roman numerals and large subsidiary seconds, gold hands, *London 1805*, 57mm. diameter. (Christie's) $21,450

A pocket chronometer movement by John Arnold & Son, London, the frosted gilt fusée movement with pierced and engraved cock, with enamel dial and silver case, diameter of top-plate 40mm. (Christie's S. Ken) $2,000

A pocket chronometer movement by John Roger Arnold, the signed and numbered enamel dial with subsidiary seconds and gold hands, 49mm. diam., circa 1820. (Phillips) $2,100

AUDEMARS PIGUET

Audemars Piguet No. 154003, gold hexagonal cased skeleton keyless lever watch, 50mm. diam. $4,125

An openface platinum dress watch with 19-jewel movement with gold train, signed Audemars Piguet & Co., no. 36541, 43mm. diam. $1,750

A skeleton keyless lever watch by Audemars Piguet & Cie, the movement with gold train, 45mm. diam. $3,750

BARRAUD & LUNDS

A gold keyless openface free sprung fusee lever watch with winding indicator, signed Barraud & Lunds, London, 1893, 51mm. diam. **$2,250**

A gold hunter-cased lever watch, signed Barraud & Lunds, London, 1882, 50mm. diam. **$1,000**

A gold open faced lever watch by Barraud & Lunds, hallmarked 1871, 47mm. diam. **$1,000**

BENSON

An 18ct. gold keyless lever chronograph, the movement with compensated balance, signed J. W. Benson, London, the case marked London 1882, 53mm. diam. (Phillips) **$950**

An 18ct. gold hunter-cased keyless chronograph, the movement signed J. W. Benson, No. 2516, London, 54mm. diam. **$2,750**

A fine and rare 18ct. gold keyless open-face split-second chronograph carousel by J.W. Benson, in plain case, the white enamel dial with Willis to the back, with chain fusée, London 1906, 59mm. diameter. (Christie's S. Ken) **$40,000**

BREGUET

A gold quarter repeating jump hour ruby cylinder watch, inscribed Breguet No. 2097, 48mm. diam. **$7,000**

A gold minute repeating keyless lever chronograph, signed Breguet No. 1310, 56mm. diam. **$11,250**

Breguet No. 58: a gold quarter repeating duplex watch, gilt Lepine calibre, 44mm. diam. **$4,750**

CARTIER

A slender gold stem wind open faced lever pocket watch, signed Cartier, Paris, 45mm. diam. $1,750

Cartier, a King George VI £5 coin containing a watch, with concealed catch in the rim, the matt silvered dial with Roman numerals and blued steel moon hands, 36mm. diameter.
(Christie's) $4,000

An 18ct. gold dress watch, silvered dial, signed *Cartier*, damascened nickel keyless lever movement signed *European Watch and Clock Co., 1929*.
(Bonhams) $1,100

COURVOISIER

A small engraved gold pocket chronometer, signed **Courvoisier & Comp'e, Chaux-De-Fonds**, 46mm. diam. $1,000

A gold hunter cased quarter repeating duplex watch, signed **Courvoisier Freres**, 18ct. gold case, 50mm. diam. $1,750

A gold quarter repeating cylinder watch, the enamel dial signed **Courvoisier & Compe**, 54mm. diam. (Phillips) $1,000

ELGIN

14ct. gold hunting case pocket watch, 'Elgin', jeweled gilt movement and white porcelain dial. $575

An Elgin watch in very narrow 14ct gold case, Swiss anchor movement, the dial with gilt Arab numerals, 17 jewels, 4.5cm. diameter, circa 1920.
(Auction Team Köln) $175

14ct. gold hunting case pocket watch, 'Elgin', lever set jeweled nickel movement and white porcelain dial. $900

FRODSHAM

Ari 18ct. gold cased key-wind pocket watch by Charles Frodsham, dated 1884, in green morocco case. $1,750

A gold hunter-cased tourbillon watch, the movement signed Chas. Frodsham, 61mm. diam. $52,500

An eight-day fusee key-less pocket chronometer, by Chas Frodsham, hall-marked 1915, 72mm. diam. $37,500

An eighteen carat gold open faced keyless lever fly-back chronograph, signed *Charles Frodsham*, presentation inscription on cuvette dated 1893, 53mm.
(Lawrence Fine Art) $1,300

An 18 carat gold half hunter case minute repeating keyless lever chronograph, signed *Cha's Frodsham 84 Strand London,* 54mm. diam.
(Phillips) $5,400

An 18ct. yellow gold three-quarter plate English key-less lever pocket watch, by Parkinson & Frodsham.
                                $625

GARON

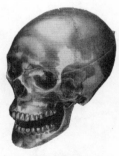

An early 18th century gold, gilt metal and shagreen pair cased quarter repeating verge watch, signed *Pet Garon, London*, with silver dust ring, 57mm. diameter.
(Phillips) $1,850

A finely modeled silver skull watch opening to reveal the engraved silver chapter ring with Roman numerals and Arabic five-minute divisions, signed *Pete. Garon, London*, 75mm. long.
(Christie's) $2,600

An engraved silver paircase verge watch by Peter Garon, London, the cock and back plate furniture pierced and engraved with leafy scrolls and mask, circa 1705, 53mm. diameter.
(Christie's) $1,450

JAQUEMART

A French gold quarter repeating erotic Jaquemart watch, with a panel below opening to reveal two lovers, 55mm. diam.
(Phillips) $4,500

A Swiss gold hunter cased minute repeating keyless lever Jacquemart watch, the movement jeweled to the center and with jeweled repeat train, 51mm. diameter.
(Phillips) $5,000

A good 19th century French gold quarter repeating Jacquemart watch, the dial with enamel chapter and skeletonised center, 64mm. diam.
(Phillips) $11,000

JURGENSEN

A gold hunter cased minute repeating watch, signed J. Jurgensen, Copenhagen, 18ct. gold case, 53mm. diam. $10,000

A gold hunter cased lever watch, signed J. Jurgensen, Copenhagen, 18ct. gold case, 50mm. diam. $2,500

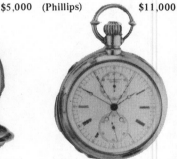

An 18ct. gold openface minute-repeating split-second chronograph with box and certificate, signed Jules Jurgensen, Copenhagen, 55mm. diam. $22,500

LE ROY

A gold French verge pocket watch, by Le Roy A Paris, white enamel dial with Roman numerals and outer Arabic minute ring, 40mm.
(Bonhams) $620

A French gold open faced key wind calendar watch, the cylinder movement with bridge cock, signed *Le Roy a Paris*, 46mm.
(Lawrence Fine Art) $2,400

A gilt metal and leather coach watch with alarm by *Jul'n le Roy à Paris*, the two-train verge movement with pierced backplate furniture, mid 18th century, 11.3cm. diameter.
(Christie's New York) $6,500

LEPINE

A gold and enamel verge watch, Lepine of Paris, circa 1790, 41mm. diam.
$3,250

A Continental gold quarter repeating ruby cylinder watch, the gilt Lepine caliber movement jeweled to the second, enamel dial signed Fourcy 3954 on the reverse, 60mm. diam. (Christie's)
$2,500

A slim gold and enamel open, faced keywind watch with Lepine caliber movement.
$1,750

LONGINES

A gold open faced keyless lever dress watch by Longines, with damascened nickel movement, 44mm. diam.
$1,300

An Art Moderne 18ct. bicolor gold open face pocketwatch, Swiss jewel movement by Longines.
$1,250

An 18ct. chased gold hunter-cased lever watch, signed Longines, with damascened nickel movement jeweled to the third wheel, 52mm. diam.
$2,250

MARTINEAU

A Dutch enamel and silver pair cased verge watch with false pendulum, signed Martineau, London, 52mm. diam.
$2,500

A gold pair case verge watch set with rubies, signed Jos. Martineau Sen., London, 53mm. diam.
$30,000

An 18th century silver pair cased quarter repeating verge watch, signed Martineau, London, the signed silver champleve dial with arcaded chapters, 50mm. diam. (Phillips)
$2,000

PATEK PHILIPPE

A large gold openface lever watch, signed Chronometro Gondolo, by Patek Philippe & Cie, 56mm. diam. $2,500

A gold openface lever watch, signed Patek Philippe & Cie, Geneva, retailed by Bailey, Banks & Biddle, Phila., 50mm. diam. $2,250

An enameled platinum openface dress watch, signed Patek Philippe & Co., Geneva, no. 810822, 39mm. diam. $2,350

PRIOR

A silver triple cased Turkish Market verge watch by E. Prior of London, hallmarked 1882, 65mm. diam. $1,400

A triple cased silver verge pocket watch for the Turkish market by Ge. Prior, London, with tortoiseshell covered outer case and shark skin covered carrying case, diameter of outer case 61mm.
(Christie's S. Ken) $1,450

A quadruple case verge watch for the Turkish market, signed Edw. Prior, London, 70mm. diam. $9,000

SMITH

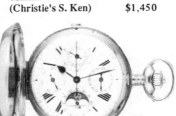

An 18ct. gold keyless lever watch, the movement jeweled to the center and signed S. Smith & Son, the case marked London, 1901, 52mm. diam. $1,250

An 18ct. gold minute repeating perpetual calendar chronograph hunter pocket watch with moonphase, by S. Smith & Sons Ltd, in plain case, 50mm. diameter. (Christie's) $8,500

A silver fusee lever watch with winding indicator, signed Smith & Son, London, the case, London, 1899, 52mm. diam. $1,750

TIFFANY

An 18ct. gold openface minute-repeating split-second chronograph, Swiss, retailed by Tiffany & Co., 54mm. diam. **$9,000**

A gold openface chronograph, Swiss, retailed by Tiffany & Co., New York, signed Tiffany, 53mm. diam. **$1,400**

A gold miniature keyless lever watch, the steel bar movement jewelled to the center and signed for Tiffany & Co., N.Y., 27mm. diam. **$800**

An 18ct. gold openface five-minute repeating watch, signed P. Philippe & Co., no. 97353, dial signed Tiffany & Co., 45mm. diam. **$4,800**

A small 18ct. gold openface five-minute repeating split-second chronograph, signed Tiffany & Co., the movement by P. Philippe, no. 111758, 42mm. diam. **$7,500**

A Swiss gold openface split-second chronograph, retailed by Tiffany & Co., N.Y., 18ct. gold case, 51mm. diam. **$2,500**

TOMPION

A silver pair cased verge watch, the movement signed Tho. Tompion, London, 2631, 55mm. diam. **$6,500**

An early 18th century quarter repeating verge watch movement, signed *Tho Tompion, London, 136,* with pierced tulip pillars and engraved cock, 56mm. diameter.
(Phillips) **$3,250**

A late 17th century silver pair cased verge watch, signed Tho. Tompion, London 0292, 57mm. diam. **$3,750**

WATCHES

VACHERON & CONSTANTIN

A finely enameled gold open-face dress watch, signed Vacheron & Constantin, 47mm. diam. $4,750

A gold openface lever watch, signed Vacheron & Constantin, Geneva, within an engine-turned 18ct. gold case, 58mm. diam. $1,750

A gold openface chronograph, signed Vacheron & Constantin, Geneve, with an 18ct. gold fob, 51mm. diam. $2,750

Vacheron Constantin, a German issue Luftwaffe watch, the silvered dial with Arabic numerals and subsidiary dials for seconds, 60mm. (Bonhams) $2,500

A silver open-face chronograph pocket watch in plain case by Vacheron & Constantin, Geneve, the white enamel dial with luminous Arabic numerals, 51mm. diameter. (Christie's S. Ken) $1,500

A 14ct. rose gold openface dress watch and chain, signed Vacheron & Constantin, Geneve, with 17-jewel nickel lever movement, 42mm. diam. $1,500

VULLIAMY

A gold and enamel duplex watch by Vulliamy No. MXRC, signed and numbered on the movement. 41mm. diam. $4,750

A late 18th century gold dumb quarter-repeating cylinder pocket watch by Just. Vulliamy, London, in engine-turned and engraved consular case, 54mm. diameter. (Christie's S. Ken) $7,000

A gold openface quarter repeating duplex watch, signed Vulliamy, London, 18ct. gold case, 1835, 45mm. diam. $2,500

AUDEMARS PIGUET

Audemars Piguet, a gold automatic wristwatch, the gilt dial with raised baton numerals, 32mm. diameter.
(Christie's) $2,000

Audemars Piguet, a ladies 18ct. gold wristwatch, the flecked gray dial with gold hands, 34 x 22mm.
(Christie's) $1,850

Audemars Piguet, a gold slim wristwatch in circular case, the white dial with baton numerals, 31mm. diameter.
(Christie's) $2,400

An 18ct. white gold wristwatch, signed *Audemars Piguet, Geneve,* **circa 1965, with lever movement, mono-metallic compensation balance, 31mm. diameter.**
(Christie's) $2,650

A gold wristwatch by Audemars Piguet, Geneve, the nickel adjusted 19-jewel movement with gold train, silvered dial, raised Arabic and abstract chapters and hands, dial and movement, 1940s.
(Christie's) $1,550

An 18ct. gold wristwatch with center seconds, signed Audemars Piguet, with nickel 20-jewel movement with gold train. $3,375

Audemars Piguet, a gentleman's slim gold wristwatch in circular case, the white dial with raised baton numerals, 31mm. diameter.
(Christie's) $2,000

A thin gold wristwatch, signed Audemars Piguet, with nickel 20-jewel lever movement. $1,900

An 18ct. gold self-winding perpetual calendar wristwatch with moonphases, signed *Audemars Piguet, Automatic,* **36mm. diameter.**
(Christie's) $10,500

BREGUET

Breguet, No. 3727, a ladies fine 18ct. gold moonphase wristwatch in drum shaped case, with signed and numbered back 25mm. diameter.
(Christie's) $4,750

A gold wristwatch, signed Breguet, no. 3150, with leather strap and 18ct. gold deployant buckle. $3,750

An 18ct. gold self-winding perpetual calendar wristwatch with moonphases and up and down indicator, signed *Breguet*, *No. 5134 A*, 36mm. diameter.
(Christie's) $45,000

Breguet, a modern 18ct. gold Tourbillon wristwatch no. 840, in drum shaped case, the silvered dial with eccentric chapter ring engraved *Brevet du 7 Messidor an IX* signed *Tourbillon Breguet No. .04*, 35mm. diameter.
(Christie's) $35,000

Breguet, No. 2128, a gentleman's fine 18ct. gold automatic, calendar, moonphase and power reserve wristwatch in drum shaped case with milled band, with signed and numbered back, 36mm. diameter.
(Christie's) $13,250

Breguet, a fine 18ct. gold calendar and moonphase and automatic wristwatch, the drum shaped case with ribbed band and cabochon winder, the silvered engine-turned dial with eccentric chapter ring, 35mm. diameter.
(Christie's) $10,000

A platinum jump hour wristwatch, signed *Breguet, No. 51/400*, circular case with coin-edged band and sapphire-set crown, 36mm. diameter.
(Christie's) $30,000

A steel wrist chronograph, signed Breguet, and another signed Henry K. Tournheim-Tourneau, without calendar.
                  $2,500

Breguet No. 3862, a gold calendar automatic Marine wristwatch, the silvered dial with Roman numerals, 36mm. diameter.
(Christie's) $9,000

BREITLING

A chronograph wristwatch, signed *Breitling Cosmonaute*, the black matt dial with Arabic numerals, 41mm. diameter. (Christie's) $1,300

Breitling, a 1950's water-resistant pink gold chronograph wristwatch, signed movement, 37mm. diameter. (Christie's) $4,850

Breitling, a steel Chronomat automatic water-resistant calendar chronograph wristwatch, 38mm. diameter. (Christie's) $1,400

Breitling, a pink gold waterproof and antimagnetic Première chronograph wristwatch, in circular case, the signed movement jeweled to the centre, 36mm. diameter. (Christie's) $3,250

Navitimer, a stainless steel Breitling chronograph wristwatch with milled rotating bezel, the signed black dial with outer calculating scales, 40mm. diameter. (Christie's) $800

A steel Breitling, Geneve, Navitimer chronograph wristwatch with rotating bezel, the black dial with outer tachymetric and telemetric scales, 40mm. diameter. (Christie's S. Ken) $825

An 18ct. pink gold calendar wristwatch with chronograph, signed *Breitling, Geneve*, circa 1950, with nickel-finished lever movement, 36mm. diameter. (Christie's) $4,250

A stainless steel chronograph wristwatch, signed *Breitling Cosmonaute, Navitime and Breitling Chronograph*, circa 1960, 36mm. diameter. (Christie's) $1,250

A gentleman's stainless steel chronograph wristwatch, the silvered dial inscribed *Breitling Premier*, Arabic numerals, 35mm. (Bonhams) $550

CARTIER

An 18ct. gold circular wrist-watch, the movement signed European Watch and Clock Co. Inc., the dial inscribed Cartier, 30mm. diam. $1,500

A gold and diamond wristwatch by Cartier, the case with diamond set shoulders, 20 x 27mm. $2,000

An 18ct. gold wristwatch by Cartier, hallmarked London 1963, 26mm.
$4,750

A steel duoplan wristwatch, signed Jaeger, with oblong nickel lever movement, the white dial signed Cartier.
$2,750

A square white gold diamond and baguette sapphire set wristwatch signed on the sil-vered dial Cartier, Paris, 23mm. square. (Christie's) $8,000

A rare tonneau-shaped single button chronograph wristwatch, signed *Cartier, European Watch & Co.*, circa 1935. (Christie's) $80,000

A Swiss gold curved rectangular wristwatch by Cartier, the signed dial with Roman numerals, the numbered case also marked *1326*, with cabochon winder. (Phillips) $5,400

An enameled gold wristwatch, retailed by Cartier, the move-ment signed European Watch & Clock Co. $11,250

Cartier, a 1930s 18ct gold 'tank' wristwatch with ruby cabochon winder, white enamel dial with Roman numerals, the back secured by four screws in the band, 31 x 23mm. (Christie's) $5,000

CHOPARD

An 18ct. white gold and hardstone skeletonised wristwatch, signed Chopard, Geneve, with original leather strap and 18ct. white gold buckle. **$10,000**

An 18ct. white gold and diamond wristwatch by Chopard, 34mm. circa 1970. **$3,250**

A Swiss gold oval lady's wristwatch, by Chopard, signed black dial with baton numerals, 26mm. wide, on a fancy link bracelet. (Phillips) **$575**

GRUEN

A gold wristwatch with nickel 17-jewel movement, signed Gruen Watch Co., Curvex Precision. **$600**

A 14ct. gold curvex wristwatch, signed Gruen, with curved cushion shaped 17-jewel movement, **$1,750**

A 14ct. gold curvex wristwatch, signed Gruen Watch Co., with curved nickel 17-jewel movement. **$2,750**

INTERNATIONAL WATCH CO.

A Swiss 18ct. gold wristwatch with center seconds, signed International Watch Co., with a 14ct. gold mesh bracelet. **$1,750**

International Watch Co., a gold waterproof wristwatch in tonneau case, the brushed gilt dial with raised baton numerals and sweep center seconds, 40 x 33mm. (Christie's) **$900**

A gold wristwatch, signed International Watch Co., Schaffhausen, with leather strap with 14ct. gold buckle and a spare crystal. **$2,250**

JAEGER LE COULTRE

A gold plated calendar
wristwatch by Le Coultre,
circa 1940, 34x40mm.
$2,500

An 18ct. gold wristwatch
with fifteen jewel movement,
signed Le Coultre Co., dated
1934. $2,500

A Swiss gold circular wristwatch, by Jaeger le Coultre,
32mm. diam. (Phillips London)
$400

A gentleman's 14ct. gold
wristwatch, 'Le Coultre',
automatic, Master Mariner,
white dial and with a leather
band. $375

A Swiss gilt metal circular
gentleman's Futurematic
wristwatch by Le Coultre, the
signed silvered dial with
subsidiaries for seconds, 35mm.
diameter.
(Phillips) $300

A gold wristwatch by Jaeger
Le Coultre, the dial signed
Duoplan, 22mm. wide,
circa 1935. $3,600

A gentleman's 14ct. gold
wristwatch, LeCoultre, 17J,
complete with a leather strap.
$775

A Swiss gold 'Mystery' wristwatch by Jaeger-le-Coultre, with
backwind movement, the bezel
with enameled baton numerals,
30mm. diam. (Phillips)
$4,000

A white gold mystery wristwatch by Le Coultre, 33mm.
diam., circa 1950. $1,750

LONGINES

A stainless steel chronograph, signed Longines, with lever movement. **$350**

A large 1930s Longines aviator's hour angle watch, the enamel chapter ring signed *A. Cairelli, Roma*, 46mm. diameter. (Bonhams) **$4,000**

A large silver and stainless steel aviator's hour angle watch, to the designs of Charles A. Lindbergh, by Longines. **$8,250**

A gentleman's rectangular Swiss gold wristwatch by Longines, the signed movement numbered 3739388, 30 x 25mm. (Phillips) **$700**

Longines, a modern steel pilot's automatic hour-angle watch in circular case, the rotating bezel engraved with hours and quarters, the white enamel dial with Roman numerals, 36mm. diameter. (Christie's) **$700**

Longines, a steel military wristwatch, the rotating bezel calibrated in minutes with a locking screw in the band, the silvered dial with Arabic numerals and sweep center seconds, 33mm. diameter. (Christie's) **$800**

MOVADO

A gent's Swiss gold wristwatch by Movado, 34mm. diam. **$2,750**

A Swiss gold circular gent's wristwatch, by Movado, the signed silvered dial with subsidiary seconds, 36mm. diam. (Phillips) **$475**

A gold wristwatch, signed Movado, with nickel 17 jewel movement, within a circular 14ct. gold case with unusual lugs. **$1,350**

MOVADO

A gold Movado calendar wristwatch made for Tiffany & Co., in circular case, the polished and matt silvered dial with outer date ring and central date hand, 31mm. diameter. (Christie's S. Ken) $1,750

A gold wristwatch with calendar, signed Movado, within a reeded 14ct. gold case, and a self-winding 14ct. gold wristwatch, signed Bulova. $1,650

Movado, a pink gold and steel wristwatch with stepped pink gold bezel and faceted lugs, the two-tone silvered dial with Arabic numerals and outer seconds ring, 29mm. diameter. (Christie's) $800

OMEGA

A stainless steel Omega Flightmaster wristwatch, the outer scale in five-minute divisions from 5 to 60, with screw back case, 53 x 42mm. (Christie's) $375

A gold wristwatch by Tissot, fitted with a gold Omega strap, circa 1970, 29mm. diam. $750

A rectangular Swiss gold gent's electronic wristwatch, by Omega, the gilt dial marked Constellation Chronometer, with center seconds, 36mm. long. (Phillips) $1,000

A Swiss gold rectangular gentleman's wristwatch by Omega, the signed silvered dial with subsidiary seconds and Arabic numerals, 34 x 21mm. (Phillips) $625

Omega, a stainless steel automatic calendar diver's watch, model Seamaster 600 Professional, the rotating bezel calibrated in five-minute marks, 55 x 45mm. (Christie's) $900

A gold self-winding wristwatch with center seconds, signed Omega Seamaster, the leather strap with 14ct. gold buckle. $475

PATEK PHILIPPE

An 18ct. gold self-winding wristwatch with perpetual calendar, signed P. Philippe & Co., Geneve, no. 1119138. $12,500

An 18ct. gold wristwatch, signed Patek Philippe & Co., Geneva, no. 743586, with an 18ct. gold mesh bracelet. $2,250

A gold center second wrist-watch with perpetual calendar, signed Patek Philippe & Co., Geneva, no. 888001. $30,000

A gold wristwatch by Patek Philippe & Co., Geneve, the nickel adjusted 18-jewel movement with black dial, gold raised Arabic chapters and hands, subsidiary seconds. (Christie's) $5,750

Patek Philippe, a 1960's white gold automatic perpetual calendar wristwatch, the matt gilt dial with raised baton numerals, subsidiary date ring with sector for the moon, apertures for day and month, 37mm. diameter. (Christie's) $23,000

An 18 carat white gold perpetual calendar wristwatch with moonphases and chronograph, signed *Patek Phillipe & Co., Geneve, No. 875348, Ref. 3970.* (Christie's) $60,000

A gold wristwatch with center seconds, signed P. Philippe & Co., Geneve, nickel eighteen-jewel cal. 27-SC movement. $3,250

A gold wrist chronograph, signed P. Philippe & Co., Geneve, no. 868978, nickel twenty-three jewel cal. 13-130 movement. $11,250

A white gold wristwatch, signed Patek Philippe, Geneva, with nickel 18-jewel cal. 23-300 movement. $4,000

ROLEX

A gold Oyster wristwatch by Rolex, with self sealing winder, 30mm., circa 1950. $2,250

An 18ct. pink gold Rolex Oyster-perpetual 'day-date' wristwatch in tonneau shaped case. (Bearne's) $2,750

A two-color calendar Oyster wristwatch by Rolex, 36mm., circa 1965. $1,350

A steel Rolex Oyster Perpetual date submariner wristwatch with black revolving bezel, the matt black dial with dot and baton numerals, 40mm. diameter. (Christie's S. Ken) $1,750

A gold steel Rolex Oyster Perpetual chronometer bubble-back wristwatch with gold bezel, the pink dial with Arabic quarter-hour marks, 30mm. diameter. (Christie's S. Ken) $1,500

Rolex, gentleman's 18ct. rose gold round cased wristwatch, nickel seventeen jewel chronometer, hand wound movement with center seconds, circa 1960, 35mm. (Bonhams) $800

An 18ct. gold self-winding wristwatch with center seconds, signed Rolex Oyster Perpetual, with gold bracelet. $2,000

A stainless steel self-winding wristwatch with center seconds, signed Rolex Oyster Perpetual, Explorer, with Oyster crown and steel bracelet. $750

A 14ct. gold self-winding wristwatch with center seconds, signed Rolex Oyster Perpetual, with a 14ct. gold bracelet. $2,750

TIFFANY

Platinum and diamond
wrist watch by Tiffany
& Co., circa 1925.
$2,500

A steel triple calendar and
moonphase wristwatch made for
Tiffany by Record Watch Co.,
the brushed steel dial with
Arabic numerals, 34mm.
diameter.
(Christie's) $600

A gold wristwatch, signed
Audemars Piguet, with
18ct. gold bracelet, signed
Tiffany & Co. $2,500

A gold wristwatch by C. H.
Meylan Watch Co., the dial
signed Tiffany & Co., 19 x
35mm., circa 1935. $1,100

A 1920's gold curvex tonneau
wristwatch, the matt white dial
with gilt Arabic numerals,
signed *Tiffany & Co.*, 35 x
26mm.
(Christie's) $2,000

A gold wristwatch, signed
Agassiz Watch Co., dial
signed Tiffany & Co., in
an 18ct. gold case. $2,500

UNIVERSAL

A stainless steel calendar and
moon phase wristwatch, inscribed 'Universal, Geneve',
the signed movement jeweled
to the third, diam. 34mm.
(Christie's) $500

Universal, a pink gold triple
calendar and moonphase
chronograph wristwatch, the
silvered dial with outer
tachymetric scale, alternating
raised pink dagger and Arabic
numerals, 36mm. diameter.
(Christie's) $2,500

A 19ct. gold chronograph
wristwatch in circular case,
the matt silvered dial signed
Universal, Geneve, 33mm.
diam. (Christie's) $1,000

VACHERON & CONSTANTIN

18ct. gold calendar
wristwatch by Vacheron
& Constantin, London,
1954, 35mm. diam.
$2,850

An 18ct. gold skeletonised
wristwatch, signed Vacheron
& Constantin, with signed
18ct. gold buckle to leather
strap. $7,000

A white gold mysterieuse
wristwatch by Vacheron
& Constantin & Le Coultre,
33mm., circa 1965. $2,500

An 18ct. gold wristwatch,
signed Vacheron & Constantin,
with nickel 17-jewel P 453/3B
movement, signed on move-
ment and case $3,250

Vacheron & Constantin,
Genève, an 18ct. gold perpetual
calendar and moonphase
automatic wristwatch, cream
dial with raised baton numerals,
35mm. diameter.
(Christie's) $11,250

An 18ct. gold wristwatch
with nickel 17-jewel movement, signed Vacheron &
Constantin, no. 421150.
                        $3,500

An 18ct. gold bracelet watch,
signed Vacheron & Constantin,
on movement, case and bracelet. $3,250

A Swiss gold circular automatic
gentleman's wristwatch by
Vacheron & Constantin,
Genève, with signed gilt dial
with center seconds and Roman
numerals, 36mm. diameter.
(Phillips) $2,600

An 18ct. white gold minute
repeating wristwatch, signed
Vacheron & Constantin,
Geneva. $60,000

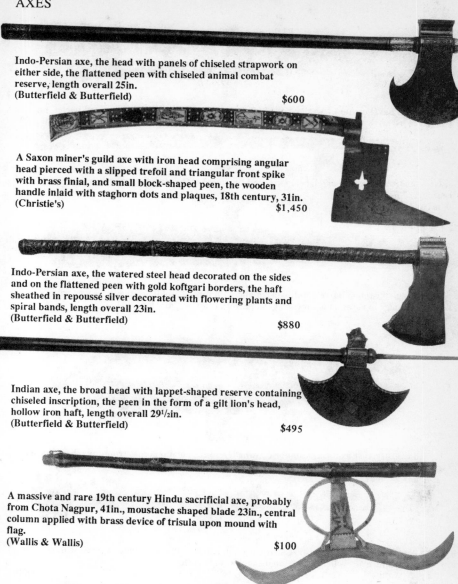

Indo-Persian axe, the head with panels of chiseled strapwork on either side, the flattened peen with chiseled animal combat reserve, length overall 25in.
(Butterfield & Butterfield) $600

A Saxon miner's guild axe with iron head comprising angular head pierced with a slipped trefoil and triangular front spike with brass finial, and small block-shaped peen, the wooden handle inlaid with staghorn dots and plaques, 18th century, 31in.
(Christie's) $1,450

Indo-Persian axe, the watered steel head decorated on the sides and on the flattened peen with gold koftgari borders, the haft sheathed in repoussé silver decorated with flowering plants and spiral bands, length overall 23in.
(Butterfield & Butterfield) $880

Indian axe, the broad head with lappet-shaped reserve containing chiseled inscription, the peen in the form of a gilt lion's head, hollow iron haft, length overall 29$\frac{1}{2}$in.
(Butterfield & Butterfield) $495

A massive and rare 19th century Hindu sacrificial axe, probably from Chota Nagpur, 41in., moustache shaped blade 23in., central column applied with brass device of trisula upon mound with flag.
(Wallis & Wallis) $100

A Silesian flintlock axe-pistol (Fokos) with two-stage barrel octagonal at the breech and with full-length flat on the top, plain beveled lock, brass head with slightly curved cutting edge and peen of rectangular section, late 17th century, 32¼in. (Christie's) $4,750

CANNON

A good iron naval cannon barrel, circa 1800, bore approximately 1¾in., stepped barrel, marked above breech with 'P' and '1.1.15', length overall 37½in., trunnion width 9in. $1,750

A German iron hackbut barrel, octagonal and swamped at the muzzle and breech, early 16th century, 47¼in. barrel.
(Christie's) $2,250

A bronze signal cannon barrel, multi-staged and with turned moldings, the chase cast with acanthus foliage in relief on a punched ground, 16th century, 24in. long.
(Christie's) $11,500

A 19th century cast iron six pounder carronade, 46in., 16½in. across trunnions, breech cast with Imperial crown and '6pr', reinforcing rings at muzzle and breech with integral loop to cascabel. $2,250

A 19th century Malayan cast bronze swivel cannon lantaka, 48½in., molded overall with sections of foliage, cylindrical swollen socket mount to rear of breech.
(Wallis & Wallis) $650

A small Continental bronze cannon barrel of tapering multi-stage form decorated with moldings in relief, those at the muzzle separated by a band of acanthus leaves, finely cast in relief, circa 1750, 18¼in. barrel, 1in. bore.
(Christie's) $2,650

A German sporting crossbow with slender steel bow, later
string and two original green woolen tassels, walnut tiller
carved at the front with a lion in the round, with iron
tongue, and inlaid with horn lines and plaques engraved
with flowerheads and foliage, early 18th century, 28½in.
(Christie's) $3,250

A German target crossbow, heavy steel bow of 89.5cm. span,
walnut stock with brass mounts including scroll trigger guard,
peephole rear sight, double set triggers, 83.5cm. overall. $1,000

A late 18th century stonebow, span 34in., fold-up 'window'
front sight, walnut stock with steel mounts, action and
lift-up cocking lever secured by a spring thumb-catch, hinge-
up aperture rear peep-sight, checkered small of stock. $1,750

A German sporting crossbow with robust steel bow retained
by its original cords, string of twisted cords, angular wooden
tiller swelling towards the middle, the top and bottom
overlaid with panels of light colored horn bordered by
darker horn, early 17th century, 25½in. (Christie's) $6,500

A German stonebow, the bow struck with a mark, cord strings,
built-in gaffle struck with the maker's mark HSB over a bird in
a shield, early 17th century, 21¼in. (Christie's) $2,500

HALBERDS

A halberd with long spike of stiff diamond section, strongly crescentic axe-blade with a fleur-de-lys in the center of the edge and decorated with chrysanthemum and V-shaped piercings, later wooden staff partly covered with textile, early 17th century, 29³/₄in.
(Christie's) $1,200

A Swiss halberd with slender spike of stiff diamond section, crescent-shaped axe-blade pierced with three shaped radiating slots and with convex edge, wooden octagonal staff, late 17th century, probably Bern, 20¹/₄in. head.
(Christie's) $1,100

A Swiss halberd with waved spear-head shaped spike and turned moldings at its base, the axe-head and fluke pierced with scrollwork, wooden staff (probably original) reinforced at the end with a ring and a short spike, late 17th century, probably Swiss, 22¹/₄in. head.
(Christie's) $1,600

A halberd, the axe-blade cusped at the back and pierced with a trefoil, flat beak-shaped fluke, cusped above and below and struck on one face with a mark, on original wooden staff, German or Swiss, early 16th century, 20in. head.
(Christie's) $1,600

A halberd with associated spear-head shaped spike, crescent axe-blade, the points of the crescents reinforced, with V- and cross-bottonée shaped piercings, and octagonal wooden staff, late 16th/early 17th century, 23³/₄in. head.
(Christie's) $800

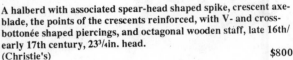

A halberd, with very long tapering spike of stiff diamond section, flat crescentic axe-blade pierced with key-hole shaped holes, two long straps, and wooden staff, late 16th century, probably German or Swiss, 34in. head. $500

HAMMERS

A Saxon horseman's hammer, entirely from iron, with small turned hammer head balanced by a long beak-shaped fluke of stiff diamond section and with spherical finial, slender haft of circular section with thicker wire-bound grip, early 17th century, 21½in. long.
(Christie's) $2,600

An Indo-Persian war hammer, iron head with pronounced curved beak, 9in. overall, decorated overall with gold damascus patterns, on a wooden haft, overall length 15½in. $400

An Indo-Persian all steel war hammer zaghnal, 18¾in., head 8½in., chiseled with flowers, foliage and stags couchant, heightened with gold damascene, on its steel haft. $400

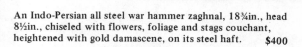

A Polish horseman's hammer, the head 16th century, the shaft later and some decoration added subsequently to the shaft, 21in. long, head 7¾in. $2,600

A Polish war hammer, iron head with traces of brass strip inlaid decoration, curved beak, overall 5½in., on a non-original wooden haft. $475

A 16th century Lucerne hammer, tapering diamond section spike, 15in., long back beak, 4½in., of diamond section, spike head 3½in., long straps with domed studs. $1,000

POLEARMS

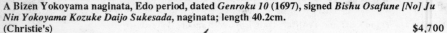

A Bizen Yokoyama naginata, Edo period, dated *Genroku 10* (1697), signed *Bishu Osafune [No] Ju Nin Yokoyama Kozuke Daijo Sukesada*, naginata; length 40.2cm.
(Christie's) $4,700

An Italian glaive, with large cleaver-shaped blade with convex main edge, back-edged towards the point with, at the bottom, a small projection formed as the outline of a dolphin's head, later velvet-covered wooden staff partly set with nails, the heads formed as bronze masks, circa 1587, probably Brescian, 36in. head.
(Christie's) $1,300

An early 18th century partizan, head 9¼in. with slightly thickened tip, baluster socket, on later brass studded wooden haft with elaborate silk tassels woven around gilt octagonal ferrule.
(Wallis & Wallis) $200

A 16th century ceremonial polearm, broad blade 28in. etched with portrait busts in medallions, crouching dogs breathing stylised flames and *IHS Mara, Vyve Le Roy 1588*.
(Wallis & Wallis) $1,850

A 17th century polearm partizan, head 9¾in. including baluster turned socket, side wings with shaped edges, raised central rib and swollen tip.
(Wallis & Wallis) $165

A Partizan head, circa 1600, of plain form, raised central rib, small projecting side lugs, overall 23in.
$325

A Bizen Yoshioka Ichimonji Naginata, Kamakura period (late 13th century), signed *Ichi*, naginata, length (nagasa), 2 shaku, 2 bu (63.8cm.), carving (horimono): naginata-hi on both sides.
(Christie's) $35,000

INDEX

INDEX

INDEX

INDEX

INDEX